COUNTER
gambits

BLACK TO PLAY
AND WIN

by

T.D.HARDING

'B.C.M. Quarterly' No. 15

British Chess Magazine Ltd.

For Gisela

First Published in 1974
by British Chess Magazine Ltd.,
9 Market Street, St. Leonards on Sea,
Sussex TN38 0DQ

Produced in Great Britain by
British Chess Magazine Ltd.

SBN 900846 13 5

Autumn 1975 Reprint

PREFACE

The aim of this book is to show you how to win your games with Black. The method is calculated aggression, right from move one.

An opening must be more than a way of moving your pieces off the back rank. It has to be a planned process of development, in which the pawn moves and piece moves complement one another. As well as laying out his own plan, a player will naturally give thought to how he may disrupt his opponent's schemes; here is the realm of the counter-gambit. White enters into a commitment (playing a move like f4 for example) and Black replies with a sacrifice of trifling material, exposing the darker side to the first player's idea.

The definition of 'counter-gambit' has been a matter of controversy, in that it has been claimed by some that only when White has already offered a gambit (however phoney) can one speak of Black's riposte as being a counter-gambit. This is fine so long as one thinks of the Falkbeer Counter-Gambit (in reply to the King's Gambit) or the Albin (in reply to the Queen's), but what of the From and the Latvian - are they not counter-gambits too? To call them, except as a convenient ellipsis, 'gambit' instead of 'counter-gambit' is to miss the point. If we accept, as I do in this book, the alternative definition of a counter-gambit as any opening sacrifice by Black then we can begin to look for deeper thematic connections among opening systems — indeed for a whole philosophy of play with the black pieces that the counter-gambits exemplify, and not only in the opening moves but right through the middle-game and ending to the triumphant moment: White Resigns.

In this book the reader will find firstly a brief account of this philosophy and how it applies to counter-gambits. The five main chapters are concerned with the counter-gambits themselves, each being favoured with as many illustrative games as it seems to me to deserve, bearing in mind the soundness of the gambit, its contemporary popularity and the intrinsic interest of the available examples: 67 games are fully annotated, and a further 25 complete games are to be found in the theoretical notes, with light comments. I have tried to present the current state of theory fairly, to suggest new ideas, and above all to entertain.

ACKNOWLEDGEMENTS

I should like to thank the following for their help in making this book possible: Firstly, Bob Wade for the use of his extensive library of foreign journals and tournament books which provided my main body of source material. Secondly to the friends who have contributed comments and even full annotations to their games included within: Bob Wade again, George Botterill, Alan Crombleholme, Peter Griffiths and Peter Markland. Thanks go also to Les Blackstock for reading the typescript and making helpful criticisms.

Lewisham
November 1973

NOTATIONS AND SYMBOLS

The notation used in this book is standard English algebraic, in the long form to distinguish the moves actually played in the text games from the variations in the notes. The use of symbols has been kept to a minimum, but the following usages should be noted:

+	check
=	equal position, or balanced chances
(Q)	pawn promotion
!	good move, or best among alternatives
!!	superb move
?	weak move
??	gross blunder
!?	interesting idea
?!	dubious idea
½-½	Draw
1-0	**Black Resigns**
0-1	**White Resigns**

CONTENTS

ERRATA & ADDENDA

page 33 — Instead of 10 ..., Nf6, Black can try the Danish improvement 10 ..., e3!! e.g. 11 Be4!, Qg1; 12 Bxe3, Qxa1; 13 Nf7+, Kc7!; 14 Qg5!, Be7!; 15 Bf4+!, d6!; 16 Bxd6+, Kd7!; 17 Bxe7, Nxe7; 18 Ne5+ when White only draws. (Analysis Botterill and Harding)

page 46 — Diagram 22. Black pawn on h7 **should be on h6**

page 85 — left col., line 31. gxf6 should read **Bxf6**

page 115 — note to Black's 14th move. **15 fxe3!** (Not 15 Ke2) is simplest.

page 134 — After 7 e4 (note b) 7 ..., exd5; 8 cxd5, g5; 9 e5 Black can play 9 ..., gxh4 e.g., 10 exf6, Qxf6; 11 Bxb5, Ba6! Perez-Pachman, Havana 1965.

page 184 — Left col., note a. **9 ..., h3** is not so clear; after 10 Ne3, Nf6; 11 Nc3 intending Qd2 and O-O-O, White may well stand better.

1   DYNAMIC COUNTERPLAY

There is more than one possible reason for offering a gambit or counter-gambit. Disregarding 'external' motivations such as the desire to surprise the opponent or unsettle him with complications, the gambiteer may hope for an attack, a strong centre, a lead in development or just for positional compensation in the form of weak pawns or a fairly long-term dis-coordination in the adversary's game. All these varieties will find their illustration in this book. Whatever the particular justification is for offering a certain gambit, one point is likely to remain the same. Black is not content to play second fiddle. He wants to win the game, and so he seeks dynamic counterplay. Counter-gambitting is one of the main ways of going about this.

How much advantage does White have by virtue of moving first? This is still a controversial question, and a player's beliefs on the matter are liable to influence his views on the correct way of playing with Black. It does not appear that many players in the early centuries of chess gave much thought to the advantage of the move. They wrote and played as if White and Black were equals. Counter-gambits were offered freely and Black's intention in doing so was essentially the same as White's in offering his gambits: to force an early tactical decision by obtaining open lines and threatening the enemy king. The leading exponents of this way of playing chess were Greco, the Italian school of the 18th Century and ultimately Adolf Anderssen (1818-1879).

A typical Anderssen sacrifice is this played in Berlin in 1851: Falkbeer was White but soon found himself defending a King's Gambit!: 1 e4, e5; 2 Nc3, f5?!; 3 exf5, Nf6; 4 g4, Bc5; 5 g5, O-O; 6 gxf6, Qxf6; 7 Qf3 and Anderssen was unable to justify his reversed Muzio. However such caprices were often successful before Morphy, Steinitz and the evolution of good defensive technique. The almost incredible 1 e4, e5; 2 Bc4, b5?! won a game in the Dundee tournament of 1867; this reversed Evans had also been pioneered by Anderssen.

Following the propagation of Steinitz's ideas and their elaboration by the next generation of grandmasters (Tarrasch, Lasker, Rubinstein etc.) there followed a decline in both gambits and counter-gambits that lasted approximately from 1890 to 1945. Frivolous sacrificing would now be punished by accurate defence, and players anyway wished to learn and add to the new positional theory. A phobia for weaknesses sprang up, now that ways of exploiting, for example, doubled pawns were known. Moreover level material became the rule rather than the exception. Many gambits were abandoned without ever being refuted by specific tactical variations (the Evans is the prime example); it was just felt that they involved self-weakening moves that could be exploited by a timely return of the pawn to stifle the gambiteer's initiative. A big shift to closed openings took place.

The classical philosophy of play with Black was now paramount. On this widely-held view, Black has to recognize that his opponent, by virtue of moving first, has an initiative of considerable but not decisive value. White, playing correctly, will be able to convert this initiative into threats that Black in his turn must counter without making permanent positional concessions. If Black succeeds in this task of patiently neutralising White's prerogative, then his reward is the draw. One plays to win with White, but with Black a draw is the goal. If White over-reaches, then perhaps Black can win in the second or third session of play. New opening lines were developed to fit these theories: the Chigorin Defence to the Lopez, Lasker's Defence to the Evans, the classical French and Caro-Kann, the Lasker and Tartakover Defences to the Queen's Gambit. These attitudes prevailed until well after the Second World War.

Then, primarily under the influence of the Soviet school of chess, a new philosophy for Black gained favour: that of the dynamic counterplay. The Soviet players, led by Botvinnik, saw the opening not as a distinct phase of a solely preparatory nature but rather 'as the threshold of the middle-game'. Kotov and Yudovich wrote (1958): '... A tense creative struggle began to take shape from the very first moves; general views on the opening that had been held for many decades were changed completely ... Soviet masters are constantly finding new possibilities in the opening as they strive to introduce elements of a tense, acute struggle beginning with the earliest moves.'

In consequence of this attitude, there occurred the discovery — and rediscovery — of various assymetric defences (e.g. the Dutch, for a long time a favourite of Botvinnik's, and the Sicilian) and of provocative systems. The aim of the latter was to induce White to set up a pawn centre that could then be counter-attacked (e.g. the King's Indian, the Pirc-Ufimtsev and the Alekhine's defences, all pioneered by Soviet players). No longer could White count on stereotyped position play to maintain control of the position; a Capablanca or Rubinstein would find it harder to reach their favourite simple positions quickly against these modern openings. A rich strategic and tactical middle-game struggle was now virtually guaranteed Black, and with it the chance of winning the game. A sterility had crept into pre-war chess. The desire to play for a win with Black from the start returned a richness to the international game that it seemed destined to have lost forever.

The new philosophy of dynamic counterplay undoubtedly stemmed in part from 'hypermodern' ideas, in that they showed how Black could avoid those openings that afforded White the opportunity of early exchanges and quiet pressure. Also important was a new appreciation of the relative value of tactics in the game, together with the concept of the 'positional sacrifice'.

The quest for dynamic counterplay led to the resurrection of many old counter-gambits (which, below master level, had perhaps never died) and the development of new ones (e.g. Volga Gambit, French poisoned pawn) which were more suited to the new ideas in chess. Counter-gambits from the old motive still sometimes appear (as do ideas best classified as 'fantasy') but the positional sacrifice has added a new direction. Numerous opening lines have been discovered in which Black offers material (usually a pawn, but sometimes the exchange or even more) for strategic reasons. These are opening variations in which early tactical play is invited not in the primary hope of quick mate, but rather to create unbalanced middle-games (e.g. the mutual destruction of the flanks in the French poisoned pawn) and/or to cut across the opponent's plan of development. The epitome of the new philosophy is surely the Volga Gambit in which, after offering a pawn, Black develops his pieces for ten moves or more before producing any threats at all of a tactical nature. This is nonetheless one of the soundest gambits.

It is notable that in the last 10 or 15 years an opposing trend, initiated by White, has grown stronger - to postpone the weight of the struggle to the middle-game again. White avoids 1 e4 and 1 d4 which are committal and allow Black splendid opportunities of complicating the position from the outset. Instead one sees 1 c4, 1 Nf3. 1 g3 or 1 b3: all moves which reserve a lot of White's options and make it harder for Black to come to grips. All these openings are good, but surely not objectively stronger than the old ones. The popularity of flank openings is partly fashion, partly a desire to innovate, and in great measure a tribute to the philosophy of dynamic counterplay in the modern opening. Perhaps it will not be long before the counter-gambit ideas are found in these openings too ...

Now it is time to proceed to the detailed discussion of the counter-gambits themselves. Black does not win all the illustrative games of course, but I think a little bias in his favour is forgivable, in view of the theme of the book.

2   COUNTER-GAMBITS IN OPEN GAMES

Until about 1880 most chess games began 1 e4, e5 and the play was largely tactical in nature, due to the rapid opening of central lines and swift piece development characteristic of the Scotch Opening, Evans and King's Gambits and the forms of the Ruy Lopez that were popular then. Each player strove to get his sacrifice in first, and then follow it up with a searing attack on the enemy king. Gambits by both players abound in the theory of the ancient openings — the 'open games' — that commence 1 e4, e5, and in most cases they have been very deeply analysed.

Counter-gambits in the open games usually involve the sacrifice of a pawn by an early ..., d5 or ..., f5, although other themes will also be seen. The move ..., d5 opens lines for Black's queen and queen's bishop and can interfere with his opponent's threats against f7. By contrast, ..., f5 is primarily a deflecting move, seeking to obtain a strong pawn centre at the cost of weakening the king's position.

Many of these counter-gambits are naive and unsound, although this does not mean that they are innocuous, while others, albeit suspect, are resistant to attempts to deal them the final theoretical death-blow. The Queen's Pawn's Counter-Gambit (2 Nf3, d5?!) and the Latvian Counter-Gambit (2 Nf3, f5!?) illustrate these categories. However where White has offended against principle (e.g. by playing 4 Ng5 against the Two Knights Defence) then a timely counter-gambit can be very effective.

The openings in this chapter are most easily to be located by consulting the alphabetical index at the back of the book. The order in which they appear is bound to be somewhat arbitrary; I have chosen the following: 2 f4; 2 Bc4; 2 Nc3; 2 Nf3 and if then 2 ..., Nc6, the order is 3 Bc4, 3 Nc3, 3 Bb5. 'Fantasy' ideas, for which there are no illustrative games, are discussed at the end of the chapter.

FALKBEER COUNTER-GAMBIT (1 e4, e5; 2 f4, d5)

The King's Gambit, it cannot be denied, holds a unique place in chess history and aesthetics. Not only is it one of the oldest recorded chess openings, but also it typically gives rise to sacrificial tactical play characteristic of the romantic movement. As such it holds a strong attraction even for modern grandmasters, having been practised by such as Bronstein, Keres, Korchnoy, Spassky and Fischer — although in the latter case it is perhaps for nostalgic reasons only, as the World Champion has claimed that the gambit is unsound.

Nonetheless the defence of the gambit is by no means easy, and Black is probably well advised not to attempt to win the game on material. He can rather play the Falkbeer Counter-Gambit, thereby making his own bid for the initiative and putting in question the strategy behind White's second move. At one time the Falkbeer (introduced in the 19th Century) was considered almost the positional refutation of the King's Gambit, although a modern master will probably reserve his judgement on this difficult question.

The idea behind the continuation 2 ..., d5; 3 exd5, e4 was best expressed by Reti:

> 'What does Black gain by making this Pawn sacrifice? Above all it achieves the complete defeat of the aims inherent in White's Gambit move. The opening of the f-file, as well as the intended establishment of a Pawn centre are thoroughly thwarted. The position of the Pawn on f4 seems now devoid of meaning.'

Let us begin our study of the Falkbeer Counter-Gambit with an example of Black successful, being (at the time of writing) the most recent grandmaster encounter in this opening.

Game 1
Planinc - Vasyukov
(Wijk aan Zee 1973)

**1 e2-e4, e7-e5
2 f2-f4, d7-d5
3 e4xd5**

This is usual and best, but other moves must also be mentioned:

a)- 3 fxe5??, Qh4+ and Black should win.

b)- 3 Nf3, dxe4 (3 ..., exf4 is also good) **4 Nxe5, Nd7** (4 ..., Bd6; 5 Qe2, Nf6! is also strong) **5 d4** (or 5 Qe2, Ngf6; 6 Nc3, Nc5!) 5 ..., exd3; 6 Nxd3, Ngf6; 7 Nc3, Nb6!; 8 Be2, Bd6; 9 O-O, O-O; 10 Bf3, c6 was equal in Lutikov - Nikitin, Tiflis 1959. Black can try to bring pressure on f4.

c)- 3 d4?! allows 3 ..., exd4; 4 Qxd4, **Nf6**; 5 exd5, Qxd5; 6 Nf3, Nc6; 7 Qe3+, Qe4 with equality; Black can also try the thematic offer **4 ...,**

Nc6!?; 5 Qxd5, Qxd5; 6 exd5, Nb4.
d)- 3 Nc3, d4; 4 Nce2, Bg4; 5 d3, Bd6; 6 fxe5, Bxe5; 7 Qd2, Nc6; 8 Nf3, Bxf3; 9 gxf3, Qh4+; 10 Kd1, f5!; 11 Qg5, Qxg5; 12 Bxg5, h6 and Black has good play, White's two bishops being of little account (Milner-Barry - Keres, Margate 1937)   **3 ...   e5-e4**

The characteristic Falkbeer idea. Black closes the f-file, and his advanced pawn restricts White to some extent. Other moves:

a)- 3 ..., exf4 transposes to the King's Gambit Accepted after 4 Nf3 (Modern Defence) or 4 Qf3! (Breyer Gambit).

b)- 3 ..., Qxd5?; 4 Nc3, Qe6; 5 fxe5, Qxe5+; 6 Be2, Bg4; 7 d4, Qe6; 8 Qd3 favours White (Tolush - Alatortsev, Moscow 1948).

c)- 3 ..., c6?! (the Nimzowitsch Variation) is only rarely seen, yet it is not clear that White can obtain any advantage against it:

c1)- 4 Qe2?, cxd5; 5 fxe5 (Not 5 Qxe5+?, Be7!) 5 ..., Nc6; 6 c3, d4; 7 Nf3, Nge7; 8 d3, Ng6; 9 Qe4, Bc5 with advantage to Black (Alekhine - Johner, Carlsbad 1911)

c2)- 4 dxc6?!, Nxc6; 5 d3 (Keres suggests 5 Nf3, exf4; 6 d4, Bd6 with a form of King's Gambit Accepted) 5 ..., Bc5; 6 Nc3, Nf6; 7 Nf3, O-O; 8 fxe5, Nxe5; 9 Bg5 (Or 9 Nxe5, Re8; 10 Bf4, Ng4!; 11 Qe2, Nxe5; 12 Bxe5, Bd4; 13 O-O-O, Rxe5 with a winning attack) 9 ..., Re8 (Lazard - Tartakover, Paris 1929). Black stands to win, e.g. 10 Ne2, Nxf3+; 11 gxf3, Qd4 or 10 Ne4, Nxe4!; 11 Bxd8, Nc3! or 10 Nxe5, Rxe5+; 11 Ne4, Nxe4! etc.

c3)- 4 Qf3 (Keres also suggests the untried **4 d3!?**) 4 ..., exf4 (4 ..., Bc5!?) 5 dxc6 (5 Nc3!? - Keres) 5 ..., Nxc6; 6 Bb5, Nf6; 7 d4!, Bd7 (Spielmann - Nimzowitsch, 1907) and now **8 c3!** (Keres) is better than 8 Nge2, Qb6 as played. Nonetheless by the simple 8 ..., Be7; 9 Bxf4, O-O followed by ..., Re8 and ..., Nd5 Black may conjure up sufficient piece activity to compensate for his pawn.

c4)- 4 Nc3, exf4!; 5 Nf3, Nf6; 6 d4, Bd6!; 7 Qe2+ (Or 7 dxc6, Nxc6; 8 Bd3, O-O) 7 ..., Kf8!? (It is also possible to dispute Keres' assessment of 7 ..., Qe7; 8 Qxe7+, Kxe7; 9 Ne5 as being slightly in White's favour; the potential weakness of the Black d-pawn after 9 ..., Nd5; 10 Nxd5+, cxd5; 11 Bxf4, f6 did not appear significant in the game Tannenbaum - Estrin, Moscow 1959) 8 Ne5, cxd5; 9 Nb5, Be7; 10 Bxf4, Nc6; 11 Nc7, Rb8; 12 c3, Bd7; 13 g4, Rc8; 14 Nxd7+, Qxd7; 15 g5, Ng8 (Cheremisin - Estrin, Moscow 1959) 16 Nxd5 (In the

game 16 Bg2, Rxc7! favoured Black) 16 ..., Qxd5; 17 Bg2, Qe6; 18 d5 (Or 18 Qxe6, fxe6; 19 O-O, Ke8; 20 Rae1, h6!) 18 ..., Qxe2+; 19 Kxe2, Na5; 20 d6, Bd8 and it is not clear how White can justify his sacrifice (Hildebrand in his Swedish monograph Falkbeers Motgambit). The critical continuation is 21 d7, Ra8, but not 21 ..., Rc4?!; 22 Bd6+, Ne7; 23 Kd3 followed by 24 Rae1 and 25 Rxe7!. So the Nimzo-witsch Variation appears to merit further attention!

1

4 Nb1-c3

A rather unusual continuation which, according to Keres, offers White little hope of obtaining an opening advantage. For other 4th moves, see the later games in this chapter.

4 ..., Ng8-f6; 5 Qd1-e2

Nor are other moves dangerous:

a)- 5 Bb5+, c6! (Hildebrand).

b)- 5 Bc4, Bc5; 6 d4 (Or 6 Nge2, O-O transposing) 6 ..., exd3; 7 Qxd3, O-O; 8 Nge2 (Or 8 h3, c6; 9 Nge2, Qc7) 8 ..., Ng4 (Or 8 ..., c6, but inferior is 8 ..., Re8) 9 Qf3 (Better than 9 Nd1, Re8; 10 h3, Nh6; 11 Ne3, c6 with the initiative for Black.) 9 ..., Re8; 10 h3, Ne3; 11

Bxe3, Rxe3+; 12 Qf1, Qh4+; 13 Kd2, Re8 (Spassky - Tumurbator, Leipzig 1960) and in Keres' opinion Black has the value of his pawn.
c)- 5 d3, Bb4+; 6 Bd2 (To Black's advantage is 6 dxe4, Nxe4; 7 Qd4, Qe7; 8 Be2, O-O; 9 Bd2, Nxd2; 10 Qxd2, Bg4 Gunsberg - Marco, Hastings 1895.) **6 ..., e3**; 7 Bxe3, O-O; 8 Bd2, Bxc3; 9 bxc3, Re8+; 10 Be2, Bg4 (Schulten - Morphy, New York 1857) 11 Kf2!= (New here is **6 ..., O-O!?**; 7 Nxe4, Re8; 8 Bxb4, Nxe4; 9 dxe4, Rxe4+; 10 Be2 with some advantage to White (Spassky - Bronstein, Moscow 1971)

5 ..., Bf8-e7

The modern continuation. Others:
a)- 5 ..., Bd6?; 6 d3!, O-O; 7 dxe4, Nxe4; 8 Nxe4, Re8; 9 Qf3, f5; 10 Be3, fxe4; 11 Qf2 with advantage to White (Rubinstein).

b)- 5 ..., Bf5; 6 Nxe4 (Zak analysed the sharp 6 h3, h5; 7 g3, c6; 8 d3, cxd5; 9 dxe4, dxe4; 10 Bd2, Nc6; 11 O-O-O.) 6 ..., Nxe4; 7 d3, Qh4+!; 8 Kd1, Qe7; 9 dxe4, Bxe4=(Keres)

6 Nc3xe4

A major alternative is **6 d3** (Or 6 b3!? — Keres) e.g.:

a)- 6 ..., exd3; 7 Qxd3, Na6; 8 a3 (8 Be3! — Keres) 8 ..., Nc5; 9 Qd4, O-O; 10 Be2 with a slight advantage to White (Keres).

b)- 6 ..., Bg4!?; 7 Qe3, exd3; 8 Qxd3, O-O (8 ..., Na6!?) 9 Be2, Re8; 10 h3? (Critical is 10 Bd2 to meet 10 ..., Na6 by 11 O-O-O.) 10 ..., Bxe2; 11 Ngxe2, Na6; 12 a3, Bc5; 13 Bd2, Qd6; 14 Rd1? (Better is 14 O-O-O, suggested in 'Revista de Sah' since 14 ..., Bxa3? fails to 15 Nb5.) 14 ..., Rad8; 15 Bc1, Re7; 16 Qf3, Rde8; 17 g3, Bb6 and Black had ample compensation for

her pawn through control of the king file and the insecurity of the White king (Nicolau - Polihroniade, Rumanian Ladies' Championship, 1970).

6 ..., O-O

An innovation. Also good is **6 ..., Nxd5**; 7 d3, O-O; 8 Bd2, f5; 9 Nc3!?, Bh4+; 10 Kd1, Re8; 11 Qf3, Be6; 12 Nge2, c5 and Black stands well (Suttles - Lengyel, Belgrade 1969).

7 Ne4xf6+, Be7xf6; 8 Qe2-f3, Rf8-e8+; 9 Ke1-d1!?

Avoiding self-pins, which would leave him very passively placed.

9 ..., c7-c6; 10 Bf1-c4, b7-b5; 11 Bc4-b3, Bc8-b7; 12 Ng1-e2, a7-a5; 13 a2-a3, c6-c5; 14 d2-d3, a5-a4; 15 Bb3-a2, Nb8-d7; 16 Ne2-c3, b5-b4; 17 Nc3-e4, b4-b3!; 18 Ne4-d6,

The variation **18 cxb3?**, Bxd5 would be swiftly won by Black. It is evident that Vasyukov's strategy of advancing pawns to expose the White king has underlined the risk taken by White on his 9th move.

18 ..., b3xa2; 19 Nd6xe8;

19 Nxb7?, Qb6; 20 d6, Bxb2 is out of the question for White.

19 ..., Qd8xe8; 20 Ra1xa2, Nd7-b6; 21 c2-c4, Qe8-d7; 22 Ra2-a1

2

22 ..., Nb6xd5!

This further sacrifice, which White cannot decline (23 Qf1, Nb6; 24 Kc2, Nxc4!), puts White's King in a wretched situation.

23 c4xd5, Bb7xd5; 24 Qf3-g3, Bd5-b3+; 25 Kd1-d2, Ra8-d8; 26 Rh1-e1, c5-c4; 27 Re1-e3, Qd7-c7;

With a new threat: 28 ..., c3+.

28 d3-d4, Bf6xd4; 29 Kd2-e2, Bb3-c2;

With the equalisation of material by **29 ..., Bxe3?**; 30 Qxe3! some of Black's advantage would disappear. The two bishops are strong.

30 Qg3-h4, h7-h6; 31 Qh4-e7, Qc7-b8; 32 Bc1-d2, Bd4-f6; 33 Qe7-b4, Qb8xf4; 34 g2-g3, Bc2-d3+; 35 Ke2-d1, Qf4-f1+; 36 Re3-e1, Qf1-f3+;37 Kd1-c1,Bd3-f5

Now Black threatens 38 ..., Qd3 and if **38 Re3** there comes 38 ..., Qf1+; 39 Be1 (39 Re1, Qd3) 39 ..., Bg5; 40 Qc3, Rd3 and wins.

38 Qb4xa4, Bf6xb2+; 39 Kc1xb2, Rd8xd2+; 40 Kb2-c1, Qf3-c3+; White resigns.

Of course White has stronger methods of play against the Falkbeer:

Game 2
Zuckerman - Reshevsky
(Netanya 1971)

1 e2-e4, e7-e5; 2 f2-f4, d7-d5; 3 e4xd5, e5-e4; 4 d2-d3!

The most dangerous continuation. Others:

a)- 4 Nc3 see Game 1.

b)- 4 Bb5+, c6; 5 dxc6, Nxc6!; **6 d3**, Nf6; 7 Nc3, Bb4; 8 Bd2, Bg4; 9 Nge2, O-O!; 10 a3 (best) 10 ..., exd3; 11 Bxd3, Bxc3; 12 Bxc3 (Or

12 bxc3) 12 ..., Nd5; 13 Qd2 (analysis of Keres). The chances after 13 ..., Re8 are in Black's favour.

In this line White can also try **6 Qe2**, Nf6; 7 Nc3 (7 d3, Qa5+; 8 Nc3, Bb4) 7 ..., Bc5; 8 Nxe4, O-O; 9 Bxc6, bxc6; 10 d3, Re8; 11 Bd2, Nxe4; 12 dxe4, Bf5 with a strong attack for Black (Rosanes - Anderssen, 1862) or **6 d4**, Nf6 (Also good is 6 ..., Qa5+) 7 h3, Qa5+; 8 Nc3, Bb4; 9 Bd2 (Better 9 Bxc6+, bxc6; 10 Ne2) 9 ..., e3! is again excellent for Black (Anderssen - Zukertort, Berlin 1868). Other moves (6 Bxc6+, 6 Nc3, 6 Ne2) also leave Black well placed.

c)- 4 d4, Nf6 (Better than 4 ..., Qxd5; 5 Be3, Nf6; 6 Nc3, Bb4; 7 Nge2, O-O; 8 a3 of Farley - Dilworth, Birmingham 1973) 5 c4 (Or 5 Nc3, Bb4; 6 Bd2, Bxc3 and 7 ..., Nxd5) 5 ..., Be7; 6 Ne2, O-O; 7 Ng3, c6; 8 dxc6, Nxc6; 10 d5, Nb4 and Black stands well (Benzinger - Henning, Bad Ems 1932).

d)- 4 c4, c6; 5 Nc3, Nf6; 6 d4, cxd5; 7 Qb3, Be7; 8 cxd5, O-O; 9 Nge2, Nbd7; 10 Ng3, Nb6 (Tartakover - Reti, Vienna 1922). White's advanced pawns are weak.

e)- 4 Qe2, Nf6 is not of independent significance.

f)- 4 Bc4, Nf6; 5 Nc3, Bc5; 6 Nge2, O-O; 7 d4, exd3; 8 Qxd3, Ng4! (Hildebrand)

4 ..., Ng8-f6!

(See Diagram 3)

5 d3xe4!

At present, this appears to be White's best chance of getting an advantage out of the opening. Others:

a)- 5 Nd2 see Game 3

3

b)- 5 Nc3, Bb4; 6 Bd2 see Game 1, note c to White's 5th move.

c)- 5 Qe2, Bg4!; 6 Nf3 (Too risky is 6 Qe3?! on account of Persitz's sacrifice 6 ..., Bb4+!; 7 Bd2?, O-O!; 8 Bxb4, Nxd5; 9 Qc5, Re8 with a strong attack; or 7 c3, O-O; 8 cxb4, Nxd5; 9 Qg3, exd3 or again 8 dxe4, Ba5.) **6 ..., Bb4+** (Or Hildebrand's untried suggestion 6 ..., Qe7!?; 7 dxe4, Nxe4 but not 6 ..., Qxd5; 7 Nbd2, Bf5?? ; 8 dxe4, Bxe4; 9 Ng5, Bb4; 10 c3 and White wins) 7 c3, O-O; 8 dxe4, Re8; 9 e5, Ba5; 10 Na3! (Filzer - Shishov, Moscow 1958) Black wins back one pawn with an unclear position resulting: will White's centre pawns prove strong or weak? (Also worth further investigation is the line **5 ..., Bf5**; 6 dxe4, Nxe4; 7 Nc3, Qe7; 8 Nb5!?, Qd7; 9 g4!? (9 Nf3! — Keres, but not 9 Nd4, Bc5) 9 ..., Bc5; 10 gxf5, O-O; 11 Be3, Re8; 12 O-O-O, Nf2 with complications (Nei - Kondratiev, Tallinn 1948).

5 ..., Nf6xe4; 6 Ng1-f3!

The young American master Zuckerman can be relied upon to find the straight and narrow way through a morass of theoretical complications. Other moves give Black fewer problems:

a)- 6 Be3, Qh4+; 7 g3, Nxg3 and now:

a1)- 8 hxg3, Qxh1; 9 Qe2, Bb4+!; 10 c3, Bd6; 11 Bg2, Qh6; 12 Bd4+ (12 Nd2!? — Tal) 12 ..., Kd8; 13 Nf3, Bg4; 14 Qf2, Re8+; 15 Kf1, Nd7; 16 Nbd2, Qg6; 17 Kg1, f6!; 18 Rc1, b6; 19 b4, a5!; 20 Nh4?, Qd3; 21 Ndf3, Re2; 22 Qf1, axb4; 23 Rd1, Rxg2+; 24 Kxg2, Rxa2+; 25 Kg1, Qxf1+; 26 Kxf1, g5; 27 Resigns (Tal - Trifunovic, Havana 1963).

a2)- 8 Nf3!, Qe7; 9 hxg3, Qxe3+; 10 Qe2, Qxe2+; 11 Bxe2, Bg4; 12 Nc3, Bb4 with an equal ending (Spassky - Matanovic, Belgrade 1964).

b)- 6 Qe2, Qxd5 (Also good is 6 ..., Bb4+) 7 Nbd2, f5; **8 Nh3** (If 8 g4?!, Nc6!; 9 c3, Be7; 10 Bg2, Qf7; 11 Nxe4, ·fxe4; 12 Bxe4, Bh4+; 13 Kf1, O-O or 8 g3, Bd7; 9 Bg2, Bc6; 10 Nh3, Nd7; 11 Nxe4, fxe4; 12 O-O, Bc5+.) 8 ..., Nc6; 9 c3, Be6; 10 Nxe4, fxe4; 11 Nf2, O-O-O; 12 g3, Bc5; 13 Bg2 and now in the game Janowski - Pillsbury, Vienna 1898, Black availed himself of the strong queen sacrifice 13 ..., e3!

6 ..., Bf8-c5

This is better than **6 ..., Bf5**; 7 Be3, c6; 8 Bc4, b5; 9 Bb3, c5; 10 d6!, c4; 11 Qd5 (Alekhine - Tarrasch, Petersburg 1914) or **6 ..., Bg4**; 7 Bd3, Bf5; 8 Qe2, Qxd5; 9 Nbd2 (Keres) or **6 ..., c6**; 7 Nd2, Nxd2; 8 Bxd2 and 9 Bd3 (Hildebrand)

7 Qd1-e2, Qd8-e7?!

Reshevsky introduces a new move. However it is probably not good enough. Current theory shows an advantage to White in all lines here:

a)- 7 ..., Bf5!; 8 Nc3 (8 g4, O-O!) **8 ..., Qe7; 9 Be3, Bxe3** (Or 9 ..., Nxc3; 10 Bxc5, Nxe2; 11 Bxe7, Nxf4; 12 Ba3! (Bronstein - Tal, Riga 1968) or 12 Bg5 with Black under heavy pressure) **10 Qxe3, Nxc3; 11 Qxe7+ Kxe7; 12 Ne4** (better than 12 ..., Bxc2; 13 Kd2) **12 Ng5!, Bxd5; 14 O-O-O** when, according to Keres' analysis, Black will have difficulty in equalising the position. A possible continuation is **14 ..., Bxa2; 15 c4, b5; 16 Kb2!** (better than 16 cxb5, h6 followed by ..., a6 and Black holds) **16 ..., Bxc4; 17 Bxc4, bxc4; 18 Rhe1+, Kf6** and now after 19 Rd4 or 19 Rd5 Black, despite his two extra pawns, is on the brink of defeat. Or **14 ..., Be6; 15 Nxe6, fxe6; 16 Bc4** with advantage to White (Krnic - Cortlever, Wijk aan Zee 1972).

b)- 7 ..., Bf2+; 8 Kd1, Qxd5+ (Or 8 ..., f5; 9 Nfd2, Bh4; 10 Nxe4, fxe4; 11 Qxe4+, Kf7; 12 Bd2) **9 Nfd2!, f5; 10 Nc3, Qd4; 11 Ncxe4, fxe4; 12 c3, Qe3** (12 ..., Qb6; 13 Nc4) **13 Qh5+!** and White is winning (Reti - Breyer, Budapest 1917).

c)- 7 ..., Qxd5; 8 Nfd2, f5; 9 Nc3, Qd4; 10 Ncxe4, fxe4; 11 Nb3 favouring White (Napier - Blackburne, 1895).

d)- 7 ..., f5; 8 Be3! (8 Nc3, O-O) **8 ..., Qxd5** (best) **9 Bxc5, Qxc5; 10 Nc3** (Spielmann - Wolf, Dusseldorf 1908). White stands better as in case of 10 ..., O-O he has the resource 11 Nxe4, fxe4; 12 Qxe4, Bf5; 13 Qc4+!.

e)- 7 ..., O-O; 8 Qxe4, Re8; 9 Ne5, f6; 10 Bd3 (Keres) e.g. 10 ..., g6; 11 Qc4, Na6; 12 b4!, Bxb4; 13 O-O, fxe5; 14 fxe5, Rxe5; 15 Bb2 and wins (analysis).

8 Bc1-e3!, Nb8-a6

Not of course **8 ..., Ng3??** because of 9 Bxc5.

9 Be3xc5

Zuckerman, in The Chess Player, claims also a slight advantage for White after **9 Nbd2, Nxd2; 10 Bxd2, Nb4**, but the move he plays is better.

9 ..., Na6xc5; 10 Nb1-d2, O-O; 11 O-O-O

Not **11 b4??** because of 11...,Qf6.

11 ..., Bc8-f5; 12 Nf3-d4, Qe7-f6; 13 Nd4xf5, Qf6xf5; 14 Nd2xe4,Nc5xe4 15 Qe2-f3, Ne4-d6!

Reshevsky defends well. He keeps the knight which will be useful for manoeuvring against the loose points in the White position (pawns on d5 and f4) and gradually steers the game into an ending which he is able to draw. Nonetheless his position cannot be considered adequate compensation for the lost pawn; perhaps Zuckerman misses a win later.

4

16 Bf1-d3, Qf5-d7; 17 f4-f5

Zuckerman mentions **17 g4!?** in The Chess Player.

17 ..., Qd7-e7; 18 f5-f6, Qe7xf6; 19 Qf3xf6, g7xf6; 20 Rh1-f1, Kg8-g7;

21 Rf1-f3, Ra8-e8; 22 Rf3-g3+,
Kg7-h8; 23 Rd1-f1, Rf8-g8; 24
Rg3xg8+, Kh8xg8; 25 Rf1xf6,
b7-b5!

Else White could advance the
queen-side pawns and dislodge the
vital knight from his watchtower.

26 Rf6-h6, Re8-e5; 27 Rh6xh7,
Re5xd5

If instead 27 ..., Nc4 (threatening
mate) 28 c3, Rxd5; 29 Rh3 —
Zuckerman.

28 Rh6-h4, c7-c5; 29 Bd3-e4,
Rd5-e5; 30 Be4-f3, Kg8-g7; 31
c2-c3, a7-a5; 32 a2-a4

In order to keep at least one
pawn on the queen-side. Also, to
play 32 Rg4+, Kh6; 33 h4, b4
might lead to a blockade.

32 ..., b5-b4; 33 Kc1-d2, b4xc3+;
34 b2xc3, f7-f5; 35 Rh4-f4, Kg7-g6;
36 h2-h4!

After 36 g3, Kg5; 37 Rh4 White
is in a tangle.

36 ..., Kg6-g7; 37 g2-g4, f5xg4; 38
Rf4xg4+, Kg7-h7

The king must not cut itself off
from the passed pawn.

39 Rg4-f4, Kh7-g7; 40 Rf4-g4+,
Kg7-h7; 41 Bf3-e2

Safety past the time control,
White tries a new tack. Zuckerman
also mentions the possible plan 41
Rg2, intending 42 h5, 43 Re2, 44
Re6.

41 ..., Kh7-h6; 42 Be2-d3, Kh6-h5;
43 Rg4-f4, Re5-e6; 44 c3-c4?

Zuckerman gives as correct 44
Be2+, Kh6; 45 h5. However after
45 ..., Kg5 the obstacles in the way
of a White victory are probably
insuperable.

44 ..., Re6-e8; 45 Bd3-e2+

If 45 Rf6 Black has 45 ..., Rd8!

45 ..., Kh5-g6; 46 Rf4-g4+, Kg6-f5;
47 Rg4-g5+, Kf5-f4; 48 Be2-d3,
Re8-e5; 49 Rg5-g6

If 49 Rxe5, Kxe5; 50 Ke3, Nc8!;
51 Bc2, Nd6

49 ..., Nd6-e4+; 50 Bd3xe4, Re5xe4
51 Rg6-a6, Kf4-e5; Draw agreed.

White cannot keep his h-pawn,
so Reshevsky only has to bring his
king back to the queen-side to
achieve a theoretical draw.

It can be seen from this game
and the analysis at Black's seventh
move, that the fate of the Falkbeer
is currently in the balance. The
other critical line is Keres' Variation, which we shall now examine.

Game 3
Sydor - Uitumen
(Poland 1971)

1 e2-e4, e7-e5; 2 f2-f4, d7-d5; 3
e4xd5, e5-e4; 4 d2-d3, Ng8-f6; 5
Nb1-d2, e4xd3!

Other moves here are not so good

a)- 5 ..., e3; 6 Nc4, Nxd5; 7 Nxe3,
Nxf4; 8 g3, Ng6; 9 Bg2, Bd6; 10
Nf3, O-O; 11 O-O and White is
rather better (Keres - Stalda,
correspondence 1933).

b)- 5 ..., Qxd5; 6 dxe4, Nxe4; 7 Bc4,
Qc5 (7 ..., Qa5; 8 Qe2) 8 Qe2, f5; 9
Nxe4, fxe4; 10 Qxe4+, Be7; 11 Nf3
is clearly better for White (Ketting -
van Nuss, Rotterdam 1938).

c)- 5 ..., Bf5; 6 dxe4, Nxe4; 7
Ngf3!, Bc5 (No better are 7 ...,
Qxd5; 8 Bc4, Qc5; 9 Qe2 or 7 ...,
Bb4; 8 c3, Qe7; 9 Ne5 or 7 ..., Be7;
8 Bc4, c6; 9 Nxe4, Bxe4; 10 d6!,
Qxd6; 11 Bxf7+, Kxf7; 12 Ng5+.)

8 Bd3, Nxd2 (8 ..., Bf2+; 9 Kf1 or 8 ..., O-O; 9 Bxe4, Re8; 10· Ne5) 9 Bxf5, Nxf3+; 10 Qxf3, O-O; 11 Bd2, Re8+; 12 Kd1 and White stands better, according to analysis by Keres.

d)- 5 ..., Bc5!? is a little-known idea of the Finnish player Niemela:

d1)- 6 Nxe4, Bxg1! (Or 6 ..., Nxe4; 7 dxe4, O-O; 8 Bd3, c6!; 9 d6, Bxd6; 10 Nf3, Re8; 11 Qe2, Na6; 12 Be3 Kaila - Niemela, Finnish Championship 1951) 7 Rxg1 (Or 7 Nxf6+, Qxf6; 8 Rxg1, O-O!) 7 ..., Nxd5; 8 Qf3, Nc6; 9 c3, O-O; 10 Bd2, f5; 11 Ng3, Nf6; 12 Be2, Be6 (threatening 13 ..., Ng4 and 14 ..., Bd5 and 15 ..., Qh4) 13 h3, Qd7; 14 Nf1, Bd5; 15 Qf2, Rad8; 16 Ne3, Be6! threatening 17 ..., Ne4 (Niemela).

d2)- 6 dxe4, Ng4; 7 Qf3, Nf2; 8 Nb3, Bb6; 9 c4, Nd7; 10 Be3, Bxe3; 11 Qxe3, Nxh1 (Böök)

d3)- 6 d4, Bxd4; 7 Ne2, Bb6; 8 Nc3, e3!; 9 Ne4 (9 Nc4!?) 9 ..., O-O! (Hildebrand)

6 Bf1xd3, Bc8-g4?!

An innovation, of unclear value. Other moves are critical too:

a)- 6 ..., Nxd5!; 7 Ne4 (Or 7 Qe2+, Qe7; 8 Ne4 or 7 ..., Be7; 8 Ne4, Nb4; 9 Bb5+ — Keres; these lines deserve close examination) 7 ..., Nb4!; 8 Bb5+, c6; 9 Qxd8+ (not 9 Qe2, Nxc2+! but 9 Ba4 is better — Keres) 9 ..., Kxd8; 10 Ba4, Bf5 and Black stands better (Castaldi - Trifunovic, Hilversum 1947).

b)- 6 ..., Qxd5; 7 Ngf3 (7 Qf3!? — Spielmann) 7 ..., Nc6 (7 ..., Bg4; 8 h3, Bxf3; 9 Qxf3, Nc6; 10 Ne4 and White is rather better — Keres) 8 Qe2+ (Or 8 O-O, Bc5+; 9 Kh1, O-O) 8 ..., Be7; 9 O-O (Keres recommends 9 Ne5.) 9 ..., O-O

(Euwe suggests 9 ..., Bg4 intending castling long.) 10 Nb3 (Spielmann - Koomen, Amsterdam 1938) and now Rausch suggested 10 ..., Bg4 with a fair game for Black.

7 Ng1-f3, Nf6xd5; 8 h2-h3, Bg4-d7?!

In Informator 12, Maric suggested 8 ..., Bxf3, e.g. 9 Qxf3, Bc5; 10 Nb3, Bb6; 11 Bd2, O-O; 12 O-O-O, a5; 13 Kb1 with an interesting game, but White's chances probably better in view of the two bishops (analysis).

9 Nd2-e4, Nb8-c6; 10 O-O, Bf8-e7; 11 Nf3-g5

White threatens 12 Bc4.

11 ..., Nd5-b6; 12 Bc1-d2

12 Qh5?! would be premature, according to Maric's analysis: 12 ..., g6; 13 Qh6, Bf8; 14 Qh4, h6; 15 Re1, Be7 followed by ..., Kf8-g7 and a good game for Black.

12 ..., h7-h6; 13 Qd1-h5, O-O;

Not now 13 ..., g6 because of 14 Nd6+, Bxd6; 15 Bxg6 etc.

14 f4-f5!

White has a dangerous attack now.

5

14 ..., f7-f6

Other moves are inferior; Maric analyses:

a)- 14 ..., hxg5?; 15 Nxg5, Bxg5; 16 f6!, Bh6; 17 fxg7 and wins.

b)- 14 ..., Bf6; 15 Nxf6+, Qxf6; 16 Ne4, Qd4+; 17 Kh1 with advantage to White.

15 Ng5-e6, Bd7xe6; 16 Bd2xh6!!

White now threatens 17 Bxg7, and he can soon infiltrate the king's rook via f4 to consummate his attack.

16 ..., Nc6-e5

Covering the vital squares g4 and g6.

17 f5xe6, g7xh6

Practically forced, else he will be a pawn down with a bad game.

18 Rf1-f5?

This gives Black a chance. After 18 Ng3!, intending 18 ..., Nxd3 (or 18 ..., f5; 19 Bxf5) 19 Nf5! Black could give up the ghost.

18 ..., Kg8-g7

Against the threatened 19 Qxh6 and 20 Rh5.

19 Rf5xe5?!, Qd8-d4+??

Black muffs it. After 19 ..., fxe5! how does White propose to justify his rook sacrifice? Maric analyses:

a)- 20 Ng5, Rf6 and White is busted

b)- 20 Qg4+, Bg5; 21 h4, Rf4 and again Black wins.

So, objectively, White should have tried **19 Raf1**.

20 Ne4-f2!

This breathes new life into White's attack. There is only one way for Black to meet the threat of Qg6+, and it is not sufficient.

20 ..., f6-f5; 21 Re5xf5, Rf8-f6; 22 Rf5xf6, Qd4xf6; 23 Qh5-g4+, Kg7-h8; 24 Qg4-e4, Qf6-g7; 25 Nf2-g4, Ra8-f8; 26 Ng4-e5, Kh8-g8; 27 Ne5-f7, c7-c6; 28 Ra1-f1, Nb6-d5; 29 Rf1-f3

Threatening 30 Rg3, Qxg3; 31 Qh7 mate.

29 ..., Nd5-f6
30 Qe4-h4, Rf8xf7

There would appear to be an easy win here by **31 Rg3!** since 31 ..., Ng4; 32 exf7+, Kf8; 33 Qxg4! and 31 ..., Qxg3; 32 Qxg3+, Rg7; 33 Qb8+ are both horrible for Black.

31 e6xf7+

This is also good enough, of course.

31 ..., Kg8xf7; 32 Rf3-g3, Qg7-f8; 33 Bd3-g6+, Kf7-e6; 34 Kg1-h1, Nf6-d5; 35 Qh4-g4+, Ke6-d6; 36 Rg3-f3, Qf8-g7; 37 c2-c4, Nd5-f6; 38 Qg4-g3+, Kd6-c5; 39 b2-b4+, Kc5xb4; 40 Rf3-b3+, Black resigns

THE BISHOP'S OPENING (1 e4, e5; 2 Bc4)

As I demonstrate in my recent monograph 'The Bishop's Opening', 2 Bc4 is a strong and flexible alternative to White's 'normal' 2 Nf3. Players of the Black side of open games may expect to meet it with increasing frequency in the next few years.

White retains the option of playing f4, either early on or after preparation by Nge2 and O-O, often obtaining dangerous pressure down the half-open f-file. Also to White's advantage are the structures which tend to result from Black's bringing about the seemingly 'natural' exchange of White's bishop by bishop or knight on b3. Nor is it easy for Black to bring about the advance ..., d5 which often leads to equality (through exchanges and the opening of central lines) in the openings stemming from 2 Nf3.

This is not the place to go into a deeper analysis of the Bishop's Opening. I shall give two games involving Black's principal countergambit replies to the Bishop's, mentioning in the notes a few other points discovered too late for inclusion in the first edition of the specific work.

Game 4
Staunton - Cochrane
(London 1842)

1 e2-e4, e7-e5; 2 Bf1-c4, Bf8-c5!?

This was the most common reply in the 19th Century — since when 2 ..., Nf6 (see Game 5) has virtually superseded it. However it can lead to original tactical situations and hence has been on occasion the choice of grandmasters Korchnoy and Portisch.

Other moves are also possible:

a)- 2 ..., f5?! (The Calabrese Counter-Gambit, also popular at one time in the last century, particularly with Steinitz) 3 d3! (For the fascinating complications developing from 3 Nf3!? see Game 9, in the section on the Latvian Counter-Gambit) 3 ..., Nf6; 4 f4!, d6; 5 Nf3 with advantage to White (Jaenisch). Black's position is hard to develop, due to possible tactical exploitations.

b)- 2 ..., b5?! (A far-fetched Anderssen idea, which has also been seen after 2 ..., Nf6; 3 Nc3.) 3 Bxb5, c6 (Also 'playable' is 3 ..., f5?!; 4 exf5, Nf6; 5 Be2, Bc5; 6 Bh5+ and now 6 ..., g6 of N.M. - Thorold, Bristol 1865, was probably better than 6 ..., Kf8 of Spens - de Vere, Dundee 1867; Black won both times!) 4 Be2! (anticipating the modern treatment of the Evans Gambit) 4 ..., Nf6; 5 d3, d5; 6 f4, exf4; 7 e5 and White stands to win (Friedlander - Anderssen, Breslau 1856).

c)- 2 ..., d5?; 3 Bxd5 and Black has lost a pawn for nothing (Jaenisch)

Other, non-gambit, defences (2 ..., Nc6, 2 ..., d6, 2 ..., c6, 2 ..., Be7) are considered in 'The Bishop's Opening'. They should be inferior to 2 ..., Nf6.

3 c2-c3!?

Philidor's interesting continuation. A modern player (e.g. Larsen) will normally choose here **3 Nc3** or seek transposition into the Giuoco Piano by **3 Nf3**. **3 b4!?** can lead to the Evans Gambit. Others:

a)- 3 Qh5?! (This is probably the place to mention the counter-gambit 1 e4, e5; 2 Qh5?!, Nf6!?; 3 Qxe5+, Be7; I should be interested to hear of any games commencing this way!) 3 ..., Qe7 (Or 3 ..., Qf6) and White has nothing.

b)- 3 Qg4?!, d5!?; 4 Qxg7, Qh4! (Bronstein) leads to complications probably favouring Black. No practical examples obtain here either.

c)- 3 Qe2!?, Nc6 (If 3 ..., d6 or 3 ..., Nf6 there comes the bizarre Lopez Gambit, 4 f4!?) 4 Bxf7+?! (Probably best is 4 Nf3.) 4 ..., Kxf7; 5 Qc4+, d5!; 6 exd5 (Not 6 Qxc5?, dxe4; 7 Qc4+, Be6; 8 Qxe4, Nf6.) 6 ..., Bxf2+! (An excellent desperado sacrifice) 7 Kxf2, Na5; 8 Qd3, e4!; 9 Qxe4, Nf6; 10 Qd4, Nc6 and Black should regain his pawns with the better position (Pachman).

A deeper analysis of these lines, together with an analysis of **3 d3, 3 f4?! and 3 d4?!**, is to be found in Chapter 13 of 'The Bishop's Opening'.

3 ..., d7-d5!?

The debonair Lewis Counter-Gambit, which excited a lot of interest in London in the early decades of the last century. Against other moves (and this includes the generally recommended **3 ..., Nf6**) White has good chances of obtaining an advantage. Whereas the Lewis is better for Black than its

reputation might suggest.

4 Bc4xd5

Instead **4 exd5?** allows 4 ..., Bxf2+!; 5 Kxf2, Qh4+ and 6 ..., Qxc4.

4 ..., Ng8-f6

6

5 d2-d4

The continuation recommended by the great chess publicist George Walker. White's choice is not easy, but Jaenisch's **5 Qf3!?** has been held to be even stronger, amounting perhaps to a refutation of Black's gambit. The analysis is tricky: **5 ..., O-O!** and now:

a)- 6 d4, exd4; 7 Bg5, dxc3; 8 Bxf6 (Staunton gives here 8 Nxc3, Nbd7; 9 O-O, c6; 10 Bb3, Qe7) 8 ..., c2; 9 Nc3, Qxf6 and Pachman holds that Black has a slight superiority.

b)- 6 Bc4, Bg4; 7 Qd3, Qe7 and now **8 f3!?** (Jaenisch) is critical. White's plan should probably be 9 b4 and 10 a4 followed by 11 Ba3 to gain space. Black can count on his safer king and rather easier development. Inferior is Staunton's **8 Qc2**, Be6; 9 Bxe6, fxe6; 10 Nf3, Nc6; 11 d3, Ng4 as Black is now threatening ..., Rxf3!

Other ideas in the diagram are

less dangerous:

x) 5 Qa4+, c6; 6 Bxf7+, Kf8; 7 Qb3, Nxe4 (Staunton)

y)- 5 Bb3, Nxe4; 6 Qe2, Nxf2; 7 Qxe5+, Qe7; 8 Qxe7+, Kxe7; 9 d4, Bxd4; 10 cxd4, Nxh1 and Black's game is at least equal (Staunton).

z)- 5 Qb3, O-O (Exchanging is also good according to Staunton.) and now:

       z1)- 6 Bxb7?, Bxb7; 7 Qxb7, Qd3 is very good for Black.

       z2)- 6 Nf3, c6 (Staunton advocated 6 ..., Nxd5.) 7 Bxf7+, Rxf7; 8 Nxe5, Bxf2+!; 9 Kf1 (9 Kxf2, Ng4++ and 10 ..., Nxe5) 9 ..., Nd5; 10 Nxf7, Qf6; 11 exd5, Bh4+; 12 Ke2, Qf2+ and Black has an overwhelming attack ('Gambits Accepted'). White's 7th move is dubious, of course, but he certainly will not find a plus.

5 ..., e5xd4; 6 c3xd4, Bc5-b4+; 7 Bc1-d2

Cook's 'Synopsis of the Chess Openings' gave 7 Nc3, Nxd5; 8 exd5, Qxd5; 9 Nf3, Bg4; 10 Be3, Bxf3; 11 Qxf3, Qxf3; 12 gxf3=. White can improve on this slightly by 10 O-O! (hoping for 10 ..., Bxc3) 10 ..., Bxf3!; 11 Nxd5, Bxd1; 12 Rxd1 but dubious is 12 Nxc7+ (or 12 Bf4!?, Bg4!) as the knight will never escape from the corner (analysis).

7 ..., Bb4xd2+; 8 Qd1xd2, Nf6xd5; 9 e4xd5, Qd8xd5; 10 Ng1-f3, O-O

Black has equalised.

11 O-O, Bc8-g4?!

According to Schlechter's (1916) edition of 'Handbuch des Schachspiels', Black should have preferred 11 ..., Nc6 and if then 12 Nc3, Qh5; 13 d5, Ne5.

12 Nb1-c3, Qd5-h5; 13 Nf3-e5, Bg4-e6?

Black's position is declining. He should complete his development by 13 ..., Nd7 followed by ..., Rad8.

14 f2-f4, f7-f6; 15 Ne5-f3, c7-c6; 16 Ra1-e1, Qh5-f7; 17 Re1-e3, Nb8-d7

White is firmly in the saddle again. Not 17 ..., Bxa2?; 18 Rfe1 and 19 Re7.

18 Rf1-e1, Ra8-e8; 19 Nc3-e4, Be6xa2

Losing a pawn, by 19 ..., Qe7; 20 Neg5!, fxg5; 21 Nxg5, is probably worse.

20 Ne4-d6, Re8xe3; 21 Nd6xf7, Re3xe1+; 22 Qd2xe1, Ba2xf7; 23 Qe1-a5!

Staunton has a very active queen for rook, bishop and pawn.

23 ..., Bf7-d5; 24 Qa5-c7, Rf8-f7

24 ..., Bxf3; 25 Qxd7, Bd5 (25 ..., Rf7; 26 Qc8+, Rf8; 27 Qe6+) 26 Qxb7, Rf7; 27 Qa8+ and White will have too many pawns.

25 Qc7-c8+?

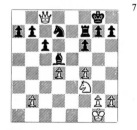

7

Insufficient technique by Staunton. According to Schlechter, 25 Qxb7 offered chances of a win. There could follow 25 ..., Bxf3; 26

gxf3, Ne5!?; 27 Qa8+, Rf8; 28 Qxa7! but not 28 Qxf8+?, Kxf8; 29 fxe5, fxe5; 30 dxe5 because of 30 ..., g5!

25 ..., Nd7-f8; 26 Kg1-f2, Bd5xf3; 27 Kf2xf3, Rf7-e7

White is in no danger, but it is hard to see how he can penetrate Black's stonewall now.

28 g2-g3, Kg8-f7; 29 b2-b4, a7-a6; 30 h2-h4, h7-h6; 31 g3-g4, Kf7-g8; 32 Qc8-b8, Kg8-f7; 33 Qb8-a7, g7-g5!?

This hardly seems necessary.

34 Qa7-c5

If **34 hxg5**, hxg5; 35 fxg5, fxg5; 36 Qc5, Ne6; 37 Qf5+, Kg7 is drawing.

34 ..., Nf8-h7; 35 f4-f5, Nh7-f8
Draw agreed

Game 5
Radulescu - Balanel
(Rumania 1958)

1 e2-e4, e7-e5; 2 Bf1-c4, Ng8-f6; 3 Nb1-c3

Other continuations, examined in 'The Bishop's Opening' are **3 d3, 3 d4, 3 f4?!, 3 Nf3!?** and **3 Qe2**. The text move gives a position that can also arise via the Vienna Gambit (2 Nc3, Nf6; 3 Bc4).

After **3 d3**, the great American tactician Frank Marshall used to play **3 ..., d5**; 4 exd5, Nxd5; 5 Nf3, Nc6; 6 O-O, Bg4 disregarding the weakness of his e-pawn, which makes this line in effect a counter-gambit. However after 7 Re1!, Be7 (7 ..., Bc5; 8 h3!, Bh5; 9 d4!) 8 h3 Black loses the pawn for insufficient compensation, whether he

retreats to h5 (Jackson - Marshall, Barmen 1905) or captures the knight (Larsen - Berger, Amsterdam 1964).

An interesting new plan for Black is **3 ..., Be7; 4 Nc3** (not f4?, d5!) **4 ..., c6** e.g. 5 Nf3, d6! (5 ..., d5 could result in weak centre pawns) 6 h3 (if 6 a4 a subsequent ..., a5 would be good for Black) 6 ..., O-O; 7 O-O, b5; 8 Bb3, Nbd7; 9 Re1!?, Qc7?!; 10 Bg5!, h6; 11 Bh4, b4; 12 Nb1, Nc5; 13 Nbd2, a5; 14 a3, Nxb3; 15 cxb3! with a balanced struggle (Harding - Orlov, Wijk aan Zee Reserves 1973). After **3 Nc3, 3 ..., Be7** allows 4 f4 as the knight covers the square d5: perhaps a good argument for preferring the text move.

3 ..., Nf6xe4!?

Objectively best for Black here is the waiting move **3 ..., Nc6**, while also possible are **3 ..., Bb4, 3 ..., Bc5, 3 ..., Be7, 3 ..., d6** and **3 ..., c6** (even **3 ..., g6** and **3 ..., b5?!** have been seen). The text move, which envisages a rook sacrifice, overthrows White's main strategic idea: but he has other good ones to take its place.

4 Qd1-h5!

Not **4 Bxf7+?**, Kxf7; 5 Nxe4, d5; 6 Qf3+, Be6.

4 ..., Ne4-d6
5 Bc4-b3

Leading, in most variations, to advantage for White in middlegame tactics; however some points have not yet become clarified by decades of practice and analysis.

Also possible for White, albeit rather drawish, is. the positional continuation **5 Qxe5+**, Qe7; 6 Qxe7+, Bxe7 and now, instead of

the **7 d3** and **7 Bb3** considered in
'The Bishop's Opening', or **7 Bd3**
of Abramson - Borisenko (correspondence 1956-7), White's best
may well be **7 Be2** (U.Andersson).

5 ..., Nb8-c6

Black could try for equality by **5
..., Be7**; 6 Nf3, **Nc6** but not **6 ...,
O-O?** as White obtains a strong
attack by 7 h4!, Nc6; 8 Ng5, h6; 9
Qg6! which is analysed in detail in
Chapter 5 of my earlier monograph.

6 Nc3-b5!

Forcing Black's reply as **6 ...,
Nxb5??** allows 7 Qxf7 mate, and 6
..., **Qe7?** loses the rook under
inferior circumstances.

6 ..., g7-g6; 7 Qh5-f3, f7-f5

The disadvantage of **7 ..., f6!?** is
that it allows White to play 8
Nxc7+, Qxc7; 9 Qxf6, b6 (Mukhin
- Bronstein, USSR Team Championship 1959) and now 10 Nf3!
when White stands better although
Bronstein, in '200 Open Games',
said that he did not know whether
it was winning.

**8 Qf3-d5, Qd8-e7; 9 Nb5xc7+,
Ke8-d8; 10 Nc7xa8, b7-b6**

8

I have called this rook sacrifice
the Frankenstein-Dracula Variation of the Bishop's Opening, in

tribute to its hair-raising complications. It is appropriate that, to
illustrate it, I should choose a game
(albeit not a very important one)
that was played in Transylvania
itself!

11 d2-d4!?

Here **11 Nf3**, Bb7; 12 d4, Nxd4
transposes back.

White has other ways of meeting
the rook sacrifice (**11 d3, 11 Qf3, 11
Nxb6**) which are all unclear,
although the former is the most
dangerous to Black. Due to the
complexity of the analyses, depen-
ding upon many fine points, I shall
not attempt to give a summary
here, but refer the reader to
Chapter 6 of 'The Bishop's
Opening'.

11 ..., Nc6xd4

White would welcome **11 ...,
exd4+?**; 12 Ne2, Bb7; 13 Bf4.

12 Ng1-f3, Bc8-b7; 13 Bc1-g5

A blunder: **13 Qxe5??**, Nxf3+
and Black wins the queen. The text
move, counter-attacking the Black
queen is a typical finesse in this
gambit.

**13 ..., Nd4xf3+; 14 Qd5xf3,
Qe7xg5; 15 Bb3-d5, e5-e4**

After a long series of practically
forced moves, Black had to make a
difficult decision. The alternatives:

a)- 15 ..., Bxd5; 16 Qxd5, Qf4
(Pikler - Hondra, 1959) and now
Barden's continuation 17 a4, Qe4+
18 Qxe4, Nxe4; 19 Ke2 probably
leads to a draw.

b)- 15 ..., Ba6; 16 Qb3! (Better than
16 Rd1, Qf4! or 16 Qc3, Nb5; 17
Qc4, Bc5 or 16 Qa3?, Ne4! but 16
c4 and 16 h4 are less clear.) 16 ...,
Ne4 (16 ..., e4 see the note to

Black's 16th move in the text game; 16 ..., Qf4, suggested by Euwe, has not been tested.) 17 Bxe4, fxe4; 18 Qa4, Bc5!; 19 Qxa6, Bxf2+; 20 Kd1, Rf8 and Black's attack proved sufficient to draw (Langer - Heilimo, correspondence 1965).

16 Qf3-b3!

White avoids the error **16 Qc3?!**, Bxd5; 17 Qxh8, Qe7; 18 Nxb6, axb6; 19 Qd4, Bc6 (Chernyshev - Kusin, Moscow Championship 1957). The position is somewhat obscure, but Black's three minor pieces eventually got the better of White's rooks.

16 ..., Bf8-h6?!

Despite its success in this game, this move is not good. Preferable:

a)- 16 ..., Bxd5; 17 Qxd5, Qxg2; 18 O-O-O, Bh6+; 19 Kb1, Bf4; 20 Rhf1! followed by the advance of either the a-pawn or the c-pawn, giving White the better game (Euwe).

b)- 16 ..., Ba6; 17 Qg3?! (17 Qa4!?, Bh6! is unclear; If 17 Qc3?!, Ne8!; 17 Nxb6, Bh6; 18 Nc4 led to a draw in Walther - Bade, Meissen 1957.) 17 ..., Qxg3; 18 hxg3, Kc8; 19 O-O-O, Bb7 and Black won on material in the ending (Zvetkov - Uitumen, Ulan Bator 1965).

17 O-O, f5-f4; 18 Bd5xb7, f4-f3 19 g2-g3, Qg5-g4

Not **19 ..., Nxb7?**; 20 Qc3 with the double threat of Qxh8 and Qc7+.

20 Qb3-c3

Other moves:

a)- 20 Bxe4, Nxe4; 21 h3! with advantage to White (Kliavin - Klovan, Latvian Championship 1953).

b)- 20 Kh1?, Rf8!; 21 Rad1, Nxb7; 22 Qd5, Kc8; 23 Qe5, d6; 24 Qe7, Qd7; 25 Qe4, Kb8 (Samarian and Troianescu).

20 ..., Rh8-f8

9

21 Kg1-h1??

A losing move in a winning position. Correct is **21 Qc7+**, Ke8; 22 Qxd6, Qh3; 23 Nc7+! (Better than drawing by 23 Qe5+ etc.) 23 ..., Kd8 (Or 23 ..., Kf7; 24 Bd5+, Kg7; 25 Qe5+, Rf6; 26 Qe7+) 24 Ne6+, Ke8; 25 Qxf8+, Bxf8; 26 Nf4 and 27 Bxe4 with decisive material advantage to White (analysis by Keres).

21 ..., Qg4-h3; 22 Rf1-g1, Rf8-f5;

Threatening mate in 2 commencing 23 ..., Qxh2+!

23 g3-g4, Bh6-f4
White resigns

The complications of the Frankenstein-Dracula Variation are such that it would be foolhardy to play 3 ..., Nxe4 without a good deal of preparation. However, even in White's best line, 11 d3!, Black has at least good practical compensation for the rook sacrificed.

VIENNA GAME (1 e4, e5; 2 Nc3)

The Vienna Game is also rarely seen in master play nowadays. In its best form it transposes into the Bishop's Opening (see Game 5) but there are also several lines in which it retains a distinctive character. There are no important counter-gambit systems against the Vienna, but the following little-known game should prove of interest.

Game 6
Kliavin - Zhuravlev
(Latvian Championship 1969)

1 e2-e4, e7-e5; 2 Nb1-c3, Bf8-b4!?

This is certainly not an usual move here.

2 ..., Nf6 allows White to transpose into the Bishop's Opening by **3 Bc4**, to play Paulsen's quiet line **3 g3** or to enter a sharp opening struggle by **3 f4, d5**, which is not a counter-gambit since no material is offered.

After **2 ..., Nc6** White again has **3 Bc4, 3 g3** or **3 f4** although in the latter case Black (instead of the invariable **3 ..., exf4**) might chance the gambit line given by Keres: **3 ..., Bc5; 4 fxe5, d6; 5 exd6, Qxd6; 6 Nf3, Bg4; 7 Ne2** (Or 7 d3!) **7 ..., O-O-O; 8 c3, f5** and White is under heavy pressure.

The old move **2 ..., Bc5** is probably inferior:

a)- 3 Na4?!, Bxf2+?! (3 ..., Be7!) **4 Kxf2, Qh4+; 5 Ke3?** (Panov and Estrin, in 'A Course of Openings', give 5 g3, Qxe4; 6 Nc3!, Qxh1; 7 Nf3 with advantage to White.) **5 ..., Qf4+; 6 Kd3, d5; 7 Kc3, Qxe4+; 8 Kb3, Na6** (Better 8 ..., Nc6 or 8 ..., d4 according to Pachman.) **9 a3, Qxa4+** led to a famous draw in Hampe - Meitner (Vienna 1873).

b)- 3 Nf3! (Also possible are 3 f4 and 3 g3) **3 ..., d6** (If 3 ..., Nc6; 4 Nxe5!) **4 d4!** (Horowitz - Kupchik, Syracuse 1931) is reputedly White's best plan. Less dangerous is **4 Na4!?**, Bb6; 5 Nxb6, axb6; 6 d4, exd4; 7 Qxd4, Qf6 (Kan - Capablanca, Moscow 1936), but here the innovation 6 ..., Qe7!? proved good for White in Benko - Larsen, Las Palmas 1972.

Finally, **2 ..., f5?!** was mentioned in Chapter 1; however, in the event of **2 ..., Nc6; 3 g3** it is reasonable to play this reversed King's Gambit. After **3 ..., f5!?; 4 exf5** (Or 4 d3, Bc5; 5 Bg2, d6; 6 Nd5! with an interesting fight in Mieses - Dus-Hotimirski, Carlsbad 1907) **4 ..., Nf6; 5 g4** a normal position has resulted, with colours reversed but no tempo lost by Black. Since this is no longer strictly a counter-gambit (White having taken upon himself the role of the second player) I shall give no further analysis of this difficult and unclear line.

3 Qd1-g4?!

This looks like a very dubious attempt to refute Black out of hand. After **3 Bc4, Nf6** a variation of the Bishop's Opening would arise, which (being in effect a reversed Ruy Lopez) is certainly not bad for White. **3 Nd5**, however.

would probably amount only to a loss of time after 3 ..., Bc5; 4 Nf3, c6 or a self-weakening after 4 b4!?, Bf8!?; 5 Bb2, c6; 6 Ne3, Qc7 or 4 ..., Bd4; 5 c3, Bb6; 6 a4!?, c6. There is at least scope for some inventiveness in these non-'book' lines.

3 ..., Ng8-f6!; 4 Qg4xg7, Rh8-g8; 5 Qg7-h6, Rg8-g6

Black's original counter-gambit is similar to that in the 'Poisoned Pawn' line of the Winawer French. He accepts the loss of a pawn and the destruction of his king-side in order to obtain an open-file for his rook, and tempi by attacking the vulnerable White queen. A conclusive evaluation will have to await further experience with the sacrifice.

6 Qh6-e3, Nb8-c6; 7 Nc3-d5

In order to exchange off at least one piece, and to play c3. It should, however, go against the grain to move his only developed piece a second time; **7 Nf3** must be better.

7 ..., Nf6-g4; 8 Qe3-d3, Bb4-c5; 9 Ng1-h3, d7-d6

10

Keres remarks that Black has now a strong initiative in return for the pawn.

10 c2-c3, Nc6-e7; 11 Nd5xe7, Qd8xe7; 12 Qd3-e2

White hopes to sort out his disorganised troops by developing the queen's side. Either here or on move 10, **Be2** would not achieve much as he dare not castle short.

12 ..., Bc8-e6; 13 d2-d3, O-O-O

Black is now ready to attack, whilst White's underdeveloped position resembles Nicaragua just before the earthquake.

14 f2-f3, Ng4-f6; 15 Nh3-f2, d7-d5

First tremor.

16 Bc1-d2, d5xe4; 17 d3xe4

The only reasonable recapture: 17 fxe4?, Ng4 or 17 Nxe4, Bb6.

17 ..., Nf6-h5

With ideas of 18 ..., Qh4 and 19 ..., Ng3, or simply 18 ..., f5.

18 g2-g4!?, Nh5-f4; 19 Bd2xf4, e5xf4; 20 h2-h4!?, Bc5-e3; 21 Ra1-d1, Be6xa2; 22 Rd1xd8+, Qe7xd8; 23 Bf1-h3

Hoping for some alleviation after 23 ..., Qxh4?; 24 Bg2.

23 ..., Ba2-c4!; 24 Qe2-c2, Rg6-d6

Threatening 25 ..., Bxf2+, winning king or queen.

25 Qc2-a4, Be3xf2+; 26 Ke1xf2, Qd8xh4+; 27 Kf2-g1, Qh4-e1+ White resigns.

A cautionary tale!

LATVIAN COUNTER-GAMBIT (1 e4, e5; 2 Nf3, f5)

The wild, anti-positional thrust 2 ..., f5 introduces one of the most infamous of chess openings. Like its analogue against the Bishop's Opening (2 Bc4, f5), it stems from Greco, the Calabrian master of the 17th Century, after whom it is sometimes named. However its resurrection by Carl Behting and other Riga analysts of the turn of the 20th Century justifies the name Latvian Gambit. It still has a few addicts who play it occasionally: e.g. Strobel of Poland and the British Master J.E.Littlewood. Furthermore, a group of analysts led by Gunderam and Latvians resident in America have published recently many arguments in favour of the gambit; but practical experience of most of their ideas is lacking.

If White is well prepared, then he should probably win. However which of the official 'refutations' is the most reliable, is not yet clear. White has a choice of two pawns to take, or he can go into the realm of fantasy with 3 Bc4 (a line that can also arise from the Bishop's Opening). These three variations will be illustrated in turn.

Game 7
Stockholm - Riga
(Correspondence 1934-6)
1 e2-e4, e7-e5; 2 Ng1-f3, f7-f5; 3 Nf3xe5

The most common reply.

3 ..., Qd8-f6

A very poor alternative is **3 ..., Nc6?!; 4 Qh5+!?** (Or Keres' simple line 4 Nxc6, dxc6; 5 Nc3.) 4 ..., g6; 5 Nxg6, Nf6; 6 Qh4 (Or 6 Qh3, Rg8 with some attacking chances for Black, according to Keres.) 6 ..., hxg6? (6 ..., Rg8 would be somewhat better.) 7 Qxh8, fxe4; 8 d4! and White is already in a winning position (Hindle - Littlewood, Hastings 1963-4).

Keres also mentions **3 ..., Qe7?!**, met by either 4 d4 or 4 Qh5+, g6; 5 Nxg6, Qxe4+; 6 Be2, Nf6; 7 Qh3.

4 d2-d4

The major alternative **4 Nc4**, fxe4; 5 Nc3 may be met by **5 ...,** c6!? e.g. 6 d3, d5; 7 Ne3, exd3; 8 Bxd3, Bc5 with equal chances according to Sokolov in Informator 13. Critical is Panov and Estrin's 6 Nxe4!, Qe6; 7 Qh5+ intending 8 Qe5 and 9 Ng5. This is untested, but other 5th moves for Black are held by most theoreticians to be bad, e.g. **5 ..., Qg6**; 6 d3!, Bb4; 7 Bd2, Bxc3; 8 Bxc3 (Smyslov - Kamyshov, Moscow 1944) 8 ..., Nf6; 9 dxe4 (Or 9 Bxf6 — Keres) 9 ..., Nxe4; 10 Bd3, O-O; 11 O-O, Nxc3; 12 bxc3, Qh5; 13 Qh5, g6; 14 Qa5, c6; 15 Rab1 with the threat of 16 Nb6. The Gunderam group here suggest 5 ..., Qf7!? (or 5 ..., Ne7!?) 6 Ne3, c6; 7 Nxe4, d5; 8 Ng3, h5, but White can improve by 8 Ng5! e.g. 8 ..., Qg6; 9 f4! followed by Bd3 (analysis).

4 ..., d7-d6

Inferior is **4 ..., fxe4** because of 5 Bc4.

5 Ne5-c4, f5xe4; 6 Nb1-c3

Played by the Stockholm club in their first game with Riga, but in another game between the same opponents **6 Ne3** was chosen. There followed 6 ..., Nc6 (Better than the 6 ..., c6; 7 Bc4, d5; 8 Bb3, Be6; 9 c4 of Nimzowitsch - Behting, Riga 1919.) 7 Nd5, Qf7; 8 Nbc3, Be6 and now 9 Nf4 should have been played (as suggested in 'Shakmaty' rather than 9 Nxc7+?!, Qxc7; 10 d5, Nf6; 11 dxe6, d5! and Black won in 26 moves.

The best move may well be **6 Be2!**, preparing to castle and preventing 6 ..., Qg6?? on account of 7 Bh5. The game Bronstein - Mikenas, Rostov 1941, took the course 6 ..., Nc6; 7 d5, Ne5; 8 O-O, Nxc4; 9 Bxc4, Qg6; 10 Bb5+ with a plus.

6 ..., Qf6-g6

Other moves are no better:

a)- 6 ..., Ne7; 7 d5, Qg6; 8 Bf4, Bf5; 9 h3, h5; 10 Qd4, a6; 11 a4, Nd7; 12 O-O-O, Nf6; 13 Bxd6! with White soon winning, was a 19th century game Mayet - Hanstein.

b)- 6 ..., Bf5; 7 g4, Bg6; 8 Bg2, c6; 9 Bxe4, Bxe4; 10 Nxe4, Qe6; 11 Qe2, d5; 12 Nf6+!, Kf7; 13 Ne5+, Kxf6; 14 Bg5+!, Kxg5; 15 Qf3 forcing mate (Petrov).

c)- 6 ..., c6; 7 Nxe4, Qe6; 8 Qe2, d5; 9 Ned6+, Kd7; 10 Nf7!, dxc4; 11 Qxe6+, Kxe6; 12 Bxc4+, Ke7; 13 Nxh8, Be6; 14 Bd3 also favours White (Keres).

7 f2-f3

White has a galaxy of strong moves at his disposal:

a)- 7 Ne3, Be7 (After 7 ..., Nf6 Keres' 8 f3! is stronger than the 8 Ned5 of A.Steiner - Apscheniek, The Hague 1928.) 8 Be2, Nf6; 9

Ncd5 (A 1945 Soviet game Zherdev - Roitman went 9 O-O, c6; 10 f3, d5; 11 fxe4, dxe4; 12 d5! but better was 10 ..., exf3.) 9 ..., Bd8; 10 Nf4, Qg5; 11 g3 with complications favouring White in Paoli - Strobel, Skopje 1972.

b) 7 Bf4, Nf6; 8 Ne3, Be7; 9 Qd2, c6; 10 Be2 (Or 10 d5 — Keres) 10 ..., d5; 11 O-O, O-O; 12 f3, exf3; 13 Bxf3 (Flohr - Vecsey, Prague 1930).

c)- 7 Qe2 (Not so good are 7 d5 or 7 h3.) 7 ..., Nc6 (Or 7 ..., Nf6; 8 f3) 8 Be3 (Or 8 d5!? — Keres) 8 ..., Be7; 9 O-O-O, Nf6; 10 d5, Nb4; 11 Na5 and White has strong threats (Kofman - Vishnatski, Kiev 1947).

11

7 ..., e4xf3

The Gunderam recommendation here is 7 ..., Nf6!?; 8 fxe4, Be7 e.g. 9 Qd3 (9 e5?, Nh5) 9 ..., Nc6!; 10 a3, O-O; 11 Be3, a6 intending ..., b5. But White can instead get a good game by returning the pawn: 10 Nd5!, Nxd5; 11 exd5, Qxd3; 12 Bxd3, Nxd4 (12 ..., Nb4!?; 13 Be4! and 14 Bd2) 13 O-O and Black's Knight is embarrassed (analysis).

8 Qd1xf3, Nb8-c6; 9 Bf1-e2?!

An experiment that has not been repeated. Also against **9 Nb5** or **9 Nd5** Black has 9 ..., Bg4 intending

10 ..., Kd7 but White has better moves:

a)- 9 d5, Nb4; 10 Ne3, Nf6; 11 a3, Na6; 12 Bd3 (Keres).

b)- 9 Bd3, Qg4; 10 Qf2! (10 Qe3+, Be7) 10 ..., Nf6 (If 10 ..., Nxd4; 11 O-O, or 10 ..., Qxd4; 11 Be3, Qf6; 12 Qe2 — Keres) 11 O-O (Yudovich - Elzov, Moscow 1941).

9 ..., Nc6xd4; 10 Qf3-e3+, Nd4-e6; 11 Bc1-d2, Ng8-f6; 12 O-O-O, Bf8-e7; 13 h2-h3, O-O; 14 Be2-d3, Qg6-e8; 15 g2-g4, Rf8-f7

As the result of White's inferior opening play, Black is in the position of defending a material advantage. His resources appear to be adequate.

16 Rd1-e1, Ne6-c5; 17 Rh1-f1, Nc5xd3+; 18 c2xd3, Be7-f8!

An ingenious way of freeing his game.

19 Qe3-g1, Bc8-e6; 20 Nc4-e3, Qe8-d7; 21 g4-g5, Nf6-h5; 22 Ne3-g4, Rf7xf1; 23 Re1xf1, Be6-f5; 24 Nc3-e4

White has to throw everything into a desperation attack.

24 ..., Qd7-c6+; 25 Bd2-c3, Bf5-g6

The Riga Chess Club avoid the trap **25 ..., Bxe4?**; 26 Nf6+!, gxf6;

27 gxf6+, Kf7; 28 Qg8+! with a strong White attack (28 ..., Kxg8?? 29 f7, mate).

26 Kc1-d2, Qc6-d5!; 27 Qg1-g2, Qd5xa2; 28 Ne4-f6+, g7xf6; 29 Qg2xb7, Ra8-e8; 30 Rf1xf6, Bf8-g7

Black defends ruthlessly.

31 Qb7-c6, Bg7xf6; White resigns.

After 32 Bxf6, Qe6 (threatening Qe3+) 33 Nh6+, Kf8 White is just a rook down.

Game 8
Vashegyi - Grobe
(Correspondence 1971)

1 e2-e4, e7-e5; 2 Ng1-f3, f7-f5; 3 e4xf5, e5-e4

In this variation, Black has to play the King's Gambit a tempo down. He has the consolation that, unlike the line 1 e4, e5; 2 f4, exf4; 3 Nf3, Nf6; 4 e5, Nh5, White cannot decentralise his knight to guard the pawn.

Weaker are **3 ..., d6**; 4 d4, e4; 5 Ng5, Bxf5; 6 f3 and **3 ..., Qf6**; 4 Nc3 (Keres).

4 Nf3-e5

Also playable is **4 Qe2**. If then 4 ..., Qe7; 5 Nd4, Qe5; 6 Nb5 or 4 ..., d5; 5 d3, Nf6; 6 dxe4 with advantage to White (Keres).

4 ..., Ng8-f6; 5 g2-g4?!

This seems too risky. White should play **5 Be2** e.g.:

a)- 5 ..., Bc5;
6 d4, exd3; 7 Nxd3, Bb6; 8 Bh5+, Kf8; 9 O-O, d6; 10 Bg5, Nc6; 11 Re1, Ne7; 12 Ne5!, Be6?! (But what else?) 13 Ng4!, Nxg4; 14 Bxg4

Resigns (Stimpson - Hall, correspondence 1970-1).

b)- 5 ..., d6; 6 Bh5+, Ke7; 7 Nf7, Qe8; 8 Nc3! (According to Keres 8 Nxh8 is also good for White.) 8 ..., Nxh5; 9 Nd5+, Kd7 (Or 9 ..., Kxf7; 10 Qxh5+, g6; 11 fxg6+, Kg7; 12 Nxc7.) 10 Qxh5, Rg8; 11 f6, Na6 (Or 11 ..., Qe6; 12 Nf4, Qxf7; 13 Qg4+) 12 O-O, c6 (If 12 ..., Qe6; 13 f3.) 13 Ne5+, dxe5; 14 f7, Qe6; 15 fxg8(Q), Qxg8; 16 Ne3 and Black is without compensation for the exchange (analysis by Keres).

13

5 ..., Qd8-e7!

A new move, not considered by Keres. His analysis ran: **5 ..., d6;** 6 Nc4, h5; 7 g5, Nd5; 8 d3! with advantage to White, e.g. 8 ..., Bxf5; 9 dxe4, Bxe4; 10 f3 or also 9 ..., Qe7; 10 f3.

6 Ne5-c4

If **6 g5,** Qxe5; 7 gxf6, Qxf5; 8 fxg7, Bxg7 favours Black, according to O'Kelly in the Dutch 'Schakend Nederland'.

6 ..., d7-d5; 7 Nc4-e3, d5-d4; 8 Ne3-g2, h7-h5!

'Pawns are the soul of chess' - Philidor!

9 g4-g5

O'Kelly analyses **9 Nf4,** Nxg4; 10 Ng6, Qc5; 11 Qe2, Bxf5!; 12 Nxh8, d3; 13 cxd3, Qxc1+; 14 Qd1, Qxd1+ with advantage to Black.

9 ..., Nf6-g4; 10 h2-h4, Bc8xf5

White has not even material advantage to console him.

11 Bf1-c4, Ng4-e5; 12 Bc4-e2, d4-d3!!; 13 Be2xh5+

If **13 cxd3** the game would proceed along much the same lines.

13 ..., g7-g6; 14 Ng2-e3, Rh8xh5! 15 Ne3xf5, Qe7xg5!

Very neat. If the queen is taken, it's mate in one.

16 Nf5-g3, Rh5xh4; 17 Rh1xh4, Qg5xh4;

Black has won a pawn, and retains an overwhelming position.

18 c2xd3, Ne5xd3+

Best, but White would also be helpless after **18 ..., exd3** (see the note to White's 13th move) in view of the threatened ..., Qh2 and ..., Bc5. 19 Qb3 would allow 19 ..., Nf3+; 20 Kd1, Qe7.

19 Ke1-f1, Qh4-h3+; 20 Kf1-g1, Bf8-c5; White resigns

If 21 Nxe4, Bxf2+!; 22 Nxf2, Qg3+ etc., or if 21 Qa4+, Kd8! and ..., Bf2+ will follow.

Game 9
Purins - Englitis
(Correspondence 1971)

1 e2-e4, e7-e5; 2 Ng1-f3, f7-f5; 3 Bf1-c4, f5xe4;

The usual move, leading to great complications which (this game suggests) favour White. Other lines:

a) 3 ..., d6 (Or 3 ..., Nc6 transposing) 4 d4, Nc6; 5 dxe5, dxe5 (Or 5 ..., fxe4!?; 6 Qd5, Qe7; 7 Bg5, Be6; 8 Qxe4 with advantage to White in de Riviere - Anderssen, London 1862.) 6 Qxd8+, Nxd8; 7 Nxe5, fxe4; 8 Bd2, Bd6; 9 Bc3 was in White's favour in the consultation game Lowenthal & Medley - Morphy & Mongredien (London 1857).

b)- 3 ..., b5!? is a new idea, seeking after 4 Bb3, fxe4; 5 Nxe5, Qg5 to have better chances as the square c4 is under Black's control, while if 4 **Bxb5?!**, fxe4; 5 Nxe5 and the bishop is skewered. Another 1971 postal game Siegers - Purins therefore went 4 **Bxg8**, Rxg8; 5 Qe2, Qe7; 6 Qxb5?! (Sokolov in Informator 13 suggested 6 Nc3!?) 6 ..., Nc6!; 7 Qd5, fxe4!; 8 Nxe5? (But after 8 Qxe4 White has no advantage) 8 ..., Qxe5; 9 Qxg8, Nb4!; 10 Qb3, Nd3+!; 11 Ke2, Ba6; 12 c4, Qd4 and 0-1 since if 13 Rf1, Bxc4 etc. So 4 Bb3 may be necessary.

4 Nf3xe5, Qd8-g5

Not 4 ..., d5?!; 5 Qh5+, g6; 6 Nxg6, Nf6; 7 Qe5+, Be7; 8 Bb5+!, c6; 9 Nxe7, Qxe7; 10 Qxe7+, Kxe7; 11 Be2, Rg8; 12 g3 and White is a sound pawn up (Keres).

Gunderam thinks this is playable for Black by 12 ...c5, but the onus of proof must be his, as 13 d3 should allow White to complete his development without having to make major concessions.

Keres does not mention the fantastic Corkscrew Counter-Gambit: 4 ..., Nf6!?; 5 Nf7, Qe7; 6 Nxh8, d5; 7 Be2 (Not 7 Bb3?, Bg4

and Black wins) 7 ..., Nc6; 8 Bh5+?! (Too greedy; correct is 8 d3 according to 'Fernschach'.) 8 ..., g6; 9 Nxg6, hxg6; 10 Bxg6+, Kd8 (now ..., Bg4 is on again) 11 Bh5, Ne5!; 12 O-O, Qh7; 13 Be2, Bd6 (Black has tremendous compensation for his exchange and two pawns.) 14 g3, Qh3; 15 f3, Neg4!!; 16 fxg4, Bxg3!; 17 Rf2 (17 hxg3 also loses.) 17 ..., Bxf2+; 18 Kxf2, Qxh2+; 19 Ke3, Qg3+; 20 Kd4, c5+; 21 Kxc5, Nd7+!; 22 Kd4, Qe5+; 23 Ke3, d4+; 24 Kf2 (amazing symmetry of the White king's marches!) 24 ..., Qh2+; 25 Kf1, Ne5; 26 Nc3!, d3!! (that theme again!) 27 cxd3, Bxg4; 28 Bxg4, Ke7!; 29 Nd5+, Kd6; 30 Ne3, Rf8+; 31 Nf5, RxRf5+!; 32 Bxf5, Qh1+ 0-1 (Morrillo - Ortiz, correspondence 1970). If 33 Kf2, Qxd1; 34 Bxe4, Ng4+ is decisive. A very fine sacrificial attack — if, for example, 26 ..., Bxg4? (instead of ..., d3!) then 27 d3! would have enabled White to defend.

5 d2-d4!

Not 5 Nf7?, Qxg2; 6 Rf1, d5!; 7 Bxd5, Nf6; 8 Nxh8, Bh3! nor 5 Bf7+?, Ke7; 6 Bxg8, Rxg8; 7 Ng4, d5 (analysis of Behting).

5 ..., Qg5xg2; 6 Qd1-h5+

6 Rf1, Nf6 is unclear (Milic in Chess Informator).

6 ..., g7-g6; 7 Bc4-f7+, Ke8-d8

Not 7 ..., Ke7??; 8 Bg5+, Nf6; 9 Qh4.

8 Bf7xg6!

White is, at best, level if he chooses 8 Qg5+, and worse are 8 Bg5+, Be7 and 8 Nxg6?, Qh1+; 9 Kd2 (9 Ke2, Qf3+) 9 ..., Bh6+ and Black wins.

8 ..., Qg2xh1+

The best move, in view of **8 ..., hxg6?**; 9 Bg5+, Be7; 10 Qxh8 or 8 ..., Nf6?; 9 Nf7+, Ke8; 10 Nxh8+ or 8 ..., d6; 9 Qg5+ (Keres)

9 Ke1-e2

As unbalanced a position as one is ever likely to see.

9 ..., c7-c6!?

The most popular choice recently. Black probably cannot do better:

a)- 9 ..., hxg6?; 10 Bg5+, Be7; 11 Qxh8, Bxg5; 12 Qxg8+, Ke7; 13 Qf7+, Kd6; 14 Nc3.

b)- 9 ..., d6; 10 Nc3!, Be7; 11 Nf7+, Ke8; 12 Nxd6+, Kd8; 13 Nf7+, Ke8; 14 Nxh8+, hxg6; 15 Qxg6+, Kd7; 16 Qf5+, Kd8; 17 Qd5+ and wins (Keres).

c)- 9 ..., Qxc1; 10 Nf7+, Ke8; 11 Nxh8+, hxg6; 12 Qxg6+, Kd8; 13 Nd2! (Keres gives 13 Nf7+, Ke7; 14 Nc3 which is apparently also sufficient) 13 ..., Qxa1; 14 Qxg8 (Milic) e.g. 14 ..., c6; 15 Qxf8+, Kc7; 16 Nf7! and soon mates.

10 Nb1-c3

Not 10 Nf7+, Kc7; 11 Nxh8, Qf3+ (Euwe).

10 ..., Ng8-f6

Or 10 ..., Kc7 (If 10 ..., hxg6; 11

Qxh8 and White obtains material advantage after all) 11 Bf4!, Qxa1; 12 Nxd7+!!, Kd8; 13 Qe5! and White wins (Purins & Sokolov in Informator 13).

11 Qh5-h4!

This move is the latest improvement for White, and it seems decisive. Other moves are either not clear or just worse:

a)- 11 Qg5, Rg8! (11 ..., e3?; 12 Qxf6+, Kc7; 13 Nf7, Resigns — Popp - Weisenburger, German correspondence 1968) and now Keres suggests 12 Bf4! is strong.

b)- 11 Bg5 (Definitely weak is 11 Nf7+, Kc7!) 11 ..., Qxa1; 12 Bxf6+, Kc7; 13 Nf7 (Not 13 Nc4? of Keller - Peperle, correspondence 1967.) 13 ..., Bb4! (Levy - Strobel, Ybbs 1968) and now critical is Milic's suggestion 14 Bxh8, hxg6; 15 Qg5!, b6; 16 Nxe4 with good attacking chances for White.

11 ..., Bf8-e7; 12 Bc1-g5!, Qh1xa1; 13 Bg5xf6, Be7xf6; 14 Qh4xf6+, Kd8-c7; 15 Ne5-c4!

The move 3 ..., b5!? in the game Siegers - Purins, given above, may have been partly motivated by the need to eliminate this resource, by which White forces mate.

15 ..., b7-b6

White threatened 16 Nd5+, cxd5; 17 Nb5 mate.

16 Qf6-e5+, d7-d6

If 16 ..., Kb7; 17 Nd6+, Ka6; 18 Bxe4!! followed by 19 Bd3+ and 20 Ncxb5.

17 Nc3-b5+!!, Black resigns.

Mate is inevitable:

a)- 17 ..., cxb5; 18 Qxd6+, Kb7; 19 Bxe4+, Nc6; 20 Bxc6+, Ka6; 21

Qa3 mate.
b) 17 ..., **Kb7**; 18 Ncxd6+, Ka6; 19
Nc7 mate.

c) 17 ..., **Kd7**; 18 Bf5+, Kd8; 19
Qf6+, Ke8; 20 Nxd6 mate.

QUEEN'S PAWN'S COUNTER-GAMBIT (1 e4, e5; 2 Nf3, d5)

If the Latvian Gambit is unsound, then this one should be even more
so, in so far as the sacrifice is of a centre pawn. It has been seen in
occasional master games in the USSR, but in nearly every case White was
the victor. Yet, again there is no consensus as to White's theoretically best
continuation.

Game 10
Gufeld - Heuer
(USSR Team Championship 1962)
**1 e2-e4, e7-e5; 2 Ng1-f3, d7-d5;
3 Nf3xe5!?,**

The major alternative is 3
exd5!, e4 (3 ..., Qxd5; 4 Nc3, Qa5; 5
d4 is a variation of the Scandinavian Defence favourable to White,
e.g. 5 ..., Bb4; 6 Bd2, Bg4; 7 a3,
Bd6; 8 Bc4, exd4?; 9 Qe2+, Ne7;
10 Nd5 Boleslavsky.) **4 Qe2:**
a) 4 ..., **f5**; 5 d3, Nf6 (5 ..., Qxd5; 6
Nbd2, Nf6; 7 Ng5) 6 dxe4 (Better
than 6 Nc3, Bb4; 7 dxe4, Bxc3+ of
Kofman-Kostiuchenko, Kiev 1956
Championship.) 6 ..., fxe4; 7 Nc3,
Bb4 (Or 7 ..., Be7; 8 Nxe4, O-O; 9
Nxf6+, Bxf6; 10 c3.) 8 Qb5+, c6; 9
Qxb4, exf3; 10 Bg5! with a big plus
to White (Tal-Lutikov, Tallinn
1964).

b) 4 ..., **Nf6**; 5 d3 (5 Nc3 is also
good.) 5 ..., Be7 (5 ..., Qxd5; 6 Nfd2
winning the pawn) 6 dxe4, O-O; 7
Bg5! (Clearer than 7 Nc3, Re8; 8
Bd2!, b5!? of Konstantinopolsky-

Ove, Moscow-Oslo telegraph match
1954-5; the line given by Keres
commencing 8 ..., Bb4?! was in fact
not the game but only an analysis
by Konstantinopolsky) 7 ..., Nxe4; 8
Bxe7, Qxe7; 9 Nbd2, Bf5; 10
O-O-O, Re8; 11 Nd4 (Clearer than
11 Qe3!?) 11 ..., Bg6; 12 Nxe4,
Bxe4 (Or 12 ..., Qxe4; 13 Qxe4,
Bxe4; 14 Nb5, Na6; 15 d6!) 13
Ne6!, Bxc2 (If 13 ..., Qh4; 14 Nxc7,
Qf4+; 15 Qe3, Qxc7; 16 Bd3, Nd7;
17 Bxe4, f5; 18 d6 intending 19
Bd5+ or if 13 ..., Bxg2; 14 Bxg2,
fxe6; 15 f4) 14 Qxc2, fxe6; 15 Bxe6,
Nc6; 16 Kb1, Rad8; 17 Bb5 and
White won with his sound extra
pawn (Pruss-Wills, correspondence
1966).

3 ..., Bf8-d6;

Other moves are probably no
better:
a) 3 ..., **Qe7**; 4 d4, f6; 5 Nd3, dxe4;
6 Nf4, Qf7; 7 Nd2 and White won
quickly (Boleslavsky-Lilienthal,
Absolute Championship of the
USSR, 1941).

b) 3 ..., **dxe4**; 4 Nxe5 (By comparison with Game 9, Black stands

clearly worse. His king is more exposed, his f-pawn en prise, and he does not have the 'corkscrew' possibility 4 ..., Nf6 since there is no prospect of building a menacing pawn centre.) 4 ..., Qg5; 5 Bxf7+, Ke6; 6 d4, Qxg2; 7 Rf1, Bh3; 8 Bc4 Nf6; 9 Bf4, Nbd7; 10 Qd2, Nb6; 11 Be2, Nbd5; 12 Nc3, Nxf4 (Or 12 ..., Be6; 13 Nxd5+, Nxd5; 14 O-O-O, Qh3; 15 Bg5+ and 16 c4 Lob-Eliskases, correspondence 1932.) 13 Qxf4, Be6; 14 h4, Rg8; 15 Nc4, Kd8; 16 O-O-O with advantage to White, as in another postal game, Feilitsh-Keres 1936.

4 d2-d4, d5xe4;

15

5 Qd1-h5!,

Not an easy decision. Other moves:

a) **5 Bc4**, Bxe5; 6 Qh5 (with advantage to White, according to Keres) 6 ..., Qe7; 7 dxe5, Nc6; 8 Bf4, Be6; 9 Bxe6, Qxe6; 10 Nc3, O-O-O; 11 O-O (Not 11 Nxe4?, Nf6.) 11 ..., Nge7; 12 Nxe4 Ng6; 13 Bg3, Ngxe5 and Black has quite a good game (Pruss).

b) **5 Bb5+**, c6; 6 Bc4, Bxe5; 7 Qh5, Qxd4?! (7 ..., Qe7; 8 dxe5, Be6 looks better.) 8 Qxf7+, Kd8; 9 Bg5+, Nf6; 10 Nc3 (Shmatkov-Marinetz, USSR 1962) and now

instead of 10 ..., Qd7?; 11 Rd1, Bd4; 12 Rxd4! Black could have played 10 ..., Nbd7 with winning chances.

Gufeld's innovation is superior by far to either of these.

5 ..., Bc8-e6;

If instead **5 ..., Qe7**, the analysis in the Soviet Chess Yearbook runs: 6 Nc3, Nf6; 7 Qh4, Bxe5; 8 dxe5, Qxe5; 9 Bf4, Qa5; 10 O-O-O, O-O; 11 Bc4 with a promising position for White in return for his pawn. In this line, not 10 ..., Be6; 11 Qg3, Nh5 on account of 12 Bxc7!, Nxg3; 13 Bxa5, Nxh1; 14 Rd8+ etc.

6 Nb1-c3, Bd6-b4;

If **6 ..., Nf6**; 7 Qe2 and the e-pawn cannot be guarded (7 ..., Bb4?; 8 Qb5+).

7 a2-a3, Ng8-f6; 8 Qh5-h4, Bb4-e7;

Not **8 ..., Qxd4**; 9 axb4, Qxe5; 10 Bf4, Qh5; 11 Qg3 with strong pressure for White. The Soviet Yearbook suggests **8 ..., Ba5!?**.

9 Nc3xe4, Nf6-g4; 10 Qh4-g3, Qd8xd4; 11 Ne5xg4, Qd4xe4+; 12 Ng4-e3, Nb8-c6; 13 Qg3xg7, O-O-O; 14 Bf1-d3, Qe4-a4;

If **14 ..., Qf4**; 15 Nf5. Similarly if **14 ..., Qh4**.

15 b2-b3, Qa4-a5+

If **15 ..., Qd4**; 16 Bb2.

16 b3-b4, Nc6xb4;

If **16 ..., Qb6**; 17 Bb2 and Black is running out of ideas.

17 a3xb4, Be7xb4+; 18 Ke1-e2, Qa5-h5+;

White is in no danger after **18 ..., Qc5**; 19 Bd2, Bxd2; 20 Kxd2.

19 g2-g4, Qh5-h3; 20 Ra1xa7, Kc8-b8;

16

21 Bc1-d2!,

If **21 Ra4**, Rhg8; 22 Qxg8, Rxg8; 23 Rxb4, Bxg4+; 24 Nxg4, Rxg4; 25 Rxg4, Qxg4+.

21 ..., Kb8xa7;

Not **21 ..., Bxd2;** 22 Rha1.

22 Bd2xb4, Rh8-g8; 23 Qg7-e5, Be6xg4+; 24 Ke2-d2, Qh3-f3; 25 Rh1-a1+, Ka7-b8; 26 Qe5-a5, Qf3xf2+; 27 Kd2-c1, c7-c6;

The Yearbook gives **27 ..., Qxe3+;** 28 Bd2, Qg1+; 29 Kb2, Qd4+; 30 Bc3, Qb6+; 31 Qxb6, cxb6; 32 Be5+, Kc8; 33 Bb5! and White wins.

28 Qa5-e5+, Black resigns.

Excellent tactical control by Gufeld. Nonetheless the lines which follow 3 exd5 are probably objectively stronger than those after 3 Nxe5.

TWO KNIGHTS DEFENCE (1 e4, e5; 2 Nf3, Nc6; 3 Bc4, Nf6; 4 Ng5)

The Two Knights Defence is Black's most combative method of meeting 3 Bc4. Against either of White's usual replies, 4 d4 (offering a pawn in many lines) or 4 Ng5 ('winning' one) the struggle immediately takes on an acute tactical nature. We are concerned here only with the lines arising from 4 Ng5 since it is here that Black offers a counter-gambit. He has several methods of doing so, and these will be examined in turn, but with greater emphasis placed on the sound lines stemming from 4 ..., d5! and 5 ..., Na5!

The Soviet analyst Y.Estrin has devoted most of his life to the study of the Two Knights, playing it frequently with both White and Black. He has also published two monographs and countless articles on the subject; nonetheless many of the lines are still unclear and susceptible of new discoveries being made. This is a tribute to the great activity that the Black forces gain upon sacrificing the pawn; White's resources appear to be adequate for a rough equality but he is not able to suppress all the ideas that the second player has at his disposal. I do not expect the issue, of the soundness of the Two Knights Defence, to be settled for many years yet. In practice, it gets excellent results.

Game 11
Porreca - Ballbé
(Correspondence 1968)

1 e2-e4, e7-e5; 2 Ng1-f3, Nb8-c6;

For counter-gambits in the Petroff Defence etc., see section on 'Fantasy' at the end of the Open Games chapter.

3 Bf1-c4, Ng8-f6;

Black counter-attacks the White e-pawn, and defers the development of his bishop since it is not yet clear where it should go.

4 Nf3-g5!?

In theory this is the only way in which White could hope to refute the Two Knights, but it offends against the principle (generally valid in open games) of moving a piece several times in the opening. Tarrasch called it a 'duffer's move', while R.G.Wade has commented that it cannot be good to force one's opponent to play well!

4 ..., Bf8-c5?!

But this isn't the way to do it! For Black's superior plans, see the subsequent games in this section.

The wild move 4 ..., Bc5 has had something of a vogue recently, but it is not really sound to expose one's own king in this way. The idea stems from the 19th Century player P.Traxler, although in the west the variation is usually referred to as the Wilkes-Barre, after a town in New England where an early game was played.

(See diagram)

5 Bc4xf7+!

The correct move; White contents himself with an extra pawn and intends to lose as little time as

17

possible.

After **5 Nxf7?!** (or 5 d4?!, d5!; 6 Bxd5, Nxd4!; 7 Nxf7, Qe7; 8 Nxh8, Bg4!) Black's idea begins to justify itself. He plays 5 ..., **Bxf2+!** and now:

a)- 6 Kxf2, Nxe4+; 7 Kg1 (7 Ke3?, Qe7!) 7 ..., Qh4; 8 g3 (8 Qf1?, Rf8; 9 d3, Nd6!) 8 ..., Nxg3; 9 Nxh8 (Or 9 hxg3, Qxg3+; 10 Kf1, Rf8; 11 Qh5, d5! and White is probably lost.) 9 ..., Nd4 (9 ..., Nxh1; 10 Qf1! should also draw; 9 ..., d5!?; 10 Qf3! is unclear) 10 hxg3 (10 c3?, d5!) 10 ..., Qxg3+; 11 Kf1, Qf4+; 12 Kg2, Qg5+; with a draw by perpetual check.

b)- 6 Kf1, Qe7; 7 Nxh8, d5!; 8 exd5 (If 8 Be2, Bb6! or 8 Qf3, Bh4!) 8 ..., Nd4! (8 ..., Bg4?!; 9 Be2, Bxe2; 10 Kxe2, Nd4+; 11 Kf2) with great complications, concerning which there is no consensus of opinion:

b1)- 9 d6!? (Bad moves are 9 Kxf2, 9 Nc3, 9 Be2 and 9 d3.) 9 ..., cxd6; 10 c3, Bg4; 11 Qa4+, Nd7 (11 ..., Bd7 should draw, according to Estrin.) and now, instead of the usual 12 Nf7 leading probably to a draw, Estrin suggests 12 Kxf2, Qh4+; 13 Kf1 e.g. 13 ..., Ke7; 14 cxd4, Rf8+; 15 Nf7, Nb6; 16 Qb3, Nxc4; 17 Qg3! and White is a rook ahead.

b2)- 9 c3, Bg4; **10 Qa4+** (Better is 10 d6! transposing to b1.) 10 ..., Nd7!; 11 Kxf2 (11 cxd4, Qf6; 12 dxe5, Qf4!) 11 ..., Qh4+; 12 Ke3 (Or 12 g3, Qf6+; 13 Ke1, Qf5; 14 cxd4, Qe4+; 15 Kf2, Qf3+!) 12 ..., Qg5+; 13 Kf2, Qf5+; 14 Kg1, O-O-O; 15 cxd4, Rf8; 16 h3, Qf2+; 17 Kh2, Bxh3!; 18 Kxh3, g5! and Black soon won in Mikyska-Traxler Correspondence 1896.

b3)- 9 h3, Bg3! (Here 9 ..., Ne4!? should draw, but other moves are bad) 10 c3, Nf5!; 11 d4 (11 d6!?) 11 ..., Bd7; 12 Qe2? (12 Bg5, Qf8! or 12 d6!?) 12 ..., Bh2!; 13 Kf2, Ng3; 14 Qe1, Nfe4+!; 15 Kf3, Nd2+; 16 Nxd2, Qf6+; 17 Resigns. (Estrin-Nun, correspondence 1965-6).

5 ..., Ke8-e7

The king must come here to make room for the rook. **5 ..., Kf8?** lost quickly in Milutinovic - Jakovljevic, correspondence 1968.

6 Bf7-b3

It is not clear whether this move is actually superior to **6 Bd5** as Estrin believes that both moves are to White's advantage. After **6 Bd5** (guarding the e-pawn and envisaging an eventual Bxc6) there can follow:

a)- 6 ..., Nb4?!; 7 d4, exd4; 8 O-O, Nbxd5; 9 exd5, Re8; 10 Qd3!, h6 (If 10 ..., g6 Estrin, in 'Schachmaty', gave 11 Nxh7!, Nxh7; 12 Qxg6, Nf6; 13 Bf4! or if 10 ..., Rh8 he intended 11 Re1+, Kf8; 12 d6!, cxd6; 13 Qc4.) 11 Qg6!, hxg5; 12 Qxg7+, Kd6; 13 Bxg5, Rf8; 14 c4, dxc3; 15 Nxc3, Resigns (Estrin-Weiss, correspondence 1971-2). White threatens 16 Bf4 mate, and Black would also get mated after 15 ..., Bd4; 16 Nb5+, Kxd5; 17 Nd4,

Kxd4.

b)- 6 ..., d6; 7 c3!, Rf8; 8 d4, exd4; 9 Bxc6, bxc6 (Estrin-Zaitsev, Moscow 1969) and now either 10 cxd4, Bb4+; 11 Bd2 (Estrin) or 11 Nc3 (Keres) offers White good play.

c)- 6 ..., h6?; 7 Nf7 (or 7 Nf3, d6; 8 Bxc6, bxc6; 9 d3! Neistadt) 7 ..., Qf8; 8 Nxh8 threatening 9 Ng6+ (Estrin)

d)- 6 ..., Rf8 (usual); **7 Nf3!** (or 7 O-O!?, d6; 8 h3, h6; 9 Nf3, Qe8; 10 d3, Qh5; 11 Nh2! Estrin, but if 8 c3, Bg4!; 9 Qa4, Qe8; 10 Bxc6, Qxc6! with a good game for Black: Larsson-Erlandsson, correspondence 1968) **7 ..., d6** (if 7 ..., Nd4!? not 8 Nxe5?, Nxd5; 9 exd5, d6 but 8 Nxd4, Bxd4; 9 O-O and 10 c3.) 8 c3 which favours White after either **8 ..., Bg4**; 9 Bxc6, bxc6; 10 d4, Bb6; 11 Qd3, exd4; 12 cxd4, Kd7; 13 Be3 (Belov-Matsukevich, Kislovodsk 1962) or **8 ..., Qe8**; 9 d4, exd4; 10 cxd4, Bb4+; 11 Nc3, Nxd5; 12 exd5, Kf7+; 13 Be3, Ne7; 14 Qb3, Ba5; 15 O-O (Elpidinski-Hasin, correspondence 1969).

6 ..., Rh8-f8; 7 O-O,

Not altogether clear is **7 d3** e.g. the game Paoli-Steiner, Reggio Emilia 1951, which continued 7 ..., h6 (Or 7 ..., d6; 8 Be3!, Bg4; 9 Qd2 with chances of an advantage for White.) 8 Nf3, d6; 9 Be3· (9 h3!? Estrin) 9 ..., Bg4; 10 Bxc5, dxc5; 11 Nbd2, Nd4; 12 h3, Bh5; 13 g4? (A blunder but also after 13 O-O, g5 with the intention of ..., g4, Black has chances.) 13 ..., Nxg4!; 14 Nxd4 (If 14 hxg4, Nxf3+; 15 Nxf3, Bxg4) 14 ..., Qxd4 and White was lost.

7 ..., d7-d6;

Another critical line is **7 ..., h6**; 8 Nf3, d6; 9 h3, Qe8 (Or 9 ..., Nxe4;

10 c3! e.g. 10 ..., Bxh3?!; 11 d4!, Qd7; 12 Nh4! Panov, or 10 ..., Nf6; 11 d4, Bb6; 12 Re1.) 10 Nc3, Qh5; 11 Nh2!, Qh4; 12 d3 and White can consolidate his king side, retaining his extra pawn (analysis by Estrin). If 7 ..., Qe8; 8 c3, Qg6; 9 d4!, exd4; 10 e5 (analysis).

8 Nb1-c3, Qd8-e8;

Not 8 ..., h6; 9 Nd5+, Nxd5; 10 exd5, hxg5; 11 dxc6 favouring White.

9 Nc3-d5+, Ke7-d8; 10 c2-c3,

This improved upon 10 Nxf6?, gxf6; 11 Nf3, Qh5; 12 d4, Bg4! of Klovan-Anzhan, Latvian Team Championship 1960.

10 ..., h7-h6;

Keres's suggestion 10 ..., Qg6; 11 d4, exd4 fails to 12 Nf4!, Qe8; 13 Nge6+ and Black has nothing for the exchange (analysis).

11 d2-d4, e5xd4; 12 e4-e5!

18

White stands clearly better, in view of the exposed situation of the Black king.

12 ..., Nf6xd5;

Other moves also fail:

a)- 12 ..., dxe5; 13 Nxf6, gxf6; 14 Ne4, Bd6 (Or 14 ..., Be7; 15 Bxh6, Rh8; 16 Be3, Bf5; 17 Ng3.) 15 cxd4, Nxd4; 16 Nxd6, cxd6; 17 Bxh6 and White wins (analysis).

b)- 12 ..., hxg5; 13 gxf6, gxf6 (Keres) 14 Nxf6!, Rxf6? (Better 14 ..., Qg6, albeit an admission that White stands better.) 15 Bg5, Qf8; 16 Qf3, Ke7; 17 Rae1+, Ne5; 18 cxd4, Bxd4; 19 Qd5, Bxb2 (Or 19 ..., Bb6; 20 Rxe5+.) 20 f4 and wins (analysis).

13 Bb3xd5, d6xe5;

Not 13 ..., hxg5?; 14 Bxg5+, Ne7; 15 cxd4 followed by exd6 and Re1, but Keres suggests the sacrifice of the exchange 13 ..., Qxe5; 14 Nf7+, Rxf7; 15 Bxf7, Bd7 is a better chance for Black. Nonetheless, White has a good plan here: 16 Qf3 followed by Bd2 and Rae1.

14 Ng5-e4, Bc5-b6; 15 c3xd4, Nc6xd4; 16 Bc1-e3

For the pawn, White has the better development and open lines for the attack against the stranded Black king.

16 ..., c7-c6; 17 Bd5-c4, Qe8-g6; 18 Ne4-g3, Kd8-c7; 19 Bc4-d3, Qg6-g4 20 f2-f3, Qg4-h4; 21 Kg1-h1, Bc8-d7; 22 a2-a4, a7-a5; 23 Ra1-b1 Ra8-d8;

If 23 ..., Qe7; 24 Bd2 forces through the advance b4.

24 b2-b4, a5xb4; 25 Rb1xb4, c7-c5 26 Qd1-c1!

After the period of preparation during which White may have missed something stronger, the decisive attack commences.

26 ..., Bd7-c6;

White was threatening to play 27 Ne4.

27 Rb4xb6!, Kc7xb6; 28 a4-a5+, Kb6-c7; 29 Qc1xc5, Rd8-e8;

How is Black to defend? Two possibilities that fail:

a)- 29 ..., Nxf3+; 30 Rxf3!, Rxf3; 31 Qxe5+, Rd6; 32 Bb6+!, Kd7; 33 Bf5+!, Rxf5; 34 Qxd6+!, Kxd6; 35 Nxf5+ and wins.

b)- 29 ..., Rfe8 (or 29 ..., Qf6; 30 Ne4) 30 Rb1, Ra8 (or 30 ..., Rb8; 31 Ne4 gives a strong attack) 31 Nf5!!, Nxf5; 32 Rxb7+!andwins(analysis).

30 Rf1-b1, Rf8xf3

Not wishing to be squashed by the kind of attack outlined in note **b** to his previous move.

31 g2xf3, Black resigns.

If 31 ..., Nxf3 White forces mate by 32 Rxb7+!, Kxb7; 33 Qa7+ etc.

In the next game, we shall look at another bizarre but ultimately insufficient plan for Black.

Game 12
Jovcic - Koshnitsky
(Correspondence 1969)

1 e2-e4, e7-e5; 2 Ng1-f3, Nb8-c6; 3 Bf1-c4, Ng8-f6; 4 Nf3-g5, d7-d5!

The best move. If **4 ..., Nxe4?** White has 5 Bxf7+!, Ke7; 6 d4!, d5; 7 Nc3!

5 e4xd5, b7-b5!?

For the orthodox **5 ..., Na5!**, see Games 13 - 16.

It is too risky to play **5 ..., Nxd5?!** because of **6 d4** (The Fegatello Attack 6 Nxf7!? is not clearly sound.) **6 ..., Bb4+** (Or 6 ..., exd4; 7 O-O!, Be6; 8 Re1, Qd7; 9 Nxf7!) 7 c3, Be7; 8 Nxf7!, Kxf7; 9 Qf3+, Ke6; 10 Qe4! (Barden-Adams, Hastings 1951-52).

Also **5 ..., Bg4?!; 6 f3** (6 Nxf7!?) **6 ..., Na5**, first played in the last century in the U.S.A. and rediscovered recently in Latvia (see 'Sahs' 1972/1), may merit further investigation. A game Belov-Gusev, U.S.S.R. 1971, continued 7 Qe2 (7 Bb5+!?), Bh5; 8 Nc3, Nxc4; 9 Qxc4, Be7; 10 d3, O-O and Black won in 30 moves after complications. White's best line may well be **7 d3!** e.g. 7 ..., Bh5; 8 Qxb5, Bd7; 7 ..., Bf5!?) 8 Bd2, b6 (If 8 ..., Nxd5 or 8 ..., h6 White has 9 Nxf7) 9 Nc3 with a clear plus.

Finally, **5 ..., Nd4!?** is possible, transposing back to the text if White plays 6 c3, b5; 7 Bf1. Other lines are not dangerous to Black:

a)- 6 d6, Qxd6; 7 Bxf7+ (Or 7 Nxf7?, Qc6!) 7 ..., Ke7; 8 Bb3, Nxb3; 9 axb3, h6; 10 Nf3, e4; 11 Ng1, Kf7 (Bogolyubov-Rubinstein, Stockholm 1919).

b)- 6 O-O, b5!; 7 Bb3, h6; 8 Nf3, Bg4 favours Black (Estrin).

c)- 6 d3, b5; 7 Bb3, Nxb3; 8 axb3, Qxd5 with a good game (Estrin).

d)- 6 Nc3, Bg4 (Or 6 ..., h6; 7 Bb3, Bg4.) 7 f3, Bh5; 8 d3, h6; 9 Nge4, Nxe4; 10 dxe4, Qh4+; 11 Kf1 and now 11 ..., Nxf3; 12 gxf3, Qh3+ leads to a draw by perpetual check.

6 Bc4-f1!

Another paradoxical move. Weaker are:

a)- 6 Bb3?!, Nd4; **7 c4** (7 Nc3, Nxb3; 8 axb3, b4 or 7 c3!?) 7 ..., Nxd5!; 8 Nxf7, Qh4! and, according to a beautiful analysisbyRadchenko Black wins: 9 O-O, Bg4; 10 Qe1, Ne2+!; 11 Kh1, Ndf4! 12 Nxe5 (Or 12 f3, Bxf3!; 13 gxf3, Qh3 threatening ..., Bc5) 12 ..., Bd6; 13 f3, Bh3; 14 gxh3, Qxh3; 15 Rf2, Ng3+; 16 Kg1, Qg2+!; 17 Rxg2, Nh3 mate.

b)- 6 Bxb5, Qxd5 is fine for Black, e.g. **7 Nc3**, Qxg2; 8 Qf3, Qxf3; 9 Nxf3, Bd7; 10 d3 (10 O-O, Nb4!) 10 ..., Nd4; 11 Bxd7+, Kxd7! or **7 Be2**, Bb7; 8 d3, Nd4 or **7 Bf1**, e4; 8 d3, Bg4; 9 Be2, Bxe2; 10 Qxe2, Nd4; 11 dxe4 (11 Qd1, e3!) 11 ..., Qc6 or **7 Qe2**, Qxg2; 8 Qxe5+, Be7; 9 Rf1, O-O 10 Bxc6, Qxc6; 11 Qc3, Qb5 (Estrin) or **7 Bxc6+**, Qxc6; 8 O-O (8 Qf3, e4!) 8 ..., Bb7; 9 Nf3 (9 Qf3!?, e4; 10 Qb3, O-O-O!) 9 ..., Bd6 with interesting complications (Volkman-Krul, correspondence 1961).

c)- 6 dxc6, bxc4; 7 Nc3 (7 Qe2, Qd5) 7 ..., h6; 8 Nge4, Nxe4; 9 Nxe4, Qd5; 10 Qf3, Be6 with good compensation for the pawn (analysis).

6 ..., Nc6-d4!

The move characteristic of Fritz's Variation. Others are risky:

a)- 6 ..., Nxd5 (Ulvestad's variation; of course not 6 ..., Qxd5? allowing 7 Nc3 and 8 Bxb5) **7 Bxb5, Bb7** (If 7 ..., Bd7; 8 d4, exd4; 9 O-O! and not now 9 ..., Be7 because of 10 Nxf7! - Keres) **8 d4** (White correctly plays for open lines and attack: 8 d3, Bc5; 9 O-O, O-O; 10 Nc3, Nd4 - Estrin - may also be good, but not 8 Qf3, Qxg5; 9 Qxd5, Qf6; 10 f4, Rd8!) **8 ..., exd4** (8 ..., f6?! is worse.) **9 O-O!, Be7** (Or 9 ..., Qf6; 10 Re1+, Be7; 11 Ne4 and 12 Nc5.) 10 Qh5! (Clearer than 10 Nf3, O-O as in Ellison-Harding, correspondence 1972.) 10 ..., g6; 11 Qh6, Qd7 (not 11 ..., Bf8; 12 Re1+, Nde7; 13 Ne4! and the queen cannot be taken because of mate in two) 12 Qg7, O-O-O; 13 Qxf7 and White stands better (Fine).

b)- 6 ..., Bg4?! 7 f3, Nxd5; 8 Nxf7, Kxf7; 9 fxg4, Nf4!?; 10 Nc3, Bc5; 11 g3, Nd4; 12 Ne4, Qd5; 13 d3!

(Honfi-Peters, 4th correspondence Olympiad 1962-4).

c)- 6 ..., h6!?; 7 Nf3 (7 Nxf7, Kxf7; 8 dxc6, Bc5!; 9 Qf3?! — 9 Be2! — 9 ..., Rf8; 10 Bxb5, Kg8; 11 h3, Bxf2+! occurred in Kurkin-Mihailovich, Moscow 1963.) 7 ..., Qxd5; 8 Nc3, Qe6; 9 Bxb5, Bb7; 10 Qe2, O-O-O; 11 Ba6? (better 11 d3 according to Estrin) 11 ..., e4 and Black had a dangerous attack in Kurkin-Neelov, Kaluga 1960). This line is almost certainly unsound, but it is as yet virtually unexplored.

7 c2-c3, Nf6xd5;

No good are **7 ..., Nf5?**; 8 Bxb5+, Bd7; 9 Qa4 and **7 ..., h6?!**; 8 cxd4, hxg5; 9 dxe5, Nxd5; 10 Bxb5+, Bd7; 11 Bxd7+ (Or 11 Qa4 Euwe) 11 ..., Qxd7; 12 Nc3!, Nf4; 13 d4!

19

8 Ng5-e4!

White has tempting alternatives here:

a)- 8 Nf3?, Nxf3+; 9 Qxf3, Rb8; 10 Qg3, Rb6!; 11 a4, Rg6; 12 Qd3, e4 (Hodzhaev-Estrin, Riga 1951) is totally inoffensive to Black.

b)- 8 Nxf7, Kxf7; 9 cxd4, exd4; 10 Bxb5 (If 10 Qf3+, Nf6! e.g. 11 Qxa8, Bc5; 12 Bxb5, Re8+! Semenenko-Perfiliev, correspondence

1947, or 11 Bxb5, Be6; 12 O-O, Rb8! Estrin) 10 ..., Qe7+ (10 ..., Be6!?) 11 Qe2, Qxe2+; 12 Bxe2, Nb4; 13 Na3! (Zachert-Vogt, 1968) 13 ..., Be6 (Or 13 ..., Bb7; 14 Bc4+, Kg6; 15 d3!, Re8+; 16 Kd1 Keres) 14 b3, Re8; 15 O-O, Bc5 (15 ..., Bxb3; 16 Bh5+) 16 Bb2, Rhf8; 17 Bc4 and White stands better (analysis).

c)- 8 cxd4, Qxg5; 9 Bxb5+ (Black is all right after 9 Nc3, Bb7 or 9 Qb3, exd4.) 9 ..., Kd8; 10 Qf3 (Or first 10 O-O) 10 ..., Bb7 (Fischer's 10 ..., e4!?; 11 Qxe4, Bd6; 12 O-O, Bb7 is risky in view of 13 Re1, c6; 14 Bf1 - Keres.) 11 O-O (White can also try 11 Nc3, exd4; 12 d3 as suggested by Keres, or if here 12 O-O then Estrin's 12 ..., Qf4! gives equal chances.) 11 ..., Rb8 (or 11 ..., e4!?; 12 Qxe4, Bd6 but less reliable is 11 ..., exd4!?; 12 d3!) 12 Nc3 (12 Qh3?, Bc8! or 12 d3, Qg6; 13 Qg3, exd4 favouring Black) 12 ..., Nxc3! (if 12 ..., Ne3!? there can come Paoli's 13 Ne4!, Qxe5; 14 Qxf7) 13 dxc3, Bxf3 (better than 13 ..., Qxg2+; 14 Kxg2!) 14 Bxg5+, f6; 15 gxf3, Rxb5!; 16 Bc1, exd4; 17 Rd1, Bd6; 18 Rxd4, Re8 with about equal chances (Estrin). A very involved tactical line!

d)- 8 h4, h6!; 9 Ne4 (9 Nxf7!? compare variation **b**; 9 cxd4, hxg5 is also fine for Black.) 9 ..., Ne6; 10 Bxb5+, Bd7; 11 Qa4, Ndf4 (11 ..., f5!? - Estrin) 12 d4, Nxg2+ with about equal chances (Fuglevich-Neistadt, correspondence 1963-5).

8 ..., Qd8-h4?!

An enterprising but, it now seems, unsound tactical continuation. However after the positional **8 ..., Ne6**; 9 Bxb5+, Bd7; 10 Bxd7+, Qxd7; 11 O-O, Be7! (Or 11 ...,

Ndf4?; 12 d4.) 12 d4, exd4; 13 cxd4 White should, following Keres, reach an advantageous endgame — although Estrin is inclined to view the chances as equal. For example: **a)- 13 ..., Nb6**; 14 Be3, Rd8; 15 Nbc3!, Nxd4; 16 Bxd4, Qxd4; 17 Qxd4, Rxd4; 18 Rad1 (Kogan-Naftalin, Vladimir 1962). White has some pressure, e.g. 18 ..., Rb4; 19 b3, O-O; 20 Rfe1, a5; 21 Ng3, Bf6; 22 Nce4, Be5; 23 Nf5 (analysis) **b) 13 ..., O-O** (14 Nc3, Rad8 (Or 14 ..., Rfd8; 15 Be3, Rab8; 16 Qe2 Spassky-Shamkovich, 27th USSR Championship, 1960) 15 Be3 (Euwe's 15 Nxd5, Qxd5; 16 Nc3, Qxd4; 17 Be3, Qxd1; 18 Rfxd1, Bc5; 19 Bxc5, Nxc5; 20 Nd5 also offers a slight edge; here Keres prefers 18 ..., a6.) 15 ..., f5!; 16 Nxd5, Qxd5; 17 Nc3, Qb7; 18 Qe2!, Rfe8 (18 ..., f4?; 19 Bc1!) 19 Qc4, Bd6; 20 d5, Nf8; 21 b3, a6 (Petik-Zhukov, correspondence 1966-7) and now after 22 Rad1 White's game is superior (Estrin).

9 Ne4-g3

Not **9 cxd4?**, Qxe4+; 10 Qe2, Qxd4 (Martin-Sanguineti, Buenos Aires 1947) but **9 d3** (Keres) and **9 Bxb5+!?** (Jovcic), hoping for 9 ..., Nxb5; 10 Qa4 with the threat of 11 Nd6+, come into consideration.

9 ..., Bc8-g4!?

Leading to exciting complications, whereas against other moves White should have little trouble: **a) 9 ..., Ne6**; 10 Bxb5+, Bd7; 11 Bxd7+, Kxd7; 12 Qf3, Nef4; 13 d4! (Timpere-Soininen, Finland 1955). **b) 9 ..., Bb7**; 10 cxd4, O-O-O; 11 Be2 (11 d3 is also very promising) 11 ..., Nf4; 12 O-O, Rxd4 (12 ..., Qh3; 13 Bf3!) 13 d3 (Or Bf3

Sax-Nunn, Norwich 1972) 13 ...,
Bc5 (13 ..., Nxg2; 14 Nf5) 14 Nd2!,
Nxd3 (14 ..., Nxg2; 15 Nf3, Nf4;
16 Bxf4) 15 Bxd3!, Rxd3; 16 Qe2 or 16
Qh5 (Keres).

10 f2-f3, e5-e4!?

This move was discovered by
the American master Hans Berliner
and was employed successfully by
him in a vital game of the 5th
World Correspondence Championship Final (an event which he won).
However the refutation has been
discovered by Estrin - 7 years too
late!

The old move **10 ..., Nf5** is
unsatisfactory on account of 11
Bxb5+ (But not 11 Qe2, Bd6! with
equal chances.) 11 ..., Kd8; 12 O-O,
Bc5+; 13 d4!, exd4; 14 Ne4 (Or 14
Nxf5, Bxf5; 15 g3 - Keres, but not
14 fxg4??, d3+!) 14 ..., Nde3; 15
Qb3!, Bd6; 16 Nxd6, Nxd6; 17
Bxe3, dxe3; 18 Qd5, Rb8; 19 Na3,
Be6; 20 Qc5 (Estrin).

11 c3xd4, Bf8-d6; 12 Bf1xb5+,
Ke8-d8; 13 O-O!

Not **13 fxg4?** (Nor 13 Kf2?, f5
'with an overwhelming attack' -
Berliner, while Estrin was afraid of
13 ..., exf3; 14 gxf3, Qf6!) 13 ...,
Bxg3+; 14 hxg3, Qxh1+; 15 Bf1,
Nb4; 16 Nc3, Nd3+ (Berliner
intended 16 ..., Re8) 17 Ke2, Qg1!;
18 Nxe4, Qxd4 (Estrin) with a very
dangerous attack for Black.

13 ..., e4xf3

(See diagram)

14 Rf1xf3!?

Not of course **14 gxf3?** because
of 14 ..., Bxg3; 15 Qe2, Nf4.
However, the move **14 Qb3!!** has
recently been discovered by Estrin.
White should be able to consolidate

a material advantage. For example:
a) 14 ..., Nf4; 15 Rxf3, Rb8; 16
Rxf4!, Bxf4 (16 ..., a6?; 17 Rxg4,
Qxg4; 18 Bd7! or 16 ..., c6; 17 Nf5!,
Qf6; 18 Nxd6!) 17 Qd5+, Bd6; 18
Nc3 or

b) 14 ..., fxg2; 15 Rxf7, Nf6 (15 ...,
Nf4?; 16 Rxf4) 16 Bc6, Rc8; 17
Rxg7, Nh5?! (What else?); 18
Rg8+, Rxg8 (18 ..., Ke7; 19 Qe3+
wins) 19 Qxg8+, Kd8 (19 ..., Kf8;
20 d3!) 20 d3!, Bxg3; 21 Qg8+ and
mates (analysis).

14 ..., Ra8-b8; 15 a2-a4!

An interesting try in this
controversial position. The aforementioned famous game Estrin-
Berliner continued:

15 Be2? (loses by force!) 15 ...,
Bxf3; 16 Bxf3, Qxd4+; 17 Kh1,
Bxg3; 18 hxg3, Rb6!; 19 d3!, Ne3;
20 Bxe3, Qxe3; 21 Bg4, h5!; 22
Bh3, g5; 23 Nd2, g4; 24 Nc4, Qxg3;
25 Nxb6, gxh3; 26 Qf3, hxg2; 27
Qxg2, Qxg2+; 28 Kxg2, cxb6!; 29
Rf1, Ke7; 30 Re1+, Kd6!; 31 Rf1,
Rc8!; 32 Rxf7, Rc7!; 33 Rf2, Ke5!
with a difficult but won ending for
Black.

The chief alternative is **15 Bf1**
(15 Bc6?, Nb4) 15 ..., Re8! (Not 15
..., Nf6?!; 16 Nc3, h5; 17 d3! as in
Kuperman-Struchkov, correspon-

dence 1971.) 16 Nc3, c6; 17 Nce2 (Recommended by Euwe in view of the line 17 d3, Nxc3; 18 bxc3, Rb5 given by Berliner, or 17 Nxd5, cxd5; 18 d3, Bxf3; 19 Qxf3, Qxd4+; 20 Qf2, Bc5.) 17 ..., Bxf3; 18 gxf3, Nf4 with the threats of 18 ..., Nxe2+ and 18 ..., Rb5 (Messere) In any case, Black seems to stand better.

15 ..., c7-c6?!

Black's main problem is, how to introduce his rooks into the attack? The alternative 15 ..., a6!?; 16 Bxa6, Rb6 (16 ..., Re8; 17 Nc3 or 16 ..., Rb4; 17 Nc3, Nf4; 18 Bb5, Rxd4; 19 Nce2, Bxf3; 20 gxf3, Nh3+; 21 Kg2) 17 Bb5, Bf4 (Or 17 ..., Nf4; 18 Nc3, Nh5; 19 Nce4.) fails to 18 Nc3, Nxc3 (Or 18 ..., Rh6; 19 Nxd5, Qxh2+; 20 Kf1,

Bxg3; 21 Ne3, Qh1+; 22 Ke2, Bxf3+; 23 gxf3, Qh2+; 24 Kd3 and Black has over-sacrificed.) 19 dxc3, Bxc1; 20 Qxc1, Bxf3 (20 ..., Rh6; 21 Qf4) 21 gxf3, Rg6; 22 Qf1, f5; 23 Re1, f4; 24 Re4, Qh6; 25 Qc4! and White wins by direct attack (analysis).

16 Bxc6, Bxf3?

A better fighting chance was 16 ..., Nf4; 17 Nc3, Rb6 but after 18 d5! it is hard to find a good continuation for Black.

17 Qd1xf3, Qh4xd4+; 18 Kg1-h1, Rb8-c8; 19 Nb1-c3, Rc8xc6; 20 Qf3xd5, Qd4-f2;

If 20 ..., Qxd5; 21 Nxd5, Re8; 22 Nge2 wins.

21 Ng3-e2!, Kd8-c7; 22 d2-d4, Bd6xh2; 23 Bc1-g5, Black resigns.

As the intriguing possibilities 5 ..., b5 and 5 ..., Nd4 are therefore perhaps not quite sound, the player who worries about such matters will have to rely upon the orthodox 5 ..., Na5. Although heavily analysed, these lines are yet rich in complications that offer Black excellent chances of winning.

Game 13
Naftalin - Fridman
(Correspondence 1971)

1 e2-e4, e7-e5; 2 Ng1-f3, Nb8-c6; 3 Bf1-c4, Ng8-f6; 4 Nf3-g5, d7-d5; 5 e4xd5, Nc6-a5!; 6 d2-d3,

This move stems from the great Paul Morphy, of whose tempo-conserving style it was typical. However, White thereby renounces any hope of refuting Black's gambit and so the more double-edged move 6 Bb5+!? (see Games 14 - 16) is the usual choice nowadays. There is nothing for White in 6 Be2?, h6; 7 Nf3, e4; 8

Ne5, Qxd5 (Kuznetsov-Volovich, Moscow 1964).

6 ..., h7-h6;

Not 6 ..., Nxd5??; 7 Qf3 nor 6 ..., e4; 7 Qe2, Qe7; 8 Nxe4 (Morphy).

7 Ng5-f3, e5-e4;

Black has other ways of playing this position:
a) 7 ..., Nxc4; 8 dxc4, e4; 9 Nd4 (Or 9 Ne5, Bd6; 10 f4, exf3 with complications; Anderssen-Dufresne Rotterdam 1861.) 9 ..., Bd6 (If 9 ..., Bg4; 10 Qd2 Estrin.) 10 h3, O-O was soon drawn in Matsukevich-

Zuhovitsky, USSR 1968.

b) 7 ..., Nxc4; 8 dxc4, Bd6 and now both **9 Be3**, Qe7; 10 Qe2, O-O; 11 h3, b5 (Karaklaic-Pilnik, Belgrade 1954) and **9 h3**, O-O; 10 Nc3, c6 (Rossetto-Gligoric, Buenos Aires 1955) were all right for Black.

8 Qd1-e2

If here **8 Nd4** Black has 8 ..., c6! e.g. 9 O-O (Or 9 Nc3, Bb4; 10 Bd2, O-O! Estrin.) 9 ..., Bd6; 10 dxc6, bxc6; 11 Ne2, Qc7; 12 h3, O-O with the initiative (Matsukevich Nikitin, Frunze 1964).

The major alternative is Bronstein's piece sacrifice **8 dxe4!?**, Nxc4; 9 Qd4 but it is unsound in view of Euwe's analysis: 9 ..., Nd6!; 10 Nc3 (Or 10 e5, Nf5; 11 Qa4+, Qd7!; 12 Qxd7+, Nxd7.) 10 ..., Nfxe4!; 11 Nxe4, Qe7; 12 O-O, Nxe4; 13 Re1, f5; 14 Nd2, Qc5!

Another way of offering the bishop is **8 Bb5+!?**, c6; 9 dxe4, cxb5; 10 Qd3 but then comes 10 ..., a6 (Or 10 ..., Qb6; 11 O-O, Bc5 Estrin) 11 O-O, Bc5; 12 c3, Ba7; 13 b3, O-O; 14 Nd4, Re8; 15 Nd2, Qd6 with advantage to Black (Pronchatov-Nekrasov, Moscow '64)

8 ..., Na5xc4

Inferior is **8 ..., Bb4+?!**; 9 c3, O-O; 10 cxb4, exf3; 11 gxf3, Re8; 12 Be3.

9 d3xc4, Bc5;

The other moves (9 ..., Bd6, 9 ..., Bg4, 9 ..., Be7, 9 ..., Bb4+) have all been weighed in the balance and found wanting.

(See diagram)

10 h2-h3,

A major decision. Other moves must be taken into consideration: **a) 10 O-O?**, O-O; 11 Nfd2, Bg4; 12

21

Qe1, Qd7; 13 Nb3, Bf3! e.g. 14 Bf4, Qg4; 15 Bg3, Nh5; 16 Nxc5, Nf4!; 17 Nxe4, Qh3!!; 18 Resigns (Field-Tenner, Chicago 1934)

b) 10 c3, b5! e.g. **11 b4**, Be7; 12 Nfd2, Bg4; 13 f3, exf3; 14 gxf3, Bh5; 15 cxb5, O-O; 16 O-O, Re8 (Grob-Keres, Dresden 1936) or **11 cxb5**, Qxd5 or **11 b3**, bxc4; 12 bxc4, O-O; 13 Nd4, Bg4 (Koch-Pahl, Berlin 1928) all favour Black.

c) 10 Nfd2, O-O; 11 Nb3 (11 h3?, e3! or 11 O-O, Bg4) 11 ..., Bg4; 12 Qf1 and now Black has two good continuations to examine:

c1) 12 ..., Bb4+; 13 c3, Be7; 14 h3, Bh5; 15 Be3, Nd7; 16 g4, Bg6; 17 N1d2, Ne5; 18 O-O-O, b5!; 19 cxb5, Nd3+; 20 Kb1 (Salwe-Marshall, Vienna 1908) 20 ..., a6! (Keres)

c2) 12 ..., Nxd5; 13 cxd5 (If 13 Nxc5, Nb4!) 13 ..., Qxd5; 14 Nc3 (Or 14 Bd2, e3!) 14 ..., Bb4; 15 Bd2, Bxc3; 16 Bxc3 (Against 16 bxc3, Black gets a strong attack commencing 16 ..., f5.) 16 ..., Rad8; 17 Nd2, Rfe8 and not now 18 Qc4? because of 18 ..., e3!; 19 Qxg4, exd2+; 20 Kd1, g6 (analysis of Keres).

d) 10 Bf4, O-O; 11 Nfd2, Bg4; 12 Qf1, c6!; 13 Nc3 (If 13 h3, cxd5) 13

..., Rfe8 and Black stands well (Ferberov-Sheremeta, Moscow '62)

10 ..., O-O; 11 Nf3-h2, c7-c6!

Also strong are **11 ..., e3** and Morphy's own move **11 ..., Nh7** but not **11 ..., b5; 12 O-O!** nor **11 ..., Re8; 12 Be3** with advantage to White.

12 d5xc6, e4-e3!; 13 Bc1xe3, Bc5xe3; 14 f2xe3, Nf6-e4;

22

15 Rh1-g1?

The previous experience with this line was the game Kopylov-Kondratiev, Leningrad Championship 1955, which had gone **15 O-O, Ng3; 16 Qf3, Nxf1; 17 Nxf1, Qb6; 18 b3, bxc6** with the better chances for Black. However, Naftalin's move is worse. The critical line must be Estrin's **15 Nf1!** since then 15 ..., Qh4+; 16 g3, Nxg3? fails to 17 Qf2. Black can probably best proceed 15 ..., Qb6 e.g. 16 c3, Be6; 17 Na3, bxc6; 18 Rd1, Rab8 and White is under heavy pressure, or here 17 cxb7!?, Qxb7; 18 Na3, Rab8; 19 Nb5, Rfd8; 20 Nd4, Bxc4 21 Qc2!, Nc5! with a difficult struggle ahead (analysis).

15 ..., b7xc6;

Black proceeds calmly, since White, even more than in the previous variation, has probably insuperable problems in trying to co-ordinate his game.

16 Nh2-f3, Qd8-f6; 17 c2-c3, Ra8-b8

Preventing the freeing attempt 18 Nbd2.

18 Nf3-d4, Rf8-d8; 19 b2-b4, c6-c5!

Crushing White's hopes of making something of his pawn majority.

20 b4xc5, Ne4xc5; 21 Nb1-d2, Rb8-b2 22 Qe2-f3, Qf6-g6

Black conjures up a threat of 23 ..., Rxd2!; 24 Kxd2, Qd3+ (25 Kc1, Qxc3+; 26 Kb1, Nd3; 27 Qe2, Bf5! or 25 Ke1, Re8) ...

23 Ra1-d1, Rd8-e8; 24 g2-g4, Bc8-b7; 25 Qf3-e2, Nc5-d3+; 26 Ke1-f1, Nd3-f4; 27 e3xf4,

White asks to see it all. If the queen moves, there comes 27 ..., Qd3+ and rapid mate.

27 ..., Re8xe2; 28 Kf1xe2, Qg6-e4+ White resigns.

If 29 Kf1 (or 29 Kf2, Qd3!) 29 ..., Qd3+; 30 Ke1, Qe3+; 31 Ne2, Bf3.

Game 14
Honfi - Zagorovsky
(4th Correspondence Olympiad 1962-4)

1 e2-e4, e7-e5; 2 Ng1-f3, Nb8-c6; 3 Bf1-c4, Ng8-f6; 4 Nf3-g5, d7-d5; 5 e4xd5, Nc6-a5; 6 Bc4-b5+, c7-c6;

An interesting and little-known alternative is **6 ..., Bd7!?; 7 Qe2: a) 7 ..., Bd6!?; 8 Nc3 (8 Bxd7+, Qxd7; 9 c4, c6!; 10 d4, O-O! - Keres) 8 ..., O-O; 9 Bxd7 (If 9 O-O,**

Nxd5!; 10 Bxd7, Nf4 or here 10 Nxd5, Bxb5; 11 Qxb5, c6 with equal chances - Keres.) 9 ..., Qxd7; 10 O-O (Better than 10 Nce4, Be7 - as in Klovan-Hermlin, USSR 1954.) 10 ..., c6 (If 10 ..., Rae8?!; 11 a3, b6; 12 Nce4 not 12 ..., Nxd5? allowing 13 Qd3!, Be7; 14 Nxh7! Romanov-Krutzberg, correspondence 1963-4.) 11 dxc6, Nxc6; 12 Nge4! (Not 12 d3? with a good game for Black in Paoli-Johannessen Skopje 1972.) 12 ..., Nxe4; 13 Qxe4, Rad8; 14 Nd5, Bb8; 15 c4, f5; 16 Qh4, Nd4; 17 d3 with advantage to White (Milev-Stoltz, Bucharest '53)

b) 7 ..., Be7! and now:

b1) 8 Nc3, O-O; 9 O-O (Or 9 Nge4, Nxe4; 10 Nxe4, Bf5!) 9 ..., c6; 10 dxc6, Nxc6 (Estrin) is as yet unexplored.

b2) 8 d4, exd4 (Or 8 ..., O-O; 9 dxe5, Nxd5; 10 h4, Bxb5; 11 Qxb5, Nb4!; 12 Bd2, Nxc2+; 13 Kd1, Nc6! Ferberov-Rustamov, Moscow 1962.) 9 Bd2 (Or 9 b4, O-O!; 10 bxa5, Bb4+; 11 Kd1, Re8; 12 Qc4, Bxb5; 13 Qxb5, Nxd5 with a strong attack; Kurkin-Manteufel, correspondence 1966-7.) 9 ..., O-O!; 10 Bxa5, Nxd5; 11 Ne4, Nf4; 12 Qf3, Bxb5; 13 Qxf4, f5; 14 Ng3, Bg5 and White will be hunted from pillar to post (Kopylov-Manteufel, correspondence 1965).

7 d5xc6, b7xc6; 8 Qd1-f3!?

The Bogolyubov Variation. For **8 Be2** see Games 15 and 16. Others:

a) 8 Ba4, h6; 9 Nf3, e4; 10 Qe2 (If 10 Ne5?, Qd4) 10 ..., Be6; 11 Ne5, Qd4!; 12 Bxc6+, Nxc6; 13 Qb5, Bc5! (Estrin).

b) 8 Bd3, Nd5; 9 Ne4 (Or 9 Nf3, Bd6; 10 O-O, O-O; 11 Be4, Nf4; 12 d4, f5 Scherzl-Kommert, correspondence 1967) 9 ..., f5; 10 Ng3,

Nf4; 11 Bf1, Bc5; 12 c3, Bb6; 13 d4, Ng6 with an active game for Black (Castaldi-Keres, Stockholm 1937).

c) 8 Bf1, h6; 9 Nh3, Bc5; 10 d3, Qb6; 11 Qe2, Bg4; 12 f3, Bxh3; 13 gxh3, O-O-O and Black stood well (Steinitz-Chigorin, 8th match game Havana 1892).

23

8 ..., Ra8-b8!

This move, discovered during the Second World War by the English player Colman and analysed by him during his long years in a Japanese P.O.W. camp, is practically a refutation of White's 8th move. Other moves are dubious and will not be considered here.

9 Bb5-d3

9 Be2 (Estrin) might be worth pursuing, but it is rank folly for White to play **9 Bxc6+?!**, Nxc6; 10 Qxc6+, Nd7 e.g.:

a) 11 d3 (No better is 11 d4) 11 ..., Be7; 12 Nf3 (If 12 h4 best is 12 ..., Rb6; 13 Qf3, O-O; 14 Nc3, Bb7; 15 Qh3, f5 Bergin-Petropavlovsky, USSR 1964.) and now Black can choose between **12 ..., O-O**; 13 Qe4, Rb4; 14 Qe2, e4! (Zicherl-Krsnic, Yugoslavia 1956) and **12 ..., Bb7**; 13 Qa4, O-O; 14 Nbd2, Nc5; 15 Qg4, f5 (Ostroverkhov-Tsai, correspondence 1957-8) when if 16 Qh3, Nxd3+!

b) 11 **Nf3**, Rb6; 12 Qe4, Bb7; 13 Qe2, Bc5 (Probably better than 13 ..., e4?!; 14 O-O, Be7; 15 Ne1, O-O; 16 d3 of Kertes-Gurskaya, Hungarian Championship 1955, won by White.) and now 14 O-O, O-O!; 15 d3, Rg6; 16 Nc3, Qa8!; 17 Kh1, f5; 18 Be3, R8f6; 19 Bg5 (19 Bxc5, Rxg2!) 19 ..., Rxg5; 20 Nxg5, Bxg2+; 21 Kg1, Rg6; 22 Qh5, Nf6; 23 Qh4, h6 gave Black a winning attack in the game D.Adams-Harding, played in a Birmingham junior tournament in 1964.

9 ..., h7-h6!; 10 Ng5-e4, Nf6-d5; 11 Ne4-g3,

Both players find their best moves. If instead 11 O-O, Nb4! (Estrin) or 11 Nbc3, Nf4; 12 Bf1, f5; 13 Ng3, g6; 14 d3, Bg7; 15 Nge2, Ne6; 16 Qg3, Kf7; 17 b3, f4 with a winning position for Black (Paoli-Kluger, Bucharest 1954).

11 ..., g7-g6; 12 b2-b3,

More usual, but not really any better, is 12 O-O e.g. 12 ..., Bg7 (12 ..., h5! should be good here too.) 13 Nc3 (If 13 Re1, O-O; 14 Nc3, Nb4! Estrin; no better are 13 Be4 and 13 c3) 13 ..., O-O (Or 13 ..., Nb4!? - Estrin) 14 Be2, Rb4; 15 Nxd5, cxd5; 16 Qa3, Nc6; 17 d3, h5 (Estrin-Ragozin, Moscow Championship 1955)

12 ..., h6-h5!

The main point of this is seen from the variation 12 ..., f5?!; 13 Nxf5, Bxf5; 14 Bxf5, gxf5; 15 Qh5+, Kd7; 16 Qxf5+ (Honfi-Kluger, Budapest 1962).

13 O-O, Bf8-g7; 14 Bc1-a3,

If 14 h3 (to prevent ..., Bg4) then comes 14 ..., h4; 15 Ne2, f5.

14 ..., Bc8-g4; 15 Qf3-e4, f7-f5; 16 Qe4-e1, h5-h4; 17 f2-f3?

This sacrifice is unsound. Correct was 17 Ne2 to answer 17 ..., e4 by 18 Nec3. Black can play instead, for example, 17 ..., Qg5 with a plus.

17 ..., h4xg3; 18 Qe1xg3

Not 18 fxg4?, Qb6+.

18 ..., Bg4-h5; 19 Rf1-e1

19 Bxf5 would be countered by 19 ..., Nf4 with a breakthrough.

19 ..., Ke8-f7; 20 Nb1-c3. Nd5-b4; 21 Kg1-h1, Nb4xd3; 22 c2xd3, Qd8-d4; 23 Ra1-c1, Bg7-f6; 24 Nc3-a4, f5-f4; 25 Qg3-h3, Bh5xf3!; 26 Qh3xf3, Rh8xh2+

Now we see why Black played his 22nd move.

27 Kh1xh2, Rb8-h8+; 28 Qf3-h3, Rh8xh3+; 29 Kh2xh3?

But also after 29 gxh3 White comes to grief: 29 ..., Bh4; 30 Rg1, Qf4+; 31 Kh1, Qf3+; 32 Kh2, f4, etc.

29 ..., Qd4-f2; White resigns.

Game 15
Fishhaimer - Gligoric
(U.S.A. 1972)

1 e2-e4, e7-e5; 2 Ng1-f3, Nb8-c6; 3 Bf1-c4, Ng8-f6; 4 Nf3-g5, d7-d5; 5 e4xd5, Nc6-a5; 6 Bc4-b5+, c7-c6; 7 d5xc6, b7xc6; 8 Bb5-e2, h7-h6; 9 Ng5-e4,

For **9 Nh3!?** see the notes to Game 16.

9 ..., e5-e4; 10 Nf3-e5,

This sequence constitutes the main line of the Two Knights

Defence. Black now has to take a major decision.

24

10 ..., Bf8-d6!

The most flexible move, and the best. However it is also possible for Black to hold his own in the complications following **10 ..., Qd4**, **10 ..., Qc7** and **10 ..., Bc5**; **10 ..., O-O** is inferior. These will not be dealt with further here since **10 ..., Bd6** is far from played out as yet.

11 d2-d4,

This is probably somewhat inferior to **11 f4** (see next game). Other moves are worse:

a) **11 Nc4?**, Nxc4; 12 Bxc4, Ng4; 13 Qe2, O-O; 14 h3, Qh4! (Estrin).

b) **11 Ng4**, with which Bronstein has had some success, should be met by 11 ..., Nxg4; 12 Bxg4, Qh4!; 13 Bxc8, Rxc8; 14 Qe2, O-O; 15 Nc3, Rce8 with advantage to Black (Bilguer) in view of the line 16 b3?, e3!; 17 dxe3, Bb4; 18 Bd2, Qf6.

11 ..., e4xd3;

Better than **11 ..., Qc7**; 12 Bd2! favouring White.

12 Ne5xd3, Qd8-c7; 13 h2-h3,

There are several other ways for White to treat this position:

a) **13 b3**, O-O (13 ..., c5!?; 14 Na3,

Rb8 is unclear.) 14 Bb2, Bf5 (Other moves giving at least equality are 14 ..., Nd5, 14 ..., Ne4 and 14 ..., Re8) 15 Bxf6, gxf6; 16 Nc3, Rad8; 17 Qd2, Rfe8 (Kovacs-Kluger, Budapest 1965). White is caught in a devastating crossfire, e.g. 18 g3, Bb4!; 19 a3, Rxe2+!; 20 Kxe2, Bxd3+; 21 cxd3, Nxb3; 22 Qb2, Qe5+ winning material (analysis).

b) **13 Na3**, Ba6!; 14 g3, O-O; 15 O-O, Rad8 with advantage to Black (Spielmann-Eliskases, match 1936)

c) **13 f4**, O-O; 14 O-O, Re8; 15 Nc3, Bf5; 16 b3 (After 16 Qe1, Nd5 Black had sufficient compensation in Belov-Hohlovkin, Yaroslavl 1954.) 16 ..., Rad8; 17 Bd2, Nb7; 18 h3, Nc5 with equal chances although White eventually won in Anderssen-von Neumann, Berlin 1866.

d) **13 g3**, O-O; 14 O-O, Bh3; 15 Re1, Rad8; 16 Bd2, Nc4; 17 Bc3, Ne4 and Black's pieces have attained their ideal positions. In the game Buzov-Borisov, Kalinin 1961, there now occurred 18 Nd2, Nxf2!; 19 Nxf2 (Or 19 Kxf2, Qb6+.) 19 ..., Ne3; 20 Qc1, Bxg3!; 21 Nxh3, Bxh2+; 22 Kh1, Qg3 and White was overwhelmed.

e) **13 Be3**, c5; 14 Nc3, Nc4; 15 Qc1, O-O favoured Black in Rodl-Bogolyubov, match 1931.

f) **13 Nd2**, O-O (13 ..., Ba6!?) 14 b4 (Nor need Black fear 14 Nf3, c5; 15 O-O, Bb7; 16 Nde1, Rad8 or 14 h3, c5; 15 b3, c4; 16 bxc4, Nxc4: see Estrin.) 14 ..., Nd5!; 15 Bb2, Nxb4; 16 Nxb4, Bxb4; 17 O-O, Rd8!; 18 Bd3, Qf4; 19 Nf3, Nc4; 20 Bc1, Qf6 (Spielmann-Cohn, Stockholm 1909).

This examination reveals that White's best chance is probably 13 f4.

13 ..., O-O; 14 O-O,

Or first **14 Nd2**, Re8; 15 O-O, Bf5.

14 ..., Bc8-f5;

Also good here is **14 ..., Rb8** (But not 14 ..., c5?!; 15 c4!) e.g. 15 Nc3, c5; 16 Bf3 (Or 16 b3, c4! Estrin.) 16 ..., c4!; 17 Ne1, Rd8; 18 Qe2, Re8; 19 Qd1, Be6 (Ekenberg-Keres, Lidkoping 1944).

15 Nb1-d2, Rf8-e8;

Estrin gives here **15 ..., Rad8; 16 b3** (16 a3 would transpose back) 16 ..., Rfe8; 17 Nf3, c5; 18 Re1, c4 with some advantage to Black.

16 a2-a3

Here at last the game diverges from another Anderssen-von Neumann struggle: **16 Nf3** (16 b3 see previous note) 16 ..., Rad8; 17 Bd2, Nc4; 18 Bc3, Nd5; 19 Nd4, Bg6; 20 Bf3, Nxc3; 21 bxc3, Ne5; 22 Rb1, Nxd3; 23 cxd3, c5!; 24 Nb5 (24 Rb7, Qc8 and White is embarrassed) 24 ..., Qa5; 25 Bc6?! (but after 25 Nxd6, Rxe1+; 26 Qxe1, Rxd6; 27 Qe8+!, Kh7; 28 Be4 — or 28 Rb8, Bxd3 — 28 ..., Re6!; 29 Qc8, Qxc3 Black is on top) 25 ..., Re6; 26 Re1, Be5; 27 Qb3, c4 and Black won in 40 moves.

16 ..., Ra8-d8; 17 b2-b4, Qc7-e7!

25

Gligoric demonstrates true grandmasterly understanding of the complications. If now **18 Re1?** there comes 18 ..., Bxd3!; 19 cxd3, Qe5 with the double threat of 20 ..., Qh2+ and 20 ..., Qxa1. So White's reply is forced.

18 b4xa5, Qe7xe2; 19 Rf1-e1?

Gligoric is ready for this too. White probably did not like **19 Qxe2**, Rxe2; 20 Rb1 (What else?) since he has many weaknesses and is practically in zugzwang after, e.g. 20 ..., Rb8; 21 Rxb8+, Bxb8.

19 ..., Bf5xd3!

Much better than 19 ..., Qxd1 although Black is no worse then.

20 Re1xe2, Bd3xe2; 21 Qd1-e1, Bd6-e5!; 22 Ra1-b1, Be5-c3; 23 f2-f3,

In the face of pins and batteries, White has to concede a piece, e.g. **23 Rb3**, Bc4; 24 Qd1, Bxd2; 25 Bxd2, Ne4.

23 ..., Be2-b5; 24 Qe1-h4,

If **24 Qd1**, Bxd2; 25 Bxd2, Re2; 26 Rxb5, Rdxd2 etc.

24 ..., Bc3xd2; 25 Bc1xd2, Rd8xd2

Rook, bishop and knight vs. queen is of course a winning material advantage.

26 a3-a4, Bb5-a6; 27 Rb1-e1, Re8-d8; 28 c2-c4, Rd2-c2; 29 Kg1-h2, Rd8-d2;

Against a grandmaster, White could resign but doubtless prefers to be taught a lesson in technique.

30 Re1-g1, Ba6xc4; 31 Qh4-f4, Nf6-d5; 32 Qf4-b8+, Kg8-h7; 33 Qb8xa7, Nd5-f4; 34 Qa7-e3, Nf4x g2; 35 Qe3-e4+, g7-g6; 36 Kh2-g3, Rd2-e2; 37 Qe4-d4, Ng2-e3;

This would probably have

been the reply wherever White put his queen. The lost tempo could not have been any use to White.

38 Qd4-d7, Ne3-f5+; 39 Ke3-f4, Bc4-e6; White resigns.

Game 16
Estrin - Strand
(Correspondence 1966)

1 e2-e4, e7-e5; 2 Ng1-f3, Nb8-c6; 3 Bf1-c4, Ng8-f6; 4 Nf3-g5, d7-d5; 5 e4xd5, Nc6-a5; 6 Bc4-b5+, c7-c6; 7 d5xc6, b7xc6; 8 Bb5-e2, h7-h6; 9 Ng5-f3,

The Steinitz continuation **9 Nh3!?** should not be under-estimated. White avoids the further losses of time involved in the main line, and hopes Black will reduce the dynamism of his set-up by playing ..., Bxh3. Almost forgotten, this variation returned into some sort of vogue after Fischer used it to defeat Bisguier in 1963 (see Game 45 in Fischer's own book 'My Sixty Memorable Games').

How should Black continue? The main line is **9 ..., Bc5** (Fischer has suggested 9 ..., Bd6; 10 d4, e4 but 10 d3 is good) and now:

a) 10 d3, O-O; 11 Nc3 (11 c3, Nb7!) 11 ..., Nd5 (Better than 11 ..., Re8 of Fischer-Radoicic, USA 1963.) 12 Na4, Bd6; 13 Ng1, f5; 14 c3, Bd7! and Black's compensation was more than adequate in Steinitz-Chigorin, cable game 1890-1.

b) 10 d3, O-O; 11 O-O, Nb7 (Fischer-Bisguier went 11 ..., Bxh3; 12 gxh3, Qd7; 13 Bf3, Qxh3 with perhaps slightly more for White; possible is 11 ..., Nd5; 12 Bf3, Nb7; 13 Nc3, Bb6; 14 Kh1, Nc5; 15 Be3, Rb8 as in Ciocaltea-Szabo, Sinaia 1964, when Wade suggests 16 d4!

with an unclear position while another Steinitz-Chigorin game went 12 c4.) **12 Nc3** (Or 12 Kh1, Bxb6; 13 c3, Bb6; 14 Be3, Nd5; 15 Bxb6, Qxb6; 16 Qd2, Bxh3!; 17 gxh3, Nf4 Makovecs-Charousek, Budapest 1896.) 12 ..., Bb6; 13 Kh1, Nc5; 14 f4, e4; 15 Nf2, exd3; 16 Nxd3, Bf5; 17 Nxc5, Bxc5 (Hamann-Geller, Kislovodsk 1966) with adequate compensation for the pawn according to Estrin. There could follow 18 Bd3, Bg4; 19 Qe1, Re8; 20 Qg3, Qd7; 21 h3, Bf5; 22 Bxf5, Qxf5; 23 Qd3, Qxd3; 24 cxd3, Rad8; 25 Rd1, Nh5 (threatening ..., Rxd3!) 26 g4, Ng3+; 27 Kg2, Ne2; 28 Nxe2, Rxe2+; 29 Kf3, Rde8! and White cannot prevent the doubling of rooks on his second rank (analysis).

c) 10 O-O, g5!? (10 ..., O-O; 11 d3 see **b**) 11 Kh1, g4; 12 Ng1, Ne4; 13 Bxg4!, Nxf2+; 14 Rxf2, Bxf2; 15 Bxc8 favours White, according to Fischer.

9 ..., e5-e4; 10 Nf3-e5, Bf8-d6; 11 f2-f4,

Perhaps stronger than **11 d4** of Fishhaimer-Gligoric etc.

26

11 ..., e4xf3!

The move favoured by Estrin

himself. As in Game 15, Black does not allow his opponent to establish a central outpost. The attempt to undermine: **11 ..., g5?!** comes amiss after 12 d4, gxf4; 13 Bxf4, Nd5; 14 O-O! while **11 ..., Qc7**; 12 O-O! and **11 ..., O-O**; 12 O-O are also liable to turn out to White's advantage.

12 Ne5xf3, O-O!

Black usually has to play this move before he is ready for action in the Two Knights. **12 ..., Qc7** is once more insufficient.

12 d2-d4,

White has the alternative of **13 O-O** after which Black's best is probably **13 ..., Re8** when **14 d4** returns to the text. Or if **14 Nc3**, Qc7:

a) 15 d4 (White has avoided the course of Estrin-Strand) **15 ..., Ng4!** (Apparently an original situation, but Black could also play 15 ..., Bg4 transposing to Magergut-Turn, Tallinn 1945, with good play according to Keres.) 16 h3, Ne3; 17 Bxe3, Rxe3 with a promising position for Black (Not 18 Qd2?, Bf4; 19 g3??, Rxf3.) - analysis.

b) 15 d3, Rb8; 16 Ne4!?, Nxe4; 17 dxe4, Rxe4; 18 Bd3, Re7; 19 b3, c5; 20 Bb2, Nc6; 21 Bc3, Bb7; 22 Re1 with about equal chances (Estrin).

Less reliable after **13 O-O ..., c5** e.g. **14 d4** (Also critical is 14 b3, Nc6; 15 Bb2, Bb7; 16 Na3, Re8; 17 Nc4, Bc7 and now Estrin's 18 Ne3 with the follow-up 19 Qe1 and 20 Qh4.) 14 ..., Qc7; 15 Nc3, a6; 16 Kh1, Bb7?! (Better 16 ..., Re8 but the situation is unclear.) and now instead of 17 Be3 as in Spassky-Geller, Gothenburg 1955, Kopylov suggests 17 d5! with attacking chances for White, e.g. 17 ..., Rfe8; 18 Nh4, Be5; 19 Nf5.

13 ..., Rf8-e8; 14 O-O, c6-c5!; ·

It was also possible to play this last move, when 14 O-O, Re8 (Or 14 ..., cxd4 with equal chances.) transposes, whilst White gets a bad game if he tries 14 dxc5, Bxc5; 15 Qxd8, Rxd8; 16 c3, Re8; 17 Kf1, Rxe2!; 18 Kxe2, Ba6+ (Mednis-Bisguier, USA Championship 1957-8)

15 Nb1-c3, c5xd4; 16 Qd1xd4, Na5-c6; 17 Qd4-h4, Ra8-b8!

This was an improvement upon **17 ..., Ne5**; 18 Kh1! of Estrin-Gurvich, 6th USSR Correspondence Championship 1963-4).

18 Kg1-h1?

The losing move. It was necessary to play **18 a3**, preventing ..., Rb4, although of course Black's position is extremely promising anyway.

18 ..., Rb8-b4; 19 Qh4-e1, Bc8-a6; 20 Qe1-d1

27

20 ..., Re8xe2!; 21 Nc3xe2, Qd8-e7 22 Ne2-g1,

If **22 Re1** then 22 ..., Ng4; 23 Kg1, Bc5+ is miserable for White.

22 ..., Nf6-e4;

Black is not to be bought off by offers of the exchange.

23 Ng1-h3, Ba6-e2!; 24 Qd1-e1,

If **24 Qxe2?** then 24 ..., Ng3+ nets the queen.

24 ..., Rb4-b5;

White is tied up, so Black increases the mobility of his rook.

25 Nf3-g1,

Against the threat of ..., Rd5-d1.

25 ..., Be2xf1; 26 Qe1xf1, Nc6-d4; 27 Ng1-f3?!,

A better try was **27 c3, Rf5; 28 Qd1** although the game is up if Black finds 28 ..., Qh4!.

27 ..., Nd4-e2!;

Threatening to win the queen by successive knight forks.

28 Qf1-e1, Rb5-h5; 29 Bc1-d2, g7-g5

Black does not hesitate to employ farmyard moves when they are appropriate.

30 Nf3-g1, Ne2-g3+; 31 h2xg3, Bd6xg3; White resigns.

To prevent ..., Nf2 mate, the queen has to go.

Thus it can be seen that the Two Knights Defence is certainly in business. The lover of combinations cannot hope for a happier hunting-ground than the Black side of the 4 Ng5 lines. Hence the popularity of this opening in correspondence play, although it is comparatively rarely seen in over-the-board play against the clock nowadays. The judgement of Tarrasch appears to be confirmed.

RUBINSTEIN FOUR KNIGHTS GAME
(1 e4, e5; 2 Nf3, Nc6; 3 Nc3, Nf6; 4 Bb5, Nd4)

Nowadays the Four Knights Game has a reputation for placidity, but in the early decades of the modern era of master tournaments it was a feared weapon. After the usual moves like 4 ..., Bb4 White was liable to get enduring positional pressure, rather as in the Ruy Lopez to which it could transpose after 4 ..., d6; 5 d4. However, just before the First World War, the great Akiba Rubinstein popularised a totally new plan for Black, involving the offer of the Black king's pawn. Within fifteen years the Four Knights had almost disappeared from master practice, tamed by Rubinstein's counter-gambit. The soundness of this idea is still unchallenged.

Game 17
Spielmann - Rubinstein
(Baden-Baden 1925)
1 e2-e4, e7-e5; 2 Ng1-f3, Nb8-c6;

3 Nb1-c3, Ng8-f6;

This is the best move here. If **3 ..., f5?!** White can transpose into the Schliemann Variation of the

Ruy Lopez by 4 Bb5, or still better play **4 d4!**, fxe4; 5 Nxe5, Nf6; 6 Bc4 with advantage, following Keres.

4 Bf1-b5

The Prussian Four Knights, characterised by **4 Bc4!?** is now virtually obsolete. It is in fact a line of the Two Knights Defence and Black can play **4 ..., Nxe4!** after which 5 Nxe4, 5 Bxf7+ and the Boden Gambit 5 O-O are all satisfactory for him as long as he is careful.

The most usual move here is **4 d4** when White intends after 4 ..., exd4 to play the Scotch Game (5 Nxd4) or Belgrade Gambit (5 Nd5!?). Black can avoid these with the sharp **4 ..., Bb4**, for which see Game 21.

4 ..., Nc6-d4!

28

5 Nf3xe5,

The natural move, and not best. White can also consider:

a) 5 Nxd4 (A 'grandmaster draw' line: the only real drawback to playing 4 ..., Nd4 against someone that you have to beat.) 5 ..., exd4; 6 **e5** (Or 6 Nd5?!, Nxd5; 7 exd5, Qf6! Wolf-Alekhine, Carlsbad 1923, or 7 ..., Qe7 Ivkov-Spassky, Belgrade-Leningrad match 1964.) 6 ..., dxc3;

7 exf6, Qxf6; 8 dxc3, Qe5+; 9 Qe2 (Or 9 Be2.) 9 ..., Qxe2+ with a quick draw following in countless games.

b) 5 O-O, Nxb5; 6 Nxb5, c6; 7 Nc3, d6; 8 d4, Qc7; 9 h3, b5!; 10 a3, a6 with about equal chances (Euwe).

c) 5 Bc4 (moving the now displaced bishop): see Game 18.

d) 5 Ba4 (... and pinning the d-pawn): see Game 19.

e) 5 Be2, d6 (or 5 ..., Bc5!?; 6 Nxe5 see note to White's 6th move in Game 20) 6 d3, Nxe2 gave White nothing in Aronin-Vistanetzkis, USSR 1962.

5 ..., Qd8-e7!

This was Rubinstein's definitive form of his variation. For **5 ..., Bc5!?** see Game 20, while **5 ..., Nxe4?** had to be abandoned after the 9th game of his match with Bogolyubov in 1920 when that grandmaster played 6 Nxe4, Nxb5; 7 Nxf7! (improving on 7 d4 of the 7th game) 7 ..., Qe7 (If 7 ..., Kxf7 comes 8 Qh5+, g6; 9 Qd5+, Kg7; 10 Qe5+, Kg8; 11 Qxb5) 8 Nxh8, Qxe4+; 9 Kf1, Nd4 (Also to be considered were 9 ..., Qf5 and 9 ..., g6 but White stands better.) 10 h4! and Rubinstein succumbed in 12 more moves.

6 f2-f4

None of White's moves are wholly satisfactory:

a) 6 Ng4, Nxg4; 7 Qxg4, Nxc2+; 8 Kd1, Nxa1; 9 Nd5, Qe5! (Reti-Balla Pistyan 1922) and now relatively best was 10 d3, f5; 11 Qg5, Be7 with complications that may favour Black.

b) 6 Nf3, Nxb5; 7 Nxb5, Qxe4+; 8 Qe2, Qxe2+; 9 Kxe2, Nd5; 10 Re1 (Or 10 c4, a6.) 10 ..., f6! and Black has the edge (A.Kubbel-Grigoriev, Moscow 1920: battle of the composers!).

6 ..., Nd4xb5;

Here **6 ..., Nxe4!?** might be worth looking at, too.

7 Nc3xb5, d7-d6; 8 Ne5-f3, Qe7xe4+;

This looks risky, but is better than **8 ..., c6**; 9 Nc3, Nxe4; 10 0-0, Nxc3; 11 dxc3 with some advantage to White, while if **8 ..., Nxe4?**; 9 0-0 and Black is lost.

9 Ke1-f2

White simply stands worse after **9 Qe2** in view of long-term factors (weak f-pawn, Black's two bishops).

9 ..., Nf6-g4+; 10 Kf2-g3!?

It would be defeatist to accept a slight disadvantage by **10 Kg1** e.g. 10 ..., Qc6; 11 Qe2+, Be7; 12 h3, Qb6+; 13 d4, Nf6; 14 Kh2, Bd7; 15 Re1, 0-0 (Barden, 'A Guide to Chess Openings').

10 ..., Qe4-g6!

This move, discovered by Teichmann, improves upon **10 ..., Kd8?** of the 3rd Bogolyubov-Rubinstein match game, continued 11 h3, Nh6; 12 d4, Qg6+; 13 Kh2, Be7; 14 Re1 with advantage to White.

11 Qd1-e2+

The alternative is **11 Nh4**, Qh5 e.g.:

a) 12 h3, Qxb5!; 13 hxg4, g5! with advantage to Black (Keres).

b) 12 f5, g5!; 13 Qxg4 (Or 13 Nf3, c6!; 14 Nxc7+, Kd8; 15 Nxa8, d5.) 13 ..., gxh4+; 14 Kf3, Qxg4+; 15 Kxg4, Rg8+ and 16 ..., Kd8 favours Black (Keres).

c) 12 Nxc7+, Kd8; 13 h3 (Or Teichmann's line 13 Nxa8, g5!; 14 fxg5, Qxg5; 15 Nf3, Qg7 with a strong attack for Black.) 13 ..., Nf6; 14 Nxa8, Qxh4+!; 15 Kxh4, Ne4 and Black stands to win, e.g. 16 Qg4, Be7+; 17 Qg5, Bxg5+; 18 fxg5, h6; 19 g6, fxg6 (Keres).

11 ..., Ke8-d8; 12 Rh1-e1

Spielmann originally tried here (against Rubinstein at Scheveningen, 1923) **12 h3**, Ne3+; 13 Kh2, Nxc2 but Black stood better.

12 ..., Bc8-d7; 13 Nb5-d4, Ng4-e3+ 14 Kg3-f2, Ne3xc2; 15 Nd4xc2, Qg6xc2

29

White is without tangible compensation for the pawn. Rubinstein's powerful handling of his advantage in this game is an object lesson.

16 b2-b4, a7-a5!; 17 Bc1-a3, a5xb4; 18 Ba3xb4, Qc2-f5;

Rubinstein, having created a target for his queen rook, goes back to play on the king side. Naturally he rejects the foolhardy pawn 'win' **18 ..., Rxa2?!**; 19 Rec1, Qb3; 20 Nd4, Qa4; 21 Rxa2, Qxa2; 22 Nb5 with a strong attack for White.

19 Qe2-e3

Guarding the f-pawn.

19 ..., h7-h6!

Preparing to open lines against Spielmann's king.

20 Ra1-c1, Rh8-g8!; 21 Kf2-g1, g7-g5!; 22 Qe3-c3, Ra8-c8;

Consolidation, as he can win the game on the other flank.

23 f4xg5, h6xg5; 24 Kg1-h1, g5-g4; 25 Nf3-d4, Qf5-d5; 26 Qc3-e3,

Against the possibility of ..., Bh6.

26 ..., g4-g3!; 27 Bb4-c3, Rc8-a8; 28 Nd4-f3, g3xh2; 29 Bc3-f6+, Kd8-c8; 30 Qe3-c3,

That mate threat again.

30 ..., Qd5-c5; 31 Qc3-d3, Qc5-h5; 32 Nf3-e5!?

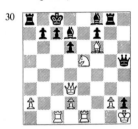

30

32 ..., Rg8xg2!!

Spielmann had hoped for **32 ..., dxe5??** when 33 Rxe5 threatens 34 Re8+! and then mate by 35 Qd8. The exposure of the White king makes all the difference.

33 Kh1xg2, d6xe5; 34 Re1xe5, Qh5-g4+; 35 Qd3-g3,

White has to exchange queens in view of the lines **35 Kh1?**, Bc6+; 36 Rxc6, Qg1 mate or **35 Kxh2**, Qf4+; 36 Qg3, Qxc2+ and 37 ..., Qxc1 (But not here 36 ..., Qxf6?? in view of 37 Re8+ and 38 Qxc7 mate).

35 ..., Qg4xg3+; 36 Kg2xg3, Bf8-d6; 37 Kg3xh2, Ra8xa2; 38 Kh2-g1, Ra2xd2!

Rubinstein reckons that the elimination of the last White pawn, together with the absolute control of the seventh rank, is well worth the exchange he could have taken instead.

39 Re5-h5, b7-b6;

Establishing a post for his bishop, as well as forestalling Rh8+.

40 Bf6-e5, Bd6-c5+; 41 Kg1-f1, Kc8-b7; 42 Be5-g3, Bd7-b5+; 43 Kf1-e1, Rd2-e2+; 44 Ke1-d1, Re2-g2; 45 Rc1-c3?

Loses outright, but if **45 Rh3**, Bd7 or **45 Rg5**, Be2+; 46 Ke1, Be3.

45 ..., Bb5-e2+

White resigns, as the Rh5 goes.

Game 18
Nimzowitsch - Alekhine
(St. Petersburg 1914)

1 e2-e4, e7-e5; 2 Ng1-f3, Nb8-c6; 3 Nb1-c3, Ng8-f6; 4 Bf1-b5, Nc6-d4; 5 Bb5-c4, Bf8-c5!

This was Rubinstein's own method, but others are:

a) 5 ..., Nxe4?!; 6 Nxd4, exd4; 7 Bxf7+ (Veinger-Zeitlin, Leningrad Championship 1966) with White emerging half a pawn up, winning in 42 moves.

b) 5 ..., Nxf3+ (similarly 5 ..., d6) is dull and moreover slightly better for White (Miyasaka-Martinez, Skopje 1972).

c) 5 ..., c6!? is more thematic. A game Schubert-Baturinsky (correspondence 1958-9) continued 6 Nxe5 d5; 7 exd5, Bd6; 8 Nxf7?! (Baturinsky gives 8 O-O, Bxe5; 9 Re1, Qe7; 10 f4, Qc5.) 8 ..., Kxf7; 9 dxc6+, Kf8; 10 d3, Bg4; 11 f3, Qe7+; 12 Ne4, Nxe4; 13 dxe4, Bc5! with advantage to Black.

6 Nf3xe5?!

Acceptance of the sacrifice, as we shall see, is dubious here. The best move for White is probably **6 d3**, d5! (Better than 6 ..., d6; 7 Na4, b5; 8 Nxd4, bxc4; 9 Nf3, Bb4+; 10 c3, Ba5; 11 dxc4, Bb7; 12 c5 of Iambshire-Davie, British Championship 1967.) 7 Nxd5, Nxd5; 8 Bxd5 (Not 8 Nxd4, Bb4+; 9 Kf1, Nb6 favouring Black.) 8 ..., Bg4 and now, according to analysis by Keres, 9 Be3 with rough equality, but not 9 Bxf7+?, Kf8; 10 c3, Nxf3+; 11 gxf3, Bh3; 12 Bh3, Qh4.

6 ..., Qd8-e7;

6 ..., O-O?! is too quiet, and leaves White better off.

7 Ne5-d3

This may be marginally superior to 7 Nf3, d5! (7 ..., Nxe4 is only level.) 8 Nxd5 (If 8 Bxd5?, Bg4!, or 8 Nxd4?, dxc4 as in Spielmann-Rubinstein, San Sebastian 1912.) 8 ..., Qxe4+ (8 ..., Nxd5; 9 Bxd5, c6 is equal.) 9 Ne3, Bg4; 10 Be2, Nxe2; 11 Qxe2, O-O-O; 12 d3, Qe6; 13 O-O, Nd5; 14 Re1, Nf4; 15 Qd1, Bh5 with complications that probably favour Black (Schubert - Henriksen, correspondence 1958).

7 ..., d7-d5; 8 Bc4xd5

A game Belitzmann-Rubinstein, Warsaw 1917, was to continue instead **8 Nxd5** (If 8 Nxc5?, dxc4 favours Black.) 8 ..., Qxe4+ (Alekhine gives 8 ..., Nxd5; 9 Bxd5, c6.) 9 Ne3, Bd6; 10 O-O, b5! and Black won quickly.

8 ..., Nf6xd5; 9 Nc3xd5, Qe7xe4+; 10 Nd5-e3, Bc5-d6; 11 O-O, Bc8-e6

Black's lead in development, and the possession of the two bishops, assure him of adequate dynamic compensation for the pawn sacrificed.

12 Nd3-e1, O-O-O; 13 c2-c3, Nd4-f5; 14 Qd1-c2?,

Until this point, it was not clear that Nimzowitsch should have lost. Alekhine gives as superior here 14 d3!, Qh4; 15 Nf3, Qh5 with balanced chances.

14 ..., Qe4-h4!

This is better than 14 ..., Qf4 immediately, in view of the line 15 g3, Qg5; 16 d4, Qf6; 17 N1g2 or 17 Nd3 (Alekhine).

15 Ne1-f3

The knight has been diverted (15 g3?, Qh3) as only in a formal sense does it stand well here.

15 ..., Qh4-f4; 16 Ne3xf5, Be6xf5; 17 d2-d3, Qf4-g4; 18 Nf3-d4, Qg4-h5;

The mate threat gains a tempo and forces a weakening of White's king position, and also of the king's file (point e3!).

19 f2-f4, Rh8-e8; 20 b2-b4,

Commencing the pawn-storm that is the theoretically indicated way of handling positions with opposite-side castling. But Alekhine is ready in the centre ...

20 ..., c7-c5!

Only apparently a weakening; White must exchange his best piece.

21 Nd4xf5, Qh5xf5; 22 Qc2-d2,

In order to cover e1.

22 ..., Bd6-c7; 23 Rf1-f3, c5xb4; 24 c3xb4, g7-g5!; 25 f4xg5,

Slightly better was **25 Bb2** but then would come 25 ..., gxf4; 26 Qc3, Kb8 with heavy pressure on the d-pawn (Alekhine).

25 ..., Qf5-e5; 26 Bc1-b2, Qe5xh2+ 27 Kg1-f1,

32

27 ..., Bc7-g3??

Black throws away the win, which could have been his by **27 ..., Qh1+; 28 Kf2, Qh4+; 29 Kf1, Bg3!; 30 Qc3+, Kb8; 31 Qc5, b6; 32 Qg1, Rxd3!; 33 Rxd3, Qf4+; 34 Rf3, Qc4+** and mate next move (Alekhine).

28 Bb2-d4!,

Threatening to put everything right for White by 29 Bg1.

28 ..., Rd8xd4!;

Fortunately for Black, he still has the draw well in hand.

29 Qd2-c3+, Kc8-b8; 30 Qc3xd4, Bg3-e5; 31 Qd4-d7, Re8-c8; 32 Rf3xf7!,

White threatens mate, and so eliminates all danger — except from his own ambition.

32 ..., Qh2-h1+; 33 Kf1-f2, Qh1-h4+; 34 Kf2-e2, Qh4-h5+; 35 g2-g4?

This move only helps Black. After **35 Kf1** the draw must follow.

35 ..., Qh5-h2+; 36 Ke2-f3, Qh2-g3+; 37 Kf3-e4, Be5-c7;

Evidently Nimzowitsch had overlooked something — probably this 'quiet move' which threatens 38 ..., Qe5+ and 39 ..., Qxa1.

38 Ra1-c1,

Alekhine, in 'My Best Games of Chess 1908-23', does not mention the possibility **38 Raf1**, after which 38 ..., Qg2+ would come to naught by 39 R1f3. However Black has adequate checks on the Black squares to ensure the draw.

38 ..., Qg3-g2+; 39 Ke4-e3, Bc7-b6+; 40 d3-d4?,

Alekhine says the only reply was **40 Rc5**, e.g. 40 ..., Rd8; 41 Qf5 (against ..., Qg3+) 41 ..., Re8+; 42 Kd4, Qb2+; 43 Kc4, Qxa2+; 44 Kc3 and Black cannot win because of the looming threat of Rxb7+ and Qc8 mate.

40 ..., Rc8-d8!

Black is winning again. Queen moves now are met by ..., Bxd4+ and then ..., Qf2+ etc.

41 Rc1-c7, Qg2-g3+; 42 Rf7-f3, Qg3-e1+; 43 Ke3-d3, Qe1-d1+;

44 Kd3-e3, Bb6xc7; White resigns

Game 19
Tarrasch - Rubinstein
(San Sebastian 1912)

1 e2-e4, e7-e5; 2 Ng1-f3, Nb8-c6; 3 Nb1-c3, Ng8-f6; 4 Bf1-b5, Bf8-c5!?

This move, intending a subsequent ..., Nd4, was Rubinstein's original idea, which however he came to consider unsound. This is perhaps the place also to set right the historical record on another point: the move 4 ..., Nd4, universally credited to Rubinstein, seems in fact to have been the idea of Frank Marshall, who played it in 1903 (against Tarrasch at Monte Carlo) and again in 1905 (against Janowski at Paris). However, shortly thereafter Marshall took up the Petroff Defence and took no further part in the debate on the Four Knights, his two games not having attracted much contemporary attention.

5 Nf3xe5, Nc6-d4!;

Not 5 ..., Nxe5; 6 d4, Bd6 (Or 6 ..., Bb4!? Friedmann-Villasante, Skopje 1972) on account of Keres's 7 O-O! e.g. 7 ..., c6; 8 Be2, O-O; 9 f4!, Ng6; 10 f5!, Ne7; 11 e5 with advantage to White (analysis).

White could also have played 5 O-O, O-O; 6 Nxe5, Nd4 transposing into the first note to White's 6th move in the next game.

6 Bb5-a4

Thus the game returns to the main line of the Rubinstein variation; this position being normally reached by the sequence 4 ..., Nd4; 5 Ba4, Bc5; 6 Nxe5. Here 6 d3 and 6 O-O are met by 6 ..., O-O with

good play for Black.

It is often stated that White should play instead **6 Be2** and obtain an advantage; this is indeed why Rubinstein abandoned 4 ..., Bc5. However, the analysis is far from clear: see note to White's 6th move in the next game, and for **6 Nd3** see that game itself.

6 ..., O-O;

33

7 d2-d3?!,

This is one of the main decisions that White has to take and Tarrasch, not having the subsequent experience with the variation to guide him, already plays an inferior move.

The game Havasi-Kmoch (1930) took the course 7 Nf3, d5!; 8 Nxd4, Bxd4; 9 O-O, Nxe4; 10 Nxe4, dxe4; 11 d3, exd3; 12 Qxd3, Be6 with about equal chances.

If White wishes to try for an advantage, he must play **7 Nd3!?** and then after 7 ..., Bb6 find his way through this labyrinth:

a) 8 f3?, d5; 9 Nf2, dxe4; 10 fxe4, Ng4!; 11 Nxg4, Qh4+; 12 g3, Qxg4; 13 Qxg4, Bxg4; 14 d3, f5 with advantage to Black (Keres).

b) 8 e5, Ne8; 9 O-O (Or 9 Ne2, d6 Roiter-Polyak, Kiev 1958.) 9 ..., d6; 10 exd6, Nxd6 (Better may be 10 ...,

Nf6 e.g. 11 dxc7, Qd6! or 11 d7, Bxd7; 12 Bxd7, Qxd7; 13 Ne1, Rae8; 14 d3, Ng4; 15 h3, f5!? with about equal chances - Malkin.)) 11 Kh1, c6; 12 Ne2 (12 Nf4!? - Keres) 12 ..., Nxe2; 13 Qxe2, Qh4; 14 Bb3, Bg4 and Black's game is superior (Tylor-Vlagsma, 1948).

c) 8 O-O, d5; 9 Nxd5 (Not 9 exd5?, Bg4!) **9 ..., Nxd5!** (Or 9 ..., Nxe4!?; 10 Nc3!, Nf6 as in Honfi-Pogats, Budapest 1959, and now Keres gives 11 h3, c6; 12 Nf4, Bc7; 13 d3, Qd6; 14 Ne4, Nxe4; 15 dxe4, Qe5 with about equal chances) **10 exd5** and now:

c1) 10 ..., Qh4!?; 11 Kh1!, Bf5! (If 11 ..., c6?!; 12 g3! or 11 ..., Bg4?!; 12 f3, Bxf3; 13 gxf3, Nf5; 14 b4! Keres) 12 Ne5 (If 12 Ne1, Bg4; 13 f3, Nf5) 12 ..., f6; 13 Nf3, Nxf3+; 14 Qxf3, Qc4; 15 Re1 (Or 15 d3, Qxa4; 16 Qxf2, Qxc2) 15 ..., Bxc2= (Gordeev).

c2) 10 ..., Qxd5!; 11 Nf4 (If 11 Ne1, Qc4! or 11 c3, Qe4!) 11 ..., Qg5!; 12 d3, Bg4; 13 Nd5 (Not 13 Qd2?, Nf3+) 13 ..., Qh5; 14 Ne7+, Kh8; 15 Qd2, Bc5 and Black has emerged better from the complications (Zak). The 8 O-O line was the subject of heated debate in 'Schach maty' a few years ago; the analyses of Gordeev and Zak, which have stood ever since, may be supplemented by an excerpt from the game Teodorescu-Kushnir(Moscow 1971) which went **8 ..., c6!?** (instead of 8 ..., d5) 9 Ne1, d5; 10 exd5, Bg4; 11 Nf3, Nxd5; 12 d3, Nxf3+; 13 gxf3, Bh3; 14 Re1, Qh4 and already White was lost.

d) 8 Nf4, d5 (Also playable are 8 ..., d6 and 8 ..., c6) **9 d3** (Not 9 Nfxd5?, Nxd5; 10 Nxd5, Qh4!; 11 O-O, Bg4; 12 Qe1, Nf3+! Panov & Estrin) 9 ..., Bg4 (9 ..., c6!?) 10 f3,

Nh5; 11 Nxh5!? (White has a draw by 11 fxg4, Qh4+; 12 g3, Nxg3; 13 Ng2, Qf6; 14 hxg3, Nf3+; 15 Ke2, Nd4+) 11 ..., Bxh5; 12 Nxd5, c6! (Better than 12 ..., Qh4+?! of Canal-Eliskases, Kecskemet 1933) 13 Nxb6 (Or 13 Nf4, Nxf3+; 14 gxf3, Qh4+; Black is better also after 13 Ne3, Qh4+; 14 Kf1, f5!) 13 ..., axb6 and, following an analysis by Keres, Black's compensation for the pawns will be good enough to draw at least.

7 ..., d7-d5!; 8 Bc1-g5, c7-c6; 9 Qd1-d2

There is probably not a better move:

a) 9 Nf3, Re8 or perhaps 9 ..., Bg4.

b) 9 O-O, Re8; 10 Nf3, Bg4 with an uncomfortable pin.

c) 9 h3, Re8; 10 Nf3, Nxe4!! winning the house.

d) 9 Bh4, Re8; 10 f4, Ne6; 11 Bg3, Bd4 is good for Black too, according to Panov and Estrin.

9 ..., Rf8-e8; 10 f2-f4,

Kmoch, in his anthology 'Rubinstein's Chess Masterpieces' gives here the variation **10 Nf3,** b5; 11 Bb3, dxe4; 12 Nxe4, Nxe4! regaining the sacrificed pawn with the superior game.

10 ..., b7-b5; 11 Ba4-b3, h7-h6; 12 Bg5-h4,

If **12 Bxf6,** Black has either 12 ..., gxf6; 13 Nf3, dxe4; 14 dxe4, b4 or 12 ..., Qxf6; 13 O-O-O (if 13 exd5, Rxe5+!) 13 ..., a5; 14 exd5, a4; 15 Ne4, Qe7; 16 d6!, axb3!! and wins (Kmoch).

12 ..., Nf6xe4!;

Possible now that the White queen's bishop is hanging.

13 Bh4xd8, Ne4xd2; 14 Ke1xd2,

**Re8xd8; 15 Nc3-e2, Nd4xe2;
16 Kd2xe2, Rd8-e8; 17 Ke2-f1,**

It would be preferable to play **17 Kd2**, but Black of course stands much better in view of his two bishops, safer king and more functional pawn structure. Rubinstein is in his element. Although Tarrasch keeps the struggle going a long time, there can be no doubt of the ultimate destination of the point.

**17 ..., Bc8-b7; 18 c2-c3, f7-f6; 19
Ne5-g4, h6-h5; 20 Ng4-f2, Bc5-e3;
21 Bb3-d1!, h5-h4; 22 g2-g3, a7-a5;
23 Bd1-f3, b5-b4; 24 Kf1-g2,
b4xc3; 25 b2xc3, Bb7-a6; 26 c3-c4!**

Tarrasch seeks always to defend actively.

**26 ..., Ra8-d8; 27 c4xd5, c6xd5; 28
Rh1-d1, Re8-e7; 29 Nf2-g4, h4xg3;
30 h2xg3, Be3-d4; 31 Ra1-c1,
Re7-b7; 32 Rc1-c2, Kg8-f7; 33
Ng4-f2, Rb7-b2!**

The rook exchange will increase the value of his bishops. Even the symmetrical pawn structure does not save Tarrasch.

34 Rc2xb2, Bd4xb2; 35 Rd1-d2,

Nothing to do but wait, while Rubinstein organises his long-term winning manoeuvre — penetration

with the king.

**35 ..., Bb2-d4, 36 Nf2-h3, Kf7-e6;
37 Rd2-c2, Ke6-d6; 38 f4-f5,**

White has a plan, to bring his knight to e6. Rubinstein, however, is ready to exchange the second pair of rooks and so obtain a dominating king.

38 ..., Rd8-c8!

39 Bf3-d1,

He cannot avoid the exchange, for if **39 Rd2**, Rc1 and Black, with threats like ..., Bc3, has rendered the d-pawn indefensible.

**39 ..., Rc8xc2+; 40 Bd1xc2,
Kd6-e5; 41 g3-g4,**

All four white pawns are now on the same colour as his bishop.

41 ..., Bd4-e3;

'With this move the game is won' — Kmoch.

**42 Kg2-f3, Ke5-d4; 43 Bc2-b3,
Ba6-b7; 44 Kf3-e2, Bb7-a6; 45
Bb3-c2,**

If **45 Bxd5**, Bxd3+; 46 Kf3 Black wins by 46 ..., Bf1!

45 ..., Ba6-b5;

Threatening 46 ..., a4, forcing the bishop to b1.

46 a2-a4, Bb5-d7!; 47 Ke2-f3,

Forced, in view of the threatened 47 ..., g6.

47 ..., Kd4-c3, 48 Kf3xe3, d5-d4+!; 49 Ke3-e2, Kc3xc2; 50 Nh3-f4, Bd7xa4; 51 Nf4-e6, Ba4-b3!; 52 Ne6xd4+, Kc2-b2;

The outside passed pawn decides now in any event.

53 Nd4-b5, a4-a5; 54 Ke2-e3, a4-a3; 55 Nb5xa3, Kb2xa3; 56 Ke3-d4, Ka3-b4!; White resigns

as he must give ground.

Game 20
Bobolovich - Hachaturov
(Moscow 1960)

1 e2-e4, e7-e5; 2 Ng1-f3, Nb8-c6; 3 Nb1-c3, Ng8-f6; 4 Bf1-b5, Bf8-c5!?

The original Rubinstein variation again.

5 Nf3xe5, Nc6-d4;

This position could also arise via 4 ..., Nd4; 5 Nxe5, Bc5 (compare Game 17 where Black played 5 ..., Qe7).

36

6 Ne5-d3!?,

For **6 Bc4** and **6 Ba4** see Game 18 and 19 respectively.

Another line that must be considered is **6 O-O, O-O; 7 Bc4** continued 7 ..., d6; 8 Nf3, Bg4; 9 Be2, Nxe2; 10 Qxe2 and Keres quotes Schlechter as saying that Black is without an adequate substitute for his pawn. Notwithstanding this ancient grandmaster opinion, the position arose in the game Gresser-Eretova (3rd Ladies' Olympiad, 1966) and Black won quickly: **10 ..., Nh5!** (improving on Schlechter's 10 ..., Re8; 11 d3)) **11 d3** (against ..., Nf4) 11 ..., f5; 12 exf5, Re8; 13 Qd1, Bxf5; 14 Ng5, Bg6; 15 Qf3, c6; 16 Nge4, Bb6; 17 Bg5, Qd7 (White prods Black a few times but cannot organise real resistance as she is too cramped.) 18 Rae1, d5; 19 Ng3, Rxe1; 20 Rxe1, Rf8 and White has collapsed. White could try instead **11 h3** but again after 11 ..., Nf4; 12 Qd1, Bh5 (12 ..., Nxh3+!?) 13 d3, Qf6 he is under heavy pressure (analysis).

The critical line has for a long time been held to be **6 Be2** as **6 ..., O-O** can be then met by the quiet **7 O-O!** (Not 7 Nd3?!, Nxe2; 8 Qxe2, Bd4; 9 f3, d5; 10 Nf2, dxe4; 11 fxe4, Nxe4! as in Leonhardt-Teichmann, Pistyan 1912.) **7 ..., Re8** (If 7 ..., d6 White will be a tempo better off than in Gresser-Eretova.) **8 Nf3, Nxe4; 9 Nxd4, Bxd4; 10 Nxe4, Rxe4; 11 c3, Bb6; 12 d4, d5; 13 Bd3, Re8; 14 Bf4** followed by 15 Qc2 with pressure for White. In this line **8 ..., Nxe2+; 9 Qxe2** has not been considered: if now 9 ..., d5?! White has 10 d3 intending Bg5 and White holds his pawn, but interesting is **9 ..., Nxe4!?; 10 Nxe4, d5** since 11 Nf6+, gxf6 is unclear and if 11 d3, dxe4; 12 dxe4, b6 Black has suddenly obtained strong threats. This possibility should be looked into.

Also after **6 Be2** Black has a

wild sacrifice: **6 ..., d5!?; 7 Nd3, Nxe4!?** (If 7 ..., Bb6; 8 e5, Ne4; 9 O-O with advantage to White - Keres) 8 Nxe4, dxe4; 9 Nxc5, Qg5; 10 Nxe4, Qxg2; 11 Ng3 which is now dismissed by Keres as being 'not correct'. This is not so clear, since the background to the text game is an article by Hachaturov in the December 1959 number of 'Schachmatny Bulletin' in which he analyses not only 6 Nd3 but also this sacrificial line, which he claims is good for Black; one may take it that Bobolovich, at least, believed the analysis: **11 ..., h5!** (to answer 12 c3 by 12 ..., h4; 13 Qa4+, Bd7 winning) and now:

a) **12 h4**, O-O; 13 d3 (Or 13 c3, Nxe2; 14 Qxe2, Bg4) 13 ..., Bg4; 14 Bxg4, Rfe8+!; 15 Kd2, Qxf2+ when Black wins back one piece with a dangerous attack.

b) **12 Bxh5** (If 12 Bf1, Qc6 threatening ..., Nxc2+) 12 ..., O-O; 13 d3, Re8+; 14 Kd2 (Not 14 Be3?, Rxe3+) 14 ..., Qxf2+; 15 Ne2, Rxe2+ etc.

Did Keres overlook this article while preparing his book 'Drei-springerspiel bis Konigsgambit'?.

6 ..., Nd4xb5;

In his article, Hachaturov mentioned **6 ..., Bb6?**; 7 e5, Nxb5; 8 Nxb5 as being good for White.

7 Nc3xb5,

If **7 Nxc5** then 7 ..., Nxc3 and 8 ..., Qe7 regains the pawn.

7 ..., Nf6xe4!;

Else Black has little hope of equalising.

8 Qd1-e2, O-O; 9 Qe2xe4,

If **9 f3**, Qh4+ (Hachaturov), e.g. 10 Kd1, Nf2+; 11 Nxf2, Bxf2;

12 Nxc7, Rb8; 13 Nd5, d6 and White's insecure king could compensate for the pawn (analysis). This may turn out to be critical.

9 ..., Rf8-e8; 10 Nd3xc5!,

A prepared variation? Hachaturov's article had only considered **10 Ne5?**, d6 e.g. 11 f4, dxe5; 12 fxe5, Bd7 followed by 13 ..., Bc6, or else 11 d4, Bxd4; 12 Qxd4, Rxe5+ and 13 ..., Rxb5 in either case with advantage to Black. Now, however, White obtains rook and two knights for queen and the onus is on Black again to justify his play.

10 ..., Re8xe4+; 11 Nc5xe4,

37

11 ..., d7-d5!;

Whether foreseen or not, Hachaturov handles the situation correctly as yet. He drives back the knights with gain of time and creates new attacking possibilities against the king in the centre.

Of course it is important to understand why **11 ..., Qe7?!; 12 Kd1!** (Not 12 Nxc7, Qxe4+; 13 Kd1, Qxg2; 14 Re1, Qf3+; 15 Re2, Rb8) has to be rejected:

a) **12 ..., Qxe4??**; 13 Re1 and mates.

b) **12 ..., f5?**; 13 Ng3 followed by consolidation.

c) **12 ..., c6?!**; 13 Nbc3! followed by consolidation.

d) **12 ..., b6!** offers some chances of drawing only:

d1) **13 Nxc7, Bb7!**; **14 Nxa8** (If 14 Re1 see **d2**) **14 ..., Qxe4** and now —

d11) **15 Re1**, Qg4+; 16 Re2 (16 f3, Bxf3+ draws) 16 ..., Bxg2; 17 Ke1, Be4; 18 d3, Qg1+; 19 Kd2, Qg5+; 20 Kc3, Qc5+ forcing perpetual check.

d12) **15 f3**, Qf4; 16 Rf1! (else Black draws by force) 16 ..., Bxa8; 17 d3, Qxh2; 18 Re1, Kf8; 19 Bd2 (19 b3!?) 19 ..., d6; 20 Bb4, a5; 21 Ba3, Bd5; 22 c4, Be6; 23 Rc1, Qxg2; 24 Bxd6+, Ke8 with complications, but White for preference.

d2) **13 Re1, Bb7!**; (13 ..., f5??; 14 Ned6!) **14 Nxc7** (14 Nbc3!?) 14 ..., Rc8 and Black has tactical chances, e.g. 15 c4!?, Qh4; 16 Nd6?, Bxg2 or 15 Nb5?, Bxe4; 16 d3, Qc5 (analysis by the author).

So it is hard to tell who in this game has prepared more deeply. Can any improvement be possible over White's next four moves?

12 Ne4-c3,

Not **12 Ng3?** because of 12 ..., Qe8+ picking up the other knight by the fork. So White concedes vital tempi...

12 ..., a7-a6!; 13 Nb5-d4, c7-c5; 14 Nd4-f3, d5-d4; 15 Nc3-e2, d4-d3!;

This must be stronger than **15**

..., **Bg4?**; 16 O-O, Bxf3; 17 gxf3, Rc8; 18 d3, Rc6; 19 Bf4 and White is fully co-ordinated.

16 c2xd3, Bc8-g4??;

I think he had to prevent castling by **16 ..., Qxd3!** after which the situation is still not clear, viz. 17 h3!?, Be6!; 18 Kd1!?, Re8; 19 Re1??, Qb3+!! Naturally this is not forced, but White has clearly got into difficulties on the White squares, and may even be lost (analysis).

17 O-O!,

Turning the tables.

17 ..., Bg4xf3; 18 g2xf3, Qd8xd3; 19 Ne2-g3, Qd3xf3; 20 a2-a4, Ra8-d8; 21 Ra1-a3, Rd8-d3; 22 Ra3xd3, Qf3xd3;

This ending must be won for White by material superiority.

23 a4-a5, Qd3-f3;

He might as well have tried **23 ..., Qb5; 24 Re1.**

24 d2-d3, h7-h5; 25 h2-h4, f7-f6; 26 Bc1-e3, g7-g5; 27 Kg1-h2!, f7-f5;

Since **27 ..., gxh4; 28 Rg1!** is futile.

28 Be3xg5, f5-f4; 29 Ng3-e4, Qf3x d3; 30 Rf1-e1, f4-f3; 31 Kh2-g2, Kg8-f7; 32 Re1-e3, Qd3-d7; 33 Re3xf3+, Black resigns.

A sad end for Hachaturov's innovation.

SCOTCH FOUR KNIGHTS GAME
(1 e4, e5; 2 Nf3, Nc6; 3 Nc3, Nf6; 4 d4, Bb4)

Game 21
Hort - Trifunovic
(Sarajevo 1964)

1 e2-e4, e7-e5; 2 Ng1-f3, Ng8-f6;

Trifunovic attempts to play Petroff's Defence, but the game

soon becomes a Four Knights instead. For another line that may arise from the Petroff, see the Fantasy section at the end of the Open Games chapter.

3 Nb1-c3, Nb8-c6; 4 d2-d4, Bf8-b4!?;

After the usual **4 ..., exd4**, which is perfectly playable, White plays either **5 Nd5?!** (Belgrade Gambit) or **5 Nxd4**, which is fortunately not White's strongest line in the Scotch: 4 ..., Nf6; 5 Nc3 instead of 5 Nxc6! and 6 e5.

Trifunovic's move is an interesting and relatively unexplored offer of the e-pawn. It can lead to White gambitting instead.

38

5 d4-d5,

The other main line is **5 Nxe5** with two possible continuations:

a) 5 ..., Nxe4; 6 Qg4, Nxc3; 7 Qxg7, Rf8; 8 a3, **Nxd4!?** (Here Keres analyses 8 ..., Ba5; 9 Nxc6 as leading to equality, while 8 ..., Qh4?!; 9 Nxc6, dxc6; 10 axb4, Bg4; 11 Qe5+, Kd7; 12 g3 favoured White in Drimer-J.Littlewood, 1969 Hastings.) 9 axb4, Nxc2+; 10 Kd2, Nxa1; 11 Kxc3, a5!; 12 bxa5, c5; 13 Nc4, Qe7; 14 Ne3, Qe4!; 15 Bc4, d5! and Black won in Strauss-Littlewood, Islington 1971.

b) 5 ..., Qe7; 6 Qd3! (Not 6 Nxc6?, Qxe4+) 6 ..., Nxe5; 7 dxe5, Qxe5; 8 Bd2, O-O; 9 O-O-O, **Bxc3?!** (But if 9 ..., d6; 10 f4!, Qe6 - or 10 ..., Qa5; 11 a3 - 11 Re1!, Bxc3; 12 Bxc3, Qxa2; 13 Bxf6, gxf6; 14 Qd4 and 15 Re3 is strong for White - Keres.) 10 Bxc3, Qf4+ (Worse is 10 ..., Qxe4?; 11 Qg3 Spielmann-Bogolyubov, Stockholm 1919.) and now after Portisch's suggestion 11 Rd2! Black has no good line, e.g. 11 ..., Qxe4; 12 Qg3, Qg6; 13 Qxc7 (13 Bd3!? - Littlewood) 13 ..., d5; 14 Bd3, Ne4? (14 ..., Qh6 is not quite so bad) and now instead of 15 Bxf6? as in R.Harman-Chapman (Ilford 1971) Littlewood gives 15 f3! forcing a winning endgame: 15 ..., Qd6; 16 Qxd6, Nd6; 17 Bb4, Rd8; 18 Bxh7+ etc.

Littlewood also points out the possibility **5 dxe5**, which is not mentioned by Keres. Presumably Black gets a good game by **5 ..., Nxe4**, since if 6 Bd2, Bxc3 obtaining the better pawn structure, while if 6 Qd3 there can follow 6 ..., Nc5; 7 Qc4, d5; 8 exd6, Be6; 9 Qf4, cxd6 with the more active pieces, or possibly the wild 6 ..., d5; 7 exd6, Bf5!; 8 Bd2, Ng3!?; 9 Qe3+, Kd7.

Hort's move involves only a temporary win of the pawn.

5 ..., Nc6-e7; 6 Nf3xe5, d7-d6!?

Black wins back his pawn, at the cost of the displacement of his king. The original continuation **6 ..., O-O** seems to lead to a draw after **7 Bd3** (If 7 Qd4, Bxc3+; 8 bxc3, Re8!) **7 ..., Nxd5;** 8 exd5, Re8; 9 O-O, Rxe5; 10 d6! (Better than 10 f4, Re8; 11 Qf3, c6; 12 dxc6, bxc6; 13 Be3, d5ofKusmichev -Klovan, Riga 1963.) 10 ..., Bxd6; 11 Nb5, Bf8; 12 Bf4, Rc5; 13 Be3,

Re5; 14 Bf4, Rc5 with repetition of the position (Mnatsakanian-Klovan Alma-Ata 1963).

However a genuine counter-gambit possibility lurks here: **7 ..., Qe8!?** (instead of 7 ..., Nxd5) 8 Qe2, c6!; 9 dxc6, d5; 10 cxb7 (10 O-O!?) 10 ..., Bxb7; 11 Bd2, dxe4; 12 Nxe4, Bxd2+; 13 Nxd2, Ned5 with, according to Keres, an unclear position (Mnatsakanian-Liberzon, Moscow 1964). This seems quite a plausible sacrifice and deserves further tests. However it would not be to the taste of the Yugoslav grandmaster Trifunovic, who likes to keep the draw well in hand.

7 Bf1-b5+,

Drimer-Kozma, Rejkjavik 1957, had gone instead **7 Nf3**, Nxe4; 8 Qd4, Bxc3+; 9 bxc3, Nf6; 10 c4, O-O; 11 Be2, Bf5-.

7 ..., Ke8-f8!

This is obligatory, as the plausible **7 ..., c6?!; 8 dxc6, O-O** fails to the coup **9 Nd7!**, discovered by the Dutch master Cortlever:

a) 9 ..., Bxd7; 10 cxd7, Nxe4; 11 Qd4, Nxc3; 12 Qxb4, Nd5; 13 Qb3 (Tal-Schmatlanek, simultaneous display game 1960)

b) 9 ..., Nxe4 (hoping for 10 Nxf8?, Nxc3!) **10 O-O!** and now:

b1) 10 ..., Nxc3; 11 bxc3, Bxc3; 12 cxb7, Bxb7; 13 Rb1 and White wins the exchange (Meier-Gerber, correspondence 1968).

b2) 10 ..., Bxc3; 11 Nxf8, Ba5; 12 Nxh7, Kxh7; 13 Bd3, f5; 14 Qh5+, Kg8; 15 Bxe4, fxe4; 16 Bg5! and the pin on the knight is decisive (Meier-Fechner, correspondence 1968).

8 Ne5-d3, Bb4xc3+; 9 b2xc3, Nf6xe4; 10 Qd1-f3, Ne4-f6;

11 c3-c4?!,

According to Keres, White can get a good game by **11 Bc4** and he cites the postal game Pevic-Rothgen (1967) in which **11 ..., h6?!** was played. However Black should surely play **11 ..., Bg4**, followed by 12 ..., Bh5! with a threat to capture the d-pawn. The unclear positions that can result are worthy of more study. However the move that Hort played has serious drawbacks ...

11 ..., Bc8-g4; 12 Qf3-f4, c7-c6!;

An excellent move, beginning a forced line that favours Black.

13 d5xc6,

Else the centre collapses immediately.

13 ..., b7xc6; 14 Bc1-b2,

If **14 Ba4** then simply 14 ..., Qa5+ wins it.

14 ..., Ne7-g6;

Not **14 ..., cxb5?**; 15 Bxf6 and the black bishop hangs.

15 Bb2xf6,

Also forced, since if **15 Qg3**, cxb5; 15 Bxf6, Qxf6 attacks a rook.

15 ..., Qd8-a5+; 16 Qf4-d2, Ra8-e8+!;

The immediate liquidation by **16 ..., Qxd2+**; 17 Kxd2, cxb5; 18 Bd4, bxc4 wins a pawn but leaves White in command of the black squares, and so with good drawing chances.

17 Bf6-e5, Ng6xe5!; 18 Qd2xa5, Ne5xc4+; 19 Ke1-f1, Nc4xa5;

(See diagram)

Compared with the note to Black's 16th move, he has here, besides the plus pawn (more desirably situated on c6 than on c4)

39

made White's king go back to obstruct its rook, and he has left White with his inferior bishop.

20 Bb5-a6, Re8-b8; 21 f2-f3, Bg4-e6; 22 Kf1-e2, Kf8-e7; 23 Rh1-b1, Ke7-d7; 24 Nd3-f4, Be6-c4+; 25 Ba6xc4, Na5xc4; 26 Ke2-d3, Nc4-b2+; 27 Kd3-d2, d7-d5; 28 Rb1-e1, g7-g6; 29 h2-h4, Kd7-d6; 30 Nf4-h3 h7-h6;

To prevent Ng5, but interesting is **30 ..., Rhe8!?** and if 31 Ng5, Nc4+; 32 Kc3, f5!; 33 Nxh7, Rh8; 34 Ng5, Rxh4 and not now 35 Re6+, Kc5; 36 Rxg6??, d4+; 37 Kd3, Ne5+ etc.

31 Nh3-f2, Rh8-e8; 32 h4-h5!?

Hoping to disturb the inexorable exploitation of Black's material advantage (by exchanges and a general advance), since now Black gets an extra pawn but also weaknesses.

32 ..., g6xh5; 33 Nf2-h3, Nb2-c4+; 34 Kd2-d3, Re8-e5; 35 Re1xe5, Nc4xe5+; 36 Kd3-c3, c7-c5; 37 Nh3-f4, d5-d4+; 38 Kc3-d2, Ne5-c4+; 39 Kd2-d3, Nc4-e5+;

Repeating moves to reach the move 40 time control.

40 Kd3-d2, h5-h4; 41 Ra1-h1, Ne5-g6; 42 Nf4xg6, f7xg6; 43 Rh1xh4, h6-h5; 44 g2-g4, Rb8-f8;

45 g4xh5, g6xh5; 46 Rh4xh5, Rf8xf3;

40

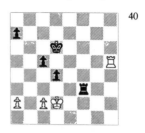

47 Rh5-h6+,

Else Black plays ..., Kc6-b5 and it's all over.

47 ..., Kd6-d5;

He should not go back, cutting off his king from the pawn majority

48 Rh6-a6, Rf3-f2+; 49 Kd2-d1,

Not 49 Ke1?, Rxc2 with an easy win. If 49 Kd3??, c4 is mate!

49 ..., Rf2-f7; 50 Ra6-a5,

Also after 50 Kd2, Kc4 White must go 51 Ra3 with similar play.

50 ..., Kd5-c4; 51 Ra5-a3, Rf7-g7;

A waiting move, edging the rook to a more favourable distance from the White king.

52 Kd1-d2, Rg7-h7; 53 Kd2-e2,

If 53 Kd1 Black can play 53 ..., Kb4; 54 Rb3+, Ka4 followed by ..., c4 and ..., a5, much as in the game. Quicker however is 53 ..., a5?!; 54 Rxa5, Kb4; 55 Ra8, Rh1+ and 56 ..., Kc3. Against 53 Kc1 (with the option of Kb2) Black would have to use the former plan, however.

53 ..., a7-a6;

Since White's c-pawn becomes en prise after **54 Rxa6?**, Kc3.

54 Ke2-d2, Rh7-h2+; 55 Kd2-d1, Rh2-h6;

Not **55 ..., Kb4?; 56 Rxa6, Kc3; 57 Ra3+, Kb2; 58 Rb3+, Kxa2; 59 Rb8-**

56 Kd1-d2, Rh6-g6; 57 Kd2-e2, a6-a5; 58 Ke2-d2, Rg6-g2+; 59 Kd2-c1, Kc4-b4; 60 Ra3-h3, c5-c4; 61 a2-a3+,

Complete passivity allows Black to win by threats of mate combined with the attack on the a-pawn, e.g. **61 Rf3, c3; 62 Rf1, Ka3; 63 Kb1, Rg5!** and **64 ...,** etc.

Rb5+ etc.

61 ..., Kb4-a4; 62 Rh3-h5, c4-c3; 63 Kc1-b1, Rg2-g1+; 64 Kb1-a2, d4-d3; 65 Rh5-c5;

Since if **65 cxd3**, c2 wins a rook.

65 ..., d3-d2;

65 ..., dxc2 also wins, as there is no stalemate ahead.

66 Rc5-d5, Rg1-c1; 67 Rd5-d8, Rc1xc2+; 68 Ka2-b1, Rc2-b2+; White resigns, in view of **69 Ka1, c2** etc.

THE RUY LOPEZ (1 e4, e5; 2 Nf3, Nc6; 3 Bb5)

The Ruy Lopez, or Spanish Opening, is one of the most respected chess openings. White immediately brings pressure on the square e5, threatens to disrupt Black's pawn structure, and prepares to castle and bring his rook to the king file before Black can challenge it. The positions which commonly arise from the Ruy Lopez involve Black in patient manoeuvring for equality against White's strategic pressure. In a desire to avoid this sort of game, numerous counter-gambit lines have been devised, by which Black brings about an open, tactical game. It is not possible here to deal in depth with many of them due to considerations of space; nor do I wish to duplicate unnecessarily any material that is due to be published shortly in the book 'Play the Marshall Attack!' by R.G.Wade and myself. So in particular the Marshall, probably the most famous of all counter-gambits in the Ruy, will be represented here by only two games, since 100 pages are needed if one is to go thoroughly into its ramifications.

Game 22
Muhamedjanov - Mordkovich
(Kazakstan Championship 1970)
1 e2-e4, e7-e5; 2 Ng1-f3, Nb8-c6; 3 Bf1-b5, a7-a6;

The most popular move by far nowadays, as the old **3 ..., d6**

(Steinitz) is too passive and the merits of Cozio's **3 ..., Nge7!?** are only just beginning to be appreciated. Many other moves are possible, of course, but (**3 ..., Nf6** perhaps excepted) they leave Black rather too exposed for the liking of most positional players. Only rarely do counter-gambits arise at this point. For example:

a) 3 ..., f5!? The Schliemann Defence, often known as Jaenisch Gambit. White must decline (by **4 Nc3** or **4 d3**) and play positionally, since if **4 exf5?**, e4!; 5 Qe2, Qe7; 6 Bxc6, **bxc6** (Or 6 ..., dxc6; 7 Nd4, Qe5; 8 Ne6, Bxe6; 9 fxe6, Bd6!; 10 Nc3, Nf6; 11 b3, O-O-O Cuellar-Bisguier, Bogota 1958) 7 Nd4, Nf6; 8 Nc3, c5; 9 Nb3, d5 (Szily-Bronstein, Budapest-Moscow 1949) with a good game for Black in either case.

b) 3 ..., d5?! (Theoretical Novelty!) will be found in the Fantasy section.

c) 3 ..., Bc5; 4 c3 (Also possible 4 O-O) and now:

c1) 4 ..., Nf6, 4 ..., Nge7 and **4 ..., Nd4!?** are not counter-gambits.

c2) 4 ..., f5!? (Cordel's Variation) was the subject of a theoretical review in 'Schachmaty' (December 1963) by V.Golenischev and Y. Kotkov, and there have been a handful of master games since. The line cannot really be recommended, but Black does get tactical chances sometimes, e.g. **5 exf5?!** (the only line in which the 'gambit' is accepted since if 5 Bxc6, dxc6; 6 Nxe5, Bd6; 7 d4, fxe4 wins the pawn back: 8 Qh5+, g6; 9 Nxg6, Nf6; 10 Qh4, Rxg2; 11 Bg5, Be7; if here 10 Qh6, Rg8; 11 Nh4, Bf8; 12 Qe3, Qe7) 5 ..., e4; 6 d4!, exf3!; 7 dxc6, Qe7+; 8 Be3, fxg2; 9 Rg1, Nf6; 10 Rxg2, d5; 11 cxd6, cxd6; 12 Qf3, O-O; 13 Nd2, Ne5; 14 Qe2, Bxf5; 15 O-O-O, a6; 16 Bc4+, d5; 17 Bd4, Rae8; 18 Qxe5, Qxe5; 19 Bxe5, Rxe5; 20 f4, Re3; 21 Nf1, Rf3 with a good ending for Black

(Kellner-Purdy, Australian Championship 1954).

c3) 4 ..., d5?! was the subject of an article in 'Chess' by the English player O.H.Hardy in 1965, but has virtually never been played. White can adopt the virtually forcing line 5 Nxe5, Qg5; 6 Qa4!, Qxg2; 7 Bxc6+, Ke7; 8 Rf1, bxc6; 9 Qxc6, Bd6 (9 ..., Be6; 10 Qxa8) 10 Qxd5, Bh3; 11 Qxf7+, Kd8; 12 Nc6+, Kc8; 13 Qe8+!, Kb7; 14 Na5+, Ka6; 15 Qc6+, Kxa5; 16 b4+, Bxb4; 17 cxb4+, Kxb4; 18 Ba3+, Ka5; 19 Qxc7+, Ka6; 20 Qc4+, Ka5 but now, if he wishes to avoid the draw, he must play 21 Nc3 obtaining an uncertain but favourable ending with two pawns for the exchange.

4 Bb5-a4,

A personal prejudice, doubtless, but I think White should play here **4 Bxc6**, although it is not proven that this brings him any significant advantage against correct play.

4 ..., Ng8-f6;

If **4 ..., Bc5; 5 O-O** ought to be a little better for White since Black loses time with the misplaced bishop. While if **4 ..., f5?!** it is in fact White who will offer material: 5 d4!, exd4; 6 e5 with a promising attack.

Black can of course play **4 ..., d6** or **4 ..., b5**, and in the latter case there is a weird counter-gambit possibility: 4 ..., b5; 5 Bb3, Nf6?!; 6 Ng5?! (White has better moves.) 6 ..., d5; 7 exd5, Nd4 (Fritz Variation of the Two Knights Defence!) 8 d6?!, Nxb3; 9 dxc7, Qd5; 10 axb3, Qxg2; 11 Qf3, Qxf3; 12 Nxf3, Bb7; 13 Ke2, Bd6; 14 Rg1, e4!? and after a complicated struggle Black attained a won ending (Scott-Harding, British Under 16 Championship, 1964).

5 O-O,

If White plays the unusual 5 Nc3 Black can offer a pawn by 5 ..., b5; 6 Bb3, d6!? e.g. 7 Ng5, d5; 8 Nxd5 (Or 8 exd5, Nd4; 9 d6, Nxb3; 10 dxc7, Qxc7; 11 axb3, Bb7 with excellent play for the pawn according to Keres) 8 ..., Nd4!:

a) 9 Nxf6+, Qxf6; **10 d3** (10 Nxf7?, Nxb3 or 10 Bxf7+?, Ke7; 11 d3, h6; 12 h4, hxg5; 13 Bxg5+, Qxg5! Keres) 10 ..., h6; 11 Nh3, Qg6! (Or 11 ..., Bxh3; 12 gxh3, Nxf3+ with some advantage: Esser-Barton, Cologne 1911) 12 Kf1, Bg4 and Black wins (Keres).

b) 9 Nc3! (If 9 d3, Nxb3; 10 axb3, Nxd5 is good for Black.) 9 ..., Nxb3; 10 axb3, b4; 11 Na4, h6; 12 Nf3, Nxe4; 13 Qe2, Bb7; 14 d3, Ng5 and, according to Keres, Black's activity compensates for the sacrificed pawn.

c) 9 Ne3, Nxb3; 10 axb3, h6; 11 Nf3, Nxe4 and Black stood better in the game Sir George Thomas-Keres Margate 1937, which may be found annotated in 'The Early Years of Paul Keres'.

5 ..., Bf8-e7; 6 Rf1-e1,

For 6 Qe2 see Game 25.

6 ..., b7-b5; 7 Ba4-b3, O-O; 8 c2-c3, d7-d5!?;

This move, instead of the usual **8 ..., d6,** inaugurates the Marshall Counter-Gambit. Black takes advantage of the slowness of White's build-up to free his game at the cost of a pawn. It is such a strong reply to the Lopez that masters often seek to avoid it by playing **8 a4** (instead of 8 c3), keeping the game in positional channels if possible. However Black can then equalise quite easily with **8 ..., Bb7,** and if then **9 d3, d6; 10 Bd2,** b4!; 11 c3!? Black can play after all 11 ..., d5! with exciting complications (Geller-Jansa, Budapest 1970). If here **10 Nc3** Black's best play is another gambit line: 10 ..., Na5!; 11 Ba2, b4; 12 Ne2, c5!; 13 Ng3, b3! with level chances.

Similarly, if White plays **8 h3** Black's best plan is 8 ..., Bb7 with the thematic ..., d5 to follow.

9 e4xd5, e5-e4!?;

For the original **9 ..., Nxd5!** see the next game, but this wild move also stems from Marshall (later in the twenties) and was introduced into international chess by his American team colleague Herman Steiner at the 1930 Olympiad.

41

10 d5xc6

After **10 Ng5?!,** Bg4!; 11 f3, exf3; 12 gxf3, Bd6! Black's attacking prospects are outstanding.

10 ..., e4xf3; 11 d2-d4!

Fischer has always played here **11 Qxf3,** Bg4; 12 Qg3 but then both 12 ..., Re8! and 12 ..., Bd6 offer Black sufficient compensation for the pawns. The text move is much more dangerous because it threatens to catch up on development; the ill-considered pawn on c6 can be quite a thorn in Black's side.

11 ..., Be7-d6!?;

Probably best is **11 ..., fxg2**, if only because it levels material for the time being. Definitely inadequate is **11 ..., Bg4?** as White plays 12 gxf3 and then consolidates with 13 Bf4.

12 Bc1-g5?!,

After this move, Black gets some attack. Others:

a) 12 g3?!, Bg4; 13 Be3 (13 Nd2 is not much improvement) 13 ..., Qc8; 14 Nd2, Qf5; 15 Bc2, Qh5; 16 Bd3, Rae8; 17 c4, bxc4; 18 Nxc4, Nd5; 19 Bd2, Bxg3!; 20 hxg3, Re2!; 21 Resigns (Scherbakov-Estrin, 1957 Moscow).

b) 12 Qxf3!, Re8 (Or first 12 ..., Bg4; 13 Qd3) 13 Bd2! (Barden) leaves Black without any tangible compensation for his pawn.

12 ..., Bd6xh2+!

White perhaps believed this to be unsound, but it is both necessary and interesting. If instead **12 .., h6?** 13 Bxf6, Qxf6; 14 Qxf3, Qg5; 15 g3 and White is winning: Pruss-Potzsch, correspondence 1961.

13 Kg1xh2, Nf6-g4+; 14 Kh2-g1, Qd8xg5; 15 Qd1xf3, h7-h5!

This move of Estrin's is necessary, to provide a bolt-hole for the Black king (White threatened 16 Qxf7+).

16 Nb1-a3,

Estrin analysed **16 Qg3**, h4; 17 Qxc7, Ra7!; 18 Qd6 (If 18 Qxa7, Qf4!) 18 ..., h3; 19 Qg3, Re7!; 20 Na3, h2+; 21 Kh1, Rxe1+; 22

Rxe1, Qd2! and wins.

16 ..., Bc8-f5; 17 Na3-c2, Ra8-e8; 18 d4-d5?,

White has to play **18 Ne3!**, Be4; 19 Qg3, Bxc6; 20 Qxc7 (Shovchov-Morozov, correspondence 1959) and it is not clear what Black can do.

18 ..., Bf5xc2; 19 Bb3xc2, Qg5-d2; 20 Bc2-e4, f7-f5; 21 Re1-e2, Qd2-g5 22 Be4-d3,

Here **22 Bc2** might be a little better.

22 ..., Ng4-e5; 23 Qf3-h3, f5-f4; 24 Ra1-d1, f4-f3; 25 Re2-e3, Rf8-f4

Black is ready to administer the coup de grace, so something desperate has to be attempted:

26 d5-d6!, c7xd6; 27 c6-c7, Rf4-g4; 28 Bd3-e4, Rg4xg2+; 29 Kg1-h1, Ne5-g4;

With a threat of ..., Nxf2 mate.

30 Be4-d5+, Qg5xd5!

If **30 ..., Kh7**; 31 Rd2 attempts a defence.

31 Re3xe8+, Kg8-h7; 32 Re8-h8+,

'Afore ye go ...'

32 ..., Kh7xh8; 33 c7-c8(Q)+, Kh8-h7; White resigns.

Game 23
Townsend - Crombleholme
(Oxford 1972)
Notes based on analysis by the winner.

1 e2-e4, e7-e5; 2 Ng1-f3, Nb8-c6; 3 Bf1-b5, a7-a6; 4 Bb5-a4, Ng8-f6; 5 O-O, Bf8-e7; 6 Rf1-e1, b7-b5; 7 Ba4-b3, O-O; 8 c2-c3, d7-d5; 9 e4xd5, Nf6xd5!; 10 Nf3xe5,

An interesting method of declining the Marshall, as yet almost unexplored, is **10 a4!?** when Black should play 10 ..., Bb7.

10 ..., Nc6xe5; 11 Re1xe5, c7-c6!;

The method favoured by Marshall towards the end of his career. But Black has other plausible moves here:

a) 11 ..., Nf6!? was Marshall's first plan. The real problem here is to find a satisfactory answer to Capablanca's idea 12 d4, Bd6; 13 Re2! which over-protects f2 and prepares doubling on the e-file. After the 'natural' 13 ..., Bg4?! the forced 14 f3 did not prove to be a significant weakening in Crombleholme-Radoicic, Southampton 1971, so best may be 13 ..., Bb7, although 'theory' holds that White stands better.

b) 11 ... Nf4!? and **11 ..., Nb6!?** have also been receiving attention recently, but it is too early to form definitive judgements on their value

c) 11 ..., Bb7?! was an early idea, not exactly refuted although 12 Qf3 forces the reply 12 ..., c6 since the long white diagonal may later be re-opened with a threat to the queen.

42

12 Bb3xd5,

This could well be the best move, although not the way it is followed up in this game. White usually plays **12 d4, Bd6; 13 Re1, Qh4; 14 g3, Qh3; 15 Be3** (15 Bxd5 transposes back) **15 ..., Bg4** (15 ..., Bf5?!) **16 Qd3, Rae8** (16 ..., Nxe3!?) **17 Nd2, Re6; 18 a4** (Or 18 Qf1 with an unclear position) **18 ..., Qh5!** with equal chances (Parma-Geller, Yugoslavia-USSR 1966).

Recently there has been a lot of fuss about the move **15 Re4?!** (instead of 15 Be3) but it is more or less unjustified. One satisfactory way of handling this line for Black was demonstrated in the game Jakobsen-Nymann, Stockholm 1972: 15 ..., g5; 16 Qf3, Bf5; 17 Bc2 Bxe4; 18 Bxe4 but now instead of 18 ..., Rae8? Black should play Jakobsen's suggestion (in 'The Chess Player') 18 ..., Qe6! and he gets at least a draw.

In all these lines there is a wealth of analytical and practical material extant (for which see the aforementioned book on the Marshall) but also there are doubtless many new ideas to be discovered.

12 ..., c6xd5; 13 d2-d4, Be7-d6; 14 Re5-e1?!,

White, having made the central piece exchange, should play the Kevitz Variation: **14 Re3!** when after **14 ..., Qh4** (14 ..., f5?!) K.B. Richardson's **15 g3!?** may well prove superior to the normal lines based on 15 h3. Here is virgin territory.

14 ..., Qd8-h4; 15 g2-g3, Qh4-h3; 16 Bc1-e3,

Marshall analysed in the thirties the consequences of **16 Qf3!?**: 16 ..., Bf5!; 17 Qg2 (too

risky 17 Qxd5?, Rae8) 17 ..., Qg4!;
18 f3, Qg6; 19 Be3, Rac8!; 20 Nd2,
b4! (Buslayev-Demuria, Tiflis 1957)

16 ..., Bc8-g4; 17 Qd1-d3, Ra8-e8;

This is better than the compromising **17 ..., f5?!**

18 Nb1-d2, Re8-e6!; 19 Qd3-f1,

If **19 a4** Black has 19 ..., b4 or
19 ..., f5, or even 19 ..., bxa4; 20
Rxa4, f5 (Fordham-Hall - Breach,
correspondence 1970-1).

19 ..., Qh3-h5; 20 Qf1-g2,

A natural move and certainly
no worse than those tried in master
play, viz:
a) 20 f4, Rfe8; 21 Qf2, f5 (or 21 ...,
Qf5=) 22 a4, g5 with good chances
for Black (Pilnik-Geller, Santiago
de Chile 1965).
b) 20 f3, Rf6!; 21 f4, g5! (Euwe).

20 ..., Rf8-e8; 21 a2-a4,

This is better than 21 **f3**, Bh3;
22 Qf2, Qg6! and the decisive entry
of Black's queen to c2 or d3 is
hardly to be prevented (Butters-
Harding, Wolverhampton 1972).

21 ..., Bg4-h3;

Black plays a probing repetition of moves, since if White
retreats the queen to h1 the ensuing
combination will be still stronger.

His plan is a clear improvement
over the 21 ..., b4 of Wills-Phillipp
(semi-final, 5th World Correspondence Championship) in which
chances were balanced.

**22 Qg2-f3, Bh3-g4; 23 Qf3-g2,
Bd6-f4!;**

Threatening to break through
on the e-file (24 Nf1??, Bf3), this is
a thematic sacrifice in the Marshall.

24 g3xf4,

If **24 axb5** Black intended 24
..., axb5; 25 Ra5, h6; 26 Rxb5,
Bxe3; 27 fxe3, Rxe3; 28 Rxe3,
Rxe3; 29 Rxd5, g5 and the killing
..., Re2 must follow.

24 ..., Re6-g6!;

Rather more efficient might
have been **24 ..., Bh3!?; 25 Qf3?,
Rg6**+; 26 Kh1, Qxf3; 27 Nxf3,
Bg2+; 28 Kg1, Bxf3+; 29 Kf1,
Rg2!; 30 Bd2, Re4! with an
amusing mating net. Better **25
Qg3!**, Rg6; 26 axb5, axb5; 27 Kh1
defending passively.

25 Kg1-h1,

White might have played 25
Qg3! although after 25 ..., Bh3 or
25 ..., Be2 White can only defend
passively and should lose eventually

25 ..., Bg4-e2!;

If **25 ..., Bh3** White plays 26
Qg3 as in the previous notes.
Black's bishop is more active here.

26 a4xb5?!,

Probably he should still give
preference to 26 Qg3.

**26 ..., Rg6xg2; 27 Kh1xg2,
Be2xb5!?;**

Black had the chance here of a
bind by **27 ..., Qg4+; 28 Kh1,
Re6!?** (28 ..., Bxb5 is still good too.)
29 Rg1, Bf3+; 30 Nxf3, Qxf3+; 31

Rg2, Rg6; 32 Rag1, axb5 and it looks as if White must reach a lost ending, since if 33 Bc1, f5!; 34 Be3, Rg4!; 35 Bc1, Rh4; 36 Be3? (Correct is 36 Re1, Rg4; 37 Rg1 forcing Black to grind on slowly.) 36 ..., Rxh2+!; 37 Kxh2, Qh5+; 38 Kg3, Qg4+; 39 Kh2, Qh4 mate.

28 Nd2-f1, Re8-e6; 29 Nf1-g3, Qh5-h4; 30 f4-f5, Re6-b6;

Now the position has become confused, although Black is still better.

31 b2-b3,

This was the sealed move. Crombleholme also analysed:

a) 31 c4?!, dxc4; 32 d5, Rd6; 33 Bc5, Rxd5; 34 Rxa6, Qd8; 35 Be7, Qb8 and wins.

b) 31 f3, g6; 32 Bf2 (32 Rg1, Bd3 also favours Black.) 32 ..., gxf5; 33 Nxf5, Qg5+; 34 Ng3, Qd2 followed by ..., Rh6 winning.

31 ..., g7-g6!;

To make the king's side situation fluid once more. White prefers to stake all on an ingenious but incorrect tactical idea.

32 Ra1-a5!?, gxf5; 33 Be3-f4?!,

Objectively he should play **33 f4.**

33 ..., Rb6-g6!;

Not 33 ..., Qxf4? on account of 34 Rxb5!, Qb8 (34 ..., axb5??; 35 Re8+, Kg7; 36 Nh5+) 35 Rxb6, Qxb6; 36 Nxf5 with an equal ending.

34 c3-c4,

If **34 Bd6** (threatening 35 Rxb5 again) Black parries with 34 ..., Qd8.

34 ..., Bb5-d7!; White resigns.

Not 35 Rxd5?, Bc6 while if the

Bf4 moves Black wins a piece by 35 ..., f4.

Game 24
Stieg - Trajkovic
(Correspondence 1967)

1 e2-e4, e7-e5; 2 Ng1-f3, Nb8-c6; 3 Bf1-b5, a7-a6; 4 Bb5-a4, Ng8-f6; 5 O-O, Bf8-e7; 6 Rf1-e1, b7-b5; 7 Ba4-b3, Bc8-b7?!;

A wild line, akin to the Marshall, which has been played a lot by Trajkovic and others in recent years. It is likely to be unsound, but there is still scope for invention.

44

8 c2-c3,

This allows Black to try his main idea. The attempt to open Black up by **8 d4** is not altogether convincing after 8 ..., Nxd4.

8 ..., d7-d5; 9 e4xd5, Nf6xd5; 10 Nf3xe5, Nc6xe5; 11 Re1xe5, Nd5-f4 12 Bb3xf7+!?,

This does not turn out too well. Another bad idea was :**12 Rf5?!,** Qd6; 13 Qg4, Nxg2; 14 Bxf7+? (Kurajica-Nunn, Islington 1971) although here White should have played 14 Rxf7!

White's best is probably **12 d4** (12 Qg4!?) **12 ...**, **Nxg2** (12 ..., Ng6!?) 13 Qe2!, h6! with great complications (Jovcic-Trajkovic, correspondence 1970). All these lines are discussed in detail in 'Play the Marshall Attack!'.

12 ..., Ke8xf7; 13 Re5-f5+, Be7-f6; 14 Rf5xf4, Qd8-d3!;

An excellent move, hindering White's developing idea 15 d4.

15 Qd1-f1,

After all, White is two pawns up. Trajkovic, in 'Informator' No.4, gives **15 Qh5+?!**, Kg8!; 16 a4, g6; 17 Qd1, Kg7; 18 axb5, Rhe8!!; 19 bxa6, Re2 and wins.

15 ..., Bb7-e4!; 16 Rf4xe4!,

The best chance, since **16 Qxd3**, Bxd3 gives a furious attack. Black's rooks come immediately into action, while White is disorganised.

16 ..., Qd3xe4; 17 d2-d4, Rh8-e8; 18 Nb1-d2, Qe4-c2; 19 Nd2-f3, h7-h6;

Covering the square g5.

20 Nf3-e1, Re8xe1!

Returning the exchange, in order to keep the initiative.

21 Qd1xe1, Ra8-e8; 22 Bc1-e3,

This is better than **22 Qf1**, Re2 or **22 Qd2??**, Re2 winning.

22 ..., Qc2xb2;

(See diagram)

According to Trajkovic, chances are level now, but in the sequel White cannot find a satisfactory plan.

23 Qe1-c1, Qb2-e2; 24 Qc1-d1, Qe2xd1!; 25 Ra1xd1, Kf7-e6; 26 a2-a4?!,

45

To eliminate one weakness before the Black king can reach it, but **26 Kf1** also comes strongly into consideration.

26 ..., Ke6-d5; 27 a4xb5, a6xb5; 28 Rd1-a1,

Now **28 Kf1** is too slow against 28 ..., Kc4, forcing 29 Rc1, Ra8! etc.

28 ..., c7-c5; 29 d4xc5, Bf6xc3;

With a dominating bishop and a strong passed pawn.

30 Ra1-b1, b5-b4; 31 Kg1-f1, Kd5-c4; 32 Kf1-e2, b4-b3; 33 Ke2-d1,

There is nothing that can be done.

33 ..., Re8-d8+; 34 Kd1-c1, Rd8-a8; 35 h2-h3, Bc3-b4; White resigns.

If 36 c6, Rc8 wins the pawn, while if White just waits, Black has the decisive plan ..., Ba3+, ..., Rd8+, ..., b2, ..., Kc3-c2 and ..., b1(Q).

Against the Worrall Attack (5 or 6 Qe2) it is also possible to play a counter-gambit analogous to the Marshall. White usually declines, but interesting play develops if he accepts:

Game 25
Borisov - Zhuravlev
(USSR 1960)

1 e2-e4, e7-e5; 2 Ng1-f3, Nb8-c6; 3 Bb1-b5, a7-a6; 4 Bb5-a4, Ng8-f6; 5 0-0, Bf8-e7; 6 Qd1-e2, b7-b5; 7 Ba4-b3, 0-0; 8 c2-c3,

White has alternatives, naturally:
a) 8 a4, b4 (8 ..., Rb8 is good, while interesting are 8 ..., Bb7!? and 8 ..., d5!?) **9 a5** (9 d4, d5! or 9 d3 are satisfactory for Black.) and now Black should probably content himself with **9 ..., d6=** (Tringov-Smyslov, Amsterdam 1964) as it is risky to play **9 ..., d5?!**; 10 exd5, e4 (Or 10 ..., Bg4 transposing) 11 dxc6, Bg4 on account of 12 d3, exf3; 13 gxf3, Bh3 (13 ..., Bh5!?) 14 Re1, Re8; 15 Nd2, Bd6; 16 Ne4, Nxe4; 17 fxe4, Qh4; 18 f4!, Bxf4; 19 Bxf4, Qxf4; 20 Qf2 and White won the ending in D.Parr-Harding Brighton 1972.

b) 8 d4?! (Alekhine) 8 ..., Nxd4; 9 Nxd4, exd4; 10 e5, Ne8; 11 c3, dxc3 (11 ..., c5 is also good.) 12 Nxc3, c6; 13 Bf4, d5 with advantage to Black (Ravinsky-Chekhover, Riga 1952).

8 ..., d7-d5; 9 e4xd5,

It is more usual to decline by **9 d3** whereupon Black gets equal chances with **9 ..., Re8!** although the game is quite complex (Keres-Geller, Budapest 1952).

(See diagram)

9 ..., Bc8-g4;

This move, which is more precise here than **9 ..., e4**, is the generally recommended - idea for Black. However it is also possible to play, as in the Marshall, **9 ..., Nxd5; 10 Nxe5, Nxe5** (10 ..., Nf4!?) **11 Qxe5, Bb7; 12 d4** and now 12 ..., a5 with

46

good chances (Kashdan-Bisguier, New York 1948-9).

10 d5xc6,

If **10 h3, Bh5; 11 g4** is unclear, but Black can also play **10 ..., Bxf3; 11 Qxf3, e4; 12 Qe2, Na5; 13 Bc2, Qxd5** (Hjorth-Keres, Lidkoping 1944).

10 ..., e5-e4; 11 d2-d4,

White might also consider **11 Qe3!?**. Compared with normal lines of the Marshall, White loses time through harassment of his queen, but his back rank is safer with the rook tucked away on f1.

11 ..., e4xf3; 12 g2xf3, Bg4-h5;

This has a better reputation than **12 ..., Bh3!?** although even that may be playable. If then 13 Re1, Re8; 14 Bg5 Black has 14 ..., Nd5! (Keres).

13 Bc1-f4,

Otherwise there comes ..., Bd6 with a dangerous attack against White's neglected king.

13 ..., Rf8-e8; 14 Bf4-g3,

Another plan worth considering is **14 Nd2**, Bd6; 15 Be5 but after 15 ..., Bxe5; 16 dxe5, Nd5 Black has evidently got good compensation for his two pawns.

14 ..., Be7-d6; 15 Qe2-d3, Bh5-g6;

47

16 Qd3-d2?,

White has to play **16 Qd1** with an interesting balanced struggle still to come.

16 ..., Nf6-h5; 17 Nb1-a3, Qd8-f6;

Gaining a tempo by attacking the unguarded f-pawn (see move 16).

18 Bb3-d1?!, Bd6-f4!;

Evidently, White should have admitted his mistake by **18 Qd1.**

19 Bg3xf4, Nh5xf4; 20 Kg1-h1, Bg6-h5; 21 Na3-c2,

In the game Vorotnikov-Havsky, Leningrad 1964, White only prolonged his agony by playing **21 Rc1, Ne2!; 22 Bxe2, Rxe2; 23 Qxe2, Bxf3+; 24 Qxf3, Qxf3+; 25 Kg1, Re8** etc.

21 ..., Nf4-e2!; White resigns,

in view of the sequel **22 Ne1, Qxf3+; 23 Nxf3, Bxf3 mate.**

This brings an end to our study of the counter-gambits of the Marshall family, but there are other lines in the closed Ruy Lopez in which Black gives up a pawn by ..., d5.

Game 26
Verlinsky - Panov
(Moscow 1944)

1 e2-e4, e7-e5; 2 Ng1-f3, Nb8-c6; 3 Bf1-b5, a7-a6; 4 Bb5-a4, Ng8-f6; 5 O-O, Bf8-e7; 6 Rf1-e1, b7-b5; 7 Ba4-b3, d7-d6;

The same position is reached by **7 ..., O-O**; 8 c3, d6.

8 c2-c3, O-O;

This is now considered more precise than Chigorin's **8 ..., Na5** which can however transpose back unless White tries a plan based on an early a4.

9 h2-h3,

To prevent the pin after **9 d4, Bg4.**

9 ..., Nc6-a5;

In the last 15 years, masters have been relying increasingly on Black's alternative moves here, especially **9 ..., Nb8** (Breyer) and **9 ..., h6** (Smyslov). Who can say what move is objectively the best?

10 Bb3-c2, c7-c5; 11 d2-d4, Qd8-c7;

Black has tried a number of moves here, of which the most reliable is Keres's **11 ..., Nd7**. The only counter-gambit line, tried in the game Suetin-Dashkevich (1959 Minsk), is the presumably unsound **11 ..., d5?!** e.g. 12 Nxe5, dxe4 (If 12 ..., Nxe4; 13 Nd2!) 13 Bg5, cxd4 (Or 13 ..., Bb7; 14 dxc5) 14 cxd4, Bb7; 15 Nc3, Rc8; 16 Bxf6, Bxf6; 17 Bxe4 with chances of an endgame win for White.

12 Nb1-d2, Bc8-b7;

Played for the first time by Panov in this game. A host of other moves are also possible of course, notably **12 ..., cxd4, 12 ..., Nc6, 12 ..., Bd7.**

13 Nd2-f1, c5xd4; 14 c3xd4,

This position can more often arise by **12 ..., cxd4;** 13 cxd4, Bb7; **14 Nf1**, although **14 d5** is also possible, preventing the sacrifice.

14 ..., Ra8-c8; 15 Bc2-d3,

The alternatives are less conducive to the soundness of Black's intended thrust. For example:

a) 15 Bb1, d5?! (However 15 ..., Rfe8 seems reasonable here.) 16 exd5!, exd4; 17 Bg5, Rfe8; 18 Qxd4! and although Black drew in Bertok-Minic (Yugoslav Championship 1966) he was lucky.

b) 15 Re2, d5!?; 16 dxe5 (If here 16 exd5, exd4; 17 Bg5 Black has the good move 17 ..., h6.) 16 ..., Nxe4; 17 Ng3, f5 (17 ..., Nxg3!?; 17 ..., Rfd8!?) 18 exf6, Bxf6; 19 Bxe4! dxe4; 20 Nxe4 and Black had to fight hard for the draw in Bulyovcic -Marovic, Yugoslav Championship 1962. In this line also Black can play **15 ..., Rfe8** with a fair game.

48

15 ..., d6-d5!?; 16 e4xd5?!,

More dangerous to Black is the alternative **16 dxe5, Nxe4; 17 Ng3!, f5** (17 ..., Bb4?!; 17 ..., Rfd8!?) 18 exf6, Bxf6; 19 Bxe4 (19 Nxe4 is level, but not 19 Nf5?, Nc4; 20 Re2, Nxb2! Ravinsky-Panov,

Moscow 1947) 19 ..., dxe4; 20 Nxe4 and now Pachman recommends **20 ..., Nc4;** 21 Rb1, Rcd8; 22 Qe2, Bxe4; 23 Qxe4, Qd7 with sufficient compensation. Even better may be **20 ..., Rad8** as played in Simagin-Heemsoth, correspondence 1960-2 but **20 ..., Bxe4** is not so good as Black is then struggling for the draw.

16 ..., e5-e4!; 17 Bd3xe4, Nf6xe4; 18 Re1xe4, Bb7xd5; 19 Re4-e1, Qc7-b7;

Black's pieces are exerting a lot of pressure and the extra white pawn on d4 does not look very strong.

20 Bc1-f4,

In a subsequent game Unzicker-Euwe, West Germany-Holland 1951, White tried to improve with **20 Ne3** but after 20 ..., Bxf3; 21 Qxf3, Qxf3; 22 gxf3, Nc6; 23 Nd5, Bh4; 24 Re4, Rcd8 Black stood better.

20 ..., Rf8-d8; 21 Nf1-d2, Be7-b4; 22 Re1-e3, f7-f6; 23 b2-b3, Bb4-a3; 24 Qd1-e2, Na5-c6; 25 Nd2-e4, Qb7-b6; 26 Ra1-d1, Bd5-f7;

White is suffering considerable aggravation, and clearly stands worse although Black has no concrete win yet.

27 Qe2-d2, Ba3-b4; 28 Qd2-b2, Qb6-a5; 29 Re3-e2, h7-h6; 30 Bf4-d2, Qa5-b6; 31 Bd2xb4, Nc6xb4; 32 Re2-d2,

Preparing Nc5, which is not possible here because of 32 ..., Rxc5.

32 ..., Nb4-d5; 33 Ne4-c5, Bf7-h5;

(See diagram)

34 Rd2-d3?,

49

A time trouble error. However, according to Wade, Blackstock and Booth (in 'The Closed Ruy Lopez') Black's positional advantage should be enough to win after 34 g4, Bf7 as he has ..., Nf4 and ...,

Bd5 to come.

34 ..., Nd5-f4; 35 g2-g4,

Only now can White have seen that if **35 Re3**, Rxc5, or **35 Rc3**, b4.

35 ..., Nf4xh3+; 36 Kg1-h2, Bh5xg4; 37 Rd1-e1, Qb6-d6+; 38 Kh2-g2, Rc8xc5; White resigns

Thus Panov's Counter-Attack represents an interesting and not well known way of playing the Chigorin Defence to the Lopez. Against inferior fifteenth moves by White he is able to offer a promising positional pawn sacrifice that has still not been analysed all that deeply. The chief drawback is that White can avoid it, by playing an early d5 himself.

FANTASY

In this section I have collected various sacrificial ideas for Black in the open games, which are not respectable enough to merit illustrative games. Some may be worth further attention however.

PETROFF DEFENCE

After 1 e4, e5; 2 Nf3, Nf6; 3 Nxe5 Black can play, instead of the usual 3 ..., d6, a move not mentioned by Keres, nor by Hooper in his study of the Petroff: **3 ..., Nc6?!** The main idea behind this is a version of the Legal trap: **4 Nxc6** (If 4 d4, Qe7!; 5 Nxc6, Qxe4+; 6 Be2! with the edge to White) **4 ..., dxc6; 5 d3, Bc5; 6 Bg5??** (6 Be2 is correct) **6 ..., Nxe4!!** and Black wins since if 7 dxe4, Bxf2+ or 7 Bxd8, Bxf2+; 8 Ke2, Bg4 mate.

PHILIDOR DEFENCE

After 1 e4, e5; 2 Nf3, d6; 3 d4, the gambit **3 ..., Bg4?!; 4 dxe5, Nd7?!; 5 exd6, Bxd6** is considered by Gunderam in his 'Neue Eroffnungswege'. For his pawn Black has only a slight lead in development and so must play for quick tactical points, e.g. **6 h3**, Bh5; **7 Be2**, Qe7; **8 Nc3**, O-O-O with compensation. More solid for White is here **7 Bd3**, and if Black now ventures out with his queen 7 ..., Qf6?!; **8 g4**, Bg6; **9 Nc3**, Ne7 then after 10 Bg5, Qe6; 11 Qe2 he will find she is in unseemly trouble.

Instead of **4 ..., Nd7** Black could also play **4 ..., Nc6** with an analogous position that may also be reached via the Scotch Game: 1 e4, e5; 2 Nf3, Nc6; 3 d4, d6?!; 4 exd5, Bg4. Here 5 exd6, Bxd6; 6 Bb5!?, Qe7 followed by ..., Rd8 or ..., O-O-O offers Black chances based on queen-winning combinations, so 6 Bd3 may again be best.

GIUOCO PIANO

After **1 e4, e5; 2 Nf3, Nc6; 3 Bc4, Bc5** White can play the wild Jerome Gambit: **4 Bxf7+?!, Kxf7; 5 Nxe5+, Nxe5; 6 Qh5+, g6; 7 Qxe5**. Now instead of clutching onto his extra material, Black does best to follow Blackburne by sacrificing the exchange: **7 ..., d6!**; 8 Qxh8, Qh4!; 9 O-O, Nf6 with a winning attack in view of the threatened ..., Ng4. If 10 h3, Bxh3!; 11 Qxa8, Qg4 mates.

Instead of 3 ..., Bc5 Black might also try **3 ..., Nd4?!** but it is of course bad. White, according to Keres, may either adopt the positional **4 O-O**, d6; 5 Nxd4, exd4; 6 c3 or the promising counter-sacrifice **4 Nxe5!?**, Qg5; 5 **Bxf7+!** (Black hoped for 5 Nxf7, Qxg2) 5 ..., Ke7; 6 O-O!, Qxe5; 7 Bxg8 followed by 8 c3 and 9 d4. The latter continuation may nonetheless be unsound, but the defence of such positions could only be to the taste of a Steinitz or a Korchnoi.

PONZIANI OPENING

The rare Ponziani, **1 e4, e5; 2 Nf3, Nc6; 3 c3**, offers Black various chances of giving up material unsoundly.

If **3 ..., d5?!; 4 Qa4!** Black's best is **4 ..., f6!** (Steinitz), but he has also tried:
a) 4 ..., Nf6 (Leonhardt) 5 Nxe5, Bd6; 6 Nxc6 (Not 6 exd5, Bxe5; 7 dxc6, O-O; 8 Be2, Re8) 6 ..., bxc6; 7 d3, O-O; 8 Be2!, Re8; 9 Bg5, dxe4; 10 dxe4 (Keres).
b) 4 ..., Bd7 (Caro) 5 exd5, Nd4; 6 Qd1, Nxf3+; 7 Qxf3, Nf6 (Against 7 ..., f5 Tartakover suggested 8 Bc4 and 9 d3) 8 Bc4, Bd6 (8 ..., c6?!) 9 d3, Bg4; 10 Qg3, h5; 11 Bg5, Qd7; 12 h3 again with advantage to White (Duckstein -Fuderer, Zagreb 1955).

Better is **3 ..., Nf6; 4 d4** (The modern 4 d3 is best met by 4 ..., g6! as in Planinc-Ghizdavu, Athens 1971) **4 ..., Nxe4; 5 d5** with another critical position. **5 ..., Nb8** is often given as best, but there is no need for this tempo loss as Black can equalise by **5 ..., Ne7!**; 6 Nxe5, Ng6. The speculative **5 ..., Bc5?!** has, supposedly, been refuted: **6 dxc6, Bxf2+** (Not

6 ..., Nxf2?; 7 Qd5.) **7 Ke2, bxc6.**

From the diagram White has:

a) 8 Nd2?!, Nxd2; 9 Kxf2 (Or 9 Bxd2, Bb6) 9 ..., Ne4+; 10 Ke1, O-O and Black has some compensation in his pawn centre and safer king.

b) 8 Qc2, d5; 9 Nd2, Nxd2; 10 Bxd2, Bb6 is similarly unclear.

c) 8 Qa4!, f5 and now:

c1) 9 Kd1?!, O-O; 10 Nxe5, Bb6; 11 Kc2, Nf2; 12 Bc4+, d5; 13 Nxc6, Qd7; 14 Bxd5+, Kh8 with advantage to Black (Mecikarov-Vukcevic, 1957).

c2) 9 Nbd2 (9 Ng5!?) **9 ..., O-O** (9 ..., Nxd2!?) **10 Nxe4, fxe4; 11 Qxe4** (Or 11 Kxf2, d5!; 12 Ke1 — 12 Be3!? Sax — 12 ..., exf3; 13 gxf3, c5! and Black won in 31 moves in Minev-Sax, Baja 1971) **11 ..., Bb6** (11 ..., d5; 12 Qxe5!, Re8; 13 Qxe8+ and 14 Kxf2 - Keres) **12 Kd1** and White has the upper hand, according to an old analysis by Maroczy. However the young Hungarian master Sax, in 'The Chess Player', says that the position is not clear after **12 ..., d5;** 13 Qxe5, Bf5 so perhaps this counter-gambit may yet be revived?

RUY LOPEZ

After **1 e4, e5; 2 Nf3, Nc6; 3 Bb5** the possibility of **3 ..., d5?!** (or, perhaps better, 3 ..., a6; 4 Ba4, d5) has apparently not hitherto been recognised. If 4 Nxe5, Qg5; 5 Nxc6, Qxg2; 6 Rf1 (Knight moves are met by 6 ..., c6) 6 ..., a6!; 7 Ba4!, Bh3 (There is nothing better, since 7 ..., Bd7 is met by 8 Qe2 and 9 exd5.) 8 Qe2, Qxf1+; 9 Qxf1, Bxf1; 10 Kxf1, dxe4 with a rough material balance (discovered checks are met by ..., b5). However White's position is surely preferable?

SCOTCH TWO KNIGHTS

After **1 e4, e5; 2 Nf3, Nc6; 3 Bc4** (Or 3 d4, exd4; 4 Bc4, Nf6) **3 ..., Nf6;**

4 d4, exd4; 5 e5 (5 Ng5?!, d5!; 6 exd5, Qe7+! but 5 O-O is also interesting)
5 ..., d5; 6 Bb5, Ne4; 7 Nxd4 Black's best move **7 ..., Bc5!** can lead to his
giving up some material:

a) 8 Nxc6?, Bxf2+; 9 Kf1, Qh4!; 10 Nd4+, c6; 11 Nf3, Ng3+; 12 Kxf2,
Ne4+; 13 Ke2, Qf2+; 14 Kd3, Bf5 and Black wins (Estrin).

b) 8 O-O, O-O!; 9 Nxc6 (Or 9 Bxc6, bxc6; 10 Nxc6?!, Qd7; 11 Nd4, Ba6 -
Estrin; White has better 10th options, F.N.Stephenson's 10 b4!? for
example, which may be best met by 10 ..., Bb6; 11 Nxc6, Qh4) 9 ..., bxc6;
10 Bxc6, Ba6!; 11 Bxa8 (Or 11 Qxd5, Bxf1; 12 Qxe4, Ba6 - Estrin) 11 ...,
Bxf1; 12 Be3 (If 12 Qxd5, Bc4!) 12 ..., Bxe3; 13 fxe3, Bxg2; 14 Qg4, Bh3;
15 Qxh3, Qg5+; 16 Kf1, Rxa8 with advantage to Black (German-Keres,
1936).

c) 8 Be3, O-O?! (Correct is 8 ..., Bd7) 9 Nxc6, bxc6; 10 Bxc5, Nxc5; 11
Bxc6, Rb8 (Or 11 ..., Ba6; 12 Nc3!, Qg5; 13 Qd4! Henkin-Vasyukov,
Leningrad 1954.) 12 O-O, Rxb2; 13 Bxd5 and White should win
(Carleton-Miles, Wolverhampton 1972).

3 BLACK SACRIFICES IN THE HALF-OPEN GAMES

This is a relatively poor field for counter-gambits, for a very good reason. Black's idea in meeting 1 e4 by moves other than 1 ..., e5 is to avoid symmetrical positions, with their all-out battle on one front, and instead to create unbalanced positions in which both sides have their chances. This is usually bought at the cost of a certain short-term insecurity (Black often has to make several pawn moves early on) which White may try to exploit by offering sacrifices himself. Provoking such sacrifices is a major element in Black's strategy in many half-open games — particularly in the Sicilian.

When Black does do the sacrificing, it is often more a matter of a thematic middle-game sacrifice than an opening gambit — consider the many and varied occasions for Black to Rc8xNc3 in the Dragon and other lines of the Sicilian. However there are a few genuine counter-gambit lines, albeit they do not stand centrally in the theory of openings in the way, for example, that the Falkbeer does in the King's Gambit.

I shall consider two sacrifices in the Sicilian, and one each in the Caro-Kann, French, and Pirc (Modern) Defences. Miscellaneous ideas are collected together at the end of the chapter.

SICILIAN DEFENCE (1 e4, c5)

The Sicilian Defence is the most popular opening at all levels of chess today, and the ways of playing it with White or Black seem to be inexhaustible. Mostly White does the honours, offering a pawn (on b2, c3 or e5 or h5) or a piece (on b5, d5, e6 or f5), but there are a few lines, notably in the Najdorf Variation, in which Black gives a pawn.

Game 27
Mestrovic - Griffiths
(Hastings Challengers 1971-2)

1 e2-e4. c7-c5; 2 Ng1-f3, d7-d6;

The most flexible move, but many others are possible. For **2 ..., Nc6** see the next game, while **2 ..., e6** and **2 ..., g6** are also well playable. But **2 ..., Nf6?!** is dubious as Black's critical pawn sacrifice has been shown to be unsound: 3 e5, Nd5; 4 Nc3, e6 (If 4 ..., Nxc3; 5 dxc3!) 5 Nxd5, exd5; 6 d4, Nc6!? (since 6 ..., d6; 7 Bb5+!, Nc6; 8 O-O, Be7; 9 c4! is greatly in White's favour) 7 dxc5, Bxc5; 8 Qxd5, Qb6; 9 Bc4, Bxf2+; 10 Ke2, O-O; 11 Rf1, Bc5; 12 Ng5!, Nxe5?! (Or if 12 ..., Nd4+; 13 Kd1!, Ne6; 14 Ne4! Unzicker-Sarapu, Siegen 1970) 13 Qxe5, d5; 14 Qxd5, Re8+; 15 Kf3, Qf6+; 16 Kg3, Bd6+; 17 Rf4!, Be6; 18 Nxe6, Rxe6; 19 Qxd6! and White won (Spassky-Ciric, Students' Olympiad 1962).

3 d2-d4, c5xd4; 4 Nf3xd4, Ng8-f6; 5 Nb1-c3, a7-a6!?;

The popular Najdorf Variation - but this is yet another move that does not contribute to the development of the pieces. **5 ..., Nc6** (see next game) would be more in accord with classical principles, while even **5 ..., g6** (Dragon Variation) and **5 ..., e6** (Scheveningen Variation) are more useful objectively. However the Najdorf, with such staunch advocates as Fischer to seek out Black's best lines, has not yet been refuted conclusively. White has to strike a nice balance between undisciplined aggression (**6 Bc4**) and timidity (**6 Be2, 6 g3**) which is not easy to do, especially confronted with a confusion of theoretical and practical study material!

6 Bc1-g5,

One of White's better moves, as it inhibits ..., e5, threatens to double Black's pawns and preserves all the options of the king bishop. Not least, it prepares long castling. Another promising move is **6 f4**, while Byrne and Hartston advocate **6 Be3!?**.

6 ..., e7-e6;

Probably best; if **6 ..., Nbd7** White still has **7 f4**, or he can play **7 Bc4** envisaging a sacrifice of the bishop on e6.

7 f2-f4,

This is the usual move nowadays, and probably the best (the threat is 8 e5 winning something).

7 ..., Qd8-c7;

Griffiths' favourite method of playing the Najdorf is not to be under-estimated, and (as this game

shows) he has found some improvements over 'book' lines. He unpins and prepares the 'unthematic' Nc6.

This is not the place to give reams of analysis on Black's alternatives, which are well-known to most chessplayers. In the (heretical) opinion of this author, Black should adopt a plan based on ..., h6 and/or ..., Qb6 as these are the only moves which can show a darker side to White's 6th and 7th moves (cutting off the queen's bishop and exposing the pawn on b2). After the popular **7 ..., Be7; 8 Qf3, Qc7!?; 9 O-O-O, Nbd7!?** White should however continue with the traditional pawn-storm **10 g4** rather than the trendy **10 Bd3**.

8 Qd1-f3, Nb8-c6;

Black could also have tried to prepare this by **7 ..., Bd7**, probably transposing since 8 e5 is met by 8 ..., dxe5; 9 fxe5, Qa5 (Euwe). However a game Florian-Petri (Budapest 1966) went instead **8 Qd2, h6; 9 Bxf6, Qxf6; 10 Bc4, Nf6; 11 Nde2, Qh4+; 12 g3, Qh5; 13 O-O-O, Qc5; 14 Bb3** with a plus to White.

51

9 O-O-O,

This is probably the most precise

move. **9 Bxf6** should transpose back, but **9 Nxc6** can be independently significant: 9 ..., Qxc6; 10 Be2 (10 O-O-O, Bd7 see the note to White's 10th move below) 10 ..., Be7; 11 O-O-O, Bd7 (or 11 ..., h6; 12 Bh4, Bd7 see the same note below) 12 Rd2, b5 with complications (Bradvarevic-Knezevic, Titograd 1965).

9 ..., Bc8-d7; 10 Bg5xf6,

The continuation recommended in the books here is **10 Nxc6** since either **10 ..., bxc6**; 11 Bc4, Be7; 12 Rd3 (Keres-Panno, Amsterdam 1956) or **10 ..., Bxc6**; 11 Bxf6, gxf6; 12 f5 (Horberg-Stahlberg, Stockholm 1956). However, Peter Griffiths' intention was to play **10 ..., Qxc6!** e.g.: **11 Be2** (Pachman claims a White plus after 11 Bxf6, gxf6; 12 f5 but then of course 12 ..., O-O-O; 13 fxe6, fxe6 transposes back into the text game) **11 ..., h6** (Or 11 ..., Be7 see the note to White's 9th, above) 12 Bh4, Be7. From here a game Miles-Griffiths (Birmingham International Tournament, 1972) continued 13 Rd3, Rc8; 14 Qg3?! (Or 14 Bxf6, gxf6; 15 Rhd1, Be7; 16 Qg3, O-O and Black won in 27 moves; Colston-Griffiths, Wolverhampton 1972) 14 ..., g5; 15 fxg5, Nxe4; 16 Qe3, hxg5; 17 Be1, d5; 18 Bf3, Nc5; 19 Rd1, b5; 20 Rf1, Ne4! with much the better game for Black.

Another possibility is **10 f5, O-O-O; 11 Be2**, Be7; 12 Qh3. The game Tarjan-Griffiths, Teeside 1972, went next 12 ..., Kb8; 13 Kb1, Nxd4; 14 Rxd4, exf5; 15 exf5, Qc5; 16 Rhd1, Bxf5; 17 Qg3, Bg6; 18 Bf4, Rhe8; 19 Rc4, Qf5; 20 Na4, Nh5; 21 Bxh5, Bxh5; 22 Bxd6+, Ka8?? (22 ..., Bxd6 wins out of

hand) 23 Nb6+, Ka7; 24 Qe3 Resigns. A sad swindle.

10 ..., g7xf6; 11 f4-f5!?, O-O-O!; 12 f5xe6, f7xe6;

This pawn sacrifice revives the 7 ...., Qc7 line for Black, unless a satisfactory quiet continuation is available for White. He could, for example, try (10 Nxc6, Qxc6; 11 Bxf6, gxf6) **12 Qh5!?**, Be7 (12 ..., b5; 13 a3) 13 f5 as in this line the sacrifice 12 or 13 ..., O-O-O is less viable, Black having less open lines and more weaknesses; however the move 12 ..., Qc5! seems adequate (analysis). So matters are not clear although Griffiths himself appears to have doubts about Black's position if White declines to win the offered pawn.

13 Nd4xc6,

Taking the pawn immediately is probably inferior; Griffiths gives 13 Qxf6?, Be7; 14 Qh6, Rdg8; 15 Kb1, Rg6 with White condemned to long defence.

13 ..., Qc7xc6; 14 Qf3xf6,

Not to take the pawn would be an admission of failure.

14 ..., Rh8-g8; 15 Qf6-d4,

An earlier example of the sacrifice was the game McFarland-Griffiths (Islington 1971) which had continued **15 Rd3**, Bg7; 16 Qf2 (Griffiths recommends 16 Qh4, Be5 with an unclear position; not 17 Qxh7?!, Rh8; 18 Qf7, Rdf8; 19 Qg6, Rf2 but 17 Qb2!, Kb8) 16 ..., Kb8; 17 g3, Rgf8; 18 Qe1, Qb6; 19 Bh3, Rf2; 20 Nd1, Rf7; 21 Rf1, Rxf1; 22 Bxf1, Qg1!; 23 Rf3, Qh2; 24 Rb3!, Rc8!; 25 Nc3, Ba4; 26 Resigns.

15 ..., Bf8-h6+; 16 Kc1-b1, Bh6-g7

.The point of checking first becomes clear at move 21.

17 Qd4xd6, Bg7xc3; 18 b2xc3,

The identical position will be brought about after **18 Qxc6+, Bxc6; 19 Rxd8+, Rxd8; 20 bxc3, Rd1+; 21 Kb2, Bxe4.**

18 ..., Qc6xe4; 19 Rd1-d4, Bd7-c6;

19 ..., Qe1+ could lead to an unclear ending after 20 Kb2, Bc6; 21 Bxa6, Rxd6 (21 ..., bxc6??; 22 Qxc6+ and wins) 22 Rxe1 (or 22 Bxb7+!?) 22 ..., Rxd4; 23 cxd4, bxa6; 24 Rxe6, Kd7; 25 Re2 White having three pawns for his piece.

20 Qd6xd8+, Rg8xd8; 21 Rd4xe4, Rd8-d1+; 22 Kb1-b2, Bc6xe4;

52

In return for his worthless extra pawn White is in a painful bind, which Black is able to intensify by bringing up his king and passed e-pawn. White is positionally lost.

23 h2-h4, h7-h5; 24 c3-c4, Kc8-c7; 25 Kb2-c3, Kc7-d6; 26 Rh1-g1, Kd6-e5; 27 Rg1-h1, Ke5-f4; 28 c4-c5, Be4-c6;

Now that his king is strongly placed, Black might even consider the materialistic **28 ..., Rc1** (29

Kd4?, e5+).

29 a2-a4?!, e6-e5?!;

It is hard to see a drawing plan for White after **29 ..., Bxa4;** 30 g3+ (presumably the intention) 30 ..., Kxg3; 31 Rh3+, Kg4; 32 Bg2 (32 Be2+, Kxh3; 33 Bxd1, Kxh4 etc) 32 ..., Rg1; 33 Bxb7 (33 Rh2, Kg3) 33 ..., Kxh3; 34 Bxa6, Kxh4 since White's passed c-pawns only represent a slight nuisance value (analysis).

30 a4-a5, e5-e4; 31 g2-g3+, Kf4xg3 32 Rh1-h3+, Kg3-g4; 33 Rh3-h1,

This move would also have been possible on move 32 in the previous note, but with a pawn less it would be quite futile.

33 ..., Kg4-f4; 34 Rh1-g1, e4-e3?;

Black had at his disposal the forcing continuation **34 ..., Bb5!;** 35 Bxb5, Rxg1; 36 c6!, bxc6! (Not 36 ..., axb5??; 37 cxb7 when White wins!) 37 Bxa6, e3; 38 Bd3, Kf3; 39 a6, e2 and wins easily.

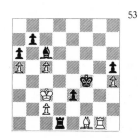

53

35 Rg1-g8!, Bc6-f3;

Since if **35 ..., Rxf1?;** 36 Rf8+, Kg4!?; 37 Rxf1, e2; 38 Re1, Bf3; 39 Kd2 or 36 ..., Kg3; 37 Rxf1, Bb5; 38 Rh1 White can probably hold out.

36 c5-c6!, b7xc6; 37 Bf1xa6,
e3-e2; 38 Ba6xe2, Bf3xe2;
39 Rg8-a8,

White seizes his chance of
counterplay, however slight.

39 ..., Rd1-a1; 40 Kc3-b2,
Ra1-a4; 41 Kb2-b3, Be2-b5;
42 c2-c4!,

Evidently best, albeit insufficient due to the relatively strong
position of Black's king in the
ensuing rook ending.

42 ..., Ra4xc4; 43 a5-a6, Bb5xa6;
44 Ra8xa6, Rc4-c1; 45 Kb3-b2,
Rc1-c5; 46 Ra6-a4+, Kf4-g3;
47 Ra4-e4,

47 Kb3 would come to the
same; Black's only winning plan is
based on the h-pawn.

47 ..., Rc5-f5; 48 Re4-c4, Rf5-f4;
49 Rc4xc6, Rf4xh4; 50 Rc6-c3+,

If 50 Kc3, Re4!; 51 Kd3, Re5;
52 Rc4 (Or 52 Kd4, Re8) 52 ..., h4
and White cannot exchange rooks.

50 ..., Kg3-f2; 51 Rc3-c2+, Kf2-e3;
52 Rc2-c3+, Ke3-f4; 53 Rc3-c8,
Rh4-h1; 54 Kb2-c2, h5-h4; 55
Rc8-h8, h4-h3; 56 Kc2-b2,

Or 56 Kd2, h2; 57 Ke2, Ra1!

56 ..., Kd4-e4; 57 Kb2-c2, Ke4-f3;
58 Kc2-c3, Kf3-g2; 59 Kc3-c2,
Rh1-g1; White Resigns.

in view of 60 Rg8+, Kh1 followed
by 61 ..., h2, then a rook check,
then Kg1 etc.

Game 28
Kriz - Markland
(Reggio Emilia 1973)

1 e2-e4, c7-c5; 2 Ng1-f3, Nb8-c6; 3
d2-d4, c5xd4; 4 Nf3xd4, Ng8-f6;
5 Nb1-c3, d7-d6; 6 Bc1-g5,

As in the Najdorf Variation,
this move is perhaps best, and was
twice employed by Fischer in his
world championship match against
Spassky in 1972. However 6 Bc4 is
also dangerous and a popular
choice here.

6 ..., Bc8-d7;

This move, permitting the
doubling of the f-pawn, has in
recent years become almost as
common as the old 6 ..., e6 after
which White most often plays 7
Qd2 (Rauser Attack). The text
move envisages an early bid for
counterplay down the c-file after
White's thematic long castling.

7 Qd1-d2,

Here it was formerly believed
that White would get the advantage
by 7 Bxf6 but this move is hardly
ever seen now. After 7 ..., gxf6; 8
Nf5 (Balogh-van der Kol, correspondence 1934) Black has the
simple and good 8 ..., Qa5!; 9 Bd3
(9 Bb5!?) 9 ..., Bxf5!?; 10 exf5,
Qe5+; 11 Qe2, Qxe2+; 12 Kxe2,
e6≈. White can also consider 8 Be2,
8 Bc4 and 8 Qd2 while Black can
counter with play based on his
half-open c and g files, and on the
weakened Black squares. The
tactical problems of these lines are
relatively unexplored as yet.

In the game Damjanovic-Stein
Tallinn 1969, another unusual idea
was tried: 7 Nb3 (Others are 7 Be2,
7 Qd3 and 7 f4!?) 7 ..., h6; 8 Bh4,
Rc8; 9 Be2, g5; 10 Bg3, h5; 11 h4,
g4 with a sharp struggle, in which
Black was ultimately victorious.

7 ..., Ra8-c8;

The logical follow-up, although
7 ..., Nxd4, 7 ..., a6 and 7 ..., e6!?
have also been played.

8 0-0-0,

White's chief alternative here is **8 f4!?**, attempting to expose Black's king in the centre. There can follow **8 ..., Nxd4** (Or perhaps 8 ..., h6 but not 8 ..., a6; 9 0-0-0, b5?; 10 Nf3, Qa5?; 11 Kb1, b4; 12 Bxf6, gxf6; 13 Nd5! Matanovic-Ivanovic, Yugoslav Championship 1969) **9 Qxd4, Qa5; 10 e5** (If 10 0-0-0 Black hits c3 as in the game) **10 ..., Ne4!?** (It may be better to transpose by playing to the text by 10 ..., dxe5; 11 fxe5, e6; 12 0-0-0 but not 10 ..., h6?!; 11 Bh4, g5; 12 exf6! Tatai-Radulov, Venice 1971) **11 Qxe4, Rxc3; 12 bxc3** (12 0-0-0!?) **12 ..., Qxc3+; 13 Kf2, Qxa1; 14 exd6** (Or 14 Bb5, Qc3!) **14 ..., f6!; 15 Bb5, Qb2!; 16 Bxd7+, Kxd7; 17 dxe7, Bxe7** with equality according to an improbable analysis by Ciric in 'Informator' No.12.

8 ..., Nc6xd4; 9 Qd2xd4, Qd8-a5;

Interesting is **9 ..., Rxc3!?; 10 Qxc3, Nxe4; 11 Qe3, Nxg5; 12 Qxg5, Qb6** (Bednarski-Simagin, Polanica Zdroj 1968).

10 f2-f4,

This is White's last chance to avoid the coming exchange sacrifice:

a) 10 Be3?!, a6; 11 f3, e6; 12 Qb6, Qxb6; 13 Bxb6, Bc6!= (Suetin-Gheorghiu, Hastings 1967-8)

b) 10 Bxf6, gxf6; **11 f4** (Or 11 Kb1, Qc5; 12 Qd2?!, f5!; 13 exf5, Bxf5 Kaplan-Gheorghiu, Hastings 1967-68) 11 ..., Bg7; 12 Kb1, Qc5; 13 f5, Qxd4; 14 Rxd4, h5 with a fair position for Black (I.Szabo-Stein, Tallinn 1969).

c) 10 Bd2, a6 (10 ..., e5!? of Radulov-Ungureanu, Skopje 1972, is probably inferior) **11 f3** (11

Kb1!?) 11 ..., e5 (11 ..., Qc5?; 12 Qxc5, Rxc5; 13 Be3 was in White's favour in Mecking-Radulov, Vrsac 1971) **12 Qa7!?** (Or 12 Qe3, Be6; 13 Kb1, Be7; 14 g4, Rxc3; 15 Bxc3, Qxa2+; 16 Kc1, Bg4; 17 Be2, Be6 with an unclear position) 12 ..., Qc7; 13 Be3, Be6; 14 Qb6, Qxb6 with a roughly equal game occurred in Gruzman-Lein, USSR 1972, which Black eventually won. Also possible here is **10 ..., Qc5** (Matulovic-Schaufelberger, Siegen 1970).

54

10 ..., e7-e6!?

It is also possible to play immediately **10 ..., Rxc3** (Not 10 ..., h6?!; 11 Bh4, g5 because of 12 e5! Karpov-R.Byrne, Hastings 1971-2) **11 bxc3,** e5; 12 Qb4! (not 12 Qe3?, Ng4! and Black soon won in Dascalov-Tringov, Bulgarian Championship 1969) 12 ..., Qxb4; 13 cxb4, Nxe4; 14 Bh4, g5! (Unzicker-Gheorghiu, Lubliana 1969). In view of his central pawns and better development, Black's chances are to be preferred. If here **11 Qxc3,** O'Kelly-Radulov (Havana 1969) continued 11 ..., Qxc3; 12 bxc3, Nxe4; 13 Bh4, g6; 14 Be1, Bg7; 15 Kb2, 0-0; 16 Bd3, Nc5; 17 Ka3, Rc8 with advantage to Black.

11 e4-e5,

White can also prevent the sacrifice by **11 Kb1** after which Unzicker-Dueball, Berlin 1971, went 11 ..., Qc5!; 12 Bxf6!? (Or 12 Qd2, Bc6=) 12 ..., gxf6; 13 Qxf6, Rg8; 14 Qh4!, h6! with about equal chances.

11 ..., d6xe5; 12 f4xe5, Rc8xc3!;

This is practically forced, since **12 ..., Bc6?!** as played in Hort-Panno, Palma Interzonal 1970, should (as Wade and Blackstock give in the tournament book) be smashed by **13 Bxf6** (Instead of 13 Bb5) 13 ..., gxf6; 14 Ne4, fxe5; 15 Nf6+, Ke7; 16 Qh4. After 16 ..., Bg7 (16 ..., Qa4!?) there can follow 17 Nd5+, Kf8; 18 Qe7+, Kg8; 19 Nf6+, Bxf6; 20 Qxf6, e4! (White threatened Rd1-d3-g3+) 21 Bc4, Qf5!; 22 Qd4! and despite his extra pawn Black cannot really hold out much hope of survival. Less clear is the ending 22 Qxf5, exf5; 23 Rhf1 on account of 23 ..., Kg7!; 24 Rxf5, Rhf8.

13 Bg5-d2,

The only move to have been tried here. If **13 exf6**, Qxg5+ or **13 Bxf6**, Rc7 and Black keeps his two bishops. If **13 Qxc3**, Qxc3; 14 bxc3, Ne4! with forced recapture of the exchange, or **13 bxc3?**, Bc5! and Black, free to castle, will get a mate.

13 ..., Qa5xa2; 14 Bd2xc3, g7-g6!;

Markland points out that **14 ..., Bc5?** is impossible on account of 15 Qxc5, Qa1+ (or 15 ..., Ne4; 16 Qa3, Nxc3; 17 Qxa2 and Black has insufficient compensation for the exchange) 16 Kd2, Ne4+!; 17 Ke3, Qxd1; 18 Kxe4 and White's extra piece will soon tell.

15 Kc1-d2,

An untried altèrnative is **15 b3!?**, using the bishop to cover a1 and meeting 15 ..., Bh6+ (15 ..., Nd5!) by 16 Rd2 (or 16 Bd2) 16 ..., Nd5; 17 Qc5 with obscure goings-on.

15 ..., Bf8-c5;

16 Qd4-d3,

White tries to improve upon the course of the game Klovan-Liberzon (USSR 1972) which was **16 Qc4** (If 16 Qh4, Nd5 is good for Black) 16 ..., Qxc4; 17 Bxc4, Ne4+; 18 Ke2, **Nxc3!**; 19 bxc3, Bc6 with roughly equal chances and an eventual draw. Yudovich's 'Informator' suggestion **18 ..., Nf2** is bad on account of 19 Rxd7!, Kxd7; 20 Rf1, Ne4; 21 Rxf7+.

16 ..., Nf6-d5;

Not **16 ..., Ng4?**; 17 Ke1 threatening 18 Qxd7.

17 b2-b3,

Threatening 18 Ra1. Black has to calculate accurately now.

17 ..., Bc5-e3+;

Not **17 ..., Nxc3?**; 18 Qxc3 and Black has nothing for the exchange but **17 ..., Bb4** was important. There can follow 18 Bxb4, Nxb4; 19 Qd6, Qxc2+; 20 Ke1, Qe4+; 21

Be2, Nc2+; 22 Kd2 with advantage to White, according to Markland. For example 22 ..., Nd4; 23 Bd3, Qxg2+; 24 Kc3 and Black's busted: 24 ..., Qc6+; 25 Kxd4 or 24 ..., Nb5+; 25 Bxb5, Bxb5; 26 Qd8 mate.

18 Kd2-e1, Qa2-a3;

For the exchange, Black has a pawn, the safer king and active minor pieces. Nonetheless White should have fair chances of holding the game, if he played now **19 Bd4** (Markland).

19 Bc3-d2?, Be3-b6;

Keeping the good bishop.

20 c2-c4, Qa3-c5;

With a blatant threat. Next move, too!

21 Qd3-e2, Nd5-b4; 22 Bd2xb4+, Qc5xb4+; 23 Qe2-d2, Qb4-e7!?;

He could cash in a positional advantage by **23 ..., Qxd2+; 24 Kxd2, Bc7** but prefers, partly in view of White's clock pressure, to play for mate.

24 Bf1-e2, Bd7-c6; 25 Be2-f3, Bc6xf3; 26 g2xf3, Qe7-h4+; 27 Ke1-f1, O-O;

According to Markland, **27 ..., Qh3+** was a little better.

28 Kf1-g2, Rf8-d8; 29 Qd2-e2,

It was better to try **29 Qe1**, Qg5+; 30 Qg3.

29 ..., Qh4-g5+; 30 Kg2-h3,

If **30 Kf1**, Rxd1+ and the e-pawn goes.

30 ..., Rd8-c8;

To introduce the rook into the mating attack; White is now completely lost.

31 Qe2-e4?!, Bb6-e3; 32 Qe4xb7, Rc8-c5; 33 Qb7-b8+, Kg8-g7; 34 Rd1-d8, Rc5xe5; 35 Rd8-g8+, Kg7-h6; 36 Qb8-f8+, Kh6-h5; 37 Rh1-f1, Qg5-h4+; 38 Kh3-g2, Be3-f4, White Resigns.

CARO-KANN DEFENCE (1 e4, c6)

The normally quiet Caro-Kann conceals a counter-gambit that Black may unleash if his opponent ventures upon the Panov Attack.

Game 29
Ljubojevic - Wade
(Teesside 1972)

Notes based upon comments by Wade in 'The Chess Player'

1 e2-e4, c7-c6; 2 d2-d4, d7-d5; 3 e4xd5, c6xd5; 4 c2-c4, Ng8-f6;

In fact Wade reached this position via the slightly unusual route of the Scandinavian Defence

(1 e4, d5; 2 exd5, Nf6; 3 c4, c6; 4 d4, cxd5), and some of the positions that can subsequently arise may also be reached via the Tarrasch or Symmetrical defences to the Queen's Gambit.

5 Nb1-c3, g7-g6;

It is this move which introduces the gambit. However Black may also play **5 ..., e6** or **5 ...,**

Nc6?!, for which he might consult Boleslavsky's book 'Skandinavisch bis Sizilianisch'.

6 c4xd5,

So far we have only a transposition of moves, since normal is **6 Qb3**, Bg7 (6 ..., dxc4?; 7 Bxc4) 7 cxd5: see the note to White's next move.

6 ..., Bf8-g7;

56

7 Bf1-b5+!?,

Ljubojevic avoids the main line **7 Qb3** when can follow:

a) 8 Nf3, Nbd7; 9 Bg5, Nb6; 10 Bc4 (If 10 Bxf6, Bxf6; 11 a4 Shatskes recommends 11 ..., e6!; 12 dxe6, Bxe6) 10 ..., Bf5; 11 Rad1 Bxf6, Bxf6; 12 Rd1 as in Tal-Lein, 29th USSR Championship 1961) 11 ..., Ne4!; 12 O-O, Nxc3; 13 bxc3, Rac8; 14 Bb5 (Hasin, in the Soviet Chess Yearbook for 1961, mentions 14 Bd3, Bxd3; 15 Rxd3, h6!) 14 ..., h6; 15 Bh4? (Hasin gives as correct 15 Bd2, Qxd5; 16 Rfe1! e.g. 16 ..., e6; 17 Qxd5, Nxd5; 18 c4!, a6; 19 cxd5, axb5; 20 dxe6, Bxe6; 21 Bb4, Rfd8; 22 a3) 15 ..., g5!; 16 Bg3, Qxd5; 17 Qb4 (If 17 Qxd5, Nxd5; 18 c4?, Nc3!) 17 ..., Bg4 and the game Tal-Bronstein, 29th USSR Championship 1961, continued: 18

Rfe1, Bxf3; 19 gxf3, e6; 20 Bd3, Qxf3; 21 Rd2, Rfd8; 22 Re3, Qc6; 23 Bb5, Qd5; 24 Re2, Nc4!; 25 Bxc4, Rxc4; 26 Qb2, Rc8; 27 Be5, Bxe5!; 28 Rxe5, Qc6; 29 Re3, b6; 30 Qa3, Rxc3; 31 Qxa7, Rxe3; 32 Rxe3, Ra8; 33 Rc3, Qe4; 34 Qc7, Rxa2; 35 Rc1, Qxd4; 36 Qg3, Kg7; 37 h4, Qxh4; 38 Qc3+, Kg6; 39 Qd3+, Kh5; 40 Qe3, Ra4; 41 Resigns.

b) 8 Bg5, Qa5; 9 Bxf6, exf6; 10 O-O-O, Nd7; 11 Kb1, Nb6; 12 Bd3, Bg4; 13 Rc1, Bh6; 14 Rc2, Rad8= (Vasyukov-Bronstein, Kislovodsk 1968)

c) 8 Be2, Nbd7; 9 Bf3, Nb6; 10 Bg5 (10 Bf4!?) 10 ..., a5; 11 a4 (If 11 Bxf6, exf6!; 12 Nge2, Bf5 Bagirov-Gurgenidze, 36th USSR Championship, 1968) 11 ..., Bf5!; 12 Rad1, Qd6 with equal chances, according to Boleslavsky.

d) 8 g3, e6!; 9 dxe6, Nc6!? (Or 9 ..., Bxe6; 10 Qxb7, Nbd7 Boleslavsky) 10 exf7+, Kh8; 11 Nge2, Qe7; 12 Be3, Ng4; 13 Kd2, Be6 (13 ..., Rxf7!?) 14 d5, Bxf7; 15 Bh3, Ne5; 16 Rad1, Na5 with good compensation for Black (Gheorghiu-Johannessen, Havana 1966).

e) 8 Nge2, Re8!; 9 g3 (9 Bg5!?) 9 ..., e6; 10 dxe6, Bxe6; 11 Qxb7, Nbd7; 12 Bg2, Rb8 with the initiative to Black (Boleslavsky).

Another important possibility, also neglected by Boleslavsky in his 'Skandinavisch bis Sizilianisch', is **7 Bc4**, O-O; 8 Nge2, Nbd7; 9 Nf4, Nb6; 10 Bb3 e.g.:

a) 10 ..., Qd6; 11 O-O, Bd7; 12 Rfe1, a5; 13 a4 (13 a3!? Tal) 13 ..., Rfc8; 14 h3, h6; 15 Re5, Nc4; 16 Qe2, Qb4; 17 Ba2 (Tal-Wade, Tallinn 1971) with great complications after either Wade's continua-

tion 17 ..., Ncxe5; 18 dxe5, Nh5!?
or Tal's suggestion 17 ..., Nd6; 18
Rxe7, Nf5; 19 Rxf7, Re8!
b) 10 ..., Bf5; 11 O-O, Nc8; 12 Re1,
Nd6; 13 h3, Rc8; 14 Bd2?, Nfe4; 15
Nxe4, Nxe4; 16 Bb4, Qb6!? with
complications that led to an unusual draw in Tseitlin-Roitov,
USSR 1972.

7 ..., Nb8-d7; 8 d5-d6!,

White would now get an
excellent position in the event of
either **8 ..., exd6; 9 Bf4** or first **9
Qe2+,** Qe7 and then 10 Bf4.

**8 ..., O-O!;
9 d6xe7+, Qd8xe7;**

With an original situation, in
which Black has surely got compensation for his pawn.

10 Bb5-e2,

Retrieving the bishop, which is
out on a limb. If instead **10 Nge2**
(to force castling) Wade was un-
decided between **10 ..., a6** and **10
..., Nb6**, in either case with an
unclear position.

10 ..., b7-b5!?;

To accelerate his pressure on
the White squares, Wade gives up a
second pawn, although the quieter
10 ..., a6!? may also be adequate.

11 Nc3xb5,

Otherwise 11 ..., b4 will undermine the piece anyway (**11 a3**, a5!?).

**11 ..., Bc8-b7;
12 Ke1-f1,**

Since **12 Nf3**, Bxf3; 13 gxf3,
Rfe8 devalues his pawns and leaves
Kf1 still obligatory.

12 ..., Nd7-b6; 13 Be2-f3!?,

It was impossible to play the
quiet **13 Nc3** when Black must
decide upon a concrete plan of

attack. One possibility is **13 ...,
Rad8**; 14 Nf3, Ng4, with ideas like
Nh6-f5 and Bxf3 followed by Rxd4
(analysis).

13 ..., Bb7-a6; 14 a2-a4, Ra8-d8!;

White's d-pawn is the natural
target.

15 Ng1-e2, Qe7-d7; 16 b2-b3,

It is no longer possible to
remain two pawns ahead, but is **16
h3** better?

16 ..., Rf8-e8;

Development comes first.

17 h2-h3,

Making a home for his king.

**17 ..., Ba6xb5; 18 a4xb5, Qd7xb5;
19 Ra1xa7, Nf6-e4;**

Sealing the fate of the d-pawn,
by unrobing the cleric.

20 Kf1-g1!,

It would be morbid to contem-
plate **20 Bb2?**, Ng5 when after the
capture on f3 the other knight
serves his lady well by making a
pilgrimage to f4. Ljubojevic unpins
just in time.

20 ..., Nb6-d5; 21 Bf3xe4,

Black threatened 21 ..., Nec3
picking off the d-pawn, and if **21
Bb2**, Ng5 is still effective.

**21 ..., Re8xe4; 22 Ne2-g3, Re4xd4;
23 Qd1-f3, Be7-f6;**

Improvising a defence of f7.

24 Kg1-h2?!,

Here Wade gives the variation
24 Ne4, Rxe4; 25 Qxe4, Nc3; **26
Qf3**, Qb8 and Black wins. However
also possible is **26 Qb7!** when Black
must play 26 ..., Rd1+; 27 Kh2,
Rxh1+; 28 Kxh1, Qf1+; 29 Kh2,
Be5+; 30 f4! (30 g3?, Qxf2+; 31
Kh1, Ne2 and wins) 30 ..., Bxf4+;

31 Bxf4, Qxf4+; 32 Kh1 (32 Kg1??, Ne2+ mates) and Black has no more than a draw.

24 ..., Rd4-d3; 25 Qf3-e4,

57

25 ..., Qb5xb3?;

Here Black missed **25 ..., Bd4** with the double threat of 26 ..., Bxa7 and 26 ..., Bxf2. Black at least regains his second pawn and retains pressure.

26 Ra7-a3, Qb3xa3; 27 Bc1xa3, Rd3xa3;

Black has only rook and bishop for queen, but with pawns only on one side of the board he has little to worry about.

28 Rh1-d1, Ra3-a5; 29 Qe4-f3, Kg8-g7; 30 Ng3-e4, Bf6-e5+; 31 g2-g3, h7-h6;

Preventing 32 Ng5.

32 h3-h4, Rd8-a8?;

After the correct **32 ..., Rb8** (not under indirect fire from the queen) the following combinative liquidation would have been impossible. But White has the softening-up move 33 h5 and a draw seems the likeliest outcome. Now Black loses another pawn, but not the game.

33 Rd1xd5!, Rd8xd5; 34 Ne4-g5, h6xg5; 35 Qf3xd5, Ra8-e8; 36 h4xg5, Kg7-g8; 37 Kh2-g2, Be5-g7; 38 f2-f4, Re8-e6; 39 g2-g4, Bg7-f8; 40 f4-f5, Re6-d6; 41 Qd5-b7, Kg8-g7; 42 Kg2-f3, Kg7-g8; 43 Kf3-e4, Bf8-g7; 44 Qb7-b8+,

If ever **44 f6**, Bf8 followed by ..., Re6 or **44 fxg6**, Rxg6 Black would have only to move his rook back and forth to draw.

44 ..., Bg7-f8; 45 Ke4-e5, Rd6-c6; 46 Qb8-a8, Rc6-b6; 47 Qa8-d8, Rb6-c6; 48 Qd8-d7, Rc6-b6; 49 Ke5-d5, Rb6-a6;

Not **49 ..., Rd6+??** losing the pawn ending.

50 Qd7-c7, Kg8-g7; 51 Qc7-d8, Kg7-g8; 52 Kd5-c4, Ra6-d6; 53 Qd8-b8, Kg8-g7; 54 Qb8-b7, Kg7-g8; 55 Kc4-b5, Kg8-g7; 56 Qb7-e4, Kg7-g8; 57 Qe4-e5, Kg8-h7; Draw agreed.

FRENCH DEFENCE

The French Defence has a reputation for great solidity rather than exciting tactics. Nonetheless it embraces one major counter-gambit theme: the offer of the g-pawn in various lines of the Winawer Variation, in reply to White's sortie Qd1-g4. A thorough study of these lines was published in 1971, in English, by two Danish analysts S.Zeuthen and

E.Jarinaes, under the title 'French Poisoned Pawn'. I give here one of Black's most celebrated victories, but cannot hope to cover the whole theme in much detail.

Game 30
Dueball- Uhlmann
(Raach 1969)

1 e2-e4, e7-e6;

It is fitting that the French should be represented by Uhlmann, the defence's most loyal and inventive exponent among the currently active grandmasters.

2 d2-d4, d7-d5; 3 Nb1-c3,

After **3 exd5, exd5; 4 Bd3, Nc6; 5 c3, Bd6; 6 Qc2** the move **6 ..., Bg4?!** was played in the game Harding-Vogel (Wijk aan Zee Reserves 1973) but White now played the conservative **7 Ne2** with a level game. The critical line is **7 Bxh7!?, Qe7+** (7 ..., Qh4?!; 8 Bf5!) 8 Kf1, O-O-O (8 ..., g6?; 9 Bxg6) 9 Bf5+, Bxf5; 10 Qxf5+, Kb8; 11 Bg5, f6; 12 Bf4, Nh6; 13 Bxd6, Rxd6; 14 Qg6, Re8; 15 Nd2 with an unclear position.

3 ..., Bf8-b4; 4 e4-e5,

The most common, and almost certainly the best, reply to the Winawer Variation. Poisoned pawn ideas occur in other lines too:

a) 4 Qg4?!, Nf6 (not 4 ..., e5?) 5 Qxg7, Rg8; 6 Qh6, c5; 7 a3, Rg6; 8 Qe3, Ba5; 9 Bd2, cxd4; 10 Qxd4, Nc6 favours Black ('F.P.P.').

b) 4 Bd2?!, dxe4; 5 Qg4, Nf6; 6 Qxg7 does not involve Black in sacrifices.

c) 4 a3!?, Bxc3+; 5 bxc3, dxe4; 6 Qg4, Nf6; 7 Qxg7 is also just an exchange.

4 ..., c7-c5;

Uhlmann actually played **4 ..., Ne7** but, as usual, this transposed back at move 6. Here **4 ..., b6** and **4 ..., Qd7** involve quite different ideas

5 a2-a3,

Another interesting idea is the 'Russian Variation' **5 Qg4!?** Now after **5 ..., Ne7** (in all these lines Black avoids the defensive 5 ..., g6 or 5 ..., Kf8 which would just leave him passively placed) **6 Qxg7** (If 6 a3, hoping to transpose back to the main line, there can come 6 ..., Qa5!? as in Jansa-Korchnoy, Luhacovice 1969; Or if 6 dxc5, Nc6!; 7 Nf3, d4!= Archives) **6 ..., Rg8; 7 Qh6** (7 Qxh7?, cxd4; 8 a3, Qa5! again) **7 ..., cxd4; 8 a3** and now, as the White queen protects the Bc1 Black should forego **8 ..., Qa5?!;** 9 axb4, Qxa1; 10 Nb5! in favour of one of the following: **8 ..., Bxc3+;** 9 bxc3, Qc7; 10 Ne2, Nbc6 or **8 ..., Ba5;** 9 b4, Qc7 (or 9 ..., Bc7!?) 10 Nb5, Qxe5+; 11 Ne2!, Bb6; 12 Bf4, Qg7 in each case with virtually unexplored complications ('F.P.P.')

5 ..., Bb4xc3+;

It is well known that **5 ..., Ba5?!** is dubious on account of **6 b4!, cxd4** (6 ..., cxb4; 7 Nb5!) 7 Qg4, Ne7; 8 bxa5 (8 Nb5!?) 8 ..., dxc3; 9 Qxg7, Rg8; 10 Qxh7, Nbc6 (Nor is 10 ..., Nd7 superior) 11 Nf3, Qc7; 12 Bb5! with virtually a forced win for White (Fischer-Tal, Leipzig 1960). **11 ..., Qxa5!?** is also critical here.

6 b2xc3, Ng8-e7; 7 Qd1-g4!?,

In this position, however,

Black has an extra tempo and White's forces do not achieve the same degree of co-ordination. In playing for the 'win' of the Black king side pawns, White expects that his ace of trumps will be the passed h-pawn that he thereby obtains.

However it is almost certainly better for White to play **7 Nf3**, as Dueball himself appears to do nowadays. The themes that then arise are quite outside the scope of this survey.

7 ..., Qd8-c7;

This could have been played last move, perhaps with the intention of meeting White's sortie by ..., f5!?. The major disadvantage of that order of moves is that it reduces Black's options against 7 Nf3!

8 Qg4xg7, Rh8-g8; 9 Qg7xh7, c5xd4;

58

Compared with the Fischer-Tal line, this move comes with a threat of ..., Qxc3+ and ..., Qc3xa1. White has two distinct ways of trying to cope with this.

10 Ng1-e2,

The Konstantinopolsky Variation, named after the Soviet master

who suggested this move. The alternative is the Euwe-Gligoric **10 Kd1** and then:

a) 10 ..., **Qxe5?**; 11 Nf3, Qf6; 12 cxd4 and White is winning — 'F.P.'.

b) 10 ..., **Nc6/d7; 11 Nf3, Nxe5**; 12 Bf4, Qxc3; 13 Nxe5, Qxa1+; 14 Bc1, **Rf8!?** (Or 14 ..., d3!?; 15 Qxf7+, Kd8; 16 Qf6! is promising for White, but not quite clear) 15 Bb5+ (15 Bd3?!) 15 ..., Nc6 (15 ..., Kd8; 16 Qg7, Rf8; 17 Qf6 with a powerful White initiative - Euwe) 16 Nxc6!, Bd7 (16 ..., a6?; 17 Qh4!) 17 Nxa7, Rxa7; 18 Bxd7+, Kxd7; 19 Qg7 followed by advancing the h-pawn (Euwe).

c) 10 ..., **Nd7; 11 Rb1**, Nc5; 12 Bd3, dxc3; 13 Nf3, Bd7; 14 Bg5, Bc6; 15 Rb4!? (better than 15 h4? of Yanofsky-Uhlmann, Havana 1966) with an unclear game - Euwe.

d) 10 ..., **Nc6; 11 Nf3, dxc3; 12 Ng5** (12 Rb1!?; 12 Bd3!?) **12 ..., Nxe5!?** (12 ..., Rf8?!; 13 f4, Bd7; 14 Bd3, Qb6; 15 Re1 with some advantage to White: O'Kelly-Pietzsch, 1965 Havana; 12 ..., Qxe5!?; 13 Qxf7+, Kd7 - Korchnoy) 13 f4, Rxg5!? (13 ..., f6!? - Euwe) 14 fxg5, Ng6; 15 Be2 (or 15 h4!? 'F.P.P.') 15 ..., e5; 16 Rf1, Be6; 17 Bb5+, Kd8 with complicated play (Matulovic-Tatai, Venice 1969).

10 ..., Nb8-c6;

Black's alternative here is **10 ..., dxc3; 11 f4** and now:

a) 11 ..., **Nbc6**; 12 Qd3 transposes back.

b) 11 ..., **Bd7**; 12 Nd4!, a6!? (12 ..., Qb6 favoured White in Padevsky-Portisch, Tel Aviv 1964) 13 Qd3, Nbc6; 14 Qxc3, Rc8 (Euwe) is unclear.

c) 11 ..., b6; 12 Ng3!, Nd7; 13 Nh5! should favour White (Ivkov).

11 f2-f4,

Probably best, in view of:

a) 11 Bd2, dxc3; 12 Bxc3, Nxe5; 13 h4, Bd7; 14 Qh6, Ng4; 15 Qd2, e5 (Akopjan-Vaijser, Kiev 1970).

b) 11 Bf4 (11 cxd4?, Nxd4!) 11 .... Bd7; 12 Rb1, dxc3; 13 h4, O-O-O; 14 Qd3, Ng6; 15 Bg5, Ngxe5 (Bakali-Uhlmann, Lugano 1968)

11 ..., Bc8-d7;

59

Of this position, the authors of 'French Poisoned Pawn' have this to say: 'It is difficult to make a final evaluation as to the prospects for either side. The position is a good example of a modern Black system: White is given certain concessions, in this case an extra pawn. In return, Black has the possibility of continuing with his own strategy, which certainly is not restricted to 'equalising'.'

The conscientious reader is also referred to Suetin's pioneering work 'Modern Chess Opening Theory', in particular the section entitled 'Operations on the flanks and play over the whole board in the opening'.

12 Qh7-d3,

White threatens 13 cxd4, attempts to consolidate.

Others:

a) 12 Rb1, O-O-O (Or 12 ..., dxc3; 13 Qd3!, Nf5!? with complications; Soska-Kupka, Czechoslovakia 1967) 13 Qd3, dxc3 14 Nxc3, Na5; 15 Nb5, Bxb5 is unclear (Sherbakov-Krasnov, USSR 1959).

b) 12 g3, dxc3 (12 ..., O-O-O!?) 13 Be3, O-O-O; 14 Qxf7 and now 14 ..., Nf5; 15 Bf2, Rh8 secures the draw ('F.P.P.').

c) 12 h3, dxc3; 13 g4, O-O-O; 14 Qd3, d4 (R.Byrne-Uhlmann, Monte Carlo 1968) and now 15 Ng3!? or 15 Bg2!? but not 15 Rb1?, Nxe5! (Uhlmann).

12 ..., d4xc3; 13 Ne2xc3,

White has many crucial tries here; a brief summary:

a) 13 Qxc3?, Nf5; 14 Rb1, Rc8! ('F.P.P.').

b) 13 Rb1 (maybe best) 13 ..., O-O-O (13 ..., d4 also gives equal chances) 14 Nxc3 (14 Be3?!) 14 ..., Na5! (14 ..., a6?; 15 Qxa6! and wins) 15 Nb5 (or 15 Be3!?) 15 ..., Bxb5; 16 Rxb5 with equal chances (Keres).

c) 13 Ng3, O-O-O; 14 Be2, Nf5 (14 ..., Rg6!?) 15 Nxf5, exf5; 16 O-O, d4; 17 Rb1 (17 Bf3!?) 17 ..., f6 (17 ..., Be6!?) 18 exf6, Rf8; 19 Bf3, Rxf6; 20 Re1, Re6 with an equal position (Ivkov-Sofrevski, Yugoslav Championship 1966).

d) 13 h4, Nf5; 14 h5 (14Rb1!?, d4; 15 h5 - Keres 'Spanisch bis Franzosisch') 14 ..., O-O-O; 15 h6, Rg6!; 16 h7, Rh8 should be no worse for Black (Vasyukov-Doroshkevich, Moscow 1967).

e) 13 Ra2?!, O-O-O! ('F.P.P.')

f) 13 Be3, Nf5 (13 ..., Qa5?!) 14 Bf2, d4!? (14 ..., O-O-O Fuchs-Uhlmann Dresden 1956) 15 Ng3 (15 Nxd4!?) 15 ..., O-O-O; 16 Nxf5 (16 Ne4, Nxe5 'F.P.P.') 16 ..., exf5; 17 Bh4 (17 g3!?) 17 ..., Rde8; 18 Kf2, Rg4 (Cobo-Ivkov, Havana 1963) and now even after the correct 19 Bg3 Black should stand better, on account of 19 ..., Nxe5! (Euwe).

13 ..., a7-a6;

Schwarz suggests the alternative **13 ..., Nf5!?**.

14 Ra1-b1,

White has never done well with **14 g3** or **14 Bd2**.

14 ..., Nc6-a5;

Other difficult lines are **14 ..., Nf5**; 15 g4!?, Rxg4; 16 Bh3, Nxe5!? and **14 ..., Rc8**; 15 h4!, Nf5 (Schmid-del Corral, Lausanne 1963).

15 h2-h4, Ne7-f5; 16 Rh7-h3, O-O-O; 17 h4-h5,

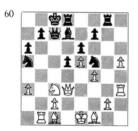

60

This is another critical position which Uhlmann has reached twice. Black's pressure in the centre and queen side should be a match for White's outside passed pawn, but as yet there is no clearer indication that masters believe such positions to favour Black, than that 7 Qg4 has hardly been seen in the last couple of years.

17 ..., Rg8-g4;

In the subsequent game Hort-Uhlmann, Hastings 1970-1, the East German grandmaster selected instead **17 ..., Nc4**, which does not seem an improvement: perhaps an indication of his confidence, that he believed he had more than one adequate plan? Or it may have been an instance of what D.N.Levy, in his book on Gligoric, calls the 'fear of an improvement syndrome'.

The Hort-Uhlmann game continued 18 Rb4, Bc6; 19 Ne2, Bb5; 20 a4, Nxe5; 21 Qc3, Bxe2; 22 fxe5, Bxf1; 23 Qxc7+, Kxc7; 24 Kxf1 a difficult ending that White won in 59 moves.

18 h5-h6?!,

This pawn becomes weaker as it is advanced. Hort intended 18 Qf3!, while another interesting possibility is **18 Rb4** and if then 18 ..., Rh8; 19 g3 (preventing ..., Nh4) 19 ..., Ng7??; 20 Be2. Black must therefore seek queen side play, with an obscure position.

18 ..., Rd8-h8; 19 h6-h7, Rg4-g7; 20 Rb1-b4, Na5-c4;

Black now has some advantage according to the authors of 'French Poisoned Pawn'. It was not possible to play **20 ..., Rxh7??** on account of 21 Rxh7, Rxh7; 22 g4 winning a piece, but the h-pawn cannot long be held.

21 Qd3xf5?!,

A desperate queen sacrifice. He might still have tried **21 g3**, to continue with Be2 and g4, but he would have to reckon with the thematic sacrifice 21 ..., Nxe5?!, or better 21 ..., Qc5! intending ..., Qg1 **21 ..., e6xf5; 22 Nc3xd5, Qc7-a5; 23**

Bf1xc4, Rh8xh7; 24 Rh3-c3, Rh7-h1+; 25 Bc4-f1+, Kc8-d8; 26 Nd5-b6, Bd7-b5; 27 Nb6-c4, Bb5xc4; 28 Rc3xc4, Rg7xg2;

Uhlmann exploits another pin neatly.

29 Bc1-e3, Qa5xa3; 30 Be3-b6+, Kd8-e7, White Resigns.

PIRC DEFENCE   (1 e4, g6 or 1 ..., d6)

Game 31
Penrose - Perkins
(British Championship 1972)

1 e2-e4, g7-g6;

Although the system arising in this game could be brought about after **1 ..., d6**; 2 d4, g6; 3 c3, Bg7 etc., Black can avoid it by the more strictly Pirc move-order (1 ..., d6; 2 d4) **2 ..., Nf6** forcing White to defend his e-pawn. Then after 3 Nc3, g6; 4 f4 (Of course there are other moves) 4 ..., Bg7; 5 Nf3, c5!?; 6 e5!? Botterill and Keene, in their book 'The Pirc Defence', recommend 6 ..., Nfd7; 7 exd6, O-O, an interesting and barely tested pawn sacrifice, leading to great complications after **8 dxc5**, Qa5!? or **8 dxe7**, Qxe7+ (8 ..., Re8!?) 9 Qe2! (Eley-Adorjan, Canterbury 1973) 9 ..., Qd6!? (Botterill).

2 d2-d4, Bf8-g7; 3 c2-c3,

White wants to play f4 but fears the good reply 3 ..., c5= He can also play **3 c4** or **3 Nc3** or **3 h4?!** with different intentions.

3 ..., d7-d6; 4 f2-f4,

The Geller Quiet System, characterised by **4 Nf3**, Nf6; 5 Nbd2 and the subsequent Be2 or Bd3 presents Black with relatively few problems.

4 ..., Ng8-f6;

The most reliable move, although also available are **4 ..., c6!?**, **4 ..., Nd7?!** (Hubner-Suttles, Palma 1970) and **4 ..., e5?!** (Portisch-Suttles, Siegen 1970) and **4 ..., c5**; 5 dxc5, Nf6!?; 6 cxd6, exd6; 7 e5, dxe5; 8 Qxd8+, Kxd8; 9 fxe5, Re8; 10 Nf3 (Stein-Suttles, Sousse 1967). Black is rather optimistic in hoping that this pawn sacrifice might be sound.

5 Bf1-d3,

Here 5 e5 is a critical alternative, but Black's resources are good, e.g. **5 ..., dxe5** (5 ..., Nd5 is also possible) 6 fxe5, Nd5; 7 Nf3, O-O; 8 Bc4, c5!; 9 dxc5 (If anything 9 Qb3, Nb6 and 9 O-O, cxd4 are worse for him) 9 ..., Be6; 10 Na3!? (10 Ng5, Nc6! or 10 O-O, Qc7 or 10 Bxd5, Qxd5 or 10 Qd4, Nc6 all good for Black) 10 ..., Nc6; 11 Qe2 (R.Byrne-Botterill, Hastings 1971-2) and now best is 11 ..., Qb8! assuring Black a slight advantage (Botterill).

5 ..., e7-e5;

The only good move; White's centre must be challenged.

6 Ng1-f3,

The main alternative is **6 Ne2** (If 6 fxe5, dxe5; 7 dxe5, Ng4-) 6 ..., O-O; 7 O-O and now Black can try 7 ..., c6, 7 ..., exf4 or 7 ..., exd4!?; 8 cxd4, Nc6; 9 Nbc3, Bg4 (Botterill and Keene, 'The Modern Defence')

6 ..., O-O!?;

Perkins finds an original tactical solution to the problems of Black's position, since he is not satisfied with the **6 ..., exf4** of R.Byrne-Donner, San Juan 1969.

7 d4xe5,

Penrose tries to refute the gambit, but the quieter **7 fxe5,** dxe5; 8 Nxe5, Nxe4!; 9 O-O!, Nd6 (intending ..., Bf5) or simply **7 O-O,** also should come into consideration. Then, instead of (7 O-O) 7 ..., exf4, returning to Byrne-Donner, or 7 ..., Nc6; 8 fxe5, dxe5; 9 d5, Ne7; 10 Nxe5 (Botterill and Keene), Perkins intended to play **7 ..., Nbd7** when Black stands, in his opinion, very well. There might occur the sharp interchange 8 fxe5, dxe5; 9 dxe5?! (9 d5, Nc5 or 9 Bg5, h6) 9 ..., Ng4; 10 e6, fxe6; 11 Nd4, Qh4!; 12 h3, Nf2; 13 Qe2, N7e5 with a promising attack for Black (analysis).

7 ..., d6xe5; 8 Nf3xe5, Nb8-a6!;

The White Ne5 is to be a target soon: not **8 ..., Nbd7**; 9 Nxd7, Qxd7 (intending ..., Rd8) because of 10 e5!

61

9 Bc1-e3?!,

The critical test of the whole line must be **9 Qe2!?** which overprotects the e-pawn and leaves the position quite obscure after **9 ..., Nc5** (9 ..., Qe7!?) 10 Bc2, b6 (Botterill).

9 ..., Qd8-e7; 10 O-O, Na6-c5;

Black wins the first skirmish, since this strong knight must be exchanged.

11 Be3xc5, Qe7xc5+; 12 Kg1-h1, Nf6-h5;

Threatening 13 ..., Nxf4 as the White knight is exposed.

13 Ne5-c4, Bc8-e6; 14 Nb1-d2, Ra8-d8; 15 Qd1-c2!?,

White's position is already difficult. He could here play **15 Qe2** which prevents Black's combination in the game by controlling h5, and so threatens 16 Nb3. However Black might then play 15 ..., Bg4!; 16 Qxg4, Rxd3; 17 Qe2 (If 17 Rad1, b5; 18 Na3, b4; 19 cxb4, Qxb4; 20 Qe2, Rfd8 and b2 falls) 17 ..., Rfd8; 18 a4 (Not 18 Rf3?, Rxf3; 19 Qxf3, b5, while 18 b4 is possible but weakens the queen side pawns considerably) 18 ..., Bh6 with advantage to Black since 19 g3? allows 19 ..., Rxg3! (analysis).

15 ..., b7-b5; 16 Nd2-b3?,

This is prettily refuted. Other weak moves are **16 Ne5, Nxf4** or **16 b4,** Qc6; 17 Ne5, Bxe5; 18 fxe5, Qd7; 19 Rf3, Bg4; 20 e6, fxe6; 21 Rxf8+, Kxf8; 22 h3, Bxh3 or **16 Na3,** Qd6; 17 Rf3, Bg4; 18 Nb5, Qd7; 19 Re3, Nxf4 (Perkins in 'Chess').

However Perkins points out that White's best move **16 Na5!** (with the threat of Nb7) is not so easy to refute. Black's best is probably 16 ...,Qd6!; 17 Rf3, Qb6!

to meet either 18 b4 or 18 N5b3 by 18 ..., Bg4; 19 Rf1, Qd6 winning the f-pawn. White can still play on, though, by 18 f5!, Qxa5; 19 fxe6, fxe6 with about equal chances (Botterill).

62

16 ..., Nh5-g3+!;

A resource which Penrose had overlooked. Now he must lose a piece, but decided not to resign yet since Black was already running short of time.

17 h2xg3, Qc5-h5+; 18 Kh1-g1, b5xc4; 19 Bd3-e2, c4xb3; 20 a2xb3, Be6xb3!; 21 Be2xh5, Bb3xc2; 22 Bh5-f3, a7-a6; 23 Rf1-f2,

Not **23 Rxa6?**, Bb5.

White is of course quite lost.

23 ..., Bc2-d3; 24 Ra1-a5, Rd8-b8; 25 e4-e5,

Perkins suggested **25 Rc5!?**, Re8; 26 e5, Re7; 27 g4 trying to embarrass the bishop.

25 ..., Rb8-b5; 26 Ra5-a4,

If **26 Rxa6** there is 26 ..., Rxb2 or 26 ..., Rxe5.

26 ..., c7-c5;

Intending ..., c4 and ..., Rfb8; a good plan.

27 c2-c4, Rb5-b4; 28 Ra4xb4, c5xb4; 29 b2-b3,

Hoping to be allowed g4 and Rd2 with perpetual attack on the bishop.

29 ..., Bd3-f5; 30 Rf2-d2, Rf8-b8; 31 g3-g4, Bf5-e6; 32 Rd2-d6, Be6xc4?;

The game ceases to follow its logical course now; the correct technical continuation was **32 ..., Bf8!**; 33 Rxa6, Rd8.

33 b3xc4, b4-b3; 34 Bf3-e4, b3-b2; 35 Be4-b1, Bg7-f8; 36 Rd6-d1,

If **36 Rxa6**, Rd8 wins. Black still stands better; here or next move he should bring his rook around to a1 via b4.

36 ..., a7-a5; 37 Kg1-f2, a5-a4?; 38 Bb1-a2, Bf8-c5+; 39 Kf2-f3, Kg8-f8; 40 Kf3-e4, Kf8-e7;

Here Black contemplated the ravages created by his time trouble errors and offered the draw. After **41 f5**, a3 this would be certain, but Penrose declined and sealed what he thought was a non-committal move ...

41 Rd1-d5?,

But is actually a terrible blunder ...

63

41 ..., Rb8-b3!;
Black is winning again!

42 Rd5xc5, Rb3-a3; 43 Ba2-b1,
Ra3-a1; 44 Ke4-d3,

It is worse to move the bishop,
allowing ..., a3.

44 ..., Ra1xb1; 45 Kd3-c2, Rb1-g1;
46 Kc2xb2, Rg1xg2+; 47 Kb2-a3,
Rg2xg4; 48 Rc5-c7+, Ke7-e8;
49 e5-e6,

Best, since if 49 Kxa4, Rxf4;
50 Kb5, Re4.

49 ..., Rg4xf4; 50 Rc7-c8+, Ke8-e7
51 e6xf7, Ke7xf7;
52 Ka3xa4, h7-h5;

Here or on the next move 52
...,g5! makes the win simpler, since
that pawn now stands in the way of
the king. Black is going to give up
his rook for the White pawn and
should advance his own pawns
together.

53 Ka4-b5, h5-h4?!; 54 c4-c5,
Rf4-f1; 55 c5-c6, Rf1-c1; 56 Rc8-h8
g7-g5; 57 c6-c7, Rc1xc7; 58 Rh8-
h7+, Kf7-g6; 59 Rh7xc7, g5-g4;

Not 59 ..., h3?; 60 Rc8, g4; 61
Rh8, Kf5; 62 Kc4- (Perkins).

60 Rc7-c8!, g4-g3; 61 Rc8-g8+,
Kg6-f5; 62 Kb5-c4, Kf5-f4?;

Only now does the win
disappear! Penrose gave in 'Chess'
the winning line 62 ..., Ke4!; 63
Rg4+, Kf3; 64 Rxh4, g2; 65 Rh3+,
Kf4; 66 Rh4+, Kf5; 67 Rh5+, Kf6;
68 Rh6+, Kg7!

63 Kc4-d4, Kf4-f3;

Or 63 ..., h3; 64 Rf8+, Kg4; 65
Ke4, h2; 66 Rg8+, Kh3; 67 Kf4=
(Penrose).

64 Rg8-f8+, Kf3-g2;

Or 64 ..., Ke2; 65 Re8+, Kd2;
66 Rg8= (Penrose).

65 Kd4-e3, h4-h3;

Events now move by force to
their droll conclusion.

66 Rf8-h8, Kg2-h2;

Or 66 ..., h2; 67 Kf4, Kf2; 68
Rh3.

67 Rh8-g8, g3-g2; 68 Ke3-f2,
Kh2-h1; 69 Rg8-g7, h3-h2;
70 Rg7xg2 Stalemate!

MISCELLANEOUS

A few other counter-gambit possibilities in the half-open games
deserve brief consideration.

SCANDINAVIAN DEFENCE

After 1 e4, d5; 2 exd5, Nf6 White can try to hold on to his pawn, but
masters usually do not, preferring 3 c4 (see Game 29) or 3 d4. However the
following possibilities should be noted:a) 3 c4, c6!; 4 dxc6?! (Instead of 4
d4) 4 ..., Nxc6; 5 d3, e5; 6 Nc3 (6 Nf3, e4) 6 ..., Bf5 (6 ..., Bc5?!) 7 Nf3, Bb4
(7 ..., e4?! or 7 ..., Qd7; 8 Be2, Rd8 - 8 ..., O-O-O!? - 9 O-O, Bxd3; 10
Bxd3, Qxd3; 11 Qa4! are better for White) 8 Be2, e4; 9 Nh4 (Or 9 dxe4,

Qd1+; 10 Kxd1, Nxe4 with an initiative for Black) 9 ..., Be6; 10 O-O, exd3; 11 Bxd3, Bxc3; 12 bxc3, Ne5; 13 Be2, Qxd1; 14 Rxd1, Rc8 and Black wins his pawn back with a good game (Boleslavsky).

b) 3 Bb5+, Bd7 (Here 3 ..., c6 is not good, but Wade suggests 3 ..., Nbd7! to answer 4 c4 by 4 ..., g6; If White captures on d7 there will be a lasting weakness on g2) **4 Bc4, Bg4** (4 ..., c6 is still dubious, but Bronstein's 4 ..., b5 may be satisfactory) **5 f3, Bf5; 6 Nc3** (If 6 g4 Boleslavsky recommends 6 ..., Bc8!; 7 Nc3, c6 while 6 Ne2 simply returns the pawn) **6 ..., Nbd7; 7 Qe2** (If 7 g4, Nb6; 8 Qe2, Bc8; 9 Qd3 Black can play 9 ..., g6 following Aronin-Shamkovich, USSR 1960 or Gawlikowski's 9 ..., Nxc4; 10 Qxc4, e6; 11 dxe6, Bxe6; 7 Nge2, Nb6 is also fairly innocuous) **7 ..., Nb6; 8 Bb3, Qd7; 9 d6!** (Or 9 d3, Nbxd5=) and according to Boleslavsky White stands better, e.g. 9 ..., cxd6; 10 a4, a5; 11 d3, Be6 (11 ..., d5; 12 Qe5, e6; 13 Nb5, Rc8; 14 Bd2) 12 Bxe6, Qxe6; 13 Qxe6, fxe6; 14 Nb5, Kd7; 15 c4! If Black cannot find an improvement in this line, he still has the recommendations on moves 3 and 4 (although the immediate 3 Bc4 avoids the former).

ALEKHINE'S DEFENCE

After **1 e4, Nf6; 2 e5, Nd5; 3 d4, d6; 4 c4, Nb6; 5 f4** some Cambridge players experimented for a time with Planinc's **5 ..., g5?!**. However it is unsound: **6 exd6** (also good are 6 Nf3 and 6 Qh5 according to Eales and Williams in their book 'Alekhine's Defence') **6 ..., gxf4** (Or 6 ..., Qxd6; 7 c5, Qe6+; 8 Qe2) 7 dxc7, Qxc7; 8 Nc3, e5; 9 dxe5, Nc6; 10 Bxf4, Be6; 11 Ne4, Bb4+; 12 Kf2 with a winning position for White (Tringov-Planinc, Varna 1970).

QUEEN'S FIANCHETTO DEFENCE

The irregular defence **1 e4, b6** has occasionally been played, the intention being to initiate complications in the event of **2 d4, Bb7; 3 Bd3?!** (Better 3 f3 or 3 Nc3 reaching a favourable French or Pirc, according to Black's reaction) by **3 ..., f5!?** Play can then go **4 exf5, Bxg2; 5 Qh5+, g6; 6 fxg6, Bg7** (Not 6 ..., Nf6??; 7 gxh7+, Nxh5; 8 Bg6 mate!) **7 gxh7+, Kf8; 8 hxg8(Q)+, Kxg8; 9 Qg4, Bxh1; 10 h4.**

Two examples are available from recent Soviet praxis:

a) 10 ..., Bd5?!; 11 h5, Be6!; 12 Qg2, Rxh4; 13 Qxa8, Bd5 with complications that probably favour White (Schmit-Vitolinsh, Latvian Championship 1969).

b) 10 ..., Qf8!; 11 h5, Qf6; 12 h6, Rxh6! (If 12 ..., Qxd4; 13 Qxg7+ White should be better, having two pieces against a rook - D.Levy) 13 Bxh6, Qxh6; 14 Nd2, Bd5; 15 O-O-O, Nc6! and the chances are balanced. The game Gendlek-Radchenko (USSR 1970) continued drastically: 16 Ngf3, Rf8; 17 Nh4? (Levy recommended 17 Kb1 e.g. 17 ..., Rf4; 18 Qg3, Nxd4; 19 Nxd4, Rxd4; 20 Qxc7 with an obscure position) 17 ..., Be6; 18 Qg3, Rf4; 19 Nhf3, Bg4; 20 Be2, Bxf3; 21 Bxf3, Nxd4; 22 Kb1, Nxf3; 23 Resigns, for if 23 Nxf3, Qf6.

An analogous possibility, arising from an unusual idea (tried by Spassky in the 1966 World Championship!) in the queen's pawn opening, should also be noted: **1 d4, b5?!; 2 e4?!, Bb7!; 3 Bxb5, f5!?** (Since if 3 ..., Bxe4; 4 Nf3 followed by O-O and Nc3 with the initiative to White) 4 exf5, Bxg2; 5 Qh5+, g6; 6 fxg6, Bg7! (Not 6 ..., Nf6; 7 g7+, Nxh5; 8 gxh8(Q), Bxh1; 9 Qxh7 and wins) 7 gxh7+ etc. as in Gendlek-Radchenko. White has a pawn more here, but his bishop is misplaced on b5 so Black would vary on move 15 by ..., Qb6; 16 Bd3, Na6 (or 16 ..., Nc6!?) with attacking chances down the b-file (analysis). Pachman, in 'Queen's Gambit and other Close Games' gives **3 Bd3** and claims that 3 ..., f5 is now incorrect (citing an exhibition game Flohr-Prins, Amsterdam 1933), but in view of the Radchenko game this opinion must be held in question. However one might also respect the judgement of Kushnir in rejecting these frolics in favour of **3 f3**, versus Kurajica at Wijk aan Zee 1973. Probably still better is 2 c3! when White is playing, with an useful extra tempo, the favourable Out-Flank (since White intends 3 a4!) Defence to the Sokolsky Opening.

4   COUNTERS TO THE QUEEN'S GAMBIT

There are several sharp counter-gambits that can arise after the opening 1 d4, d5; 2 c4. However their soundness is not easy to establish ...

ALBIN COUNTER-GAMBIT (1 d4,d5; 2 c4, e5)

This rather optimistic doppelganger to the Queen's Gambit is not so fearsome as his first cousin the Falkbeer on the other side of the board. Black's king is even more exposed than that of his opponent, while it is also hard to demonstrate that the white pawn on c4 is weak. Nonetheless it has had a fair run for its money, having been tried by many tacticians eager to avoid the slow positional manoeuvring of the Orthodox and Slav Defences. Two illustrative games will be given.

Game 32
Malich - Muller
(21 st East German
Championship 1972)

1 d2-d4, d7-d5;

The Englund Gambit, **1 ..., e5?!** is an inferior form of the Albin or Budapest gambits. After 2 dxe5, Nc6; 3 Nf3 (If 3 f4, f6 gives Black chances) 3 ..., Qe7; 4 Bf4! (Also good is Spielmann's 4 Qd5) 4 ..., Qb4+ (Or 4 ..., f6; 5 exf6, Nxf6; - 5 ..., Qxf6; 6 Qc1 - 6 Nc3, d5!; 7 e3 and Black is without adequate compensation) 5 Bd2, Qxb2; 6 Nc3! (Not 6 Bc3?, Bb4!) and White has a clear advantage, e.g. 6 ..., Bb4; 7 Rb1, Qa3; 8 Rb3, Qa5; 9 a3!, Bxc3; 10 Bxc3, Qc5; 11 e4 (Pachman).

2 c2-c4, e7-e5;

The alternatives **2 ..., dxc4, 2 ..., c6** and **2 ..., e6** will be considered in subsequent sections of this chapter.

3 d4xe5, d5-d4; 4 Ng1-f3,

This natural move, guarding

White's advanced pawn and attacking Black's, is almost invariably seen at this point. **4 a3** is playable, but unlikely to lead to original lines (4 ..., Nc6; 5 e3, a5! and 6 ..., Bc5 - Euwe). The chief alternative is **4 e4** e.g. **4 ..., Nc6;** 5 f4, **g5;** 6 f5!, Nxe5; 7 Nf3, Bb4+; 8 Kf2!, Ng4+; 9 Kg1, Bc5; 10 b4! with a positional advantage to White (Spassky). However Black has better in **5 ..., f6** e.g.:

a) 6 exf6, Nxf6; 7 Bd3, Bb4+; 8 Nd2, O-O; 9 Nf3, Qe7; 10 O-O, Ng4; 11 a3, Ne3 with a difficult struggle; White, the stronger player, won in 43 moves after Black committed an elaborate hari-kiri (Vasyukov-Gusev, Moscow 1959).

b) 6 Nf3, fxe5; **7 Bd3** (Or 7 f5, Bb4+; 8 Kf2, Nf6; 9 Bd3, g6; 10 a3, gxf5!; 11 axb4, fxe4; 12 Re1, exf3! and Black won quickly in Szilagyi-Forintos, Budapest 1964) 7 ..., Bb4+ (Or 7 ..., Bg4; 8 O-O, Nge7 Euwe) 8 Nbd2, exf4; 9 O-O, Nf6; 10 Nb3, O-O; 11 c5, Qe7; 12

Qc2, Nd7 and the sharp play led eventually to a draw in Spassky-Lutikov, USSR 1963.

4 ..., Nb8-c6;

64

5 a2-a3,

According to Pachman, this move is the most troublesome for Black to meet. **5 Nbd2** will be examined in the next game.

The other move that has been occasionally seen is **5 g3** (In addition, there is Fine's innocuous suggestion 5 Bf4) and now:

a) 5 ..., Bc5; 6 Bf4, Nge7; 7 Bg2, Ng6; 8 Nbd2, f6; 9 exf6, Nxf4; 10 f7+, Kxf7; 11 gxf4, h6; 12 Nb3!, Qd6; 13 Ne5+! to White's advantage (Sterk-Adams, Ventnor City 1943).

b) 5 ..., Bg4; 6 Bg2 (6 Nbd2 see game, note to White's 6th move) 6 ..., Qd7; 7 h3 (Also after 7 O-O Black failed to equalise with any of: 7 ..., h5!? Sokolsky-Simagin, Soviet Championship 1953; 7 ..., Nge7; 8 b4!, Nxb4; 9 e6! Tolush-Horne, Hastings 1953-4; 7 ..., O-O-O; 8 Qb3!, Bh3; 9 e6! Spassky-Forintos, Sochi 1964) 7 ..., Bf5; 8 a3, O-O-O; 9 Nbd2, f6; 10 Qa4, Kb8; 11 Nh4 with the better position for White (Simagin-Gereben, 1949).

c) 5 ..., Be6; 6 Nbd2, Qd7; 7 Bg2,

O-O-O; 8 O-O, Nge7 (8 ..., f6! 'Teorijski Bilten') 9 Qa4, a6; 10 b4 and White has an attack (Gligoric-Leban, Novi Sad 1965)

d) 5 ..., Bf5; 6 a3?! (Better to proceed as in **c**) 6 ..., Qd7; 7 Bg2, O-O-O; 8 O-O, Bh3; 9 b4, h5; 10 b5, Nce7; 11 e6, Bxe6; 12 Qa4, Kb8; 13 Ne5, Qc8; 14 c5, f6; 15 b6, a6 and Black's resources are more than adequate (Solochina-Borisenko, Sverdlovsk 1958).

5 ..., Bc8-g4;

The most usual move, but maybe not the best:

a) 5 ..., Be6; 6 Nbd2 (6 e3?, dxe3; 7 Qxd8+, Rxd8; 8 Bxe3, Nge7!; 9 Bf4? - better Euwe's 9 Nc3 - 9 ..., Ng6; 10 Bg3, h5 Simonson-Opocensky, Folkestone 1933) 6 ..., Qd7; 7 g3 see next game, note **a** to Black's 5th move.

b) 5 ..., Nge7; 6 Nbd2, Be6; 7 b4, Ng6; 8 Bb2, Ngxe5; 9 b5, Nxf3+; 10 exf3, Na5; 11 Bd3 and White stands very well (Bogolyubov)

c) 5 ..., a5 (recommended by Euwe):

c1) 6 Bf4, f6; 7 exf6, Nxf6 and now Euwe recommends 8 g3, 9 Bg2, 10 O-O.

c2) 6 Nbd2, Bg4 (Probably superior to 6 ..., Be6 of Ekstrom-Mieses, Hastings 1945-6) 7 g3 (7 h3?, Be6!) 7 ..., Bc5; 8 Bg2, Nge7; 9 h3, Be6!; 10 O-O, h6; 11 Ne4, Ba7; 12 Qd3, Ng6; 13 Bf4, Qe7!; 14 Kh2, Rad8; 15 Qb3, Bc8 with good play for Black (Toth-Balogh, Budapest Championship 1964).

c3) 6 h3 (6 e3 and Ulvestad's 6 Qd3 have also been tried) 6 ..., Bc5; 7 Bg5, Nge7; 8 Nbd2, h6; 9 Bh4, Be6; 10 Rc1, a4; 11 g4, Qd7; 12 Bg2, Ng6; 13 Bg3, h5 and Black got the upper hand, but was outplayed in complications (Janowsky-Tarrasch, Monte Carlo 1902).

d) 5 ..., f6; 6 exf6, Qxf6; 7 g3, Bf5; 8 Bg2, h6; 9 O-O, O-O-O; 10 Nbd2, g5; 11 Ra2, h5; 12 b4, h4; 13 b5 (Lundholm-Rojahn, Sweden-Norway 1948) and now after 13 ..., Nce7 followed by ..., Kb8 and ..., Nc8 the editor of the Swedish booklet 'Albins Motgambit' considers Black's game to be playable. However he comes under heavy pressure in the line 14 Qa4, Kb8; 15 c5!, Nc8; 16 Nc4 (threatening Bxg5) 16 ..., Rh5; 17 c6, Nb6; 18 Nxb6, cxb6; 19 Ne1, hxg3; 20 fxg3, Qe6; 21 Rc2!, e.g. 21 ..., Bxc2; 22 Qxc2, Rc8?; 23 cxb7!, Rxc2; 24 Rxf8+ and wins (analysis).

6 Nb1-d2,

The main alternative here is **6 b4** e.g. 6 ..., Qe7!; 7 Qa4, O-O-O; 8 Bf4, Bxf3; 9 gxf3, Kb8; 10 Nd2, Nxe5; 11 Qb3 (Petrosian-Porreca, Belgrade 1954) and now Euwe recommends 11 ..., Nf6 followed by ..., Nh5.

6 ..., Qd8-e7;

Here Black could also try **6 ..., a5** (6 ..., f6?; 7 exf6, Nxf6; 8 Nb3! Samisch-Becker, Mittweida 1927) with transposition into note **c2**, above, to Black's 5th move. It is probably more precise to play it on this move, and one may then consider this one of the critical lines of the Albin. Until the next White improvement is found, Black may be all right.

7 h2-h3, Bg4xf3;

The possibility **7 ..., Bh5!?**, mentioned by Lilienthal in 'Schachmaty' is apparently quite unexplored.

8 Nd2xf3, O-O-O; 9 g2-g3!?,

The usual move here is **9 Qd3** e.g.:

a) 9 ..., Nxe5; 10 Qf5+, Nd7; 11 Nxd4, g6 (Lilienthal-Hildebrand, Uppsala 1964) and now according to Euwe 12 Qc2 would have maintained White's advantage.

b) 9 ..., h6; 10 g3, g6; 11 Bg2, Bg7; 12 O-O, Nxe5; 13 Nxe5, Bxe5; 14 b4, f5; 15 c5 with good attacking chances to White, who won in 35 moves (Lasker-Alekhine, 1914 St. Petersburg).

9 ..., Nc6xe5; 10 Nf3xe5, Qe7xe5; 11 Qd1-d3, f7-f5; 12 Bf1-g2, Ng8-f6 13 O-O, g7-g6?!

After this rather passive move, White is able to make use of his two bishops and queen side pawns to launch an attack. Black should therefore have preferred **13 ..., h6** Continuing the fight for the f4 sq.

14 b2-b4, Bf8-g7; 15 c4-c5, Rh8-e8; 16 Rf1-e1,

65

Black appears to have a strong centralised position, whereas White as yet is disorganised. However his inability to bring a pawn lever against White's position entails virtual impotence.

16 ..., Nf6-e4;

This looks impressive, but

what good does it actually do? He might have considered **16 ..., Nd5** and 17 ..., f4 whereon White is more or less forced to accept the sacrifice by 18 Bxd5 and 19 Bxf4, but at the cost of White square weaknesses near his king and another half-open file for Black.

Lilienthal only considers the line **16 ..., c6?**; 17 Bxc6!, bxc6; 18 Qa6+, Kd7; 19 Bf4, Qe7; 20 Bd6!, Qf7; 21 b5, cxb5 (21 ..., Ke6; 22 bxc6!) 22 Qxb5+, Ke6; 23 Qc4+, Nd5; 24 e4, dxe3; 25 Rxe3+, Kf6; 26 Qd4+, Kg5; 27 Qh4 mate.

17 Bc1-f4, Qe5-e6; 18 c5-c6!, b7xc6; 19 Ra1-c1, Kc8-b7;

Black is anyway in grave danger. Lilienthal analyses:
a) 19 ..., Kb8 (19 ..., Kd7; 20 b5 followed by catching the king in the centre by 21 f3 etc.) 20 Rc5!, Nxc5; 21 bxc5, Rd5; 22 Qa6 etc.
b) 19 ..., Nc3; 20 Bf3, Kb8; 21 Qa6 with threats of Bxc6 and b5.

20 b4-b5!, c6-c5; 21 Rc1xc5, Rd8-d7; 22 Qd3-c2, Re8-e7; 23 Re1-c1, Qe6-f7;

23 ..., Qb6 would have offered a somewhat longer resistance.

24 Qc2-a4, Kb7-b8; 25 b5-b6!, Black resigns.

If 25 ..., axb6; 26 Ra5!, bxa5; 27 Qb5+, Ka7 (27 ..., Kc8; 28 Qa6+, Kd8; 29 Qa8 mate) 28 Qxa5+, Kb7; 29 Rb1+, Kc6; 30 Qb5 mate.

Game 33
Toth - Balogh
(Correspondence 1943-4)

1 d2-d4, d7-d5; 2 c2-c4, e7-e5; 3 d4xe5,

There is no good way to decline the gambit, e.g. **3· e3**, exd4; 4 Qxd4/exd4, Nf6 or 3 **cxd5**, Qxd5; 4 Nc3, Qxd4; 5 Qxd4, exd4; 6 Nb5, Bb4+; 7 Bd2, Bxb2+; 8 Kxd2, Kd8 (Pachman).

3 ..., d5-d4; 4 Ng1-f3, Nb8-c6; 5 Nb1-d2, Bc8-g4;

The most reliable move, which seems to guarantee equality. Others:

a) 5 ..., Be6; 6 g3 (6 a3 is also good) 6 ..., Qd7 (6 ..., Bb4; 7 Bg2!, Bxc4; 8 O-O, and White has the two bishops or else the win of the d-pawn in hand) 7 a3 (Or 7 Bg2 as in Pirc-Kostic, Zagreb 1947) 7 ..., Nge7; 8 Qa4, Ng6; 9 Bg2, Be7; 10 O-O, O-O; 11 b4, Rad8; 12 Bb2, b6; 13 Rac1, a5; 14 b5, Nxe5; 15 Bxd4 and White keeps his gambit pawn (Spielmann-Kostic, Bled 1931).

b) 5 ..., Bb4; 6 a3 (Or 6 g3) 6 ..., Bxd2+; 7 Bxd2, Bg4; 8 Qb3, Nge7; 9 g3, d3 (If 9 ..., O-O Grunfeld gave 10 Bg2, Rb8; 11 O-O, Ng6; 12 h3, Bxf3; 13 exf3, Nxe5; 14 f4, Nd7; 15 Qd1 with advantage to White) 10 h3, Bxf3; 11 exf3, Nxe5; 12 Bg2, N7c6 (Bernhardt-Haller, correspondence 1912-13) and now Euwe says that White stands well after 13 O-O with f4 to follow.

c) 5 ..., f6; 6 exf6, Qxf6 (6 ..., Nxf6?; 7 a3, Bg4; 8 h3) 7 g3, Bg4 (Pachman prefers this to the usual 7 ..., Bf5; 8 Bg2, O-O-O; 9 Nh4! or 8 ..., Nb4; 9 O-O which favour White according to old analyses) 8 Bg2, O-O-O (8 ..., d3?! looked unsound in Anzin-Fodor, Hungary 1961) 9 O-O, Nge7; 10 Qb3 (Or 10 h3! Euwe) 10 ..., Ng6; 11 a4, Bb4; 12 a5!, Bxa5; 13 Qa4, Rhe8! with complications (Emmrich-Moritz, Oeynhausen 1922).

d) 5 ..., Bf5 and **5 ..., Qe7** also come into consideration.

6 h2-h3,

Here **6 a3!?** would transpose into the previous game. Others:

a) 6 g3! (Currently seems White's most promising line against the Albin):

a1) 6 ..., Qd7; 7 Bg2, O-O-O; 8 h3, Bf5; 9 a3, f6 (If 9 ..., Nge7; 10 b4, Ng6; 11 Bb2!, d3; 12 e3 'Albins Motgambit') 10 exf6, Nxf6; 11 b4, Re8 (11 ..., Ne4; 12 Nxe4, Bxe4; 13 O-O) 12 Bb2!, Bd3; 13 O-O!, Bxe2; 14 Qa4, Bxf1; 15 Rxf1, Kb8; 16 b5, Nd8; 17 Nxd4 and White's thematic attack means more than the exchange, e.g. 18 ..., Bxd4; 19 Bxd4, b6 (19 ..., a6; 20 Qa5!) 20 c5, Re7; 21 cxb6, cxb6; 22 Bxb6, axb6; 23 Qa8+, Kc7; 24 Qa7+, Kd6; 25 Rd1+, Ke5; 26 Rxd7, Nxd7; 27 Qc7+, Ke6; 28 Nd4+, Kf7; 29 Nf5, Re1+; 30 Kh2, Rd1; 31 Qc2, Resigns (Bondarevsky-Mikenas, 17 USSR Championship 1950).

a2) 6 ..., f6; 7 exf6, Qxf6; 8 Bg2, O-O-O; 9 h3, Bh5; 10 O-O, and according to Hans Muller's analysis Black is without compensation for his sacrificed material: 10 ..., d3?!; 11 exd3, Rxd3; 12 g4, Bg6; 13 Qa4!, Bb4; 14 a3, Bxd2; 15 Nxd2.

b) 6 Qb3, Nge7; 7 h3, Bf5; 8 a3, Rb8; 9 g4, Bg6; 10 e4, h5; 11 g5, h4; 12 Qd3, Bh5; 13 b4, Ng6 unclear, eventually drawn in Ivanov-Tarasevich, USSR 1965.

6 ..., Bg4xf3;

Inferior is **6 ..., Bh5**; 7 a3 (or 7 g3 Pachman) 7 ..., Qe7; 8 Qa4! (Balogh), but Black might try **6 ..., Be6!?**; 7 g3, Qd7.

7 Nd2xf3, Bf8-b4+!;

The pre-war treatise Collijn's

'Larobok' gave a line against **7 ..., Bc5**, viz. 8 a3, a5; 9 g3, Nge7; 10 Bg2, Ng6; 11 O-O, Rb8; 12 Qc2, Qe7; 13 Bd2, while if 12 ..., Ngxe5; 13 Nxe5, Nxe5; 14 b4! (Euwe).

8 Bc1-d2, Qd8-e7!;

66

9 a2-a3,

After **9 Bxb4**, Qxb4+; 10 Qd2, Qxd2+; 11 Kxd2, Nge7! there comes:

a) 12 e3?, O-O-O!; 13 exd4, Nxd4; 14 Nxd4, Rxd4+ better for Black.

b) 12 e4, dxe3+; 13 Kxe3, Ng6 and now either:

b1) 14 e6 (Szabo-Krenosz, Budapest 1939) 14 ..., O-O!; 15 exf7+, Rxf7 and Black stands better (all sources).

b2) 14 Bd3!, Nxe5; 15 Nxe5, Nxe5; 16 f4, Nxd3; 17 Kxd3, O-O-O+; 18 Kc3, Rd7; 19 Rad1, Rxd1; 20 Rxd1, Re8 (Fuster-Balogh, correspondence 1944).

9 ..., Bb4xd2+; 10 Qd1xd2, O-O-O; 11 O-O-O,

If **11 Qf4** Black gets a positional plus by 11 ..., f6!; 12 exf6, Nxf6.

11 ..., Nc6xe5; 12 Nf3xe5,

Not **12 Nxd4**, Nxc4; 13 Qc3, Nd6 with attacking chances.

12 ..., Qe7xe5; 13 e2-e3, c7-c5; 14 e3xd4,

Avoiding the trap **14 Qa5,
Ne7; 15 Qxa7?, Nc6!**

14 ..., Rd8xd4; 15 Bf1-d3, Ng8-e7;

To cover f5, and so make his
17th move possible. However **15 ...,
Nf6** also seems to be perfectly
playable.

**16 Rh1-e1, Qe5-d6;
17 Qd2-g5, Rd4xd3;**

With the knight on f6, Black
could play here **17 ..., g6** (not then
17 ..., Rxd3?; 18 Qf5+) and leave
some life in the position (18 Qe5,
Re8!).

18 Rd1xd3, Qd6xd3; 19 Qg5xe7,

Qd3xc4+; 20 Kc1-b1,

Now White has just a little
pressure himself.

**20 ..., Qc4-f4; 21 Qe7xc5+, Kc8-b8
22 g2-g3,**

Pachman gives the possible
line: **22 Re7, Rc8; 23 Qb5, b6; 24
g3, Qd4; 25 Rxf7, Qe4+; 26 Ka2,
Rc1!; 27 Rf8+ (27 Rxg7, Qb1+; 28
Kb3, Qc2+ draws) 27 ..., Kb7; 28
Qd7+, Rc7** with an equal game.

22 ..., Qf4-f6; Draw agreed.

After 23 Re7, Rc8; 24 Qe5+,
Qxe5; 25 Rxe5, b6; 26 Re7, Rc7 it's
dead.

QUEEN'S GAMBIT ACCEPTED (1 d4, d5; 2 c4, dxc4)

The Q.G.A. is not the sort of opening in which one expects to find
Black offering material. However the line seen in the following game did
for a time have the theoreticians arguing about its soundness.

Game 34
Foguelman - Bronstein
(Amsterdam Interzonal 1964)

**1 d2-d4, d7-d5; 2 c2-c4, d5xc4; 3
Ng1-f3, Ng8-f6; 4 e2-e3, Bc8-g4!?;**

An interesting alternative to
the normal **4 ..., e6** leading to
positions that hang on the strength
or weakness of White's isolated
queen pawn.

5 Bf1xc4, e7-e6; 6 Qd1-b3,

The departure of Black's QB
for foreign lands has left a weakness on b7, which is indeed a decoy
to lure White into time-wasting
queen expeditions. White can avoid
the complications by **6 Nbd2** or **6**

Nc3 and the latter is the main
reason why 4 ..., Bg4 is a rarity.

A variant form of the gambit
arises after **6 h3, Bh5; 7 Qb3** (7 g4,
Bg6; 8 Ne5, Nbd7; 9 Nxg6, hxg6
Portisch-Padevsky, Havana 1964) 7
..., Bxf3; 8 gxf3, Nbd7; 9 Qxb7, c5
reaching the same position except
that the White pawn stands on h3
instead of h2.

6 ..., Bg4xf3; 7 g2xf3, c7-c5;

More usual is **7 ..., Nbd7** first,
but the difference does not appear
to be important; the sacrifice
(instead of 7 ..., b6 or 7 ..., Qc8) was
an original idea of Larsen's.

8 Qb3xb7, Nb8-d7;

67

9 d4xc5!?,

The main parting of the ways. Others:

a) 9 Nc3, Be7 (Not **9 ..., cxd4**; 10 exd4, **Be7**; 11 Bf4!, O-O; 12 Bc7 but **10 ..., Bd6** according to Euwe offers good counterplay, e.g. 11 Rg1, Rb8!? or 11 Bd2, O-O or 11 Ne4, Nxe4) 10 d5, exd5 (10 ..., Rb8!?) 11 Nxd5, O-O; 12 Bd2 (Better than 12 f4) 12 ..., Rb8; 13 Nxe7+, Qxe7; 14 Qxa7, Rxb2 and now according to Euwe 15 Rd1! offers White the better chances.

b) 9 Rg1 (an attempt to improve upon note **a**) 9 ..., g6; 10 Nc3, Be7!; 11 dxc5 (11 d5, Ne5; 12 dxe6, Rb8) 11 ..., Nxc5; 12 Qc6+ (12 Qb5+ - Euwe) 12 ..., Kf8; 13 f4, Nfe4!; 14 Ba6, Rb8! and White loses material (Hodos-Tal, USSR Championship 1962).

c) 9 O-O, cxd4; 10 Rd1, dxe3 (Neistadt's 10 ..., Bc5; 11 exd4, Bb6 is met by Euwe's 12 Bf4 and 13 Nc3) 11 Bxe3, Qc8; 12 Ba6, Qxb7; 13 Bxb7, Rb8; 14 Bc6, Rc8 (14 ..., Rxb2?; 15 Bd4 and 16 Bxf6) 15 Bxd7+, Nxd7; 16 Bxa7, Rc2 (Volovich-Gurevich, Yalta 1964) and now Euwe's 17 Na3!, Rxb2; 18 Rac1 retains a clear advantage for White (Euwe) since after the more or less forced 18 ..., Rb7; 19 Rc8+, Ke7; 20 Be3 and 21 Nc4 White retains an outside passed pawn. If there is a clear refutation of Black's gambit, it is probably to be found here.

9 ..., Bf8xc5; 10 f2-f4,

Another possibility is **10 Nc3,** O-O; 11 Qb3, Qc7 (threatening ..., Rab8 followed by ..., Bxe3) 12 Be2, Rab8; 13 Qc2, Bd6 (to prevent O-O, but if White's pawn is on h3 - see note to White's 6th - Black might prefer another tactic here) 14 Bd2, Nd5 and now if 15 O-O-O there comes 15 ..., Nb4 or 15 ..., Rfc8 (Euwe).

With the intermediate 5 h3, Bh5, and therefore the White pawn now standing on h3, a game Rubtsova-Gaprindashvili (USSR Women's Championship 1965) went **11 O-O** (instead of 10/11 f4) 11 ..., Rb8; 12 Qc6, O-O; 13 f4, Rc8; 14 Qa6? (But if 14 Qg2 Black regains his stake by 14 ..., Bxe3; 15 fxe3, Rxc4) 14 ..., e5!; 15 fxe5, Nxe5; 16 Be2, Ne4; 17 Nc3? (17 Qa4!?) 17 ..., Nxc3; 18 bxc3, Qh4 (This would still be strong with the pawn on h2) 19 Kh2, Rc6; 20 Qb7, Rh6; 21 Qg2, Rg6; 22 Qd5, Bd6; 23 Resigns.

10 ..., O-O; 11 O-O,

Black also gets a good game after either:

a) 11 Nc3, Rb8; 12 Qf3, Qc7 (12 ..., Bb4!? Euwe) 13 Bd3 (13 Bb3!? Euwe) 13 ..., Bb4; 14 Bd2, Nc5; 15 Bc2, Ba5; 16 Rb1, Rfd8 (Tal-Shianovsky, USSR Championship 1962)

b) 11 Qg2, Rc8; 12 O-O (12 b3?, Nb6 and ..., Nxc4) 12 ..., Bxe3; 13 fxe3, Rxc4; 14 b3, Rc7; 15 Bb2, Qa8 (Foguelman-Smyslov, Amsterdam 1964).

11 ..., Nf6-d5!; 12 Rf1-d1?;

Not **12 Bxd5**, Rb8; 13 Qc6, Rb6; 14 Qa4, exd5, but Euwe says **12 Qb3** would be better. Nonetheless White is condemned to a life of diligent defence as his king is vulnerable and he dare not open more lines by capturing the knight on d5.

12 ..., Ra8-b8; 13 Qb7-c6, Qd8-h4!;

See Diagram

14 Nb1-c3,

If immediately **14 Qxd7?** then 14 ..., Nxf4! forces mate.

14 ..., Rb8-b6!; 15 Qd6xd7, Nd5xf4!; 16 Nc3-e2,

16 exf4 still gets mated in 2,

68

while if **16 Be2**, e5 the rook decides.

**16 ..., Nf4-h3+; 17 Kg1-g2, Nh3xf2
18 Rd1-d4, Nf2-g4!; 19 Rd4-f4,
Qh4xh2+; 20 Kg2-f1, Bc5xe3; 21
Bc4-d5, Be3xf4; White resigns.**

SLAV DEFENCE (1 d4, d5; 2 c4, c6)

**Game 35
Langeweg - Donner**
(Amsterdam 1965)
**1 d2-d4, d7-d5; 2 c2-c4,
c7-c6; 3 Nb1-c3,**

A somewhat unusual continuation, which was employed by Alekhine in his second world championship match against Euwe. Usual is **3 Nf3** (Or 3 cxd5) 3 ..., Nf6 (3 ..., e6 Semi-Slav Defence) 4 Nc3, dxc4; 5 a4 (5 e4!?) 5 ..., Bf5 and now a sacrificial line can arise by 6 Ne5!?, e6!; 7 f3, Bb4; 8 e4!?, Bxe4; 9 fxe4, Nxe4 after which White's best is probably to take a draw by 10 Qf3 (10 Bd2!?, Qxd4; 11 Nxe4, Qxe4+! is very complicated but about equal) 10 ..., Qxd4; 11 Qxf7+, Kd8; 12 Bg5+, Nxg5! (12

..., Kc8; 13 Qxe6+!, Nd7; 14 Qxd7+! reaches a promising ending for White) 13 Qxg7, Bxc3+; 14 bxc3, Qxc3+; 15 Ke2, Qc2+!; 16 Ke1! and Black takes perpetual check.

3 ..., e7-e5!?

Winawer's Counter-Gambit, of which the current game is about the only modern example. Other moves are **3 ..., dxc4** and **3 ..., e6**.

4 c4xd5,

If **4 dxe5**, d4; 5 Ne4, Qa5+; 6 Nd2 (Not 6 Bd2, Qxe5 and Black is well off) Black must be accurate:
a) **6 ..., Qxe5?**; 7 Ngf3 with some advantage to White.
b) **6 ..., Nd7**; 7 e6 (7 f4?, Nh6 and 8 ..., Nf5 while 7 Nf3, Nxe5; 8 Nxe5,

Qxe5; 9 Nf3, Qa5+; 10 Bd2, Qb6;
11 Qb3, c5; 12 e3, dxe3; 13 Bxe3
gives White a slight plus according
to Pachman 7 ..., fxe6; 8 g3 led
White to a positional advantage in
Simagin-Nei, USSR Championship
1960, says Euwe.

c) 6 ..., Nh6! is recommended as a
good plan by Euwe, who analyses 7
Ngf3, Nf5; 8 g3, **Ne3?!**; 9 fxe3,
dxe3; 10 Bg2, Bc5! but then 11 a3!
(Taimanov) so the critical line is the
latter's **8 ..., Nd7**; 9 e6, fxe6; 10
Bg2, Ne3.

4 ..., c6xd5;

69

5 e2-e4,

White opens the centre, hoping
for a slight edge. Others:

a) 5 e3, exd4; 6 Qxd4, Nf6 followed
by 7 ..., Nc6 with equal chances
according to Euwe. The position is
a form of Tarrasch Defence; Black
cannot afford to play here the
gambit 6 ..., Nc6?! since he is a
whole tempo (5 e3!) behind normal
lines of the Hennig-Schara Gambit.
b) 5 dxe5, d4; 6 Ne4, Qa5+; 7 Nd2,
Nc6!; 8 Ngf3 (Or 8 f4, Nh6 with a
plus) 8 ..., Bg4   (all sources)
c) 5 Nf3, e4; 6 Nd2 (If 6 Ne5 correct
is 6 ..., Nc6!; 7 Nxc6, bxc6 or
Taimanov's 7 Qa4!; and not 6 ...,

f6?; 7 Qa4+, Ke7; 8 Qb3, fxe5; 9
Bxg5+, Nf6; 10 dxe5 Bernstein-
Marshall, Ostend 1906) 6 ..., Nc6; 7
e3, Nf6; 8 Qb3, Be7= (Pachman)

5 ..., d5xe4;

Black could try **5 ..., exd4**
hoping for a kind of Hennig-Schara
Gambit after **6 Qxd4,** Nc6; 7 Qxd5,
Be6 but Euwe considers that **6
Nxd5** gives White rather the better
game.

6 Bf1-b5+,

More dangerous than **6 d5,**Nf6
7 Bg5, Qb6 (Marshall-Winawer,
Monte Carlo 1901).

6 ..., Bc8-d7; 7 d4xe5, Bf8-b4;

Other moves have also been
tried here:
a) 7 ..., Bxb5; 8 Qxd8+, Kxd8; 9
Nxb5, Bb4+; 10 Ke2, a6; 11 Nd4,
Ne7; 12 Ke3 with an endgame
advantage to White (Muller-Haas,
correspondence 1924).
b) 7 ..., Nc6; 8 Qd5! (8 Qe2?, Bb4
was good for Black in Weber-
Ullrich, Leipzig 1960) 8 ..., Bb4; 9
Ne2, a6 (9 ..., Qe7; 10 O-O) 10 Bc4,
Qe7; 11 Bf4 also favoured White in
a 1922 postal game of Muller and
Haas.

**8 Bc1-d2, Bb4xc3; 9 Bb5xd7+,
Qd8xd7; 10 Bd2xc3, Ng8-e7; 11
Ng1-e2, Ne7-d5; 12 O-O, Nb8-c6;**

Black suffers from a deficit in
development; if he loses a further
tempo by exchanging on c3 he will
surely lose his e-pawn.

**13 Qd1-a4, e4-e3; 14 f2-f4, O-O;
15 Ra1-d1,**

Despite the eventual result of
this game, White surely stands
better here, the pawn on e3 being
more likely weak than strong.

15 ..., Ra8-d8; 16 Qa4-b3, Qd7-g4;

17 Rd1xd5, Qg4xe2; 18 Rd5xd8, Nc6xd8;

To protect the b-pawn, until the knight's position can be improved.

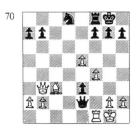

70

19 a2-a3?,

It is not clear why Langeweg plays this waiting move, when he could win the e-pawn by **19 Bd4**.

19 ..., Nd8-e6!; 20 Qb3xb7, Rf8-d8; 21 g2-g3,

Black threatened ..., Nxf4.

21 ..., Qe2-c2; 22 Qb7-g2,

If **22 Qxa7** then 22 ..., e2; 23 Re1, g5! protects the back rank and creates many new threats in one shot (analysis). Or 23 ..., Qe4 as in the game.

22 ..., e3-e2; 23 Rf1-e1, Rd8-d1; 24 Qg2-a8+, Rd1-d8; 25 Qa8-f3, Rd8-d1; 26 Qf3-a8+, Rd1-d8; 27 Qa8xa7?,

Evidently annoyed at missing a win, White goes for the risky line which he rejected on move 22.

27 ..., Qc2-e4!?;

This hardly seems to be stronger than **27 ..., g5!** with White in big trouble. The move Donner plays is more obscure.

28 Qa7-f2, Rd8-d1; 29 h2-h4!?,

Here **29 Qg2** might be better.

29 ..., h7-h5; 30 Kg1-h2, Rd1xe1; 31 Qf2xe1, Ne6-c5;

Threatening 32 ..., Nd3 winning a piece.

32 Qe1-h1, Qe4-c2; 33 Qh1-g2, Nc5-e4;

Now the idea is ..., Nxc3 followed by ..., Qd2.

34 Bc3-e1, Qc2-d3;

Threat: ..., Nd2-f3+.

35 a3-a4,

There is probably no defence.

35 ..., Ne4-d2; 36 Qg2-f2, Nd2-f3+; 37 Kh2-g2, Nf3-d4; 38 a4-a5,

Also after **38 Bc3** Black can force the win: 38 ..., Qe4+; 39 Kg1 (If 39 Kh2, e1(Q)! followed by a knight fork, or if 39 Kh3, Qh1+; 40 Qh2, e1(Q)) 39 ..., Nf3+ forces promotion.

38 ..., Qd3-e4+; 39 Kg2-h2,

Other moves lose the bishop.

39 ..., Nd4-f3+; 40 Kh2-h3, Nf3xe1
White resigns.

After 41 Qxe1, Qf3 Black wins easily. An instructive attack with attenuated material, despite the errors.

THE HENNIG-SCHARA GAMBIT
(1 d4, d5; 2 c4, e6; 3 Nc3, c5; 4 cxd5, cxd4)

This is one of the most seductive of Black's suicide attempts in the Queen's Gambit. The efforts of the Rumanian master Samarian to find new resources for Black mean that this gambit must once again be taken seriously, even if there are doubts about its absolute validity. Therefore three illustrative games will be given, in order to present a complete picture of the current state of theory.

Game 36
Smyslov - Estrin
(Leningrad 1951)

1 d2-d4, d7-d5; 2 c2-c4, e7-e6; 3 Nb1-c3, c7-c5;

The Tarrasch Variation of the Orthodox Defence, which is being rejuvenated by Spassky, Samarian and others.

4 c4xd5,

The only move that is likely to be dangerous; White hopes to saddle Black with a weak central pawn structure, while Black, following the usual **4 ..., exd5** hopes that his d-pawn (and in some lines c-pawn) will have a restricting effect and so offer him good dynamic chances. But Black can also play the gambit devised by the Viennese player Schara which was much analysed by the German von Hennig:

4 ..., c5xd4!?; 5 Qd1xd4,

The natural move, but **5 Qa4+** is also seen quite often, bowing to the inevitable (since Black can force the position that arises in the next two games, after the text move too) and saving the trouble of preparing two sets of variations.

5 ..., Nb8-c6;

This tempo gain is the first point of the gambit.

6 Qd4-d1, e6xd5;
7 Qd1xd5, Bc8-e6!?;

It is here that Black, playing **7 ..., Bd7!**, may force transposition into the 5 Qa4+ variation.

8 Qd5xd8+, Ra8xd8;

71

9 e2-e3!,

Only after this game was this move recognized to be best. On the other hand, no other plan offers White an advantage:

a) 9 f3?, Nb4; 10 Kf2, Nc2; 11 Rb1, Bc5+; 12 e3, Nh6 (12 ..., Ne7!? Samarian — Taimanov prefers it) 13 Bb5+, Ke7; 14 g4, f5; 15 g5 (Kashdan-Tartakover, Bled 1931) 15 ..., Nf7; 16 Nh3, h6!; 17 g6, Ne5 with adequate counterplay for Black ('Schachmaty').

b) 9 Bg5, f6; 10 Bd2, Nb4; 11 Rc1, Nxa2 with equality (Terpugov-Estrin, Moscow 1949).

c) 9 e4, a6! (Neither 9 ..., Nb4? nor 9 ..., Nd4? but Pachman suggests 9 ..., Bb4!? or 9 ..., Bc5!?) 10 Be2, Nb4; 11 Kf1, Bc5 with active play (Samarian).

9 ..., Nc6-b4;

A little-known plan here is **9 ..., a6!?**, preventing White's check and retaining the threat of ..., Nb4. The only example of this, (Trifunovic-Kozomara (Sarajevo 1957) continued 10 a3, g6!; 11 Nf3, Bg7; 12 Be2, Nge7; 13 O-O, O-O when in Samarian's opinion Black still retains some positional compensation for the pawn. Trifunovic failed to find any advantage for White, playing 14 e4, Nd4; 15 Nxd4, Bxd4; 16 Bh6, Rfe8; 17 Rfd1, Bb3; 18 Rd2, Nc6; 19 Rc1, Na5; 20 g3, Bg7; 21 Rxd8, Rxd8; 22 Bxg7, Kxg7 (threat ..., Rd2) 23 Nd5, Bxd5; 24 Rd1, Bc4; 25 Rxd8, Bxe2 with a complicated ending, eventually drawn.

10 Bf1-b5+, Ke8-e7; 11 Ke1-f1!,

Only this move tends to White's advantage:

a) 11 Ke2?!, Nc2; 12 Rb1, a6; 13 Ba4, Bc4+; 14 Kf3, Ne1+; 15 Kg3, Rd6; 16 f4, Rg6+; 17 Kf2, Nd3+ with perpetual check (Smyslov-Aramanovich, Moscow 1945).

b) 11 Ba4?!, Bc4! (Not 11 ..., b5?; 12 Nxb5! but Pachman recommends 11 ..., a6!?) 12 Nge2, b5!; 13 Bd1, Nd3+; 14 Kf1, b4 and Black has a powerful initiative (Poliansky-Estrin, Moscow 1938)

11 ..., Ng8-f6; 12 Ng1-f3, Nb4-c2?!;

Pachman considered the position after White's 11th move to be 'about even', but suggested no continuation. After this move Estrin loses quickly, but he might have tried **12 ..., a6** as suggested by Samarian. Black's main problem is the position of his king, obstructing his natural development so that he is ill-placed for acute tactics - hence Kozomara's 9 ..., a6.

13 Ra1-b1, Be6-f5; 14 Bc1-d2, g7-g5?!;

If **14 ..., Nxe3+!**; 15 Bxe3, Bxb1 Black appears to have won material back, but the refutation is certainly not so simple as to justify Taimanov's comment (after White's 14th) that 'White defends himself from the attack and maintains his material advantage.' For the correct solution is the mating attack 16 Ke2!, Bg6 (16 ..., Bf5?; 17 Bc5+, Ke6; 18 Nd4+) 17 Re1! hoping for 17 ..., a6?; 18 Bc5+, Ke6; 19 Kf1+, Kf5; 20 Re5+ or 17 ..., Ng4!; 18 Bxa7! with rough material equality and a difficult, if not impossible, defensive task for Black (analysis).

72

15 Rb1-c1, h7-h6;

Not 15 ..., g4?; 16 Nh4, Rxd2; 17 Nxf5+, Ke6; 18 Rxc2!, Rxc2; 19

Nd4+ or 17 ..., Kd8; 18 Nb1.

16 e3-e4!, Nf6xe4;
17 Rc1xc2, Ne4-d6;

If **17 ...,** Nxf2; 18 Bxg5+
leaves White a piece up.

18 Nf3-d4,

18 Bxg5+, f6; 19 Re2+ is also
good.

18 ..., Nd6xb5;

Because if **18 ...,** Bxc2 then 19
Nd5 is mate!

19 Nd4xf5+, Ke7-f6; 20 Nc3xb5,
Kf6xf5; 21 Kf1-e2, Black resigns.

Game 37
Gufeld - Nikolaevsky
(Ukraine Championship 1968)

1 d2-d4, d7-d5; 2 c2-c4, e7-e6;
3 Nb1-c3, c7-c5; 4 c4xd5, c5xd4;
5 Qd1-a4+, Bc8-d7;

Not **5 ...,** Qd7?; 6 Nb5! (Or
simply 6 Qxd4) 6 ..., Na6; 7 d6!
(Havasi-Tartakover,   Budapest
1929), nor **5 ...,** b5?; 6 Qxd4, b4; 7
Nb5, a6 (7 ..., exd5; 8 Qxd5!) 8
dxe6! and wins (Samarian).

6 Qa4xd4, e6xd5; 7 Qd4xd5,

White can only get difficulties
by declining the pawn. A game
Katz-Harding, Hastings 1971-2,
ran **7 Nf3,** Nc6; **8 Qd1?** (8 Qxd5
would transpose into the next
game) 8 ..., Bb4; 9 Bd2, Nf6; 10 e3,
Qe7; 11 Be2, a6; 12 O-O, O-O
(Black has a typical Hennig-Schara
attacking position plus his d-pawn
so there is no need to risk long
castling) 13 a3, Bd6; 14 Na4, Rad8;
15 Rc1, Rfe8; 16 b4, d4 and Black
had a strong attack.

7 ..., Nb8-c6;

With the same position that

could be reached by 7 ..., Bd7 in the
previous game. Here **7 ...,** Nf6 is a
dubious alternative, since Samarian (in 'Chessman Quarterly 15')
quotes with approval analysis by
the Swiss master W.Henneberger
from 'Deutsche Schachzeitung',
1932: **8 Qxb7** (Also good is 8 Qb3 of
Dake-Makarczik, Folkestone 1933,
while 8 Qd1, Nc6; 9 Nf3 transposes
into the next game) 8 ..., Nc6; 9
Qb3!, Nd4; 10 Qd1, Bf5; 11 e4!,
Nxe4; 12 Nf3! (correcting Tartakover's 12 Qa4+?, Ke7!; 13 Qa3+,
Kf6 when Black wins) 12 ..., Bb4!
(If 12 ..., Bc5; 13 Nxe4, Bxe4; 14
Nxd4, Bxd4; 15 Bb5+, Kf8; 16
O-O or 12 ..., Nxc3; 13 Qxd4, Bb4!;
14 Bd2) 13 Qxd4, Qa5 (13 ..., Nxc3;
14 Bd2, Qe7+; 15 Qe5, Nd5!; 16
Bb5+ etc.) 14 Bd2 in each case with
positional advantage to White.

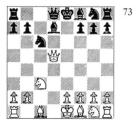
73

8 Bc1-g5,

Other moves are also important
here:

a) 8 Nf3, Nf6 etc. see the next game.

b) 8 a3, Nf6; 9 Qd1, Bc5; 10 e3,
Qe7; 11 Nf3, see note **a** to White's
11th move in the next game.

c) 8 e3, Nf6; **9 Qb3** (9 Qd1, Bc5; 10
Nf3, Qe7 see next game) 9 ..., Bb4
(9 ..., Bc5!?) 10 Bb5, Qa5; 11 Bd2,
a6; 12 Be2, Be6; 13 Qc2, Bf5; 14

Qb3, Ne4; 15 Nf3, Nc5; 16 Qd5, Bd3; 17 Ng5 (17 Bxd3?, Rd8) 17 ..., Bg6; 18 a3, Rd8; 19 Qa2, Rxd2! (Dulin-Starkov, USSR 1960). White's centralised king presents a sitting target: 20 Kxd2, Bxc3+; 21 bxc3, h6 etc (analysis).

d) 8 Bd2, Nf6; 9 Qb3, Bb4; 10 Nf3, O-O; 11 e3, Be6; 12 Qc2, Rc8; 13 Be2, Re8; 14 O-O, Bg4 (Havasi-Merenyi, Budapest 1932). White is in a bind and will probably be forced to weaken his king side pawns.

e) 8 Bf4?!, Nf6; **9 Qd1?** (9 Qd2 is necessary - Littlewood) 9 ..., Qb6; 10 Qc1, Bc5; 11 e3, Nb4!? with complications (Lorber-Stolear, British Boys Championship 1971) but anyway Black has a good game.

8 ..., Ng8-f6; 9 Qd5-d2;

Samarian quotes here a game Gaister-Zaitsev, Moscow Championship 1960, which went **9 Bxf6?**, Qxf6; 10 e3, O-O-O; 11 Qb3, Be6; 12 Qa4, Bb4; 13 Rc1, Rd2!; 14 Kxd2, Qxf2+; 15 Ne2, Bf5! (cutting off the flight square) 16 Qxb4, Rd8+; 17 Qd4, Nxd4; 18 Nb5+, Nc6+; 19 Nd4, Kb8; 20 Kd1, Qxe3; 21 Resigns.

9 ..., h7-h6;

A playable alternative is **9 ..., Qa5; 10 Qe3+** (Better than 10 Bxf6, gxf6; 11 e3, O-O-O of Grushevsky-Gusev, 1955) 10 ..., Be7; 11 Bxf6, gxf6; 12 Nf3, Nb4; 13 Rc1, Nd5; 14 Qd2, Rc8; 15 Rd1, Nb6; 16 e3, Bb4 (Lilienthal-Aramanovich, Moscow 1959).

10 Bg5-h4,

In the game Pirc-Alekhine, Bled 1931, White went badly wrong by **10 Bxf6?!**, Qxf6; 11 e3, O-O-O; 12 O-O-O? (Necessary was 12 Nd5!,

Qg6; 13 Ne2 followed by Nef4 or Nec3 with possibilities of defence, according to Alekhine) 12 ..., Bg4; 13 Nd5, Rxd5!; 14 Qxd5, Ba3! and Black won quickly by direct attack.

10 ..., g7-g5; 11 Bh4-g3, Qd8-a5;

Alekhine's intention was **11 ..., Bb4** with about equal chances.

12 e2-e3, O-O-O; 13 Ng1-e2, Bf8-b4;

Black has an excellent game, according to Samarian. In fact, it looks rather like a forced win for him.

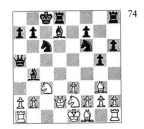

74

14 a2-a3!?,

As **14 f3?!**, Rhe8; 15 Kf2 fails to 15 ..., Bc5; 16 Nd4, Rxe3!, **14 O-O-O!?** to 14 ..., Bf5; 15 Qe2, Ne4 and **14 Qc2** to 14 ..., Bf5, it is hard to find a better move.

14 ..., Nf6-e4; 15 Qd2-c1, Ne4-c5!; 16 a3xb4, Nc5-d3+; 17 Ke1-d1, Qa5xb4; 18 Ra1xa7!?,

This threatens mate, e.g. 18 ..., Nxa7??; 19 Nb5+, Nxc1; 20 Nxa7. But White could also have tried passive resistance:

a) 18 Ra4?, Nxb2+ and 19 ..., Nxa4

b) 18 Qd2?, Bf5!

c) 18 Qc2, Bf5!; 19 e4, Nxf2+! and **18 Qb1** would just be worse.

18 ..., Bd7-e6!; 19 Ra7-a8+, Kc8-d7; 20 Ra8xd8+, Rh8xd8; 21 Qc1-a1,

If **21 Qc2** or **21 Qd2** then 21 ..., Bb3 wins outright, while **21 Qb1** is merely a more hopeless version of the text.

21 ..., Kd7-e7; 22 Kd1-c2,

Not **22 Qa3** because of 22 ..., Nxb2+ winning the queen.

22 ..., Qb4-b3+; 23 Kc2-d2, Nd3xb2+; White resigns.

Game 38
Polugaevsky - I.Zaitsev
(36th USSR Championship 1969)

1 d2-d4, d7-d5; 2 c2-c4, e7-e6; 3 Nb1-c3, c7-c5; 4 c4xd5, c5xd4; 5 Qd1-a4+, Bc8-d7; 6 Qa4xd4, e6xd5; 7 Qd4xd5, Nb8-c6; 8 Ng1-f3!, Ng8-f6; 9 Qd5-d1,

This represents White's only hope of refuting the Hennig-Schara Gambit. If instead **9 Qb3** all sources agree that 9 ..., Be6; 10 Qa4, Bc5 offers Black the initiative in compensation for his pawn.

9 ..., Bf8-c5!;

The usual move nowadays. The others:

a) **9 ..., Bb4**; 10 Bd2, O-O; 11 g3!, Re8; 12 Bg2, Qb6; 13 O-O, Rad8; 14 Qc2 (analysis by Euwe). White has a sound extra pawn and does not have concrete threats to meet.

b) **9 ..., Qb6**; 10 e3, O-O-O; 11 Bd2!, Qxb2; 12 Rb1, Qa3; 13 Bc4! and White has the initiative. (Lisitsin).

10 e2-e3,

75

A critical position for the whole of the Queen's Gambit. Black has to choose between ..., O-O, in which case we have a positional initiative which White may however be able to neutralise slowly, or the preparation of long castling, with the likelihood of a violent tactical struggle. Doubtless more practical experience of the various key lines are required, since, writing in 1970 on the basis of much the same evidence, Samarian considered Black's resources to be sufficient whilst Taimanov, who here doubtless represents grandmaster opinion in general, prefers White's solid position. Let us say that the onus of proof is on Black ...

10 ..., Qd8-e7;

Usual, but in the game Vladimirov-Ravinsky, USSR 1955, the slow plan **10 ..., O-O; 11 Be2, Qe7; 12 O-O** was seen. There followed **12 ..., Rfd8** (Not 12 ..., Bf5; 13 Bd2, Rad8; 14 Rc1 and White stands better - Lisitsin) 13 a3, Bf5; 14 Qa4, Ng4 (Or 14 ..., a6!? Prokhorovich-Ravinsky, USSR 1968) 15 h3, Nge5; 16 Qf4 (Not 16 b4?!, Bb6; 17 b5, Nxf3+; 18 Bxf3, Ne5 with a strong attack for Black) 16 ..., Nxf3+; 17 Bxf3, Bd3; 18 Rd1 (Too passive is

18 Re1?, Bd6! with a strong attack for Black) 18 ..., Bc2 (If 18 ..., Bd6?!; 19 Nd5!, Qe6 - the ending after 19 ..., Bxf4 should be lost - 20 Qg5! and White beats off the attack) 19 Rxd8+, Rxd8; 20 Bxc6, bxc6 (20 ..., Bd6?!; 21 Qf3, Qe5; 22 g3!, bxc3; 23 Qxc6) 21 e4 (21 Qf3?, Rd6!) 21 ..., Bd6 (21 ..., Rd6?; 22 Be3) 22 Qg4, Be5; 23 Be3 (If 23 Ne2?, Bxe4! or 23 f3?, Qc5+) 23 ..., Bxc3; 24 bxc3, Bxe4 with a clearly drawn ending.

11 Bf1-e2!,

Other moves appear to offer Black good chances:

a) 11 a3 and now:

a1) 11 ..., O-O-O; 12 Qc2 (Or Bd2, g5!; 13 h3?!, Rg8; 14 g4, h5 as in Lloyd-Nicholson, England 1971, but better here is Littlewood's suggestion 13 b4, Bb6; 14 Be2, g4; 15 Nh4!?) 12 ..., Kb8; 13 Be2 (Also good for Black is 13 b4, Nd4; 14 Nxd4, Bxd4; 15 Be2, Ba4; 16 Qb2, Be5; 17 f4, Ne4; 18 fxe5, Qh4+; 19 g3, Nxg3; 20 hxg3, Qxh1+ Garnev-Babitchuk, USSR 1959) 13 ..., g5; 14 O-O, g4; 15 Nd2, Rhe8; 16 Nb3, Bb6; 17 Bd2, Qe5 and Black has strong threats (Gurevich-Safonov, Moscow Championship 1960).

a2) 11 ..., O-O; 12 Qc2?! (Or 12 Be2, Rfd8; 13 O-O see the note to Black's 10th move) 12 ..., Ne5; 13 Be2, Rac8 and Black got good play all over the board (Burlaev-Aramanovich, Moscow 1957).

b) 11 Bd2, O-O-O (Here also Aramanovich has been successful with a plan based on ..., O-O) 12 Qb3, Bf5; 13 Rc1, Kb8; 14 Na4, Bb4!; 15 a3, Bxd2+; 16 Nxd2, Nd4! with a dangerous attack against White's king in the centre

(Hanov-Gusev, Stalinabad 1955).

11 ..., O-O-O!?;

Until the text game, the normal move here, but others are better:

a) 11 ..., O-O! is Black's most reliable plan - see note to his 10th move.

b) 11 ..., g5!? is Gusev's idea, recommended by Samarian, e.g. 12 O-O!?, g4; 13 Nd4, h5; 14 b4 (14 Ncb5!?) 14 ..., Bd6; 15 b5, Ne5 with sufficient counter-chances. But why did Gusev's opponents reject the critical 12 Nxg5?!: it is not entirely clear what will happen. After 12 ..., Rg8; 13 Nf3! (13 Nh3?!, Rxg2?; 14 Nf4 and 15 Ncd5 but better 13 ..., Bd6 or 13 ..., Bxh3; 14 gxh3, Qe6) 13 ..., Rxg2 (13 ..., O-O-O!?) 14 Rg1, Rxg1+; 15 Nxg1, O-O-O; 16 a3 (16 Qc2?) with b4 to follow (analysis). However White's position could not be to the taste of many players. Taimanov considers the correct reply to 11 ..., g5 to be 12 Nd4! e.g. 12 ..., g4; 13 Nxc6, Bxc6; 14 Bb5 (Bagirov-Kudryashov USSR 1969), but Samarian did not comment on this possibility.

12 O-O,

If 12 Bd2, g5; 13 Rc1, Kb8; 14 O-O (Stolyar-Gurevich, USSR 1955) then Samarian recommends 14 ..., Bf5 with unpleasant threats.

12 ..., g7-g5;

See Diagram

13 Nf3-d4,

Other moves to be considered:

a) 13 Nxg5?!, Rhg8 with ..., Bh3 in reserve.

b) 13 a3?!, g4; 14 Nd4, Qe5!; 15 b4, Nxd4; 16 bxc5, Nf3+! (Borisenko-

76

Spassky, USSR 1959) and Black has a devastating attack.

c) 13 b4!? (also critical) **13 ..., Nxb4** (13 ..., Bxb4; 14 Bb2, g4; 15 Nd4 see the text game) **14 Bb2**, h5 (Or first 14 ..., g4) 15 Qb3, g4; 16 Nd4, h4; 17 Rac1, Kb8 (Sales-Patterson, England 1971) and now instead of 18 Na4? Kottnauer in his 'Schackend Nederland' column recommended 18 a3, Nc6 and now either 19 Ncb5 or 19 Nd5.

13 ..., g5-g4;

Other possibilities:

a) 13 ..., h5; 14 a3, g4; 15 b4, Bd6; 16 Ncb5, Bb8; 17 Bb2, Ne4; 18 Qc2 and White stands better (Novotelnov-Spassky, USSR 1956).

b) 13 ..., Qe5!? (Samarian) along the lines of Borisenko-Spassky above.

14 b2-b4!?,

Not **14 a3?**, Qe5 but Petrosian and Suetin's untried recommendation **14 Bb5!?** looks dangerous. There might follow 14 ..., Qe5; 15 Qc2 (15 Qa4!?) 15 ..., Bxd4 (If 15 ..., Nxd4; 16 exd4, Bxd4?; 17 Nd5+ or 16 ..., Qxd4; 17 Ne2) 16 Bxc6, Bxc6 (If 16 ..., Bxc3; 17 Bxd7+ remaining a pawn up) 17 exd4 and 18 Be3 (analysis).

14 ..., Bc5xb4;

The possibility **14 ..., Nxb4!?** has also to be considered. If then 15 Qb3 Black can seek transposition to Sales-Patterson by 15 ..., h5 (yet White might not play 16 Bb2) but if Samarian is right Black's correct plan lies in avoiding this move. However he made no concrete suggestion in his article; a good working assumption is that the Black king is in the greater danger, since White has Bb2, Ncb5 and Rac1 in his locker as well as g3 (to meet ..., Qe5 and ..., Bd6). Barden believes this to be satisfactory for Black, though.

15 Bc1-b2, h7-h5;

Holmov says that **15 ..., Kb8** is better. That is quite plausible, but does not alter the fact that Black will have to meet a sharp attack.

16 Nc3-b5!, Kc8-b8;

Black cannot endure the exposure involved in **16 ..., a6**; 17 Nxc6, Bxc6; 18 Na7+, Kc7; 19 Nxc6.

17 Qd1-a4!?,

According to Polugaevsky, **17 Qb3!** was the most accurate move, as it guards the e-pawn and so prevents Black's resource at move 19.

17 ..., a7-a6; 18 Nd4xc6+, Bd7xc6; 19 Bb2xf6, Qe7xf6?;

Zaitsev overlooks the counter-attack **19 ..., Qe4!** by which he could have made White's task much more difficult. Samarian analyses 20 f3 (Or 20 Be5+, Ka8; 21 Nc7+, Ka7) 20 ..., Qxe3+; 21 Kh1, Qxe2 (21 ..., Rd2!? is suggested in the tournament book; this may stem from the players' post-mortem, as with so many other unsigned ideas that appear in books and theoretical articles.) 22 Qxb4, gxf3; 23 Qf4+, Ka8; 24 Nc7+, Kb8 'and now it seems that White has no better than to go for the win of the exchange by 25 Nd5+, Ka8; 26 Qxf3, Qxf3; 27 Rxf3, Bxd5; 28 Rf2 with an ending difficult to win.'

20 Qa4xb4, a6xb5; 21 Be2xb5, Qf6-d6; 22 Ra1-b1, Bc6-d5; 23 a2-a4, f7-f5; 24 Qb4xd6+, Rd8xd6;

77

With pawns still remaining on both sides of the board, there is no reason to suppose White should fail to win this ending.

25 Rb1-d1, Rh8-d8; 26 f2-f3, Bd5-e6; 27 Rd1xd6, Rd8xd6; 28 f3xg4, f5xg4;

After **28 ..., hxg4** Black would have to reckon with an outside passed pawn.

29 Rf1-f8+, Kb8-a7; 30 Rf8-h8, Rd6-d5;

Or **30 ..., Rd1+;** 31 Kf2, Rd2; 32 Kg3, Bd5; 33 Bf1, Rd1; 34 Rxh5! etc. - given in the tournament book.

31 Kg1-f2, Rd5-c5; 32 e3-e4, Rc5-c2+; 33 Kf2-g3, Rc2-c3+; 34 Kg3-f4, Rc3-c2; 35 Rh8xh5!, Rc2xg2; 36 Rh5-h6!, Be6-b3; 37 e4-e5, Rg2-a2; 38 e5-e6, Bb3xa4; 39 Bb5xa4, Ra2xa4+; 40 Kf4-f5, Ra4-a2; 41 e6-e7, Black resigns.

If **41 ..., Re2;** 42 Re6 etc.

5 INDIAN COUNTER-GAMBITS

In this chapter I shall be considering those games which commence 1 d4, Nf6, characterised by Black's avoidance of Queen's Gambit structures in favour of undermining manoeuvres aimed at achieving counterplay rather than sterile equality. First come the Budapest, Blumenfeld and Volga Gambits and then follow various sacrificial lines of the Benoni, King's Indian, Gruenfeld and Nimzo-indian defences. The counter-gambits in this chapter include some of the most sophisticated positional sacrifices, as well as some highly original tactical tries. Only the Budapest can be definitely not recommended.

BUDAPEST COUNTER-GAMBIT (1 d4, Nf6; 2 c4, e5)

Game 39
Smyslov - H.Steiner
(Groningen 1946)

1 d2-d4, Ng8-f6; 2 c2-c4, e7-e5?!;

Black challenges White's centre in a manner that is direct but self-weakening. Nobody would play such a move against Smyslov now, but at this time his reputation was not well-known in the West.

3 d4xe5, Nf6-e4?!;

Only this move turns the opening into a genuine gambit: the Fajarowicz Variation. More usual is **3 ..., Ng4** with the following possibilities:

a) **4 f4?, Bc5** (4 ..., d6!? is also to be considered) 5 Nh3, d6; 6 exd6, O-O!; 7 dxc7 (Better 7 e4, cxd6; 8 Nc3, Nc6 but with advantage to Black) 7 ..., Qxc7; 8 Nc3, Bb4 (Or 8 ..., Be6; 9 Nd5, Bxd5; 10 Qxd5, Rd8 and Black has an overwhelming game - 'Chess Digest') 9 Qb3, Nc6; 10 e3 (Or 10 e4, Nd4; 11 Qd1, Rd8) 10 ..., Re8 and Black is winning (Pachman).

b) **4 Qd4?**, d6; 5 exd6, Bxd6; 6 Nf3, O-O!; 7 Nc3, Nc6; 8 Qd1, Be6 'Black having more than adequate compensation for the pawn minus' - Pachman.

Therefore White should content himself with a slight but definite positional advantage - unless Black insists on giving up the pawn:

c) **4 e4, d6?!** (4 ..., Nxe5; 5 f4 should favour White, the Chess Digest idea 5 ..., Nbc6!? being answerable, faute de mieux, by 6 Nf3) **5 exd6** (Good for White also is 5 Be2 of Reshevsky-Denker, Syracuse 1934) 5 ..., Bxd6; 6 Be2, f5 (Or 6 ..., h5; 7 Nf3!, Nc6; 8 Nc3, Qe7; 9 Bg5 Golombek) 7 exf5, Qe7; 8 Nf3, Bxf5; 9 Bg5, Nf6; 10 Nc3, Nc6; 11 Nd5 (Capablanca-Tartakover, Bad Kissingen 1928).

d) **4 Bf4, Nc6** (However 4 ..., g5!? offers Black good chances of equality, according to Pachman) 5 Nf3, **f6?!** (After 5 ..., Bb4+; 6 Nbd2 White gets a slight plus) 6 exf6 (Not 6 Qd5?, fxe5; 7 Nxe5, Ngxe5; 8

Bxe5, Qg5! 'Chess Digest') 6 ...,
Qxf6; 7 Qd2 (Or 7 Qc1, Bb4+; 8
Bd2 - Euwe) 7 ..., Bb4; 8 Nc3, Bxc3;
9 bxc3, d6; 10 e3, b6; 11 Be2, Bb7;
12 O-O, Ne7; 13 Nd4, Ne5 (Eliska-
ses-Bogolyubov, 11th match game
1939) and now Pachman's 14 Nb5
gives White a plus.

e) 4 Nf3 assures White of positional
advantage.

78

4 Ng1-f3,

Other moves are also good:

a) 4 a3 - Smyslov, 'My Best Games
of Chess'.

b) 4 Nd2, Nc5 (If 4 ..., Bb4; 5 Nf3
and 6 a3) 5 Ngf3, Nc6; 6 g3, Qe7; 7
Bg2, g6; 8 Nb1! (Alekhine-Tartako
ver, London 1932).

c) 4 Qc2! (But not 4 Qd5?, f5! nor 4
Qd4 according to Chess Digest) 4
..., Bb4+ (If 4 ..., d5; 5 exd6, Bf5; 6
Nc3! Pachman; Or if 4 ..., Nc5; 5
Nf3, Nf6; 6 Nc3 likewise) 5 Nc3!
(Not 5 Nd2?!, d5!; 6 exd6, Bf5; 7
dxc7, Qxc7 with good prospects for
Black; Plesse-Wolf, West Germany
1966) 5 ..., d5; 6 exd6, Bf5; 7 Bd2!,
Nxd6; 8 e4, Bxc3; 9 Bxc3, Be4; 10
Qd2, O-O; 11 O-O-O with advan-
tage to White (de Carbonnel-Starke
Leipzig 1953).

4 ..., Bf8-b4+;

Other moves are · perhaps
better:

a) 4 ..., d6!?; 5 exd6, Bxd6 and now
White tends to fall into the trap 6
g3??, Nxf2!; 7 Kxf2, Bxg3+ e.g.
Murphy-Wigglesworth, British
Boys Championship 1962.

b) 4 ..., Nc6 and now:

b1) 5 Nbd2, Bb4 (Or 5 ..., Nc5; 6 g3,
g6 or 6 ..., d6 with equal chances -
Chess Digest) 6 a3 (If 6 g3, d6!
Najdorf-Czerniak, Buenos Aires
1939) 6 ..., Nxd2 (Or 6 ..., Bxd2; 7
Nxd2 etc) 7 Bxd2, Bxd2+; 8 Qxd2,
Qe7 see text game.

b2) 5 Qc2, Bb4+; 6 Nd2? (Correct
is 6 Nc3! e.g. 6 ..., d5; 7 exd6, Bf5; 8
Bd2! or 6 ..., Nxc3; 7 bxc3, Bc5; 8
Bf4, h6; 9 e3) 6 ..., d5! etc. with the
better game for Black (Ziewitz-
Hagen, Schleswig 1963).

b3) 5 a3, d6; 6 Qc2, d5; 7 e3, Bg4
with good play for Black (Bisguier-
Ljubojevic, Costa del Sol 1971).

5 Bc1-d2,

Also possible is **5 Nbd2**, a
game Podgaets-Krutikhin (USSR
Olympiad 1972) continuing 5 ...,
Nc6; 6 e3, Qe7; 7 Be2, Nxe5; 8
O-O, Nxd2; 9 Nxd2, Bxd2; 10
Bxd2, d6; 11 Bc3 with advantage to
White through his two bishops and
greater pressure on the centre; he
won in 35 moves.

**5 ..., Ne4xd2; 6 Nb1xd2, Nb8-c6; 7
a2-a3, Bb4xd2+; 8 Qd1xd2,
Qd8-e7; 9 Qd2-c3, O-O; 10 Ra1-d1
Rf8-e8; 11 Rd1-d5!,**

Smyslov determines to hold on
to his strong pawn at all cost.

**11 ..., b7-b6; 12 e2-e3, Bc8-b7;
13 Bf1-e2, Ra8-d8;
14 O-O, Nc6-b8!;**

See Diagram

79

15 Rf1-c1!,

The consistent plan. Not **15 Rd2**, Bxf3; 16 Bxf3, Qxe5 (Smyslov) but in the game Bobotsov-Panlov (Students' 1953) there occurred **15 Rd4**, Bxf3; 16 Bxf3, Qxe5; 17 Re1, d6; 18 Qc2, Nd7; 19 Re4 and White still had the edge.

15 ..., Bb7xd5; 16 c4xd5, d7-d6;

The complicated alternative was **16 ..., c5**; 17 Bb5, a6; 18 d6, Qe6; 19 Bc4, Qf5; 20 Bd5, Nc6; 21 Bxc6, dxc6; 22 h3! when Black's weaknesses on the queen side make

it hard for him to resist the White pawns (Smyslov).

17 Be2-b5, Re8-f8; 18 e3-e4!, a7-a6; 19 Bb5-d3, d6xe5?;

According to Smyslov, **19 ..., Rfe8** was probably better, e.g. 20 e6, fxe6; 21 dxe6, c5; 22 Bc4 and matters are not yet simple.

20 Nf3xe5, Rd8-d6?!;

But after **20 ..., f6**; 21 Ng4 (intending Ne3-f5) White stands better.

21 Ne5-c4, Rd6-h6; 22 Nc4-e3, Qe7-h4; 23 Qc3xc7, Rh6-f6; 24 g2-g3, Qh4-h5; 25 e4-e5, Rf6-h6; 26 h2-h4, Qh5-f3; 27 Rc1-c4!,

White parries the desperation attack with economy and power.

27 ..., b7-b5; 28 Rc4-f4, Qf3-h5; 29 Ne3-g4, Rh6-g6; 30 Bd3xg6, Qh5xg6; 31 e5-e6, Qg6-b1+; 32 Kg1-h2, f7-f5; 33 e6-e7, Rf8-e8; 34 Qc7-d8, Black resigns.

BLUMENFELD COUNTER-GAMBIT
(1 d4, Nf6; 2 c4, e6; 3 Nf3, c5; 4 d5, b5)

As will be seen later in this Indian Systems chapter, there is now a proliferation of counter-gambit systems based on the idea of under-mining the White central pawn salient c4-d5 by the offer ..., b5. The Blumenfeld, which is the grandfather of the Volga and allied gambits, is distinguished from these by the early ..., e6, aimed at the creation of a pawn centre, whereas the others normally involve a king's fianchetto with the aim of long-term pressure on b2 and d5. Nonetheless it is natural that a revaluation of the Blumenfeld should be sought in recent years and not at all surprising that this old opening should be the subject of a theoretical article in 'Schachmatny Bulletin' (by B.Voronkov, January 1971).

Game 40
Alekseev - Peresipkin
(Kaliningrad semi-final,
40th USSR Championship 1972)

**1 d2-d4, Ng8-f6; 2 c2-c4, e7-e6;
3 Ng1-f3, c7-c5; 4 d4-d5, b7-b5!?;**

This move, instead of the usual Benoni continuation 4 ..., exd5; 5 cxd5, d6 characterises the Blumenfeld Counter-Gambit. This position (as in fact in this game) can also be reached by the move order 1 d4, Nf6; 2 Nf3, c5; 3 d5, b5!?; 4 c4 (Better 4 a4!, bxa4; 5 Nd2!) and now 4 ..., e6 instead of the Volga 4 ..., g6 or 4 ..., d6. Slight variants on this are also possible.

5 d5xe6,

For forms of the Blumenfeld Declined see Game 42 below.

5 ..., f7xe6; 6 c4xb5,

Bogolyubov's suggestion 6 e4, Nxe4; 7 Bd3 does not seem too dangerous in view of 7 ..., Bb7 or even 7 ..., Qa5+.

6 ..., d7-d5;

80

Of this basic position Pachman, in his book 'Indian Systems' has written: ' ... an interesting example of the interchangeability of basic chess-elements; in this case, the exchange of material (sacrifice of a pawn) for scope (command of the centre).' Indeed, although the gambit has been known for nearly 70 years, chess players and analysts have hardly begun to penetrate the secrets of this variation.

7 Nb1-c3,

This is believed to be one of the best moves here. Others:

a) 7 Nbd2 see the next game.

b) 7 Bf4 (Pachman's preference) 7 ..., Bd6 (If 7 ..., Qa5+?! White has 8 Nc3, d4; 9 Qa4 or 8 Nbd2!, Qxb5; 9 e4! Pachman) 8 Bxd6, Qxd6; 9 Nbd2, O-O! (Better than 9 ..., Nbd7; 10 e3, O-O; 11 Be2, a6; 12 bxa6, Bxa6; 13 O-O, Qb6; 14 b3 when White stands better; Rossetto -Szabo, Buenos Aires 1955) 10 e3, a6!; 11 bxa6, Bxa6; 12 Be2, Nc6; 13 O-O, Rfb8 with equal chances, e.g. 14 b3, e5; 15 e4 (15 Nc4?, Qe7!) 15 ..., dxe4; 16 Ng5, Bxe2; 17 Qxe2, Qd3! (Voronkov).

c) 7 Bg5! is strong:

c1) 7 ..., Be7; 8 e3, O-O (Or 8 ..., Nbd7) 9 Be2, Nbd7 (9 ..., a6!?) 10 Nc3, Bb7; 11 O-O with transposition to the text game.

c2) 7 ..., Bd6; 8 e4!, dxe4 (8 ..., Nbd7; 9 exd5, exd5; 10 Nc3, Bb7; 11 Bd3 Voronkov) 9 Nfd2!, Be5; 10 Nc3, Bb7; 11 Bc4 followed by Qe2 with the better game for White (Holmov).

c3) 7 ..., Qa5+; 8 Qd2, Qxb5; 9 e4!, Qb7; 10 Bxf6, gxf6; 11 exd5, Qxd5; 12 Qe3 is also good for White (Holmov).

d) 7 e3?!, Bd6; 8 Nc3 and now:

d1) 8 ..., O-O; 9 e4! (Euwe's move, which is stronger than 9 Be2 of Tarrasch-Alekhine of Pistyan 1922, which continued 9 ..., Bb7; 10 b3, Nbd7; 11 Bb2, Qe7; 12 O-O, Rad8;

13 Qc2, e5! and 'White's game is already far too compromised by the strategic error of the opening, ceding the centre to his opponent in exchange for a pawn of little value' - Alekhine) and White is better, e.g. 9 ..., d4; 10 e5! or 9 ..., dxe4; 10 Ng5! or 9 ..., Nxe4; 10 Nxe4, dxe4; 11 Ng5!

d2) 8 ..., Bb7!; 9 e4 (9 Be2, O-O see Tarrasch-Alekhine) 9 ..., Nbd7! (Better than 9 ..., d4; 10 e5!, Bxf3; 11 Qxf3, Bxe5; 12 Ne4! of Rethy-Rellstab, Brno 1931) 10 exd5, exd5; 11 Be2 (Or 11 Qe2+, Kf8!; 12 Ng5, Qb6 etc - Hildebrand in his tiny monograph 'Blumenfeld Gambiten') 11 ..., O-O and Black has sufficient compensation for his pawn (Hildebrand and Voronkov).

7 ..., Nb8-d7!?;

Apparently an entirely new move in this position, although by move 11 we reach the well known critical line of the 7 Bg5 variation. Others:

a) 7 ..., Bd6?; 8 e4!, Be7 (8 ..., d4; 9 e5!) 9 Bd3 or 9 e5 (Hildebrand).

b) 7 ..., Bb7?; 8 e4, Be7 (If 8 ..., Nbd7 9 e5, Ng4; 10 Bf4, Qc7; 11 h3! or 8 ..., d4; 9 e5! Nattorp-Karlsson, Sweden 1964) 9 e5!, Nfd7; 10 Bd3 with better play for White: 10 ..., d4 11 Nb1! (Hildebrand).

c) 7 ..., d4; 8 Nb1, Qa5+ (Not 8 .., Bd6; 9 e3!, e5; 10 exd4, exd4; 11 Bc4! Hildebrand) 9 Bd2! (If 9 Nbd2, Bd6; 10 g3, Bb7; 11 Bg2, Qxb5 Voronkov) 9 ..., Qxb5; 10 Na3, Qxb2; 11 Nc4! (Euwe's idea: if now 11 ..., Qb5; 12 e3 is good for White) 11 ..., Qb7; 12 g3 (Hildebrand here says White stands better) 12 ..., Nc6; 13 Bg2, Nd5! with an interesting position, White being able to get some counter-

chances for his pawn by the move e3 (Voronkov).

8 Bc1-g5,

Surely the most critical try. If White played **8 e3?!** etc. he would soon find himself back in Tarrasch-Alekhine.

8 ..., Bf8-e7; 9 e2-e3,

Black is watching the central black squares too well for e4?!, either here or last move, to be effective.

9 ..., Bc8-b7;

Black could of course try **9 ..., a6!?** on the lines of the Volga Gambit, but the text is more in accord with the needs of the position, Black having a pawn centre but no fianchettoed king bishop.

10 Bf1-e2, O-O; 11 O-O,

This is the critical position of the Blumenfeld Gambit Accepted.

81

11 ..., Qd8-e8!?;

This move is probably not best, since it does not threaten to play 12 ..., e5 (Not 11 ..., e5?; 12 Bxf6!) and if Black were to play here the waiting move **11 ..., Kh8!?** (which is usually required anyway) it may become clear that some other queen move is preferable. If then 12 Qc2 Black can play 12 ..., e5! while if 12 Rc1 then 12 ..., Qe8 is more appropriate (analysis). This idea is in need of practical testing.

In a Kan-Goldenov match game (1946) Black played instead **11 ..., Qc7?!** but after 12 Rc1, Rae8; 13 Bh4!, Bd6; 14 Bg3, e5?! (Better 14 ..., Bxg3 and 15 ..., Qd6 with an unclear position - analysis) there came 15 b4!, c4 (15 ..., cxb4; 16 Nxd5!) 16 a3, e4; 17 Nxd5! with decisive material and positional advantage to White.

12 Bg5-f4?!,

Much stronger is **12 Qc2!** e.g. **12 ..., e5**; 13 Bxf6!, Bxf6; 14 e4!, d4; 15 Bc4+ followed by 16 Nd5 (Voronkov); one point of the suggestion 11 ..., Kh8 is seen here. A game Holmov-Portisch, Balaton-fured 1959, continued instead **12 ..., Bd6** but after 13 Rfe1, Rac8; 14 Rad1, Bb8; 15 Bh4, Kh8; 16 Bf1, e5; 17 e4! White again had the better game. Peresipkin, who played the Blumenfeld at least twice at Kaliningrad, presumably had some improvement in mind and this, I would guess, was **12 ..., Qh5!** with an unclear position. In all these lines Black stands well, so long as he can maintain his centre.

12 ..., Kg8-h8; 13 Nf3-e5, Nd7xe5; 14 Bf4xe5, Nf6-d7; 15 Be5-g3, Be7-f6; 16 Ra1-c1, Qe8-e7;

Black is clearly making steady progress.

17 Be2-d3!?,

Hoping to bring about some clarification of the situation by tempting Black's advance; otherwise he will be slowly crushed into passivity.

17 ..., e7-e5; 18 e3-e4, c5-c4; 19 Bd3-b1, d5-d4; 20 Nc3-d5, Bb7xd5; 21 e4xd5, Nd7-b6;

82

22 Bb1-e4, Qe7-f7; 23 d5-d6, Ra8-d8; 24 f2-f4, e5xf4; 25 Bg3xf4, Nb6-d5; 26 Be4xd5, Qf7xd5; 27 Qd1-a4, Rd8-c8; 28 d6-d7,

Also after **28 Qxa7**, Qxb5 it's feeding time for the Black pieces.

28 ..., Qd5xd7; 29 Rc1xc4, d4-d3;

White is still a pawn up, but Black's d-pawn is a princess!

30 Rc4xc8, Rf8xc8; 31 Bf4-e3, Bf6xb2; 32 Qa4-f4,

If **32 Bxa7?**, d2, so a little mate threat instead.

32 ..., h7-h6; 33 a2-a4, Rf8-e8;

Threatens ..., Rxe3 and ..., Bd4.

34 Be3-d2, Re8-e2; 35 Rf1-d1, Bb2-f6;

Preventing the check on f8.

36 Kg1-h1, Qd7-d5; 37 Qf4-f1, Qd5-b3; 38 a4-a5, Qb3xb5; 39 Bd2xh6!,

Not that it makes any difference really ...

39 ..., Qb5xa5;

Since if **40 Rxd3**, Re1.

40 Bh6-f4, Bf6-h4; 41 Bf4-g3,

Bh4xg3; 42 h2xg3, Qa5-h5+; 43
Kh1-g1, Qh5-c5+?!; 44 Kg1-h2,
Qc5-h5+; 45 Kh2-g1, d3-d2;

He sees it this time.

46 Qf1-f8+, Kh8-h7; 47 Kg1-f1,

Or 47 Qf1, Qe5 and ..., Re1.

47 ..., Re2-e1+; White resigns.

If 48 Rxf1, Qh1+ etc.

Game 41
Furman - Panov
(Leningrad semi-final,
15th USSR Championship 1946)

**1 d2-d4, Ng8-f6; 2 c2-c4, e7-e6; 3
Ng1-f3, c7-c5; 4 d4-d5, b7-b5; 5
d5xe6, f7xe6; 6 c4xb5, d7-d5;
7 Nb1-d2,**

This move, apparently stemming from Alekhine's notes to his
game with Tarrasch, may only have
been played in the present game.
Pachman and Voronkov do not
even mention it.

7 ..., Qd8-a5;

Better than 7 ..., Bb7; 8 e4! or
7 ..., **Bd6?!**; 8 e4!, Nbd7; 9 Qe2!,
Be7; 10 g3, O-O; 11 Bg2, Bb7; 12
O-O in either case with advantage
to White (Hildebrand).

8 e2-e3, Bc8-d7; 9 Bf1-e2,

The attempt to hold on to the
pawn by 9 a4?! is extremely
suspect, e.g. 9 ..., a6 (or quiet play
with about equal chances) 10 bxa6,
Nxa6; 11 Be2, Nb4; 12 b3, c4 and
Black wins either the a-pawn or the
exchange (analysis). Alekhine's
suggestion was to combine Nbd2
with a queen's fianchetto, but
whether he would have played 8, 9
or 10 b3 we shall never know.

9 ..., Bd7xb5; 10 O-O, Bb5xe2;

Presumably 10 ..., Bc6!?; 11
Ne5 is promising for White.

11 Qd1xe2, Qa5-a6!;

It is important to maintain the
white squares.

**12 Qd1-e1, Nb8-c6;
13 e3-e4, Nc6-b4;**

Threatening a fork on c2.

14 Qe1-d1, O-O-O!?;

If 14 ..., Be7; 15 exd5, exd5; 16
Re1 could be awkward (Panov in
'Schachmaty').

83

A difficult position - is Black's
centre strong or weak? How vulnerable is his king? Hildebrand holds
that Black stands rather better
(certainly his development is superior) but equally Black has some
nasty moments in the sequel.

**15 Nf3-e5, Qa6-b7; 16 e4xd5,
e6xd5; 17 Nd2-f3, Bf8-d6; 18
Qd1-a4, Rh8-e8; 19 a2-a3!,**

Commencing the plan of opening Black up. If 19 ..., Na6; 20 Nf7!

**19 ..., Bd6xe5; 20 a3xb4, c5-c4; 21
Nf3xe5, Re8xe5; 22 Bc1-f4, Re5-e4;
23 Bf4-d2, Rd8-d7; 24 Qa4-d1,
Qb7-c7; 25 Ra1-a5, Kc8-d8;**

Panov looks for a safer roof
over his head.

26 Qd1-f3, Qc7-d6; 27 Rf1-a1,

Nf6-g4; 28 g2-g3, Ng4-e5;
29 Qf3-f5?,

White embarks on a bad plan.
He should play **29 Qg2** although
there comes then 29 ..., Nd3
(Panov).

29 ..., g7-g6; 30 Qf5-g5+?,

One mistake intends another!
Panov gives as preferable **30 Bg5+**,
Ke8; 31 Qf6 when he intended 31
..., Qxf6; 32 Bxf6, Nc6 threatening
..., d4 and ..., Nb4.

30 ..., Kd8-e8; 31 Kg1-g2, Ne5-f7;
32 Bd2-f4, Nf7xg5; 33 Bf4xd6,
Rd7xd6; 34 Ra5xa7, Re4-e2;
35 Ra7-g7,

Threatening the win of a rook,
commencing Ra8+.

35 ..., Ke8-f8; 36 Ra1-a7, Rd6-f6;
37 g3-g4,

Mate is inevitable.

37 ..., Rf6xf2+; 38 Kg2-g3,
Ng5-e4+; **White resigns.**

Game 42
Botterill - Bellin
(Robert Silk Fellowship,
Paignton 1971)
Notes marked (B) are specially
contributed by George Botterill.

1 d2-d4, Ng8-f6; 2 c2-c4, e7-e6;
3 Ng1-f3, c7-c5; 4 d4-d5, b7-b5;
5 Bc1-g5!,

This move of Dus-Hotimirski
is generally considered to be the
best reply to the Blumenfeld
Counter-Gambit.

Other methods of declining
the pawn are:

a) 5 Nc3, b4; 6 Nb1 (Better than 6
Na4, exd5; 7 cxd5, d6; 8 Bg5, Be7;

9 e3, O-O; 10 Bc4, Nbd7; 11 O-O,
Bb7; 12 h3, Nb6; 13 Nxb6, axb6
with advantage to Black; H.Steiner
-Samisch, Berlin 1930) **6 ..., d6!** (If
6 ..., exd5; 7 cxd5, Bb7 comes 8
Bg5!, h6; 9 Bxf6, Qxf6; 10 e4! and
White got excellent compensation
for his pawn in Yudovich-Gusev,
Moscow 1948; 6 ..., Bb7? comes to
the same, while if 6 ..., Be7
Hildebrand gives 7 d6, Bf8; 8 Bf4,
Ne4; 9 Qd3, Bb7; 10 Nbd2, f5 with
an unclear position) 7 Bg5, Be7; 8
Bxf6 (Black threatened ..., Nxd5) 8
..., Bxf6; 9 Qc2, O-O; 10 e4, Nd7;
11 Nbd2, a5 (analysis of Hildebrand). Black can choose between
two good plans: ..., Nb8-d7-b6 with
..., a5-a4-a3 and ..., exd5, or ..., e5,
..., g6, ..., Bg7 preparing ..., f5.

b) 5 e4!?, Nxe4 (Not 5 ..., Bxc4?; 6
Nc3, exd5; 7 e5! Vukovic-Spiel-
mann, Vienna 1922) 6 dxe6 (If 6
Bd3, Nf6 transposes, but 6 ...,
Qa5+? was crushed in Yahin-
Popov, Frunze 1964) 6 ..., fxe6; 7
Bd3, Nf6 (7 ..., Nd6!? Hildebrand)
8 Ng5, Qe7! (8 ..., bxc4?; 9 Bxh7!) 9
cxb5 (Not 9 Bxh7?, Rxh7; 10 Nxh7,
Nxh7; 11 Qh5+, g6; 12 Qxg6+,
Qf7 Pachman) 9 ..., d5 (Hildebrand
recommends 9 ..., Bb7; 19 O-O, g6)
10 O-O, g6; 11 Re1, Bg7; 12 Qe2
(Or 12 Nc3!?, O-O; 13 f4, c4?!; 14
Bf1 - Grunfeld) 12 ..., c4!; 13 Bc2,
O-O; 14 Nxe6, Re8 and now after
15 Nf4?, Qf7! in the game
Rubinstein-Tartakover, Teplitz-
Schonau 1922, Black stood well
and won. An old analysis of
Grunfeld, however, shows that 15
Nd4! would have assured White of
a large advantage: 15 ..., Qc5; 16
Be3, Ng4; 17 Ne6! or 15 ..., Qc7; 16
Qf1. The absence of comment on
this dangerous possibility of 5 e4 is
a major omission of Voronkov's

article.

c) 5 a4, b4! (No other move here is satisfactory; for 5 ..., bxc4 see for example the game Rubinstein-Spielmann, Vienna 1922) 6 Bg5, d6; 7 e4, h6! (Not 7 ..., Be7; 8 Bd3, Nxd5?; 9 exd5!, Bxg5; 10 dxe5 with 11 Be4 in hand) 8 Bxf6, Qxf6; 9 Qc2, e5 and Black, continuing ..., g6, ..., Bg7 and ..., O-O gets a good game whilst White has potential weaknesses on the queen side (Euwe).

d) 5 g3, Bb7; 6 dxe6, fxe6; 7 cxb5, d5; 8 Bh3, Qb6; 9 a4, Nbd7; 10 Bf4 (Stolberg-Konstantinov, USSR 1937). Black now played the positional blunder 10 ..., a5?, whereas continuing with the normal 10 ..., h6 (or may be 10 ..., Be7 even) the threat to win a piece by ..., g5-g4 he could have undercut White's plans completely: e.g. 11 Ne5, Nxe5; 12 Bxe5, d4! and if 13 f3, O-O; 14 O-O then the positional sacrifice 14 ..., Nd7; 15 Bf4, Rxf4 followed by ..., Nf6-h5 puts White under heavy pressure (analysis).

5 ..., e6xd5;

Other moves are suspect:

a) 5 ..., Qa5+?; 6 Qd2, Qxd2+; 7 Nbxd2, bxc4 (Or 7 ..., exd5; 8 Bxf6, gxf6; 9 cxd5, Bb7; 10 e4, a6; 11

Nh4 Marshall-Hanauer, New York 1937) 8 Bxf6, gxf6; 9 e4, f5; 10 Bxc4 Bb7; 11 O-O, Bh6; 12 Rfe1, O-O; 13 Rad1, Kh8; 14 Nb3, Ba6; 15 Na5 both favouring White (Grunfeld-Rabinovich, Moscow 1925)

b) 5 ..., Qb6?; 6 Bxf6 (Or 6 Nc3, bxc4; 7 e4 Gereben-Balogh, Budapest 1936) 6 ..., gxf6; 7 e4, b4; 8 Be2, d6; 9 O-O, Bh6; 10 Ne1!, e5; 11 Bg4! with great advantage to White (Macht-Spielmann, Kaunas 1934).

c) 5 ..., h6!?; 6 Bxf6 (If 6 Bh4?! then 6 ..., bxc4; 7 Nc3, d6; 8 e4, Be7; 9 dxe6, Bxe6; 10 Bxc4, O-O Roessel-Scheipl, match Amsterdam-Munich 1961, or 6 ..., exd5!; 7 cxd5, Bb7 given in the Latvian magazine 'Sahs') 6 ..., Qxf6:

c1) 7 Nc3, b4 (Or 7 ..., bxc4; 8 e4!, d6; 9 Bxc4, e5; 10 Qa4+ Januschko -Igel, Austria 1922, or probably better 9 dxe6, Bxe6; 10 Bxc4!, Nd7; 11 Bxe6, Qxe6; 12 O-O, Nb6; 13 a4!, Be7; 14 a5, Nc8; 15 Nd5, Bd8 Chukaev-Chesnauskas, Vilnous 1961, as White could now play 16 Re1, O-O; 17 e5 instead of 16 b4?!) 8 Nb5, Na6; 9 e4!, Qxb2 (No better 9 ..., e5) 10 Bd3, d6 (Worse luck for Black after 10 ..., Qf6?; 11 e5!, Qd8; 12 dxe6! with a quick win for Grunfeld against Bogolyubov at Vienna 1922) 11 O-O, Bd7; 12 Qa4 with a plus for White (Helling-Leonhardt, Berlin 1928).

c2) 7 Qc2?!, Na6; 8 e4 (8 a3!? 'Sahs') 8 ..., Nb4; 9 Qd2, bxc4; 10 Bxc4, Qg6; 11 O-O, Qxe4; 12 Na3, Be7; 13 Rfe1, Qf5 with complications (Dzhindzhihasvili-Peresipkin, Kaliningrad 1972).

c3) 7 Qd2, exd5; 8 cxd5, g5?! (Rosenfeld-Heinra, Estonia 1965).

d) 5 ..., bxc4; 6 e4!, Qa5+; **7 Nc3?!** (Best may be Hildebrand's 7 Qd2, Qxd2+; 8 Nbxd2) 7 ..., Nxe4 (7 ..., Ba6; 8 dxe6! Dus-Hotimirski - Levenfish, USSR 1922) 8 Bxc4, Nxc3; 9 Qd2, Qb4!; 10 Qxc3, Qxc3+; 11 bxc3, d6 (11 ..., Be7?; 12 O-O-O! Moritz-Gilg, Oeynhausen 1922) and in Grunfeld's view we might well ask where White's compensation is? Another Grunfeld idea here is **7 Bd2**, Qb6; 8 Nc3, Ba6; 9 Ne5.

e) 5 ..., Bb7; 6 e4, Qa5+; 7 Qd2, Qxd2+; 8 Nfxd2, b4 (8 ..., Be7!?) 9 Bd3, d6; 10 O-O, Nd7; 11 f4 and White was on top (Grunfeld-Michell, Margate 1923).

6 c4xd5, d7-d6!?;

An interesting alternative, devised by Tartakover, to the usual move **6 ..., h6** when can follow:

a) 7 Bxf6, Qxf6; 8 Qc2 (Not 8 Nc3?, b4!; 9 Nb5?, Qb6 or 9 Ne4, Qxb2; 10 d6, Na6! or 9 Na4, d6 while if 8 e4?!, Qxb2; 9 Nbd2, c4! Hildebrand) 8 ..., d6; 9 e4, a6; 10 a4!, b4 (10 ..., bxa4!? Yudovich in 'Informator 4') 11 Nfd2 (11 Nbd2, Bg4!; 12 Be2, Bxf3! or 12 e5!?, Qe7!, or 11 h3, g5!; 12 Nbd2, Nd7; 13 Nc4, Bg7 Voronkov; or 11 Bd3, Nd7; 12 Nbd2, g5!? with complications: Tatai-Rodriguez, Skopje 1972) 11 ..., Be7 (Or 11 ..., Nd7; 12 Nc4, g5; 13 Bd3, Bg7; 14 O-O, Qe7; 15 e5! Shashin-Bastrikov, USSR 1967, or Euwe's suggestion 13 a5, Bg7; 14 Nbd2 intending Bd3, O-O and an eventual f4) 12 Nc4, Nd7; 13 Nbd2, O-O; 14 Bd3, a5 (14 ..., Ne5!? Voronkov) 15 O-O, Ne5; 16 Nxe5!, dxe5 (16 ..., Qxe5; 17 f4, Qd4+; 18 Kh1 and Nf3) 17 Nc4! and White has a big positional advantage, although he made nothing of it in

the game Lipnitsky-Tolush, 18th USSR Championship 1950.

b) 7 Bh4 may be better than was once held:

b1) 7 ..., g5 (Pachman suggested 7 ..., d6; 8 e4, holding ..., g5 in reserve) 8 Bg3, d6; 9 e4, a6 (9 ..., Nxe4!?; 10 Bxb5+, Bd7 Hildebrand) 10 a4, b4; 11 Nfd2!, Bg7; 12 Bd3, O-O, Ne8; 14 Nbd2, Nbd7; 15 O-O, Nb6; 16 Nxb6, Qxb6; 17 Nc4, Qd8; 18 f4, g4; 19 e5! and White had a strong attack (Geller-Szabo, Stockholm 1952).

b2) 7 ..., Bb7; 8 e4!, g5; 9 Bg3, Qe7 (Not 9 ..., Nxe4?!; 10 Qe2, Qe7 because of 11 Be5!, f6; 12 Qxe4, fxe5; 13 Bxb5, Bg7; 14 Nc3, Qf6; 15 h4! Sakharov-Goldenov, Kiev 1946) 10 Qe2, Qxe4; 11 Be5!, Qxe2+; 12 Bxe2, Bg7; 13 Nc3, a6; 14 h4! with a sharp position in which Voronkov holds White's chances to be better. But in view of the myriad possibilities following 14 ..., b4, 14 ..., g4 and 14 ..., d6!? one can only consider the case 'not proven'.

85

7 e2-e4,

A correspondence game Runstrom-Svensson (1964) went instead **7 Nc3**, b4; 8 Ne4, Be7; 9 Bxf6, Bxf6; 10 Qc2, O-O; 11 e3,

Ba6!; 12 Bxa6, Nxa6; 13 O-O, Nc7 and Black stood well.

7 ..., a7-a6; 8 Nb1-d2?!,

More precise is **8 a4!** which after **8 ..., Be7** (8 ..., b4; 9 Nbd2, Be7; 10 Bc4!, O-O; 11 O-O, Nbd7; 12 a5! Voronkov) **9 Nbd2** would transpose back to the game. However White could also try, instead of 9 Nbd2, one of:

a) 9 axb5?, Nxe4!; 10 Bxe7, Qxe7; 11 Be2, O-O; 12 O-O, Bb7; 13 Nc3, a6; 14 Rxa8, Bxa8; 15 Bxb5, Nf6 and Black had a good game (Milev-Portisch, Moscow 1959).

b) 9 Bxf6!, Bxf6; 10 axb5 (10 Qc2 was also good in Bobotsov-Drimer, Leipzig 1960) 10 ..., Bxb2; 11 Ra2, Bf6; 12 Nbd2, O-O; 13 Bd3, Bb7; 14 O-O, Re8; 15 Qb3!, Re7; 16 Rb1 with advantage to White (Fuchs-Radovic, Bucharest 1959).

8 ..., Bf8-e7;

Now Black has caught his opponent in an inferior line.

9 a2-a4, b5xa4;

Better seems 9 ..., Nxd5!? and now:

a) 10 Bxe7, Qxe7; 11 axb5, O-O. In 'Indian Systems' Pachman says 'Black having a satisfactory game.' But it is probably more than satisfactory, e.g. 12 Be2, Nf4 (12 ..., Nf6 is also good) 13 O-O, d5! with advantage to Black, for if 14 e5 there comes 14 ..., f6.

b) 10 exd5! (This is not considered by Pachman) 10 ..., Bxg5; 11 Qe2+, Be7 (Best, I think) 12 axb5, O-O; 13 Qd3, Re8; 14 Be2 with an unclear position.(B)

10 Qd1xa4+, Nf6-d7; 11 Bg5-f4?!,

Better 11 Bxe7, Qxe7; 12 Bd3 with an edge for White (B).

11 ..., O-O; 12 Bf1-d3, Nd7-b6; 13 Qa4-a5,

At the time I thought this was very strong, having quite overlooked the reply. However, **13 Qc2**, a5!; 14 O-O, Na6 does not look very much more inviting (B).

13 ...., f7-f5!;

Winning a pawn. Black stands better (B).

14 e4xf5, Bc8xf5; 15 Bd3xf5, Rf8xf5; 16 Bf4-g3,

This bishop has proved an embarrassment, but it returns to life later.

16 ..., Rf5xd5; 17 O-O, Nb8-c6; 18 Qa5-a2, Kg8-h8;

The alternative was **18 ..., Nb4!?** (B).

19 Ra1-d1, Nc6-b4; 20 Qa2-b1, Qd8-f8; 21 Nd2-e4, h7-h6; 22 Rd1xd5, Nb6xd5; 23 Rf1-d1, Nd5-f4; 24 Ne4-c3,

Now White has - very luckily - compensation on the White squares (B).

24 ..., Nf4-h5; 25 Bg3-h4!, Nh5-f6; 26 Qb1-g6, Ra8-d8; 27 h2-h3, Nb4-c6; 28 Nc3-e2,

Intending to go to f4 (B).

28 ..., Nf6-d7; 29 Qg6-e4, Nc6-e5; 30 Nf3xe5, Nd7xe5; 31 Bh4-g3, Be7-f6; 32 Qe4-b7, Qf8-f7!; 33 Qb7xa6, Qf7-c4; 34 Qa6xc4, Nd5xc4; 35 b2-b3, Nc4-a5; 36 Ne2-c1, d7-d5?;

See Diagram 86

Time trouble. **36 ..., Bb2**; 37 Nd3, Bd4; 38 b4, Nb3 is about equal, maybe better for Black (B).

37 Bg3-c7, Rd8-a8; 38 Rd1xd5, Na5-b7; 39 Bc7-f4, Ra8-a1; 40

86

Kg1-h2, Ra1-b1; 41 Bf4-d2,
    Kh8-h7; 42 f2-f4,

Possible was **42 Rd3!?** intending 43 Ne2 (B).

42 ..., Bf6-d4; 43 Nc1-e2, Rb1-b2!;

Not **43 ..., Rxb3?**; 44 Nxd4,
Rd3; 45 Be3! (or 45 Bc3!) 45 ...,
Rxe3; 46 Nf5 and White is winning
(B).

**44 Ne2xd4, Rb2xd2; 45 Rd5-d7.
Draw agreed.**

NIMZO-INDIAN DEFENCE (1 d4, Nf6; 2 c4, e6; 3 Nc3, Bb4)

Game 43
Spassky - Tal
(Tallinn 1973)

**1 d2-d4, Ng8-f6; 2 c2-c4, e7-e6;
3 Nb1-c3, Bf8-b4; 4 Bc1-g5!?,**

This has long been Spassky's
favourite way of meeting the
Nimzo. It was much analysed in the
1950s by his former trainer, Zak.

Another line of the Nimzo-
Indian in which Black may sacrifice
a pawn is suggested by Bronstein.
After **4 Qc2**, c5; 5 dxc5, O-O!; 6
Be3?! (Instead of 6 Bf4) Averbakh,
against Bronstein at Leningrad in
1963, played 6 ..., Qe7; 7 Nf3,
Bxc5; 8 Bg5! and White stood
better, but he could have tried **6 ...,
b6!**; 7 cxb6, d5! endangering
White's king.

**4 ..., h7-h6; 5 Bg5-h4, c7-c5;
6 d4-d5,**

This seems necessary because
if **6 e3**, Qa5; 7 Qb3, Ne4 favoured
Black in Reti-Marshall, Brno 1928,
whereas if now **6 ..., Qa5?** White

can play 7 Bxf6, gxf6; 8 Qc2
'resulting in a serious weakness of
Black's king side' (Pachman).

6 ..., b7-b5!;

An interesting solution, which
has long been known to be best.
Compared with the analogous
system in the Blumenfeld Counter-
Gambit (Game 42), Black has
better chances because of the
powerful pin on the White knight.
Other moves are at best merely
adequate:

a) 6 ..., exd5; 7 cxd5, O-O (Or 7 ...,
d6 when either Korchnoy's 8 e3 or
Pachman's 8 e3 offer White some
advantage) 8 e3, d6; 9 Bd3, Nbd7;
10 Nge2, Ne5; 11 O-O with an edge
for White (Spassky-Filip, Interzonal 1955).

b) 6 ..., d6; 7 e3 (7 Qc2!?
Purevshav-Sakhalkar, Tel Aviv
1964) 7 ..., e5; 8 Ne2 (8 Qc2 was
only equal in Morra-Keres, Tel
Aviv 1964) 8 ..., Nbd7; 9 a3, Ba5; 10
Qc2, O-O; 11 Nc1, Re8; 12 Na2,

Qe7; 13 f3, e4 (Spassky-Keres, match 1965).

c) 6 ..., Bxc3+; 7 bxc3, e5? (Better 7 ..., d6 - Spassky in 'Chess') 8 d6! (Zak's move, which improved upon 8 e3 of Keres-O'Kelly, Budapest 1952) 8 ..., g5 (8 ..., Qa5; 9 Rc1, Qxa2; 10 Bxf6, gxf6; 11 e3 Spassky, or 8 ..., O-O; 9 e3, Re8; 10 Be2, Nc6; 11 Nh3, b6 favouring White - Pachman) 9 Bg3, Nc6; 10 Qc2, Qa5? (Better 10 ..., Nh5 intending ..., Qf6, ..., b6 and ..., Bb7 - Spassky) 11 Rc1, Qa3; 12 Nf3 with a big plus for White (Spassky-Lee, Hastings 1965-6).

d) 6 ..., Nxd5?!; 7 Bxd8, Nxc3; 8 Qb3, Ne4+; 9 Kd1, Nxf2+; 10 Kc1!, Nxh1 (Or 10 ..., Kxd8; 11 Qf3, Nxh1; 12 Qxf7!) 11 a3!, Ne4; 12 Nf3, Bf2; 13 Bc7, d5!; 14 cxd5, exd5; 15 e4! with advantage to White (Zak).

e) 6 ..., O-O; 7 Nf3!, exd5 (Or 7 ..., b5; 8 e4!, g5; 9 Nxg5) 8 cxd5, d6; 9 e3, Nbd7; 10 Nd2! favours White too - another Zak analysis.

87

7 d5xe6?!,

This move is even riskier here than in the Blumenfeld. Others:

a) 7 Rc1!?, bxc4; 8 e4, Ba6!?; 9 Qf3, g5; 10 Bg3, exd5; 11 Be5,

Nxe4!; 12 Bxh8, Qe7; 13 Qe2?! (According to Hartston, 13 Kd1 was correct) 13 ..., d4; 14 f3 with wild complications (Keene-K.Lloyd Ilford 1965).

b) 7 e4, exd5 (Or 7 ..., g5!?; 8 Bg3, Nxe4; 9 Be5, O-O!; 10 Qh5, d6; 11 Bd3, Nxc3!; 12 Qxh6, Ne4+; 13 Kf1, dxe5; 14 Bxe4, f5; 15 Qg6+ with perpetual check - Zak) **8 cxd5!** (After 8 exd5?, O-O! Black stands well, e.g. 9 cxb5, Bb7! Bagirov-Demuria, Tiflis 1957; or 9 Bd3, cxb4 Zak-Shaposnikov, Sochi 1952 although here Pachman says 10 Bc2 is better than Zak's 10 Bxc4) 8 ..., g5; 9 e5!, Qe7 (Pachman's analysis shows that 9 ..., gxh4 is inferior) 10 Bg3, Nxd5; 11 Qf3, Nxd5; 12 O-O-O!, Bxc3; 13 bxc3, Qe6; 14 c4, bxc4; 15 Bxc4, Nb4!; 16 Bxe6, Bxf3; 17 Bxf7+, Kxf7; 18 Nxf3, Nxa2+; 19 Kb2, Nb4; 20 h4 with about equal chances, following Pachman's analysis in 'Indian Systems'. One wonders whether there may be a flaw in it, since Spassky has always played the text move in preference.

7 ..., f7xe6; 8 c4xb5,

If **8 e4**, O-O; 9 Qc2 (9 e5?, Qa5) 9 ..., Qa5; 10 Bxf6, Rxf6; 11 cxb5, a6; 12 e5, Rf7 and Black has excellent attacking chances (Zak-Averbakh, Moscow 1947)

8 ..., d7-d5!;

Now Black has a very good game, and it is puzzling that this move (recommended by Pachman over a decade ago) had not previously been tried. For example the much weaker **8 ..., Qa5?** was played in Spassky-Posner, Canadian Open 1971.

9 e2-e3, O-O;

After **9 ..., d4?!**; 10 exd4, cxd4; 11 a3, Ba5; 12 b4, dxc3; 13 bxa5, Qxa5; 14 Bxf6, gxf6; 15 Qc2 White has some advantage since he has fewer weaknesses.

10 Ng1-f3, Qd8-a5;

Tal didn't like **10 ..., g5**; 11 Bg3, Ne4; 12 Qc2, Qf6 (12 ..., Qa5; 13 Nd2!) 13 Rc1, g4; 14 Nh4.

11 Bh4xf6, Rf8xf6; 12 Qd1-d2,

According to Tal's notes for 'The Chess Player' he intended to meet **12 Qc2** by 12 ..., d4; 13 exd4, Rxf3; 14 gxf3, cxd4 and **12 Qc1!?** by 12 ..., c4! (Not 12 ..., d4 because of 13 a3).

12 ..., a7-a6!;

The most dynamic way to complete his development.

13 b5xa6,

Or **13 Be2**, axb5; 14 O-O, c4 with some advantage (Tal).

13 ..., Nb8-c6!;

From a6 the knight would have little scope.

14 Bf1-e2?!,

A further error, after which Spassky is probably lost. Tal gives **14 a3**, d4; 15 Qc1! (Not 15 exd4, Rxf3; 16 gxf3, Nxd4!) 15 ..., Bxc3+; 16 bxc3, dxc3; 17 Be2 keeping White's arrears within reasonable bounds.

14 ..., d5-d4!; 15 e3xd4,

See Diagram 88

15 ..., Rf6xf3!

After **15 ..., cxd4?!**; 16 Nxd4, Nxd4; 17 Qxd4, Bc5; 18 Qa4, Bxf2+; 19 Kd1 the position is unclear (Tal).

16 Be2xf3, c5xd4; 17 O-O,

Alternatives hardly bear thinking about. For instance, **17 Rc1?**, Bxa6!; 18 Bxc6, Rd8; 19 Qc2, dxc3; 20 bxc3, Qe5+ and Black wins (Tal).

17 ..., d4xc3; 18 b2xc3, Bb4xc3; 19 Qd2-d6, Ra8xa6!;

Not **19 ..., Bxa1?**; 20 Qxc6 (Tal).

20 Bf3xc6, Bc3-b4!;

It is necessary to win the bishop. Weaker is **20 ..., Bxa1?** (Or 20 ..., Be5?; 21 Qe7) 21 Rxa1, Qb6; 22 Rc1, Rxa2; 23 Qf4 and White wins (Tal).

21 Qd6-b8, Ra6xc6;

Rough material equality for the first time.

22 Ra1-c1, Bb4-c5;

Evidently forced.

23 Rc1-c2, Qa5-a4!;

The only winning move, e.g. 23 ..., Ba7?; 24 Rxc6! (Tal).

See Diagram 89

24 Qb8-b3,

If **24 Rfc1** Tal intended 24 ..., Bxf2+!

24 ..., Qa4-f4; 25 Qb3-g3,

89

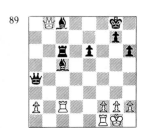

Other moves analysed by Tal:

a) 25 Qb5, Qd6; 26 Rfc1, Ba6; 27 Qa5, Bxf2+; 28 Kxf2, Qf4+; 29 Kg1, Qe3+; 30 Kh1, Qxc1+

b) 25 Qf3!?, Qxf3; 26 gxf3, e5; 27 h4!? with endgame advantage to Black.

25 ..., Qf4-f5; 26 Rf1-c1, Bc8-b7!; 27 Qg3-f3,

If 27 Qb8+, Kh7; 28 Qxb7, Bxf2+ and Tal wins.

27 ..., Qf5-g5; 28 Qf3-b3,

Not 28 Qg3?, Bxf2+! e.g. 29 Kxf2, Qf5+ or 29 Qxf2, Qxc1+.

28 ..., Rc8-c7; 29 g2-g3,

If 29 Qxe6+, Rf7; 30 Qh3, Rxf2 etc.

29 ..., Bc5xf2+!; 30 Kg1xf2, Qg5-f6+?!;

According to Tal, more precise was **30 ..., Qf5+!** meeting 31 Kg1 by 31 ..., Qe4. He is winning anyway.

31 Kf2-e1, Qf6-e5+; 32 Ke1-f1,

Or 32 Kd1, Qd4+; 33 Ke1, Qe4+ (Tal).

32 ..., Bb7-a6+; 33 Kf1-g1, Qe5-d4+; 34 Kg1-g2, Qd4-e4+; 35 Kg2-g1,

If 35 Kh3, Rxc2; 36 Qxc2, Bf1+ (Tal).

35 ..., Ba6-b7;

Reaching the same position as after the note to Black's 30th move.

36 h2-h4, Qe4-h1+; 37 Kg1-f2, Rc7-f7+; 38 Kf2-e2, Qh1-e4+; White resigns.

GRUNFELD DEFENCE (1 d4, Nf6; 2 c4, g6; 3 Nc3, d5)

The Grunfeld leads, in many cases, to an early tactical struggle and there are several more or less sound counter-gambits which Black can offer if White gives him the opportunity. These arise in a wide variety of ways, but a common theme in the justification behind most of them is: the White king in the centre.

**Game 44
Ocampo - Najdorf**
(Buenos Aires 1968)

1 d2-d4, Ng8-f6; 2 c2-c4, g7-g6; 3 Nb1-c3, d7-d5; 4 Ng1-f3,

The most flexible move, although White has many others to choose from, e.g. **4 Bf4** (see Game 47), **4 cxd5**, **4 Bg5**.

Quite interesting but not very

good is **4 f3?!** against which Black, if he wishes to play safe, can transpose into a good line of the Four Pawns Attack in the King's Indian Defence, by **4 ..., Bg7**; 5 e4, dxe4; 6 fxe4, e5. Or he can try for complications with **4 ..., c5!?**; 5 dxc5, d4; 6 Nb5, Nc6; 7 Bf4, e5; 8 Bg5 (This is where Hartston's analysis in 'The Grunfeld Defence' ended, in an assessment favourable to White) 8 ..., Bxc5! offering a rook. White is advised not to play 4 f3 unless he can find an improvement upon the following variation: 9 Bxf6, Qxf6; 10 Nc7+, Kd8; 11 Nxa8, Be6!; 12 e4, Bb4+; 13 Kf2, d3!; 14 Qxd3+!?, Kc8 and Black will capture the Na8 before long with a vehement attack in compensation for his exchange and pawn.

4 ..., Bf8-g7; 5 Bc1-g5,

This is one of White's sharper possibilities, but also critical are **5 Qb3** (see Game 46), **5 Bf4** and **5 cxd5** while **5 e3** (see Game 45) can lead to a variety of slower lines.

5 ..., Nf6-e4; 6 c4xd5, Ne4xg5; 7 Nf3xg5, e7-e6!;

The best move, since Hartston shows that **7 ..., e5?!** can be well met by 8 Nf3, exd4; 9 Nxd4, c5; 10 Nf3, b5!; 11 Nxb5, Bxb2; 12 Rb1, Bg7; 13 d6! while the alternative gambit **7 ..., c6?!** (mentioned in an article by the present author in 'The Chess Player') can now be categorically stated to be unsound. The inaugural game Gunnell-Harding (London 1972) went 8 dxc6, Nxc6 (Not 8 ..., e5?? as misprinted in that article, on account of 9 cxb7, Bxb7; 10 Qb3) 9 e3?! (The refutation begins 9 d5!) 9 ..., e5; 10 Nf3, exd4; 11 exd4, O-O; 12 Be2 and White's sterile attitude

was rapidly rewarded by a drawn ending.

90

8 Qd1-d2,

White can also play the quiet **8 Nf3** but **8 Qa4+!?** is risky on account of **8 ..., c6!**; 9 dxc6, Nxc6; 10 Nf3, Bd7; 11 Qd1, O-O with about equal chances as in Blagidze-Gurgenidze, USSR 1959, or here 11 ..., Qb6! (Prybil).

8 ..., h7-h6!?;

This is where the fun really begins, since Black can also get a good game by **8 ..., exd5**; 9 Qe3+, Kf8; 10 Qf4, Bf6; 11 h4, h6 (or maybe 11 ..., c6) as first played in Stein-Spassky, 31st USSR Championship, 1963.

9 Ng5-h3, e6xd5; 10 Qd2-e3+,

If **10 Nf4!?** the correct course is **10 ..., O-O!** (to meet 11 Nfxd5 by 11 ..., c6! in e3, c5! as in Pytel-Adorjan, Polanica Zdroi 1971. But in a London league match game Cooke-Harding Black forgot this analysis and played instead **10 ..., c5?!**; 11 dxc5, d4; 12 Rd1, Nc6; 13 Ne4, O-O; 14 g3!, Qe7; 15 Bg2, b6!; 16 O-O, Rd8 (welcoming White's forthcoming attack on f7, since I was at the time convinced of the logicality of my play) 17 Nd6, Bd7; 18 Bd5, Ne5!; 19 Bxa8, Rxa8;

20 Nd5, Qf8; 21 b4, Bc6; 22 Nf4, Rd8; 23 Nd3. Unfortunately Black was now in time trouble and so, instead of the promising 23 ..., Nd7!, played the absurd 23 ..., Rxd6 and quickly lost. An unusual struggle.

10 ..., Ke8-f8;

Not **10 ..., Be6**; 11 Nf4 with advantage to White.

11 Nh3-f4, c7-c5!;

Here **11 ..., Nc6**; 12 Rd1, Ne7; 13 Qd2, c6 (Adorjan) may be all right, but **11 ..., c6?!** is too passive and obstructs development.

12 d4xc5!?,

It is rather unusual for White to accept this pawn, but of course it must be critical. After **12 Qf3, cxd4** White dare not play **13 Nxg6+?!**, Kg8; 14 Nxh8, dxc3; 15 Nxf7, cxb2; 16 Rb1, Qa5+ and so play goes **13 Ncxd5**, Kg8; 14 e4, Nc6 (If 14 ..., dxe3 recapture with the pawn is promising) 15 Be2 (To avoid the coming liquidation White played in Ripley-Harding, Brighton 1972, the original 15 a3!?, Kh7; 16 Be2 but after 16 ..., Qd6!; 17 O-O, Bd7 he was already having to face the threat of ..., f5) 15 ..., Qa5+; 16 b4, Nxb4 with equal chances (Kiarner-Nei, USSR 1962).

12 ..., d5-d4; 13 Qe3-d2,

Malich suggested, in 'The Chess Player' that White could get a slight advantage here by **13 O-O-O**, Nc6; 14 Qf3 however after 14 ..., Qa5 Black's resources in the ensuing complications certainly look no worse.

13 ..., Nb8-c6; 14 Nc3-e4, Bg7-e5;

There is no progress to be made by routine moves, so Najdorf

prepares to dislodge at least one of the strong white knights. He stands well.

15 g2-g3?!,

A natural move, but there may be better. Probably **15 Nd3**.

15 ..., Be5-c7;

Threatening the queen.

16 O-O-O, g7-g5; 17 Nf4-d3, Qd8-d5; 18 Bf1-g2, Qd5xa2;

In one form or another, this was hard for White to prevent even back at move 15.

19 Qd2-c2, Bc8-f5; 20 b2-b3, Qa2-a3+; 21 Qc2-b2, Qa3-a6; 22 Kc1-b1, Ra8-e8; 23 f2-f3, Bc7-e5; 24 Qb2-a2, Qa6-b5; 25 Qa2-a4, Qb5xa4; 26 b3xa4, Kf8-g7;

91

This ending is much in Black's favour since he has good control of the centre and targets on the queen side.

27 Kb1-c2, Bf5-d7; 28 Rd1-b1, Nc6-a5; 29 Ra4-b4, f7-f5; 30 Ne4-f2 Be5-f6;

Now it will pay to conserve the two bishops, since White is covering everything for the time being.

31 Kc2-d2, Re8-e7; 32 Rh1-b1, Rh8-e8; 33 Bg2-f1,

What a miserable piece this is.

33 ..., Bd7-e6; 34 Nf2-d1, Be6-d5; 35 Rb4-b5, Na5-c4+; 36 Kd2-c1, Nc4-a3; 37 Rb1-b2, Na3xb5; 38 a4xb5, Re7-c7; 39 Kc1-d2, Bd5-c4; 40 Nd1-f2, Bf6-e7; 41 b5-b6 and **White Resigns.**

Game 45
Taimanov - Boleslavsky
(USSR Trade Union Championship 1964)

1 d2-d4, Ng8-f6; 2 c2-c4, g7-g6; 3 Nb1-c3, d7-d5; 4 Ng1-f3, Bf8-g7; 5 e2-e3, O-O; 6 Bc1-d2,

Opocensky's Variation, which is one of the many moves in this quiet line: White has also **6 Be2, 6 Qb3, 6 b4** and **6 cxd5** but all are level.

6 ..., c7-c5!;

The move White thought he was preventing. It is also possible to play **6 ..., c6** with positions akin to the Slav Defence in the Queen's Gambit.

7 d4xc5, Nb8-a6; 8 c4xd5,

White might as well accept the pawn, since there is nothing in **8 Be2,** dxc4; 9 O-O, Nxc5; 10 Bxc4, Bg4 (Lyavdansky-Bukhman, 33rd USSR Championship 1965).

8 ..., Na6xc5;

This is clearly superior to **8 ..., Nxd5**; 9 Bxa6, Nxc3 (Worse is 9 ..., bxa6); 10 Bxc3, Bxc3; 11 bxc3, bxa6; 12 O-O, Bb7; 13 Rb1, Qc7; 14 Nd4, Be4 and Black's strong bishop gives Black chances of equalising (Taimanov-Kristiansson Rejkjavik 1968).

9 Bf1-c4,

Any other move simply allows

Black to recapture the pawn and a slight lead in time which be might be exploited on the queen side.

92

9 ..., a7-a6;

Threatening 10 ..., b5 and the regain of the pawn. However a very sharp possibility in this position is **9 ..., b5!?** when there can follow:

a) 10 Bxb5, Rb8 or possibly 10 ..., Bb7!?

b) 10 Nxb5, Nxd5; 11 Bxd5 (If 11 Rb1, Nb6 with the initiative) 11 ..., Qxd5; 12 Nc7 (12 Nc3?!, Nd3+; 13 Kf1, Qc4; 14 b3, Qa6; 15 Kg1, Bb7 with enormous minor pieces to compensate for the pawn) 12 ..., Nd3+; 13 Kf1, Qc4; 14 Nxa8 (If 14 Qe2 Black has either the safe 14 ..., Qxc7; 15 Qxe2, Bxb2 or the wild 14 ..., Bxb2!?) 14 ..., Nf4+; 15 Kg1 (15 Ke1??, Nxg2 mate) 15 ..., Ne2+; 16 Kf1, Nc3+ and wins. Although the text move is also quite satisfactory, undoubtedly this new possibility is worthy of serious attention (analysis). Another idea is **9 ..., Bf5;** 10 O-O, a6?!; 11 Nd4 (Zuhovitsky-Tukmakov, USSR 1971) but better here is 10 ..., Rc8! (Gufeld).

10 b2-b4,

The alternative is **10 a4, Bf5;**

11 O-O, Rc8 and Black has rather the better of the position, e.g.:

a) 12 Qe2, Nfe4; 13 Rfd1, Nxc3; 14 Bxc3, Bxc3; 15 bxc3, Qa5! (Dementiev-Tukmakov, USSR '71)

b) 12 Nd4 (Holmov-Shamkovich, Moscow 1968) 12 ..., Bd3!; 13 Bxd3, Nxd3; 14 Qb3, Nc5 (Hartston).

10 ..., Nc5-e4; 11 Ra1-c1, Bc8-g4; 12 Nc3xe4, Nf6xe4; 13 O-O, e7-e6!; 14 d5xe6!,

Since Black will otherwise regain his pawn with strong pressure, the chances are equal, according to Hartston.

14 ..., Bg4xf3; 15 g2xf3, Ne4xd2; 16 e6-e7,

After **16 exf7+?**, Kh8; 17 Re1, Nxc4 White ends up with only two pawns for a strong bishop. If now **16 ..., Nxf3+?!**; 17 Qxf3, Qxe7; 18 Bd5 with the initiative.

16 ..., Qd8xe7!; 17 Qd1xd2, Ra8-d8 18 Qd2-e1, Rd8-d6; 19 Bc4-b3, Qe7-h4; 20 Rc1-c4, Qh4-h3; 21 Qe1-e2, Bg7-e5; 22 f3-f4, Rd8-d2! Draw agreed.

Game 46
Ivkov - Ree
(Wijk aan Zee 1971)

1 d2-d4, Ng8-f6; 2 c2-c4, g7-g6; 3 Nb1-c3, d7-d5; 4 Ng1-f3, Bf8-g7; 5 Qd1-b3, d5xc4; 6 Qb3xc4, O-O; 7 e2-e4,

Reaching the main branching point of the Russian System.

7 ..., a7-a6!?;

Currently fashionable, this move which spent over 30 years in obscurity after its original (unsuc-

cessful) adoption by Alekhine in the 12th game of his first world championship match with Euwe (1935). Its revival is due to the young Soviet master Lukin and to various Hungarian players. As yet, no way of demonstrating an advantage for White is known. And why should there be one? Black logically prepares ..., b5 and ..., Bb7 gaining time against White's queen and his e-pawn. In some lines this plan involves Black in the sacrifice of a pawn.

Black's playable alternatives are 7 ..., Bg4, 7 ..., Nc6, 7 ..., Nfd7 (variants of the Smyslov system), 7 ..., Na6 (Prins) and 7 ..., c6 (Hort). In each case very difficult positional and tactical problems can be posed to both players, which makes the Russian System perhaps the richest and most sophisticated realm within the Grunfeld Defence.

93

8 Bc1-f4?!,

The comment upon this move is that of Ivkov himself, in 'Informator 11'. He was hoping to improve upon an earlier game (see move 12) but he has not repeated the experiment.

White has several critical alternatives:

a) 8 a4?!, b5!; 9 Qb3 (Only now does White see that 9 axb5 loses a rook!) 9 ..., c5; 10 dxc5, Be6! (10 ..., b4?!) 11 Qa3? (11 Qc2 - Jovcic) 11 ..., b4 with quick wins for Black in both Pyzhkov-Lukin, USSR 1969, and Hybl-Barczay, correspondence 1971.

b) 8 Qb3, b5; **9 e5** (9 a4? see **a** and 9 Be2! see **e**) **9 ..., Nfd7!; 10 e6?!** (If 10 Be2, Nb6=) 10 ..., fxe6; 11 Qxe6+ (Or 11 Ng5, Nb6; 12 Nxe6, Bxe6; 13 Qxe6+, Kh8; 14 Be3, Qd7; 15 Qxd7, Nbxd7; 16 Be2, Nb6; 17 Bf3, Rad8; 18 O-O, Nc4 Adorjan) 11 ..., Kh8 with great complications, if anything better for Black (Portisch-Adorjan, IBM 1971). Quite critical is the 'end-game' position that can be reached by force, according to analysis by Horton in 'The Chess Player': **12 Ng5** (Portisch played 12 Qe4, Nb6; 13 Be2) 12 ..., Ne5; 13 Qd5!, Qxd5; 14 Nxd5, Ne6; 15 Nxc7, Ra7; 16 Nce6, Nxd4!; 17 Nxf8, Nc2+; 18 Kd1, Nxa1. After White's virtually forced move 19 Nfe6 Black has many simple good moves, but it seems to me probable that White cannot avoid the ultimate loss of a piece after 19 ..., h6!; 20 Nf7+, Kg8; 21 Nfd8, Rd7+; 22 Ke2, Rd6; 23 Nxg7, Kxg7; 24 b3, Nc2 (analysis). On the other hand the middle-game is very dangerous to White

The latest word is **10 Be3, Nb6** (10 ..., c5!?) 11 a4, Be6; 12 Qd1, c5! (Portisch-Vadasz, Hungarian Championship 1971).

c) 8 a3, b5; 9 Qd3, c5; 10 dxc5, Qc7; 11 Be3, Rd8; 12 Qc2, Bb7; 13 Be2, Ng4 and Black had good chances for the pawn (Forintos-Ribli, Hungary 1969).

d) 8 e5, Nfd7!? (Simplest is 8 ..., b5; 9 Qb3 transposing to **b**, but not 8 ..., Be6?! when 9 exf6! is known to be a virtually winning queen sacrifice for White) **9 e6?!** (Or 9 Be2, b5; 10 Qd5, Nb6 with about equal chances) 9 ..., fxe6; 10 Qxe6+, Kh8; 11 Ng5?!, Nc6!; 12 Nf7+?, Rxf7; 13 Qxf7, Nxd4 and Black's threats cannot be met (analysis by Horton).

e) 8 Be2!, b5; **9 Qb3** (Horton gave 9 Qd3, reckoning about equal chances) 9 ..., c5; 10 dxc5, Be6; 11 Qc2, Qc7!; 12 O-O, Qxc5; 13 Be3, Qc7 with about equal chances (Sosonko-Stean, Islington 1972).

8 ..., b7-b5!; 9 Qc4xc7, Qd8xc7;

Alekhine played **9 ..., Qe8?** and got a terrible game.

10 Bf4xc7, Bc8-b7!; 11 e4-e5, Nf6-d5;

94

In return for the sacrificed pawn, Black appears to have excellent compensation. These stem from his lead in development, the displaced situation of the white Bc7 and the general looseness of White's position which is best demonstrated by examples.

12 Nc3xd5,

The game Balashov-Barczay,

Skopje 1970, had gone instead **12 Ba5, Nf4; 13 O-O-O?**, Nh3! with advantage to Black. However even after the correct **13 h4**, Nc6; 14 Bb6, Nb4; 15 O-O-O, Rfc8; 16 Kb1 Black has a good game, especially if 16 ..., a5!? is sound. On the other hand Black can also follow another of Horton's analyses: **12 ..., Nc6?!** (instead of ..., Nf4) 13 Nxd5, Nxa5; **14 Nxe7+?**, Kh8; 15 d5, Rfe8; 16 d6, Bxf3; 17 gxf3, Bxe5 and wins. White's improvement here is **14 Ne3!** (14 Nc3?!, Rac8 followed by ..., Rfd8 and ..., Nc4) when Black's pressure is only sufficient for the recovery of his pawn at the cost of (eventually) making the undesirable exchange ..., Bxf3 (analysis).

It is also necessary to consider the tempo-saving move **12 Bxb8** and after 12 ..., Rxb8; 13 Rc1 (13 Nxd5, Bxd5 and 13 Ne4??, Nb4 are both good for Black) but again 13 ..., Nf4 has a quite crippling effect on White (analysis).

12 ..., Bb7xd5; 13 Bf1-e2, Rf8-c8; 14 Bc7-a5,

Ivkov rejects **14 Bxb8**, Raxb8 since there is no longer any good way to hold both his centre and his second rank (15 Kd1?!; 15 b3!?).

14 ..., Nb8-c6; 15 Ba5-c3, b5-b4; 16 Bc3-d2,

The rover's return.

16 ..., f7-f6!;

Since if **17 exf6**, Bxf6!; 17 Be3, e5! and the position is completely opened up in favour of Black's raking bishops and c-file control.

17 O-O, Draw agreed!

Unfortunately clock times for this game are not on record, but Ivkov is a leading grandmaster against whom most I.M.s are happy to draw with Black. In the 'Informator', he admits that Black stands rather better in the final position; against one's equals, such positions are played on.

Game 47
Dzieciotowski - Schmidt
(Poland 1971)

1 d2-d4, Ng8-f6; 2 c2-c4, g7-g6; 3 Nb1-c3, d7-d5; 4 Bc1-f4, Bf8-g7; 5 e2-e3,

White need not play this, but can try instead:

a) 5 Nf3, O-O; **6 Rc1** (6 cxd5 etc. would be much worse here than in the text) **6 ..., c5** (6 ..., dxc4!? is also interesting) 7 dxc5, Be6 (only move) 8 Nd4 (If 8 Ng5, d4; 9 Nb5, Nh5! Borisenko-Estrin, 5th World Correspondence Championship) 8 ..., Nc6; 9 Nxe6, fxe6; 10 e3 (10 cxd5, Nxd5!) 10 ..., Qa5; 11 Be2 (Or 11 Qa4) 11 ..., e5!; 12 cxd5, exf4; 13 dxc6, bxc6; 14 exf4, Ne4; 15 O-O, Nxc3; 16 bxc3, Rxf4; 17 Qb3+, Kh8; 18 Qb7, Raf8! and the draw is almost certain (Wexler-Tschudinovsky, Perm 1967). Another lively Grunfeld counter-gambit!

b) 5 Rc1 is unlikely to be independently significant after 5 ..., c6 from non-gambit lines already known.

5 ..., O-O;

If Black does not wish to offer the Grunfeld Gambit then he can play **5 ..., c6** or **5 ..., c5** with fair chances of equalising. The latter may be viewed as a counter-gambit, after **5 ..., c5**; 6 dxc5, Qa5; **7 Rc1** (Not 7 cxd5?, Nxd5!; 8 Qxd5, Bxc3+; 9 bxc3, Qxc3+; 10 Ke2,

Qxa1; 11 Be5, Qb1! and Black is winning - Rawie) 7 ..., dxc4 (7 ..., Be6!? Euwe and 7 ..., Ne4 Fischer are both risky) 8 Bxc4, O-O, Nf3, Nc6; 10 O-O, Bg4! (Better than 10 ..., Qxc5?!) 11 h3, Rad8; 12 Qe2, Bxf3; 13 Qxf3, Qxc5 with equal chances (Martz-Smejkal, Ybbs '68).

6 c4xd5,

If White declines the gambit by **6 Rc1** (best) then Black has **6 ..., c6**, or can repeat the theme of the two previous notes by **6 ..., c5**; 7 dxc5, **Be6!**; 8 Nf3, Nc6; 9 Be2 (Not 9 Ng5, Bg4; 10 f3, e5! Botvinnik-Gligoric, Tel Aviv 1964) 9 ..., **Ne4!** with probably equal chances, but the game Portisch-Schmidt, Skopje 1972 (with the new 10 O-O) is critical.

6 ..., Nf6xd5; 7 Nc3xd5, Qd8xd5; 8 Bf4xc7,

95

Black has a lead in development, while the white king is not yet in safety. It is probable that Black's chances are good, but not so clear which way he should play this position.

8 ..., Nb8-c6;

The main alternative is **8 ..., Na6**, obtaining the two bishops since White does not have time for 9 Bg3?, Bf5 with strong threats on the queen side. After **9 Bxa6** there are two main lines:

a) 9 ..., bxa6; 10 Nf3 (Not 10 Qf3?, Qb5!) 10 ..., Bb7! (Or 10 ..., Bf5) 11 O-O, Rac8 with compensation for the pawn (Boleslavsky).

b) 9 ..., Qxg2; 10 Qf3, Qxf3; 11 Nxf3, bxa6; 12 Rc1, Bb7; 13 Ke2, f6 (13 ..., f5!? Hort) 14 Rhg1, Rc7; 15 Ba5, e6 with a level ending (Lengyel-Gligoric, Enschede 1963).

Probably inadequate, though, is **8 ..., Bf5?!**; 9 Ne2, Na6; 10 Nc3, Qc6; 11 Ba5!, b6; 12 Qf3! and Black could not get sufficient compensation for his pawn (Gastonyi-Haag, Budapest Championship 1966).

9 Nf3-e2,

The only sound move, since 9 **Be2** may be met by 9 ..., Bf5!; 10 Bf3, Qb5; 11 Ne2, Rac8 (Hartston), and **9 Nf3**, Bf5 (9 ..., Bg4!?) 10 Be2, Rac8; 11 Bg3, Qa5+; 12 Nd2, Nb4; 13 O-O, Bf2 with a good attack for Black (Jiminez-Simagin, Moscow 1963).

9 ..., Bc8-g4;

Other moves are suspect:

a) 9 ..., e5; 10 dxe5, Qb5; 11 Qb3!, Qxb3; 12 axb3, Nxd5; 13 Nd4, Nc6; 14 Nxc6, bxc6; 15 Bc4! and White gets a good ending (Portisch).

b) 9 ..., Qb5; 10 Qd2, Bg4 (10 ..., e5?; 11 d5) 11 Nc3, Qb4; 12 Bd3, Rac8; 13 Bg3, Rfd8; 14 b3 with advantage to White (Hartston).

10 f2-f3, Ra8-c8;

Not 10 ..., Bxf3?! (Nor 10 ..., Qd7?; 11 Bg3, Be6; 12 Nf4!) 11 gxf3, Qxf3; 12 Rg1, Qxe3 (Or 12 ..., Rac8; 13 Bf4, e5; 14 dxe5) 13 Bf4, Qe4; 14 Bg2, Qf5; 15 Bxc6!, bxc6; 16 Qd2, c5!; 17 d5, Rfd8; 18

O-O-O, e6; 19 Qc2! and Black has nothing concrete for his piece (Kyzhukov-Saligo, semi-final 4th USSR Correspondence Ch'ship).

11 Ne2-c3!,

Much weaker is the immediate **11 Bf4** on account of **11 ..., e5!** (Or first 11 ..., Qa5+) 12 dxe5, Qa5+; 13 Kf2 (Also after 13 Nc3, Be6 Black got good play in Keres-Lilienthal, Leningrad 1939) 13 ..., Be6; 14 Nd4, Rfd8; 15 Be2, Qb6; 16 Qe1, Nxd4; 17 exd4, Qxd4+; 18 Be3, Qxe5; 19 Qb4, Rc2; 20 Rhd1, Re8; 21 Rd2, Bc4!; 22 Bf4, Qxf4; 23 Rxc2, Qe3+; 24 Resigns (Chernikov-A.Zaitsev, USSR 1964).

11 ..., Qd5-e6; 12 Bc7-f4;

96

A critical position. Black must act drastically, since if **12 ..., Rfd8?** White wins a piece by 13 Be2!, Bf5; 14 g4.

12 ..., Bg7xd4!?;

A relatively new move here, not mentioned in Hartston's book. There he gives as the main line the continuation **12 ..., Nxd4!;** 13 fxg4, Rfd8; 14 Bd3! (Not 14 Kf2?, Qb6 nor 14 Be2, Nxe2) 14 ..., Nc6!; 15 Qb1 (Or 15 Qe2, Nb4; 16 Rd1, Bxc3+; 17 bxc3, Nxa2, unclear) 15 ..., Ne5! and Black has probably at least equal chances (Simagin). Only

time and further experience will tell whether Schmidt's move is stronger.

13 f3xg4, g7-g5!;

So that the subsequent ..., Qxg4 will gain time by hitting this bishop, and also to clear e5 for the knight. If instead **13 ..., Rfd8** not 14 Bd3?, Nb4 but 14 Qf3.

14 Bf4xg5,

Others:

a) **14 Kf2??**, gxf4; 15 exd4, Qe3 mate.

b) **14 Bg3?**, Rfd8; 15 Qf3, Bxe3 with very heavy threats (analysis).

14 ..., Rf8-d8; 15 Qd1-b3!,

The only move, as the threat to exchange queens prevents ..., Bxe3.

15 ..., Qe6xg4; 16 Bg5-f4, e7-e5; 17 h2-h3, Bd4xc3+;

If **17 ..., Qd7** White might dare to castle.

18 b2xc3,

If **18 Qxc3**, Qf5 and the threat of ..., Nd4 is awkward.

18 ..., Qg4-d7;

Threatening mate and so regaining the piece.

19 Ra1-d1, Qd7xd1+; 20 Qb3xd1, Rd8xd1+; 21 Ke1xd1, e5xf4; 22 e3xf4, Nc6-e7; 23 c3-c4,

If **23 Kd2** or **23 Kc2** then 23 ..., Nd5 forks two pawns, and Black stands better. White therefore makes sure of a rook ending.

23 ..., Ne7-f5; Draw agreed.

Black threatens to regain the pawn by ..., Ng3, ..., Ne3 or ..., Nd6.

MODERN BENONI DEFENCE (1 d4, Nf6; 2 c4, c5; 3 d5, e6)

Although the main Benoni counter-gambit is the Volga (3 ..., b5), given an extensive coverage in Games 49 to 56, there are sometimes other ways for Black to give up material for tactical chances. Indeed for many years the defence was a favourite with ex-World Champion Tal, who always prefers to play openings which are rich in combinative possibilities. The young Yugoslavian grandmaster Planinc is not unlike the young Tal in this respect, but his ideas are, if anything, even more bizarre ...

**Game 48
Donner - Planinc**
(Wijk aan Zee 1973)
**1 d2-d4, Ng8-f6; 2 c2-c4, c7-c5;
3 d4-d5, e7-e6;**

To loosen White in the centre and obtain an half-open e-file. One used to play **3 ..., d6**, followed by the king's fianchetto, but in that case White is liable to obtain a slight edge and the move is rarely seen today.

4 Nb1-c3,

To exchange pawns is of course bad, giving Black a central pawn majority, while if **4 Nf3** play would probably continue much as in the game, although Black could also essay the Blumenfeld Counter-Gambit by **4 ..., b5!?**

4 ..., e6xd5; 5 c4xd5, d7-d6;

The answer to **5 ..., g6** might be 6 d6!?

6 Ng1-f3,

The most flexible move, although also possible are the king's fianchetto **6 g3** or **6 e4** intending 7 f4 or 7 Nge2.

6 ..., g7-g6; 7 Nf3-d2,

White has a variety of alternatives: **7 g3, 7 e4, 7 Bf4, 7 Bg5**. After this game, Donner switched to 7 e4 against Najdorf!

7 ..., Bf8-g7;

Recently the popularity of this move has been challenged by Fischer's **7 ..., Nbd7** which intends to meet 8 Nc4 by 8 ..., Nb6, relieving the pressure on his d-pawn. The reader is referred to the third game of the Spassky-Fischer world championship match 1972 for an example.

8 Nd2-c4, O-O; 9 Bc1-f4,

The main idea behind White's knight manoeuvre, although the English international player Whiteley has had some successes with **9 Bg5**.

97

9 ..., b7-b6!?;

Offering the d-pawn, Black guards his c-pawn and also prepares the development of his bishop to b7 or a6. This is a complete novelty; a game Borisenko-Suetin (25th USSR Championship 1958), for example, had gone **9 ..., Ne8; 10 Qd2, b6 (10 ..., Bxc3!?; 11 bxc3, b5) 11 e3, Ba6; 12 a4, Bxc4; 13 Bxc4** and White stands better.

10 Bf4xd6,

If instead **10 Nxd6!?**, however, Black's sacrifice is harder to justify as White's advanced knight obstructs development. After **10 ..., Ba6; 11 g3!** (Not **11 Qd2?, Qe7!** threatening ..., Rd8 and ..., Rxd6) **11 ..., Qe7!?** (Not **11 ..., g5?; 12 Be5** while if **11 ..., Nh5?!** White must play **12 Bg2** allowing ..., Nxf4 but he would still stand better) **12 Ndb5!** with complications in which Black will be obliged to sacrifice. However Black has many other possibilities, e.g. **10 ..., Nh5!; 11 Qd2, Bxc3!; 12 bxc3, Qf6; 13 Nxc8!, Nxf4; 14 Ne7+, Kh8** with a position hard to assess (analysis).

10 ..., Rf8-e8; 11 Bd6-g3;

Since the bishop would soon become embarrassed on d6, while **11 Bxb8**, though playable, would leave Black getting an excellent game by straight-forward moves. Donner proposes to play his knight to d6, creating some more complications.

11 ..., Nf6-e4;

To activate the king bishop and rook.

12 Nc3xe4,

If **12 Rc1**, Ba6; 13 e3, b5 with good play for Black.

12 ..., Re8xe4; 13 e2-e3, b7-b5; 14 Nc4-d6, Re4-b4; 15 Bf1xb5?!;

After this move, Black's initiative swiftly becomes decisive. White might have tried **15 Nxc8**, Bxb2; 16 Be2! (Or **16 Rc1!?**) 16 ..., Bxa1?; 17 Qxa1, Qxc8; 18 a3! with good compensation for the exchange, although the intermediate check 16 ..., Bc3+ should tip the scales in Black's favour (analysis).

15 ..., Bg7-f8!; 16 Bb5-c6,

In view of **16 Nxc8**, Rxb5 winning a piece.

98

16 ..., Bc8-a6!; 17 Bc6xa8, Rb4xb2!

Black is a rook and pawn down, but is threatening to win material in at least two ways, as well as mating by ..., Qa5+.

18 Qd1-a4, Qd8-f6!;

Hunting big game.

19 Ra1-c1, Bf8xd6;

Now that f2 is under fire.

20 f2-f4,

If instead **20 f3!?** the end could take the form: 20 ..., Bxg3+!; 21 hxg3, Qf5; 22 e4, Qg5; 23 Qe8+, Kg7; 24 Rxh7+! and White saves himself, but instead 20 ..., Qg5; 21 f4, Qg4 leaves no doubt (analysis).

20 ..., Qf6-f5;

Threatening rook checks followed by queen mates.

21 e3-e4, Rb2-e2+; 22 Ke1-d1, Qf5-h5!; White resigns.

VOLGA GAMBIT (1 d4, Nf6; 2 c4, c5; 3 d5, b5)

This is the most important chapter of the book. The gambit offered by Black's 3rd move is a positional sacrifice envisaging, in return for the pawn, persistent pressure down the half-open a and b files in co-operation with the fianchettoed king side bishop. In addition the White d-pawn may become vulnerable. White on the other hand finds king side counterplay hard to arrange and even if he can establish a solid position a draw is still the most he can usually hope for, as he will have several pieces bound to the defence of his weak pawns. Therefore the Volga Gambit has become increasingly popular at all levels of chess in the last three years and as yet no refutation has been discovered. At the 1972 Skopje Olympiad Black scored 10 wins, 5 draws and no losses!

The gambit was invented in the USSR, and made sporadic appearances in the fifties; the first survey of it appeared in 'Schachmaty' in 1961. However, not many of these early games are of theoretical significance, as Black almost always played an early ..., e6 (on the lines of the Blumenfeld), an idea which is no longer usual and is probably not good. Black should try to undermine the d-pawn only when he has made concrete progress, since the rigidity of the centre helps his flank manoeuvres (the exception is when White exposes his king, as in the well-known game Avram-Benko, US Open 1968).

The American grandmaster Benko, and his disciple Browne, are primarily responsible for the gambit in its modern form, hence the name Benko Gambit which is often used synonymously with Volga Gambit. Benko experimented with the defence in the late sixties and published many of his games and ideas in a series of articles in 'Chess Life and Review' between 1967 and 1969, under the title Benoni Counter-Gambit. Since then two collections of Volga material have been published, one in Sweden (by Akvist & Berglund), the other by 'Chess Digest' in the USA (editors Zechiel & Crane) but they make very few critical comments and so leave the average player very much on his own. It is hoped that this chapter will make it rather clearer what is going on, as well as providing more recent material. The need for a good introduction to the Volga Gambit, together with its great current popularity, justify the large amount of space devoted to it here.

Game 49
Kuzmin - Georgadze
(U.S.S.R. 1972)

**1 d2-d4, Ng8-f6; 2 c2-c4, c7-c5;
3 d4-d5, b7-b5; 4 c4xb5,**

For ways of declining the Volga Gambit, see Game 56.

4 ..., a7-a6;

The invariable follow-up nowadays, seeking to open more lines and accelerate the development of Black's queen side. The old **4 ..., e6?!** is considered in the note to Black's 4th move in Game 54.

However 4 ..., **d6**; 5 Nc3, g6 is sometimes seen, the disadvantage being that Black will soon find himself obliged to play ..., a6 without it giving White as many problems as if he had played it here. See the Lundin Counter-Gambit.

5 b5xa6,

For the important alternative 5 e3 see Game 55, while **5 b6** and others are dealt with in notes to White's 5th in that Game.

5 ..., Bc8xa6;

The controversial **5 ..., e6!?** is the subject of Game 54. On the other hand **5 ..., d6!?**, retaining the possibility of recapturing with the knight, is very interesting and as yet little explored. There can follow **6 Nc3** (Or 6 g3, d6; 7 Bg2, Bg7; 8 Nf3 - better than 8 e4 of Nedeljkovic-Bertok, Yugoslav Championship 1953 - 8 ..., O-O; 9 Ne2, Nxa6; 10 O-O, Qb6; 11 Nd2, Ng4; 12 Rb1, Nc7; 13 Nc3, Ne5; 14 Nf3, Ba6 Marovic-Bertok, Yugoslav Championship 1967; compare the sort of positions arising in Game 53 and notes.) **6 ..., g6** (Or 6 ..., Nxa6 as yet is too committal; it was also possible to play 5 ..., g6 and 6 ..., d6 however) **7 e4, Bg7** and now:

a) 8 Bd3, O-O; 9 Nge2, Bxa6; 10 Bxa6, Nxa6; 11 O-O, Qc7; 12 Bf4, Rfb8; 13 Qd2, Rb4; 14 f3, Rab8; 15 Rab1, Qb7; 16 a3, Rb3; 17 Rfc1, Nd7; 18 Rc2, Nb6; 19 Nd1, Na4; 20 Nec3, Nxc3; 21 Nxc3, Nc7; 22 Be3, Nb5; 23 Nxb5, Qxb5 and Black breaks through (Gustafsson-Akvist, Vaxjo 1963). Such inexorable slow-motion attacks are typical of successful Volga Gambit strategy; Black's moves are gener-

ally much easier to find that White's.

b) 8 Nf3, O-O; 9 h3 (Other plans are: 9 Nd2 - Euwe; 9 Be2, Bxa6; 10 O-O, Nbd7; 11 Nd2, Nb6; 12 a4! Van Seters-Lundvall, Biel 1970; 9 Bg5, Nfd7; 10 Qd2, Re8; 11 Be2, Bxa6; 12 O-O Kluger-Lundin, Olympiad 1954) 9 ..., Nfd7; 10 Be2, Bxa6; 11 O-O, Qb6; 12 Re1, Rc8; 13 Qc2 (Gligoric-Udovcic, Yugoslav Championship 1967). None of these examples seem very logical as Black can improve his play by following normal plans - but in that case why not 5 ..., Bxa6. The crucial test in all these cases would be to play ..., Nxa6, keeping on the white bishops and reserving the option of a ..., Bb7, ..., Nc7 and ..., e6 plan.

c) 8 Qa4+, Bd7 (8 ..., Nfd7!?) 9 Qc2, O-O; 10 Nf3, Qb6; 11 Be2, Nxa6; 12 O-O (Vaganian-Parma, USSR-Yugoslavia 1972) is also fairly irrelevant as Black tried the manoeuvre ..., Bc8-a6 with two tempi down on normal lines. His 8th move seems at fault.

6 Nb1-c3, g7-g6;

99

At this point, White has to decide whether to fianchetto (see Game 53) or to allow the exchange of his king bishop. The latter may

be done forthwith, as in this game and the next, or he may first play the elegant Ng1-f3-d2 followed by e4, Nxf1 and Nf1-e3. That plan, and Black's attempts to cut across it, are to be found in Game 52 and notes.

7 e2-e4, Ba6xf1;

The consistent move, although 7 ..., d6 and 7 ..., g6 would doubtless transpose into lines considered elsewhere, after 8 Bxa6.

8 Ke1-f1, d7-d6;

Not 8 ..., Bg7?!; 9 d6!

9 g2-g3,

Formerly this was the most usual continuation (or 9 Nf3, Bg7; 10 g3 transposing), but the plan of finding a home for the king on h2 instead of g2 is perhaps stronger - see Game 51. 9 Nge2 has also been played, and after 9 ..., Bg7; 10 h3 (as above) or 10 g3 (see Gross-Benko, note to White's 11th move in the present game).

Here 9 g4?! is too loose. After 9 ..., Bg7 Black stands better:

a) 10 Kg2, O-O; 11 h3 (If 11 h4, h5) 11 ..., e6; 12 dxe6, fxe6; 13 e5!, Ne8!; 14 exd6, Nxd6; 15 Qe2, Qd7; 16 f4, Nc6 (Avram-Benko).

b) 10 f3, O-O; 11 Nge2, e6; 12 Kg2, exd5; 13 Nxd5, Nc6; 14 N2c3 (If 14 Bg5, Nxd5) 14 ..., Nxd5; 15 exd5 (Or 15 Nxd5, f5) 15 ..., Nb4! (Visier-Benko, Malaga 1969)

Also after the similar 9 f3, Bg7; 10 Nge2, O-O; 11 Be3, Nbd7; 12 Kf2, Ne5; 13 g4?! Black might try ..., e6 although in Kchouk-Fuller, Skopje 1972, 13 ..., Qa5 and thematic queen side play also was seen to be good.

9 ..., Bf8-g7; 10 Kf1-g2,

O-O!; 11 Ng1-f3,

Black's last move has to be precise since 10 ..., Nbd7 instead could be met by 11 f4!, O-O; 12 Nf3, Qb6; 13 Re1, c4; 14 Re2!, Nc5; 15 Be3 (Rabar-Milic, Zagreb 1955) or 12 ..., Nb6; 13 Re1, Qd7 also with some advantage to White (Parma in 'Informator' 12).

But if now 11 f4!? Black has better in 11 ..., Na6 (Not 11 ..., e6?; 12 dxe6, fxe6; 13 Nf3, Nc6; 14 Re1 Gerusel-Schaufelberger, Luxembourg 1971) 12 Nf3, Qb6; 13 Re1, Rfb8 (or 13 ..., Nb4 Malich-Ciocaltea, Vrnjacka Banja 1972); 14 Re2, Nb4; 15 Be3, Qa6; 16 Rd2, Qc4; 17 Qf1, Qxf1+; 18 Kxf1, Nd7; 19 e5, Nb6; 20 b3, Ra3; 21 Re1, Rba8; 22 Ree2, Nc4! with advantage to Black (Gerusel-Markland, Wijk aan Zee 1973).

Also possible is 11 Nge2 e.g. Gross-Benko, U.S.Open 1968, which went 11 ..., Qb6; 12 Rb1, Na6; 13 b3, Nc7; 14 f3, e6; 15 dxe6?!, fxe6; 16 Be3, Qc6 and now White could keep roughly level by 17 b4, cxb4; 18 Rxb4, d5; 19 Rb6, Qc4; 20 Qb3, Qd3 (Benko).

11 ..., Nb8-d7;

Several other moves come into consideration here:

a) 11 ..., Ng4!? with some advantage to Black (Gheorghiu in 'The Chess Player).

b) 11 ..., Nfd7!?; 12 Re1, Qb6; 13 Re2, Na6 led to a draw in Gligoric-del Corral, Siegen 1970.

c) 11 ..., Qb6!?; 12 Re1, Nbd7 see note to Black's 12th move below. Or 12 ..., Na6!? as in Kane-Vogt, Skopje 1972.

d) 11 ..., Qa5; 12 Re1, Nbd7 see game continuation.

e) 11 ..., Na6!?; 12 Qe2, Qb6; 13 Bf4, Rfb8; 14 Rab1, Nc7; 15 Rhe1, Nb5; 16 Nxb5, Qxb5; 17 b3 with advantage to White (Camara-Hook Siegen 1970).

12 Rh1-e1,

For alternatives, see the note to White's 12th move in the next game.

100

12 ..., Qd8-a5!?;

Probably not best, but this game has been chosen for thematic reasons. The best move is generally held to be **12 ..., Ng4!?** but there has yet to be a clear demonstration of this; after 13 Re2 what is Black's best?:

a) 13 ..., Qa5; 14 Bg5, Rfe8; 15 Qc2 (Better may be 15 Rc1 of Bagirov-Zilberman, USSR 1972) 15 ..., h6; 16 Bd2, Qa6; 17 Rad1, Reb8; 18 Bc1, Rb7 with a difficult balanced struggle, eventually won by Black, the stronger player (Popov-Vasyukov, Varna 1971). Also critical is **14 h3**, Nge5; 15 Nxe5 (see below).

b) 13 ..., Qc7; 14 Rc2, Rfb8; 15 h3, Nge5; 16 Nxe5, Nxe5 (16 ..., Bxe5!?) 17 Qe2, Qb7; 18 f4 and White was on top (Holm-Pytel, Polanica Zdroi 1972).

Black has also tried various queen moves here:

a) 12 ..., Qb6; 13 Re2 (Or 13 Qc2, Ng4; 14 Re2, Qa6; 15 Bd2, Rfb8; 16 Be1, Nge5; 17 Nxe5, Nxe5; 18 Rd1, c4! (Another Volga theme) 19 b3, Nd3; 20 bxc3, Nb4 and Black eventually drew in Holmov-Platonov, Uzhgorod semi-final, 40th USSR Championship 1972) 13 ..., Rfb8 (13 ..., Ng4!?) 14 Bf4 (14 h3! - Keres) 14 ..., Ng4; 15 Rc1, Qa5 (Keres-Pokhla, Parnu 1971) and now 16 a3! (Keres) leaves White somewhat better.

b) 12 ..., Qb8 achieved nothing in Kuzmin-Albert, USSR 1971.

c) 12 ..., Qc7; 13 Re2, Rfb8 (Holm-Toran, Skopje 1972) 14 h3! and White is better.

From these examples, it is clear that Black gets into trouble if he omits ..., Ng4-e5 and if he loses time with his queen, and that the best square for the latter piece is a6. White must defend his queen side with economy (avoiding moves like Rc2 and Bd2) and strive for e5; he may be able to harass Black by moves like Bg5 but timing is important.

13 Bc1-d2?,

White should play **13 h3!**, preventing ..., Ng4, and thereby transposing into the next game. Another reasonable move is **13 Re2**, Ng4 transposing to the first note to Black's 12th move, e.g. 14 h3, Nge5; 15 Nxe5, Nxe5 (Or 15 ..., Bxe5!?) 16 f4!, Bd4; 17 a3 with complications) 16 f4, Nc4; 17 Qd3, Qa6 (Or 17 ..., Na3; 18 e5, c4; 19 Qe4) 18 b3, Na3; 19 Qxa6, Rxa6; 20 e5, Rfb8; 21 Bb2, c4; 22 Bxa3!, Rxa3; 23 Rb1, cxb3; 24 axb3,

Rbxb3; 25 Rxb3, Rxb3; 26 exd6!,
exd6; 27 Re8+, Bf8; 28 Ne4, Kg7;
29 Rd8, Re3! (Instead 29 ..., Rb6;
30 Rd7, h6; 31 Kf3 and White can
still play on) 30 Nxd6, Bxd6; 31
Rxd6, Rd3! with a book draw
(analysis).

13 ..., Rf8-b8; 14 Qd1-c2, Nf6-g4!;

According to Georgadze in
'The Chess Player', Black now
stands slightly better.

15 a2-a4,

It is not clear that this move is
desirable, since Black gains the
point b3 - another typical theme in
this gambit.

**15 ..., Qa5-b4; 16 h2-h3,
Ng4-e5; 17 Nf3xe5, Bg7xe5!;**

Georgadze shows that 17 ...,
Nxe5?! is inferior: 18 Nb5, Qc4; 19
Bc3, Nd3? (Or 19 ..., Qd3; 20
Qxd3, Nxd3; 21 Reb1, Bxc3; 22
bxc3, Ra5 with only a small plus to
White) 20 b3, Nxe1+ (20 ..., Nb4?;
21 Qb1, Qd3; 22 Bxb4, Qxb1; 23
Raxb1 and wins) 21 Rxe1, Bxc3; 22
bxc4, Bxe1; 23 f4 winning.

**18 Nc3-d1, Qb4-b3; 19 Qc2xb3,
Rb8xb3; 20 Re1-e3,**

If 20 Ra2, Nb6; 21 a5, Nc4 and
Black wins a pawn (analysis).

20 ..., Be5xb2!; 21 Ra1-a2,

If 21 Rxb3, Bxa1; 22 Rb7 (Or
22 a5, Kf8) 22 ..., Nf6; 23 Rxe7,
Rxa4; 24 Nc3?!, Rd4; 25 e5, dxe5;
26 Bh6, Bxc3; 27 Ra7, Ne8; 28 Ra8,
f6; 29 Rxe8+, Kf7 and Black wins
(Georgadze).

**21 ..., Rb3xe3; 22 Nd1xe3,
Bb2-d4; 23 Ne3-c4, f7-f5;**

Here 23 ..., Ne5 would be level
but Black, having regained his
pawn without having to exchange
his king bishop, is justified in

trying to win.

24 e4xf5, g6xf5; 25 Bd2-g5?!,

Probably 25 Be3 would hold
the draw.

25 ..., Kg8-f7;

101

26 f2-f4, Ra8-b8!;

White cannot make anything
of his passed pawn (27 a5, Rb4; 28
a6, Rxc4; 29 a7, Nb6 - Georgadze)
so Black stands clearly better.

27 Nc4-a5, h7-h6!!;

To prevent a subsequent Nxe7.

**28 Bg5xh6, Nd7-b6; 29 Na5-c6,
Rb8-a8; 30 g3-g4,**

Hoping to create a new passed
pawn. But he is lost.

**30 ..., Nb6xd5; 31 Nc6xd4, c5xd4;
32 a4-a5, Kf7-g6; 33 Bh6-g5,
e7-e5!; 34 a5-a6, Nd5-e3+!;**

He could also win by 34 ..., e4;
35 gxf5+, Kf7 (Georgadze).

**35 Kg2-g1, e5-e4; 36 Bg5-e7, d4-d3
37 Be7xd6, Ne3-c2!;
38 g4xf5+, Kg6-f7;**

Not 38 ..., Kxf5?; 39 Ra5+.

**39 Ra2-b2, d3-d2; 40 Rb2-b7+,
Kf7-g8; White resigns.**

Game 50
Malich - Ciocaltea
(Skopje 1972)

1 d2-d4, Ng8-f6; 2 c2-c4, c7-c5; 3 d4-d5, b7-b5; 4 c4xb5, a7-a6; 5 b5xa6, Bc8xa6; 6 Nb1-c3, g7-g6; 7 Ng1-f3, d7-d6; 8 e2-e4, Ba6xf1; 9 Ke1xf1, Bf8-g7; 10 g2-g3, O-O; 11 Kf1-g2, Nb8-d7;

102

12 h2-h3!?,

Perhpas the best move, preventing ..., Ng4. Others:

a) 12 Re1 see the previous Game and notes.

b) 12 Qc2, Qb6; 13 Rb1, Rfc8; 14 b3?!, Ng4 with equal chances and a quick draw in Donner-Benko, Palma de Mallorca 1971.

c) 12 Qe2, Qa5; 13 Bd2 (Or 13 Bf4, Ng4!; 14 Nd2, Nge5; 15 Be3?! - better 15 Rhc1 according to Maric - 15 ..., Rfb8!; 16 f4?, Ng4! with advantage to Black, Gerusel-Pedersen, West Germany 1971) 13 ..., Rfb8; 14 Rab1, Ne8 (14 ..., Ng4!?) 15 Rhd1, Nc7 (It is too risky to win back the pawn at the cost of a weak king by 15 ..., Bxc3.) 16 a4!?, Rb7 (16 ..., Ng4??; 17 Nb5) 17 Be1 (Roitov-Popov, Tallinn 1973) and now 17 ..., Qb4 would have been perfectly satisfactory.

12 ..., Qd8-a5!?;

Apparently 12 ..., Qb6! is more exact, for after 13 Re1 there are:

a) 13 ..., Rfb8; 14 Rb1 (Or 14 e5, dxe5; 15 Nxe5, Nxe5; 16 Rxe5, Qb7; 17 Qf3 ½-½ F.Portisch-Markland, Wijk aan Zee 1973) 14 ..., Qa6; 15 Qc2, Rb7; 16 Bg5, Ne8; 17 Bf4 (17 Bxe7?, h6 or 17 ..., f6 followed by 18 ..., Ne5) 17 ..., c4; 18 Be3 with perhaps some advantage to White, but Black soon got the upper hand and won (Cobo-Vasyukov, Polanica Zdroi 1972).

b) 13 ..., Ne8; 14 Re2, Nc7; 15 Bg5, Rfe8; 16 Qc2 (Or 16 Rc1, Qa6; 17 b3, Ne5 with balanced chances, Peev-Georgadze, Lublin 1972) 16 ..., Nb5; 17 Nxb5, Qxb5; 18 Bf4, Reb8?! (Here 18 ..., Nb6! keeps some advantage for Black) 19 e5! and White soon forced the draw (Sosonko-Witkowski, Wijk aan Zee Reserves 1973).

13 Rh1-e1,

Better than 13 Qc2, Nb6; 14 Nd2, Nfd7; 15 Nb3, Qa6; 16 Rd1, Na4! and Black had the advantage (Popov-Tringov, Varna 1972). White's knight on c3 is his lynchpin in many lines of the Volga, so it is usually worth the tempi expended in manoeuvring a knight to exchange it off.

13 ..., Rf8-b8;

Not 13 ..., Ne8?; 14 Bg5.

14 Re1-e2,

Here White might play 14 e5! (Georgadze) as Black still has 14 ..., Ne8 as if 15 exd6, exd6; 16 Re7, Qd8 and the rook must retreat (17 Qe2?, Ne5). Further analysis of this variation could be made, but if Black wants to play for a win he must adopt the alternative at move 12.

14 ..., Nf6-e8;

Velimirovic, in 'Informator' 14, analysed **14 ..., Rb7!?**; 15 Bg5 (If 15 Rc2 or 15 Qc2 Black plays 15 ..., c4) 15 ..., Rxb2; 16 Rxb2, Qxc3 with an unclear position.

15 Bc1-g5?!, h7-h6!;

White's 15th move had been believed good on account of the continuation of Knaak-Damjanovic Sombor 1972: **15 ..., Bxc3**; 16 bxc3, Qxc3; 17 Bxe7, Ne5; 18 Re3, Qb2; 19 Bh4, Nxf3; 20 Kxf3, Nf6; 21 Qc1, Qe5 and now correct was 22 g4! according to Velimirovic. But now **16 Bxe7?** loses the bishop to 16 ..., f6 and even 17 e5 is no good.

16 Bg5-f4, g7-g5?!;

Correct was **16 ..., Nc7!**; 17 e5 (Or 17 Qd2, Rxb2!) 17 ..., dxe5; 18 Nxe5, Nxe5; 19 Bxe5, Bxe5; 20 Rxe5, Rxb2; 21 Rxe7, Qxc3; 22 Rxc7, Ra3! with advantage to Black (Ciocaltea). Now White gets an edge.

17 Bf4-c1, Ne8-c7; 18 h3-h4!, g5-g4; 19 Nf3-h2, Nd7-e5; 20 Re2-c2, h6-h5; 21 f2-f3!, g4xf3+; 22 Nh2xf3, Ne5-g4; 23 Nf3-g5?!,

In 'The Chess Player' Ciocaltea mentions **23 Nh2!?** and **23 Qe2!**

23 ..., Rb8xb2!;

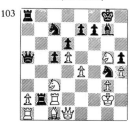

Now White has to fight for the draw.

24 Rc2xb2,

Not **24 e5?**, Qxc3! and Black wins.

24 ..., Bg7xc3; 25 Qd1-f3!,

If **25 Qc2**, c4! meeting 26 e5 by 26 ..., Qxd5 winning (Ciocaltea). Also **25 Rab1**, Bxb2; 26 Rxb2, Qc3; 27 Re2, Nb5 is very good for Black (analysis).

25 ..., f7-f6; 26 Qf3-f5!, f6xg5; 27 Qf5xg5+,

27 Qg6+!? also came into consideration.

27 ..., Bc3-g7;

The situation is extremely double-edged — if the king moves, hoping to 'win' the exchange back, his chances of getting mated would be good.

28 Ra1-b1, Ra8-f8!;

A counter-counter-attack! He could even lose after **28 ..., Nf6?!**; 29 Rb8+, N7e8; 30 Qg6!, Qxa2; 31 R1b2, Qa7; 32 R8b7! (Ciocaltea).

29 Qg5xh5, Qa5-e1!; 30 Qh5xg4, Qe1-f1+; 31 Kg2-h2, Rf8-f2+; 32 Rb2xf2, Qf1xf2+; 33 Kh2-h1, Qf2-f1+ , Draw agreed.

Game 51
Kuijpers - Dueball
(Holland - West Germany, Hitzacker 1971)

1 d2-d4, Ng8-f6; 2 c2-c4, c7-c5; 3 d4-d5, b7-b5; 4 c4xb5, a7-a6; 5 b5xa6, Bc8xa6; 6 Nb1-c3, g7-g6; 7 e2-e4, Ba6xf1; 8 Ke1xf1, d7-d6; 9 Ng1-e2!,

White intends to bring his

king to h2, and to consolidate his
queen side (no hope in exchanging
the Nc3 when there is another to
take its place). This plan was
recommended to me by the Dutch
student player F. van der Vliet, a
sceptic of the 'White has simply
won a pawn' school. However it is
true that this Dutch System is to be
treated with respect, since as yet
nobody has demonstrated a complete answer to it.

The analogous plan with **9 Nf3**
is less dangerous, e.g. 9 ..., Bg7; **10
h3**, O-O; 11 Kg1 and now:

a) 11 ..., **e6?!**; 12 dxe6, fxe6; 13 e5!,
dxe5 (13 ..., Ne8!?) 14 Qxd8, Rxd8;
15 Bg5 with clear advantage to
White (O'Kelly-Honfi, Solingen
1972).

b) 11 ..., **Na6!?** (or first 11 ..., Qb6)
12 Kh2, Qb6; 13 Qe2, Nd7; 14 Nd2,
Nb4 (Or 14 ..., Rfb8; 15 Nc4, Qd8
Loheac-Ammoun - D.Levy, Skopje
1972) 15 Nc4, Qa6; 16 Re1, Ne5
with a fair game for Black (Schau-
felberger-Parma, Luxembourg
1971).

c) 11 ..., **Nbd7**; 12 Kh2, **Qa5**
(Velimirovic suggests 12 ..., Nb6; 13
Re1, Nfd7; 14 Qc2, e6!? while
Ogaard-Gheorghiu, Helsinki 1972,
went 12 ..., Qb6; 13 Re1, Ne8!; 14
Re2, Ne5 with White slightly better
but a draw was soon agreed) 13
Re1, Rb8; 14 Qc2 (Or 14 Re2, Ne8;
15 Rc2, Nc7; 16 Bd2, Nb5; 17 a4,
Nxc3; 18 Bxc3, Bxc3; 19 bxc3,
Ne5! Hort-Jiminez, Palma 1970)
14 ..., Ne8; 15 Bd2, Qa6; 16 a4,
Rb4 (K.Pytel-Peev, Lublin 1972).
Black stands well and indeed won a
fine knight endgame.

9 ..., Bf8-g7;

See Diagram

104

10 h2-h3,

For **10 g3** see the last note to
White's 11th move in Game 49.
Another possibility here is **10 Nf4**,
O-O; 11 g4!?, Na6; 12 h4!? (since
the Benko recipe of ..., h5 and ...,
e6 is not available here!) 12 ..., Qa5;
13 h5, Rfb8; 14 hxg6, hxg6; 15 g5,
Nd7; 16 Qg4 with a strong attack
for White (Formanek-Browne,
Atlantic Open 1970). It is surprising that such caveman tactics
should work against a grand
master. A better plan was 11 ...,
Qc8!; 12 f3, Qa6+; 13 Kg2, Nbd7
and if 14 g5, Ne8; 15 h4, Nc7; 16
h5, Ne5 and White has plenty of
weaknesses capable of exploitation
in either the middle-game or the
ending (analysis).

10 ..., O-O; 11 Kf1-g1, Nb8-d7;

In the game Enklaar-Ree,
Dutch Championship 1972, Black
tried to improve by **11 ..., Qb6** but
after 12 Rb1 (This and the text
move constitute a strong manoeuvre that could also be tried with the
knight on f3 - see note **b** to White's
9th) 12 ..., Na6; 13 Be3, Rfb8; 14
Kh2, Nd7; 15 Qd2, Qa5 (intending
Na6-c7-b5, for if 15 ..., Nc7 comes
16 b4) 16 Bg5, Qc7?! (Or 16 ...,
Qd8; 17 f4, Nc7; 18 e5, dxe5?!; 19
d6!) Enklaar claims an advantage

for White by 17 f4. In his notes to the game, in 'Schakend Nederland' he suggests **11 ..., Qa5!?** which would probably transpose into the text again.

12 Kg1-h2, Qd8-a5; 13 Qd1-c2,

The main point of this move is to bring the king rook over to the queen side, since it has nothing to do on e1 and the plan Rf1, f4, Rf3 is rather loosening. For example: **13 Rb1, Rfb8; 14 Rf1, Nb6; 15 f4, Nfd7; 16 Rf3, Na4** threatening (by ..., Nxc3 etc) to win two rooks for the queen, and if **17 Qc2, Bxc3** and ..., Qxa2 will be all right here, with a likely draw. While if 16 b3 Black has 16 ..., Qa6!; 17 Rf3, c4!; 18 b4!?, Na4; 19 Nxa4, Qxa4; 20 Qxa4, Rxa4; 21 a3, Nc5! with advantage (analysis).

13 ..., Rf8-b8; 14 Ra1-b1,

A prophylactic move, which reduces Black's prospects of combinative breakthrough by over-protecting the b-pawn and removing the rook from the dangerous long diagonal.

14 ..., Nd7-e5?!;

Black is in too much haste to clarify the situation, before it can be in his favour to do so. In view of the passivity of the White pieces, he should have time for the standard manoeuvre **14 ..., Ne8!** e.g. 15 Rf1 (Or 15 b3, Nc7; 16 Bb2, c4!?; 17 bxc4, Ne5 or here 17 Na4! with complications; 16 ..., Na6 looks best) 15 ..., Nc7; 16 f4, Na6; 17 a3, Qb6; 18 Rf3 (Or 18 b3, Nc7; 19 a4, c4; 20 bxc4, Qc5 with about equal chances) 18 ..., Qb3; 19 Qxb3 (19 Qc1!?) 19 ..., Rxb3; 20 Nc1, Rb7 and White has still not solved his basic problems (analysis). The

Dutch System is clearly critical for the Volga Gambit, and further practical experience and analysis are required before a definitive judgement can be pronounced.

15 b2-b3,

If the king knight were on f3 instead of e2, this would be impossible. Now White threatens 16 f4 and so forces Black's reply.

15 ..., c5-c4;

A typical Volga idea, but played here under inferior conditions.

16 Bc1-e3,

Not **16 Bb2?!**, Nd3 with complications.

16 ..., c4xb3; 17 a2xb3, Rb8-c8; 18 Rh1-c1,

Scotching Black's plan of an eventual ..., Nf3+ with attacking chances against White's weak pawns in the ending.

18 ..., Qa5-b4; 19 f2-f3, Rc8-c7; 20 Qc2-d2, Nf6-d7; 21 Nc3-a4, Qb4xd2; 22 Be3xd2,

White has played better than Black, reaching a difficult ending in which he has winning chances.

22 ..., Rc7-b7;

Avoiding the exchange of the

rooks, since they are his best hope of restraining and attacking the passed b-pawn.

**23 Bd2-e3, Ne5-d3;
24 Rc1-d1, Nd3-b4?!;**

Here Black might well have tried to reach a drawn ending by 24 ..., N3c5!? e.g. 25 Nxc5, Nxc5; 26 Bxc5!?, dxc5; 27 Rdc1, Be5+; 28 Kh1, Ra2; 29 Nc3, Ra3 and suddenly Black has the advantage! On the other hand it is not clear that White has any more chances of winning after 26 b4, Na4; 27 Rdc1, Nb2 (analysis).

**25 Ne2-d4, Nd7-e5; 26 Kh2-g1,
h7-h5; 27 Kg1-f1, Ne5-d3; 28
Nd4-c6, Ra8-a6; 29 Kf1-e2, e7-e6;
30 Nc6xb4, Nd3xb4; 31 d5xe6,
f7xe6; 32 Be3-f4, d6-d5; 33 Na4-c5,
Ra6-a2+; 34 Rd1-d2,**

White is making steady progress. Black at move 24 might have been helped by an obiter dictum of Larsen's (heard in post-mortem at Teesside 1972): 'Passed pawns should not be blockaded; that is old-fashioned ... They should be eaten!'

**34 ..., Rb7-f7; 35 Rd2xa2, Nb4xa2;
36 Bf4-d2, d5xe4; 37 Nc5xe4,
Rf7-c7; 38 b3-b4, Bg7-d4; 39
b4-b5, Kg8-f8; 40 Ke2-d3, e6-e5;
41 b5-b6, Black resigns.**

Next we shall look at the plan in which White tries both to play e4 and to castle, by employing the stratagem Nf3-d2.

**Game 52
Karasev - Platonov**
(39th USSR Championship 1971)
**1 d2-d4, Ng8-f6; 2 c2-c4, c7-c5; 3
d4-d5, b7-b5; 4 c4xb5, a7-a6; 5
b5xa6, Bc8xa6; 6 Nb1-c3, d7-d6; 7
Ng1-f3, g7-g6; 8 Nf3-d2,**

8 ..., Bf8-g7;

The move 8 ..., Qa5!? has been advocated as best here, since the half-pin on the White knights prevents him from executing his intended manoeuvre. On the other hand the White knight will eventually reach the strong post c4 with tempo. Experience in this line is as yet inconclusive:

a) 9 e4, Bxf1 (Or 9 ..., Bg7; 10 Bxa6, Qxa6; 11 Qe2, O-O; 12 Nb5!; Nbd7; 13 a4, Rfc8; 14 Nc4, Ne8; 15 Ra3 with an edge for White, Kuzmin-Stein, USSR 1972) 10 Kxf1, Bg7; 11 Nc4 (Or 11 g3, Nbd7; 12 Nc4, Qa6; 13 Qe2, O-O; 14 Kg2 Marschalek-Wach, Poland 1971; now Pytel gave 14 ..., Nb6 in 'The Chess Player') 11 ..., Nbd7; 12 Qe2, O-O; 13 Bd2, Nbd7 (Reicher-Markland, Wijk aan Zee 1973) with balanced chances, eventually won by Black. Browne has also had two draws in this line.

**b) 9 e3, Bxf1; 10 Nxf1, Nbd7; 11
Ng3, Bg7; 12 O-O, O-O; 13 Bd2,
Rfb8** led to a nice example of sustained attack in Ungureanu-Peev, Lublin 1972: 14 b3, c4!; 15

bxc4, Qc7; 16 Rb1, Qxc4; 17 Qe2, Ne5; 18 e4, Nd3; 19 Rxb8, Rxb8; 20 Rb3, Nd7; 21 Rb3, Nd7; 22 Nf1, N7c5; 23 Ne3, Qd4; 24 Ra3, Qb4; 25 Nc2, Qb2; 26 Qd1, Nxf2! and Black won.

c) 9 g3, Nbd7; **10 Bh3** (Or 10 e4, Bxf1; 11 Kxf1, Bg7 see **a**) 10 ..., Bg7; 11 O-O, O-O; 12 Qc2, c4!?; 13 Rd1, Nb6; 14 Bg2, Bb7; 15 b4, cxb3; 16 Nxb3, Qa6; 17 e4, Rfc8; 18 Bf1, Qa7; 19 Nd4, Qa5; 20 Bd2, Qc5; 21 Nb3, Qa3 ½-½ (Szabo-Bronstein, Budapest-Moscow 1971)

9 e2-e4, Ba6xf1?!;

Experience suggests that Black should play 9 ..., O-O!; **10 Bxa6** and now:

a) 10 ..., Nxa6; 11 O-O, Nd7 (11 ..., e6!?) **12 Nc4** (12 Qe2, Nb6 led to a draw in Ghitescu-Benko, Siegen 1970) **12 ..., Nb6** (Or 12 ..., Nc7!?; 13 Qe2, Qb8; 14 Bd2, Nb5; 15 Rfc1, Nd4; 16 Qd3 with perhaps a slight plus for White in Dorosh-kevich-Georgadze, USSR 1972; Gufeld suggests now 16 ..., Ne5; 17 Nxe5, Bxe5 as perhaps even better for Black, but how would he meet 18 f4, Bg7; 19 Rab1, Rfc8; 20 b3 with apparently a sound extra pawn?) **13 Ne3** (13 Nxb6 helped Black in Weber-Delgado, Skopje 1972) 13 ..., Qc7 (Or 13 ..., Qd7; 14 a4, Rfb8; 15 Ra3, Bd4; 16 Qe2, Qb7! as in a game Vranesic-Benko, but better first 15 a5) 14 Bd2 (He could still try a4 and Ra3, but a5 would be no threat when the knight has d7) 14 ..., Rfb8; 15 Qe2, c4!; 16 Rfc1 (Or 16 a4!?, Nc5; 17 a5, Nbd7; 18 Nxc4, Nb3; 19 Rad1, Nd4; 20 Qd3, Nc5 Jakobsen) 16 ..., Nxc5 (Soos-Jakobsen, Stockholm 1972) and now White should play 17 Rab1! with about equal chances

according to Jakobsen in 'C.P.'

b) 10 ..., Rxa6!?; 11 O-O (11 Qe2!? Pytel) 11 ..., Nbd7; 12 Nc4, Nb6; 13 Ne3, Qa8; 14 a4! (14 Bd2?, Na4!) 14 ..., Nfd7; 15 Bd2 and now instead of regaining his pawn by 15 ..., Bxc3? (Pytel-Petersen, Aarhus 1972) Black should have kept the position unclear by 15 ..., c4; 16 Qe2, Rfc8 (Pytel).

The apparently innocuous possibility **10 Be2** should also be noted: **10 ..., e6** (Or 10 ..., Nfd7; 11 O-O, Qa5!? when Benko gives 12 Nc4 as favourable to White) 11 Bxa6, Nxa6; 12 O-O (12 dxe6!? and 13 e5!) 12 ..., exd5; 13 exd5, Re8; 14 Nc4, Ne4; 15 Bd2, Rb8 (Toran-Benko, Malaga 1970). If this is not convincing, there is always the standard **10 ..., Nbd7** intending ..., Nb6.

10 Nd2xf1, O-O;

In Kazilaris-Beyen, Siegen 1970, Black drew quite easily with the plan **10 ..., Qa5!**; 11 Nd2, Qa6; 12 Qe2, Qxe2+; 13 Kxe2, Nbd7; 14 Nc4, O-O; 15 h3, Rfb8; 16 Bd2, Nb6 although there is perhaps some improvement for White. The text move leads to an advantage for White, anyway.

11 Nf1-e3, Nb8-d7;

The alternative **11 ..., Na6**; 12 O-O, Nfd7 was tried in Taimanov-Benko, Wijk aan Zee 1970, but then 13 Qe2, Qc7; 14 Bd2, Qb7; 15 Rab1, Nc7; 16 b3, e6; 17 a4 and White had the edge.

12 O-O,

See Diagram

12 ..., Qd8-b6;

The difference between this

107

variation and that of Games 49 and 50 lies in the superior position of White's king (less vulnerable on g1 than g2) and king's knight (observing c4 and preventing ..., Ng4). One would therefore assess White's position (in the last diagram) as somewhat advantageous for him. Black should have reasonable drawing chances.

Other playable 12th moves for Black are:

a) 12 ..., Qa5; 13 Kh1!? (Better 13 Qc2 etc. as in the text) 13 ..., Rfb8; 14 f4?! (Denker has tried the amusing 14 Qe2 and 15 Ned1 here) 14 ..., Rb4; 15 Qc2, Qa6; 16 Bd2, Nxe4!; 17 Nxe4, Rxb2; 18 Qc1, Qd3; 19 Bc3, Re2 and Black won (Berrios-Onat, Skopje 1972).

b) 12 ..., Qc7; 13 Bd2, Rfb8; 14 Qc2, Qb7; 15 b3, Ne8; 16 Rab1, Nc7; 17 a4, Qa6 and the game bogged down into a draw (Najdorf-Garcia, Siegen 1970).

13 Qd1-c2,

A game Doroshkevich-Spassky USSR 1971, went instead **13 Rb1**, Qb4; 14 a3, Qd4!; 15 Nc2, Qc4; 16 Ne3, Qd4 and soon was drawn.

13 ..., Rf8-b8; 14 Ra1-b1!, Nf6-e8; 15 b2-b3!?,

This is more risky than **15 Bd2**, Qa6 (15 ..., Nc7; 16 a4, Qa6 and Black has even gained a tempo on Najdorf-Garcia in **b** above; or if 16 b3, Nb5) 16 b3, Nc7; 17 a4! (the same) and Black should draw, but in the game Bukic-Vukic (Yugoslav Championship 1972) he did so because he soon indulged in an unwise ..., e6. Karasev offers the gambit pawn back.

15 ..., Ne8-c7;

Black continues with the same plan, but here White has omitted the move Bd2. Gufeld suggested in 'C.P.' that Black should regain his pawn by **15 ..., Bxc3!?**; 16 Qxc3, Rxa2 although White stands better in view of the vulnerability of Black's king. A priori that seems right, but in fact it is hard to support the view with any concrete continuation as all Black's pieces are very active and he may even have the advantage, e.g. 17 Bb2, Nef6; 18 Ba1, Qb4; 19 Qxb4, Rxb4; 20 f3, Re2; 21 Nd1, Ne5 with a likely draw (analysis).

16 Ne3-c4, Qb6-a6; 17 a2-a4, Nd7-e5?!;

A further inaccuracy, after which he is lost because his king side gets exposed; he should play **17 ..., Nb6** after which it is hard for White to make concrete progress, if the Najdorf-Garcia game already cited is any indication.

18 Nc4xe5, Bg7xe5; 19 Bc1-h6!, Rb8-b7; 20 Rf1-c1, Ra8-b8; 21 Nc3-d1!,

On the way to the key point c4.

21 ..., Bd4-g7;

Inevitable in the long run.

22 Bh6xg7, Kg8xg7; 23 Nd1-e3, Qa6-a5;

Waiting.

24 Ne3-c4, Qa5-a6; 25 Qc2-c3+, Kg7-g8; 26 Nc4-a5, Rb7-b6; 27 Na5-c6, Rb8-e8; 28 b3-b4, e7-e6; 29 b4xc5, Rb6xb1; 30 Rc1xb1, Qa6xa4; 31 c5xd6, Black resigns.

In the next game, White adopts another commonly seen idea, namely the fianchetto of the king bishop. However, this probably gives Black fewer problems than in the lines so far discussed.

Game 53
Thorbergsson - Gheorghiu
(Rejkjavik 1972)

1 d2-d4, Ng8-f6; 2 c2-c4, c7-c5; 3 d4-d5, b7-b5; 4 c4xb5, a7-a6; 5 b5xa6, Bc8xa6; 6 Nb1-c3,

It is also possible to play immediately **6 g3, d6; 7 Bg2, g6** and now:

a) **8 Bd2!?**, Bg7; 9 Bc3, O-O; 10 Nh3, Nbd7; 11 O-O, Nb6; 12 Nf4, Qd7 (intending ..., Na4) 13 b3! (Benko-Berry, USA) and now Black instead of 13 ..., Ra7? might consider 13 ..., g5!? (Benko?). At any rate the grandmaster has not repeated this experiment.

b) **8 b3?!**, Bg7; 9 Bb2, Nbd7; 10 Nd2? (Now the d-pawn becomes weak) 10 ..., O-O; 11 Nh3, Nb6; 12 Nf4, g5!; 13 Nh3, h6; 14 O-O, Qd7 with a good game for Black (Kirk O'Grady-Markland, England 1973)

c) **8 Nh3!?**, Bg7; 9 O-O, O-O; 10 Nc3 (10 Na3!? Basman) 10 ..., Nbd7 and now White has tried all sorts of things:

c1) **11 f4**, Nb6; 12 Nf2 (Dipre-Berry,

USA: Chess Digest).

c2) **11 Qc2**, Qa5; 12 Bg5 (12 Bd2!? Benko - 'Chess Life & Review') 12 ..., Rfb8; 13 Rfe1, Ra7; 14 Rab1, Rab7; 15 Bd2, c4 with a hard and balanced fight (Denker-Benko, US Open 1969).

c3) **11 Nf4**, Qc7; 12 Qc2, Rfb8; 13 Rb1, c4 and Black stood well (Yanofsky-Gheorghiu, Siegen 1970)

c4) **11 Bd2**, Qb6; 12 Rb1, Rfb8; 13 b3, Ne8; 14 Qc2, Nc7; 15 a3, Nf6; 16 Nf4 (Antoshin-Mihaljcisin, Sarajevo 1970) 16 ..., Bb7!; 17 a4, g5! (analysis).

c5) **11 Re1**, Qb6?! (11 ..., Qa5 with an unclear position - Malich in 'C.P.') 12 Qc2, Rfb8; 13 Rb1 (13 b3!?, c4 is unclear - Malich) 13 ..., Ne5; 14 Ng5 with a slight advantage to White (Eroezbek-Schoneberg, Skopje 1972).

d) **8 Nc3** and **8 Nf3** (followed by Nc3) see below.

6 ..., g7-g6;

Here **6 ..., d6** should transpose.

7 g2-g3,

Instead of **7 e4** or **7 Nd2** (previous Games).

7 ..., d7-d6; 8 Bf1-g2, Bf8-g7; 9 Ng1-f3,

Besides **9 Nh3** (note c above) White has also tried:

a) **9 Qa4+?!**, Nbd7; 10 Qh4, h6!; 11 f4, Rb8; 12 e3, Qa5; 13 Nge2, Bd3! with advantage to Black (Barlay-Benko, USA 1968).

b) **9 e4?!**, O-O; 10 Nge2, Nbd7; 11 O-O, Qb6; 12 Qc2, Rfb8 with a typical good position for Black - weakness at d3! (Jones-Malagon, Skopje 1972).

9 ..., O-O; 10 O-O, Nb8-d7;

108

11 Rf1-e1,

This is nearly always played (here or next move), but it may not be best:

a) 11 Rb1, Qa5 (11 ..., Qb6!?) **12 a3?!**, Rfb8; 13 Re1, Ne8; 14 Bd2, Bc4! (Laver-Benko, USA 1968).

b) 11 Qc2, Qb6 (Or 11 ..., Qc7; 12 Rd1, Rfd8?; 13 h3 with a plus for White in Korchnoy-Gurgenidze, USSR Championship 1957) **12 Rb1** (12 Re1 see text; 12 Rd1 is suggested by Akvist and Berglund, but it is not clear that it makes any significant difference) 12 ..., Qb7! (12 ..., Bc4?; 13 Nd2, Bxa2??; 14 Ra1) 13 Bg5 (If now 13 Rd1, Bc4! is good) 13 ..., Nb6; 14 Bxf6, Bxf6; 15 Rfd1, Bxc3 (If 15 ..., Bc4; 16 b3, Bxd5; 17 Nxd5, Nxd5; 18 Ng5!, e6; 19 Ne4, Be7; 20 Nc3 - Akvist & Berglund) 16 bxc3, Bc4; 17 Rb2, Qa6; 18 Qe4, Qa4!; 19 Rbd1 (Jakobsen-Westerinen, Lidkoping 1969) and now 19 ..., Bxd5; 20 Qxe7, Nc4 with more complications ahead.

c) 11 Qc2, Qa5; 12 Rb1, Rfb8 (Or 12 ..., Nb6; 13 Rd1, Nc4; 14 Nd2, Nd7! Forintos-Browne, Skopje 1970) 13 Bd2 (13 Rd1!?) 13 ..., Nb6; 14 b3, Qa6; 15 Bc1, Qa5 with a quick draw (Padevsky-Browne, Sarajevo 1970).

d) 11 Bg5, Qc7; 12 Qc2, Rfb8; 13 b3, Nb6; 14 Rad1, h6; 15 Bd2?, Nbxd5 and Black won (Uddenfeldt-Green, Stockholm 1970).

11 ..., Qd8-b6!;

Restraining White's queen bishop. Black can also consider:

a) 11 ..., Ng4!? (Gheorghiu).

b) 11 ..., Qa5; 12 Qc2 (Or 12 Bd2, Qb6; 13 Rb1, Rfb8) 12 ..., Rfb8 (More natural than 12 ..., Nb6?! of Lorinczi-Browne, Siegen 1970) 13 Nd2, Ne8; 14 Nb3, Qb4; 15 Nd2, Nc7; 16 a3, Qa5; 17 Rb1, c4 with a complicated game, probably in Black's favour (Haigh-Vogt, Skopje 1972).

c) 11 ..., Qc7; 12 Bd2 (Or 12 Qc2, Rfb8 and 13 ..., Nb6 Vincenti-Andrewes, Skopje 1972) 12 ..., Nb6; 13 Bf4, Rfb8; 14 b3, Ng4; 15 Bd2, Nc8; 16 h3, Ne5; 17 Nxe5, Bxe5; 18 Rb1, Na7; 19 Qc2, c4 with a hard fight, drawn in 63 moves (Spassky-Szabo, Gothenburg 1971).

d) 11 ..., Nb6 has also been successful in a couple of Swedish games.

12 h2-h3,

This is necessary, e.g. 12 e4?, Ng4!; 13 Qc2, Rfb8; 14 h3 (If 14 b3 or Rb1, Benko intended 14 ..., c4!) 14 ..., Nge5; 15 Nxe5, Nxe5; 16 b3? (16 Rd1!?) 16 ..., Nd3; 17 Rd1, c4! with great advantage to Black (Aspler-Benko, Canadian Open 1972).

12 ..., Rf8-b8; 13 e2-e4, Nf6-e8; 14 Qd1-c2,

In the game Grunberg-Gheorghiu (Rumanian Team Championship 1970) there was played instead **14 Qd2** but Black still stood well: 14 ..., Qa5!; 15 h4, Nb6!; 16 Qf4, Nc4; 17 e5!, Nxb2 (declining the intended exchange sacrifice) 18 Bxb2, Rxb2; 19 Ne4, Rb4!; 20 Nfg5, f6; 21 exf6, exf6; 22 Ne6, f5!; 23 Nxg7, Kxg7!; 24 Qg5, fxe4; 25 Qe7+, Kg8; 26 Bh3, Ng7!; 27 Be6+, Kh8; 28 Qxd6, Qb6; 29 Qe5, Qb8; 30 Resigns.

14 ..., Ne8-c7; 15 Ra1-b1,

If **15 Bg5!?**, h6!; 16 Bxe7, Ne8! ensnares the bishop.

15 ..., Nc7-b5!; 16 Nc3xb5,

If **16 Bd2** (16 Na4!?) Gheorghiu gives 16 ..., Nd4!; 17 Qd1 (Or 17 Nxd4, cxd4) 17 ..., Nxf3+; 18 Bxf3, Ne5 with a big plus.

16 ..., Ba6xb5;

109

This is the critical position of the fianchetto variation, and Gheorghiu considers it to be clearly in Black's favour. Compared with the exchange variation, Black has an extra attacking piece but White does not have an additional defender.

17 Re1-e3?!,

An inaccuracy, after which there is no doubt of the final result, but White could play, as Gheorghiu recommends, **17 a3!** (Not 17 b3?, Qa6) and now after **17 ..., Ba4** there has occurred:

a) 18 Qc4, Bb3; 19 Qe2, Ra4; 20 Nd2, Ne5; 21 Nxb3, Qxb3; 22 Qd1, Qxd1; 23 Rxd1, Rxa3 and soon the b-pawn went too (Charpentier-Hook, Virgin Islands 1970).

b) 18 Qe2, Qb3?! (18 ..., Bb3 keeps a small positional plus, e.g. 19 Bg5, h6! or 19 g4, Qa6; 20 Qxa6, Rxa6; 21 Bf1, Ba2!?; 22 Ra1, Rxa3!; 23 bxa3, Bxa1; 24 Bg5, Bf6 with a good ending) 19 Bg5, Kf8; 20 Nd2, Qa2 (20 ..., Qb5!?) 21 Qc4 and now instead of 21 ..., Rxb2?! (when 22 Qxa2, Rxa2; 23 Nc4! gives White a big plus, although he lost in Radford-Harding, Woolacombe 1972) Black should play 21 ..., Bb3!; 22 Nxb3, Ne5!; 23 Qe2, Rxb3 with the edge (analysis).

Possibly White can even hold the balance with 17 a3, but he has to play a tricky defence in view of his opponent's control of the queen side white squares, files and long black diagonal.

17 ..., Ra8xa2;

He was bound to win a pawn in the end.

18 Re3-a3, Ra2xa3;

Not **18 ..., Rba8?**; 19 Qb3! and White equalises.

19 b2xa3, Qb6-a6!; 20 Nf3-d2, Bg7-d4!; 21 Bg2-f1, Bb5xf1; 22 Rb1xb8+, Nd7xb8; 23 Ne2xf1, Nb8-d7; 24 Bc1-b2!?,

Better to play **24 Kg2** but he has little hope.

24 ..., Nd7-e5!; 25 Kg1-g2, Ne5-d3!; 26 Bd2-c3?,

In view of 26 Bxd4?, Ne1+ he had to lose the f-pawn.

26 ..., Qa6-c4; White resigns.

In the next game, the plan which Black adopts is not so

theoretically pure. It is here that the Volga betrays its Blumenfeld ancestry.

Game 54
Razuvaev - Pytel
(Polanica Zdroi 1972)

1 d2-d4, Ng8-f6; 2 c2-c4, c7-c5; 3 d4-d5, b7-b5; 4 c4xb5, a7-a6;

The alternative 4 ..., e6?!; 5 Nc3 is very good for White:

a) 5 ..., Bb7; 6 e4!, a6; 7 Nh3!?, Qb6; 8 Bf4, axb5; 9 Nxb5, Na6; 10 Qb3, Qa5+; 11 Bd2, Qb6; 12 e5!, Nxd5 (Or 12 ..., Bxd5; 13 Nd6+, Qxd6; 14 exd6, Bxb3; 15 axb3, Nc7; 16 dxc7, Rxa1+; 17 Bc1! Pachman) 13 Bc4, Qc6; 14 f3, Be7; 15 O-O (Dobias-Maximovic, Prague 1947).

b) 5 ..., exd5; 6 Nxd5, Bb7 and now:

b1) 7 Nxf6+!?, Qxf6; 8 Nf3, d5; 9 g3, Qb6; 10 a4 (Alatortsev-Ratner, 14th USSR Championship 1945) and now Zechiel & Crane claim that 10 ..., a6; 11 bxa6, Nxa6; 12 Bg2, Be7; 13 O-O, O-O is a little better for Black - unclear!

b2) 7 Bg5?, Bxd5!; 8 Bxf6, Qxf6; 9 Qxd5, Qxb2 (Sirkia-Grigorian, Riga 1967).

b3) 7 e4!, Nxe4 (Slightly better 7 ..., Nxd5; 8 exd5, Qe7+; 9 Be3, Qe4; 10 Nge2! Rovner-Orlov, Riga 1954) 8 Bc4!, Nd6 (8 ..., Bd6; 9 Qg4! or 9 Nf3) 9 Qe2+, Be7; 10 Bg5, f6; 11 Bf4, Nxc4; 12 Qxc4 and White should win (Boleslavsky-Alexeev, USSR 1959).

5 b5xa6, e7-e6!?;

If 5 ..., Bxa6; 6 Nc3, e6?! White could follow the game Averbakh-Kuznetsov, USSR 1960:

7 e4, Qa5; 8 Bd2, c4!?; 9 Be2, Qb6; 10 Rb1, Bc5; 11 Nh3 and Black's position is too loose.

Taimanov has called 5 ..., e6 'the modern way of handling the Volga Gambit', but this seems unhistorical. For example, Pachman's 'Indian Systems' (1962) gives some analysis of 5 ..., e6 but of 5 ..., Bxa6 he only comments 'also playable'.

110

6 Nb1-c3,

White has probably made enough pawn moves already. After 6 dxe6, fxe6:

a) 7 e3, Be7!; 8 Nc3, O-O; 9 Nf3, d5; 10 Be2, Bxa6 (If Argunov's 10 ..., Nxa6; 11 O-O, Bb7 'Chess Digest' give 12 Ng5 as a plus for White) 11 Ng5 (Or 11 O-O, Nc6 and ..., e5) 11 ..., Qd6 with an unclear position ('Chess Digest').

b) 7 Bg5, Be7?! (Better 7 ..., Bxa6 Chess Digest) 8 e3, O-O; 9 Nc3; 10 Nf3, Nc6; 11 Bb5 with a good game for White (Kotov-Bialas, USSR-East Germany, 1960).

c) 7 g3, d5; 8 Nf3, Bd6 (8 ..., Be7?; 9 Bf4!) 9 Bg2 (Nikolaevsky-Zilberman Ukraine Championship 1968) 9 ..., Rxa6; 10 O-O, e5; 11 Nc3, Bb7; 12 Ng5, h6?; 13 Nxd5! ('Chess Digest')

Other 12th moves for White allow equality.

6 ..., Nf6xd5;

The alternative is **6 ..., exd5; 7 Nxd5, Rxa6** (7 ..., Nxd5 see text) 8 Nf3, Nxd5; 9 Qxd5, Nc6; 10 e4!, Be7; 11 Bc4, O-O; 12 O-O, Nb4; 13 Qd1 (13 Qh5 - Euwe) and not now 13 ..., Rg6?; 14 Ne5, Rf6; 15 a3 with advantage to White (Lengyel-Bilek, Budapest 1965). 'Chess Digest' also recommend **7 e3!**, Nc6; 8 Nf3, Be7; 9 Be2, O-O; 10 O-O.

7 Nc3xd5, e6xd5; 8 Qd1xd5, Nb8-c6; 9 e2-e4!?,

This is new; one used to play **9 e3** and now:

a) 9 ..., Rxa6!?; 10 Bxa6 (Or 10 Bc4, Qf6; 11 Ne2!, Nb4; 12 Qe4+, Be7; 13 Nc3, Re6! with complications) 10 ..., Qxa6; 11 Ne2, Nb4; 12 Qe4+, Be7 (Akvist & Berglund).

b) 9 ..., Be7 with the following possibilities:

b1) 10 Bd2!?, O-O; 11 Bc3 followed by Rd1 (Pytel).

b2) 10 Nf3, Bxa6 (10 ..., O-O; 11 Ne5, Nb4! Pachman) 11 Bxa6, Qa5+; 12 Qd2, Qxa6; 13 Qe2, Bf6! and a draw at move 19 (Mikenas-Ungureanu, Lublin 1972).

b3) 10 Bc4, O-O; 11 Nf3 (Or 11 Ne2, Bxa6; 12 Bxa6, Rxa6 - 12 ..., Nb4! Chess Digest - 13 Bd2, Qb6; 14 Rb1, Nb4! Dementiev-Pokrovsky, Irkutsk 1964) 11 ..., Bxa6 (Or 11 ..., Rxa6!?; 12 O-O, Nb4!?; 13 Qd1 and White has an edge - Argunov) 12 Bd2 (Or 12 Bxa6, Qa5+; 13 Bd2 Chess Digest) 12 ..., Qb6; 13 O-O, Qxb2 (If 13 ..., Bxc4; 14 Qxc4, Qxb2; 15 a4! intending Bc3 with a slight plus - Pytel) 14 Bxa6, Rxa6; 15 a4 and

White has the advantage (Pytel-Ungureanu, Lublin 1972).

9 ..., Bf8-e7; 10 Bf1-c4, O-O; 11 Ng1-e2,

If instead **11 Nf3**, hoping for **11 ..., Rxa6** which transposes into the favourable note to White's 8th move, Black can play instead **11 ..., Bxa6!**:

a) 12 Bd2, Qb6; 13 O-O, Qxb2; 14 e5!, Nd4; 15 Nxd4, Qxd4; 16 Qxd4, cxd4 with about equal chances (Sadomsky-Pokrovsky, semi-final 8th USSR Correspondence Championship).

b) 12 e5? (Or 12 a3!?, Bb7 and ..., Na5) 12 ..., Nb4; 13 Qe4, d5; 14 exd6, Bxd6; 15 O-O, Re8; 16 Qg4, h5; 17 Qxh5, Bxc4 (Chess Digest).

c) 12 b3?, Nb4; 13 Qd2, d5!; 14 Bxa6 (14 Bxd5?, Nxd5; 15 exd5, Bf6 and wins) 14 ..., Rxa6; 15 e5, Qa8; 16 a3, c4 with advantage to Black (Chess Digest).

However the text move does not seem to lead to a clear advantage for White either, so perhaps 9 e3 is stronger than 9 e4. I am sceptical about the 5 ..., e6 variation because its virtues are primarily tactical, and it appears to lack the sound strategic basis of the main lines, or even of the Blumenfeld.

11 ..., Bc8xa6; 12 Bc4xa6,

Not **12 O-O?**, Nb4.

See Diagram

12 ..., Qd8-a5+!

Other plans:

a) 12 ..., Rxa6; 13 Bd2, Qb6; 14 Rb1, Nb4; 15 Bxb4, Qxb4+; 16 Nc3, Bf6 since not now 17 e5?, Bxe5; 18 Qxe5?, Re6 (Chess Digest)

111

---

b) 12 ..., Nb4?!; 13 Qc4 (Or 13 Qb3, Rxa6; 14 O-O with advantage - Chess Digest) 13 ..., Rxa6; 14 O-O, d5; 15 exd5, Qxd5; 16 Qxd5, Nxd5; 17 Rd1, Nb4; 18 a3, Bf6; 19 Rb1 and Black had nothing for his pawn (Kakagel'diev-Gel'dymamedov, Turkmenian Championship 1972).

13 Qd5-d2, Qa5xa6; 14 O-O, Be7-f6; 15 Ne2-c3,

Not **15 Qxd7?,** Rfd8; 16 Qg4, Ne5; 17 Qh5, g6 winning the knight

15 ..., Nc6-b4; 16 Qd2xd7,

White is unable to complete his development normally, e.g. **16 Nd5,** Nxd5; 17 exd5, Bd4 followed by the demise of his d-pawn.

16 ..., Nb4-c2!;

Not **16 ..., Rfd8?;** 17 Qf5, Nc2; 18 e5 (Pytel), White winning two pieces for a rook.

17 Ra1-b1, Rf8-d8; 18 Qd7-g4,

Since **18 Qb5,** Qxb5; 19 Nxb5, Rdb8! should lead to a draw (Pytel).

18 ..., Nc2-a3!; 19 b2xa3,

White could play **19 Ra1,** acquiescing in a draw by repetition.

19 ..., Bf6xc3; 20 h2-h4!?,

Pytel does not mention **20 Rb3!** (to meet 20 ..., Qd3? by 21 Bb2). After this move it is not clear

to me that Black has adequate play for his two pawns. He must try to make something of his c-pawn, but that is not easy as White can use threats against g7 to gain time for the co-ordination of his position: 20 ..., Bf6 (20 ..., Be5; 21 Bf4 or 20 ..., Bd4; 21 Be3, c4?!; 22 Bxd4!) 21 Rg3, g6; 22 Bf4, c4; 23 e5, Bg7; 24 Rc1 (analysis).

20 ..., Qa6-d3!;

Now things become unclear.

21 Bc1-g5,

If **21 h5** Pytel intended 21 ..., Ra4.

21 ..., Rd8-e8; 22 f2-f3, Bc3-d4+; 23 Kg1-h2, Qd3xa3; 24 Rf1-d1, Qa3xa2; 25 Rb1-b6,

If **25 Rxd4,** Pytel gives 25 ..., h5!; 26 Qg3, cxd4; 27 Bf6, g6; 28 Qg5, Kh7.

25 ..., Re8-e6; 26 Rb6-b7?,

It would be better to exchange heavy pieces on e6, although the ending favours Black in view of his passed c-pawn.

26 ..., h7-h6; 27 Rd1-d2?,

Not **27 Bf4,** Rg6; 28 Qh3, Qe2 and ..., Ra2 but his last chance resided in **27 Bd2!** (Pytel).

27 ..., Qa2-a6; White resigns.

With White's recent failure to demonstrate any advantage by 5 bxa6, attention is beginning to shift back to an older plan of simply guarding the advanced pawn by 5 e3. Black will eventually have to make the pawn exchange himself, if he is not to fall behind on development, but if he waits until the White king bishop has moved then it does not cost him a tempo. Besides it is not clear that any White piece is well placed on b5.

Game 55
Blumin - Benko
(Atlantic Open, USA 1969)

1 d2-d4, Ng8-f6; 2 c2-c4, c7-c5; 3 d4-d5, b7-b5; 4 c4xb5, a7-a6; 5 e2-e3,

Other 5th moves (besides 5 bxa6) are:

a) 5 Nc3, axb5; **6 Nxb5,** e6?! (Simplest is 6 ..., Ba6!; 7 Nc3 with a normal position) 7 Nc3, exd5; 8 e3?! (8 Nxd5 could lead to certain lines discussed in the previous game) 8 ..., Bb7 and Black stood well (Hanov-Gusev, USSR 1962). Also poor is **6 e4?,** b4; 7 e5, bxc3; 8 exf6, cxb2; 9 Bxb2, Qa5+ and Black wins a pawn.

b) 5 f3, g6 (If 5 ..., axb5; 6 e4, d6; 7 Nc3 or if here 6 ..., b4; 7 Bc4 or 7 Nd2 - Gheorghiu in 'Revista de Sah') 6 e4, d6; 7 Nc3, Bg7; 8 Bg5! and now instead of 8 ..., O-O? (Viner-Gheorghiu, Adelaide 1971) the Rumanian grandmaster recommends 8 ..., h6; 9e3, O-O; 10 Qd2, e6; 11 Bxh6, Nxe4!; 12 fxe4, Qh4+; 13 g3, Qxh6 with an unclear position.

c) 5 b6!? (keeping some lines closed):

c1) 5 ..., Qxb6; 6 Nc3, g6; 7 e4, d6; **8 Nf3** (Or 8 Rb1, Bg7; 9 Qa4+, Nbd7; 10 Bd2, O-O; 11 Nf3, Rb8; 12 Bd3 Mendoza-Benko, Malaga 1969; 12 ..., Ng4! with a good game for Black - analysis) 8 ..., Bg7; 9 Nd2, O-O; 10 Be2, Nbd7; 11 O-O, Qc7; **12 Qc2,** e6 with a balanced struggle (Steinberg-Georgadze, USSR 1972), or here **12 Nc4,** Nb6; 13 Bg5, Nxc4; 14 Bxc4, Re8 (Saidy-Popov, Tallinn 1973).

c2) 5 ..., d6; 6 Nc3, Nbd7; 7 Nf3, g6; 8 e4, Bg7; 9 Be2, O-O; 10 O-O,

Nxb6 (10 ..., Qxb6 see **c1**) 11 Bf4, Bg4; 12 Nd2 soon drawn in Pfleger-Benko, Skopje 1972.

5 ..., g7-g6!;

Once more, **5 ..., d6** will transpose, but there is also the old 5 ..., e6!?; 6 Nc3 and now:

a) 6 ..., Bb7!? (Milic, 'Informator No.4').

b) 6 ..., axb5?!; 7 Bxb5, Qa5 (7 ..., Bb7; 8 Bc4 and 9 e4) 8 dxe6! (The only good move) 8 ..., fxe6; 9 Qb3!, Qb6 (9 ..., Bb7; 10 Bxd7+) 10 e4 and White stands better (Pachman)

c) 6 ..., Qa5!; 7 Bd2 is unclear:

c1) 7 ..., **Qb6;** 8 Qb3!? (8 dxe6!? Milic) 8 ..., axb5; 9 Bxb5, exd5; 10 Nxd5, Nxd5; 11 Qxd5, Bb7 (Equally obscure is Milic's 11 ..., Qxb5!?; 12 Qxa8, Ba6; 13 O-O, Be7!?) 12 Qe5+, Be7; 13 Bd3, O-O!? (13 ..., Qf6!?; 14 Qxf6, Bxf6; 15 Nf3, O-O!? Milic) 14 Qxe7, Bxg2; 15 Bc3!? (Or 15 Be4!?, Nc6!; 16 Qh4!, Bxe4; 17 Qxe4, Qxb2 Milic) 15 ..., Bxh1 (15 ..., Qh6!? Milic) and now instead of 16 Ne2?, Qh6! favouring Black (Martens-Rajkovic, Harrachov 1967) White could have got on top with Milic's 16 Qg5!.

c2) 7 ..., axb5; 8 Bxb5, Na6; 9 dxe6, fxe6; 10 Qb3 (10 Nf3!?) 10 ..., Nb4!; 11 Qxe6+ (Or 11 a4, Be7; 12 Nf3, O-O Tarasov-Pokrovsky, semi-final 10th USSR Correspondence Championship) 11 ..., Kd8; 12 Qb3, Rb8; 13 a4, Ba6; 14 Rd1 (Or 14 Rb1, d5!; 15 Nxd5, Rxb5; 16 Nxf6, c4; 17 Qxc4, Qxa4; 18 Qd4+, Kc8; 19 Rc1+, Kb7; 20 Qd7+, Ka8; 21 Ne8, Bd6!; 22 Qxd6, Rxe8 Riskov-Pokrovsky, Quarter-final, 9th USSR Correspondence Championship) 14 ..., Nd3+; 15 Ke2 (If 15 Kf1, Qc7 or 15 ..., Qb6 Prokovsky)

15 ..., c4; 16 Nd5 (16 Qc2!?, Bb4; 17 Nf3 Pokrovsky) 16 ..., Qxd2+; 17 Kxd2, cxb3; 18 Nxf6, Bxb5; 19 axb5, Nxf2; 20 Nd5, Nxd1; 21 Kxd1, Rxb5; 22 e4, Ra5; 23 Ne2, Ra1+; 24 Nc1, Ba3!; 25 Resigns (Efimov-Pokrovsky, USSR Masters & Candidate Masters Tourney 1971).

It appears from these examples that 5 ..., e6 may be playable, but as yet there have been no grandmaster games and judgement should be deferred. Benko played the move in the 1966 US Open, but his opponent was not a master and the game not critical.

112

6 Nb1-c3, d7-d6;

In a few games **6 ..., Bg7** has been played first, which avoids some of White's alternatives. However the critical reply 7 d6!, e6; 8 Qf3! appears to throw doubt on the validity of that move-order (analysis). Also **6 ..., Qb6?!** looks unsound after 7 Na4!

7 Bf1-c4,

To follow up with Nge2 rather as in the Dutch System. White has quite a range of possibilities here, and few have been explored deeply:

a) 7 b6?!, Nbd7; 8 a4, Qxb6; 9 a5, Qc7; 10 Nf3, Bg7; 11 h3, O-O; 12

Bc4, Rb8; 13 O-O, Ne8 and Black is O.K. (Reshevsky-Browne, Skopje 1970).

b) 7 Nf3, Bg7; **8 Be2** (8 bxa6, O-O and 9 ..., Bxa6 or 9 ..., Qa5 is quite innocuous) O-O; 9 O-O, axb5; 10 Bxb5, Ba6; 11 Bxa6, Rxa6 or 11 ..., Nxa6 with positions of a balanced nature akin to those in the note to Black's 9th move in Game 52. It is of course in Black's favour that White has his pawn on e3 rather than e4. Portisch and Benko have both played 7 Nf3 without making any real impact.

c) 7 e4?!, Bg7; 8 bxa6?!, O-O; 9 f3!?, Nxa6; 10 Bc4, Nd7; 11 Nge2, Ne5; 12 Bb3, c4; 13 Ba2, Qb6; 14 Na4, Qa4; 15 a3, Bd7; 16 Nc3, Nc7 with great advantage to Black (Kchouk-Toran, Siegen 1970).

d) 7 a4!, Bg7; 8 Qb3!, axb5 (Not 8 ..., O-O??; 9 b6! and 10 a5 with a cold win) 9 Bxb5+ is a very dangerous plan, introduced by Korchnoy against Calvo at Palma 1972. Black played **9 ..., Bd7?!**; 10 Ra3!, O-O; 11 Nge2, Na6; 12 O-O, Nc7; 13 Bc4, Rb8; 14 Qc2, Bc8; 15 b3, Ba6; 16 Bb2 and White was always on top. The critical line may be: **9 ..., Nfd7!**; 10 Nge2, O-O; 11 O-O, Na6!; 12 e4, Nb4! followed by ..., Ba6 and attack against White's weak squares on the queen side; the Bb5 is best ignored (analysis).

e) 7 bxa6 (Seems rather inconsistent) **7 ..., Bg7** and now:

e1) 8 e4?!, O-O; 9 f4, Qa5!; 10 Bd2, Bxa6; 11 Bxa6, Nxa6; 12 Nf3, Nb4; 13 O-O, c4; 14 Kh1, Nd3; 15 Qe2, Rfb8 and Black stands well (Hamann-Gheorghiu, Skopje 1972)

e2) 8 Nf3, O-O; 9 e4 (9 Nd2!?) 9 ..., Qa5!? (9 ..., Bxa6 Benko) 10 Nd2,

Bxa6; 11 Bxa6, Qxa6; 12 Qe2, Nfd7; 13 Nc4, f5!? with a sharp game (Kaufman-Benko, US Open 1968)

e3) 8 Bb5+! (The only way to give point to his 7th move) 8 ..., Nfd7; 9 Nge2, O-O; 10 O-O, Nxa6 (10 ..., Bxa6!?) 11 e4, Nc7; 12 Bd3, Ne5; 13 Bc2, Ba6; 14 f4, Nc4; 15 Rf3, e6 with balanced chances although Black lost after over-optimistic play (Kuijpers-Benko, Wijk aan Zee 1970).

7 ..., Bf8-g7; 8 Ng1-e2, O-O; 9 O-O, Nb8-d7!;

The threat of ..., Ne5/..., Nb6 obliges White to make the pawn exchange at last. Instead **9 ..., axb5**; 10 Bxb5 followed by 11 a4 could leave White in control (compare Korchnoy-Calvo).

10 b5xa6, Nd7-b6; 11 Bc4-b5,

He has to concede a tempo, since **11 Bd3** costs the d-pawn and **11 Bb3**, Bxa6 is positionally undesirable.

11 ..., Bc8xa6; 12 Bb5-c6?,

The bishop is badly out of play here. He had to play **12 Bxa6**, Rxa6 when Black continues with ..., Qa8, ..., Rb8 with about equal chances according to Benko.

12 ..., Ra8-b8; 13 Ra1-b1?,

A further inaccuracy, of which Black takes immediate advantage. He should play **13 Re1**, unpinning his king knight.

13 ..., Nf6-g4!;

This threatens 14 ..., Ne5 and subsequent ..., Nxc6, or ..., Nd3.

14 f2-f4, Bg7xc3!;

This would have no effect if White could play 15 Nxc3.

15 b2xc3, Nb6-c4; 16 Rb1xb8, Qd8xb8;

113

17 Qd1-a4,

If **17 Rf3** Benko would play 17 ..., Qb1 threatening ..., Ngxe3!

17 ..., Qb8-b6; 18 e3-e4,

In 'Chess Life & Review' Benko mentions **18 Rf3**, Nd2!; 19 Bxd2, Bxe2 followed by ..., Qb1+.

18 ..., Nc4-d2;

Opening lines.

19 Rf1-d1, Ba6xd2; 20 Rd1xd2, c5-c4+; 21 Rd2-d4, Qb6-b1!;

Now White is lost, but not 21 ..., e5? because of 22 dxe6, fxe6; 23 Qb5 holding the balance.

22 Qa4-a3, Rf8-b8; 23 h2-h3, Ng4-e3; 24 Bc6-a4, Be2-d3; 25 Kg1-f2, Ne3-c2; 26 Ba4xc2, Qb1xc2+; 27 Kf2-g3, Qc2-e2;

Bishops of opposite colour attacks are deadly.

28 f4-f5, Bd3xe4; 29 Rd4-d2, Qe2-e3+; 30 Kg3-h2, Qe3-f4+; 31 Kh2-g1, Rb8-b1; 32 Rd2-d1, Qf4-g3; 33 Rd1-d2, Qg3-e1+; White soon resigned.

Because of the success of the Volga Gambit, ways are being

sought to decline the pawn and keep lines closed on the queen side. Most of these lines are virtually unexplored but the Volga gambiteer must know how to handle them. The old saying that 'the only way to refute a gambit is to accept it' is not necessarily applicable in this case. The following illustrative game is particularly important to study, in view of the conflicting notes given by two masters in 'The Chess Player'.

Game 56
Hartoch - Keres
(IBM Tournament, Amsterdam 1971)

1 d2-d4, Ng8-f6; 2 c2-c4,

Another way of reaching standard Volga Gambit lines is **2 Nf3, c5; 3 d5, b5; 4 c4** (as in fact was the case in this game). The disadvantage for Black is that White may play **4 a4!** (If 4 Bg5!? of Larsen-Browne, Hastings 1972-3, the author has been successful with 4 ..., Qb6!?) to follow up with Nbd2 and Nc4. This is as yet untested, but similar to certain positions that could arise in the note to White's 4th move in the game. There however, White has played c4 which is a positive disadvantage to him.

2 ..., c7-c5; 3 d4-d5, b7-b5; 4 Ng1-f3,

White has already ways of varying at this point:

a) 4 cxb5 see earlier Games.

b) 4 g3, bxc4; 5 Bg2, g6; 6 Nc3, Bb7; 7 Nf3, Bg7; 8 O-O, O-O; 9 Ne5, d6; 10 Nxc4, Nbd7; 11 Re1, Ba6 (Johannessen-Fischer, Olympiad 1956)

c) 4 f3, bxc4; 5 e4, d6 (5 ..., e6!?) 6 Bxc4, g6; 7 Nc3, Bg7; 8 Nge2, O-O; 9 O-O, Nbd7; 10 Be3, Ne5; 11 Bb3, Ba6 and Black had the edge (Lim-Browne, 1971).

d) 4 b3, bxc4; 5 bxc4, g6; 6 Bb2, d6; 7 e4, Bg7; 8 Bd3, O-O; 9 Ne2, Nbd7 (Torner-Berglund, Linkoping 1970).

e) 4 Na3, b4 (4 ..., a6!?) 5 Nc2, e5!?; 6 g3, d6; 7 Bg2, Be7; 8 e4, O-O!?; 9 Ne3 and White stood slightly better in this unusual Czech Benoni (Velimirovic-Njegovan, Yugoslavia 1966). Black might have tried **8 ..., a5!?** intending to exchange all the heavy pieces on the a-file and then play against b3 and other weaknesses in the ending (analysis).

f) 4 Bg5, Ne4 (4 ..., Qb6!?) 5 Bf4, Qa5+; 6 Nd2, d6; 7 b4!?, Qxb4; 8 Rb1, Qc3; 9 Rxb5, Nxd2; 10 Bxd2, Qxc4; 11 e3, Qxa2; 12 Bc3, e6 (12 ..., Ba6!?) 13 Bd3, Bd7; 14 dxe6, Qxe6; 15 Ne2 and White had, according to Kotov in 'Informator No.11', fair compensation for his sacrifices. Black did not take the exchange and went on to lose (Shashin-Domes, USSR 1971).

g) 4 a4, bxc4; 5 Nc3 (5 Na3 fails to 5 ..., Bb7) 5 ..., d6; 6 e4, Ba6; 7 f4, Nbd7 (If 7 ..., e6; 8 Nf3, exd5; 9 e5, dxe5; 10 fxe5, Ne4; 11 Qd5 Peev-Alburt, Lublin 1972) 8 Nf3, Qb8; 9 Qe2, Qb7; 10 g3, e5; 11 dxe6, fxe6; 12 e5, Nd5 and Black triumphed (Peev-Pedersen, Skopje 1972).

See Diagram

4 ..., Bc8-b7;

This is the most thematic move. Others:

a) 4 ..., e6 Blumenfeld Counter-Gambit.

114

b) 4 ..., bxc4; 5 Nc3 (If 5 a4, Bb7 see note to Black's 5th move) 5 ..., g6; 6 e4, d6; 7 Bxc4 (Or 7 Nd2, Bg7; 8 Nxc4, O-O; 9 Be2, Nbd7; 10 O-O, Ba6; 11 Re1, Rab8; 12 a3? - Better 12 Ne3 Shatskes - 12 ..., Qc7; 13 h3, Rb7; 14 Qa4, Bxc4; 15 Qxc4, Rfb8; 16 Qa4, Nb6; 17 Qc2, c4! Doda-Forintos, Belgrade 1961) 7 ..., Bg7; 8 e5, dxe5; 9 Nxe5, O-O; 10 O-O, Nfd7; 11 Nc6, Nxc6; 12 dxc6, Nb6; 13 Be2, Qc7; 14 Bf3, Ba6; 15 Re1, Rad8; 16 Qb3, Bc4 and Black certainly stands no worse (Balashov-Stein, Moscow 1971).

c) 4 ..., d6; 5 a4, bxc4; 6 Nc3, Nbd7; 7 e4, Ba6; 8 Qc2, Qb6; 9 a5, Qb7; 10 Nd2, Ne5 (Malich-del Corral, Siegen 1970).

d) 4 ..., g6; 5 g3 (5 cxb5, a6 etc) 5 ..., bxc4; 6 Bg2, Bb7; 7 Nc3, Bg7; 8 O-O, O-O with no problems for Black (Castagna-Lundvall, Biel '70)

5 e2-e3?!,

A somewhat unusual move, and not the best:

a) 5 g3, g6; 6 Bg2, Bg7; 7 O-O, d6; 8 Re1, bxc4; 9 e4, O-O; 10 Nfd2, Nbd7; 11 Nxc4, Rb8; 12 Bd2, Nb6; 13 Na5, Ba8; 14 Na3, Nfd7; 15 Rb1, e6 with about equal chances (Klaman-Keres, USSR Championship 1957).

b) 5 cxb5?, Bxd5; 6 Nc3, Bb7; 7 Qa4, d5; 8 Ne5, e6; 9 Nc6, Qb6; 10 Na5, Nbd7; 11 e3, Bd6; 12 Nxb7, Qxb7; 13 Qa6, Qb8; 14 Be2, O-O with some advantage to Black (Tarasevich-Zaitsev, Moscow 1964).

c) 5 Nbd2, d6; 6 e4, b4 (6 ..., bxc4!?) 7 Bd3, g6; 8 O-O, Bg7; 9 Re1, Nbd7; 10 Nf1, O-O; 11 Rb1, a5; 12 a4 (He must prevent ..., a4) 12 ..., bxa3 with an early draw (Kolarov-Peev, Varna 1971).

d) 5 Nc3, b4 (5 ..., bxc4; 6 a4 see **e**) 6 Qb3, Qa5 (6 ..., Qb6!) 7 Nd1, e6; 8 e4!? (Better 8 Ne3 and 9 g3) 8 ..., Nxe4; 9 Bd3, Nf6; 10 O-O, g6; 11 Bg5, Bg7; 12 Ne3, O-O; 13 h4, Qc7? (Better 13 ..., d6 or 13 ..., Nbd7) 14 Rae1, d6; 15 Bxf6, Bxf6; 16 Ng4, Bg7; 17 h5! with advantage to White (Guimard-Keres, Gothenburg 1955).

e) 5 a4! could be critical:

e1) 5 ..., a6!?; 6 axb5!?, axb5; 7 Rxa8, Bxa8; 8 Nc3 (Kan-Keres, USSR Championship 1955) 8 ..., b4; 9 Qa4 (Or 9 Nb5, Qb6) 9 ..., bxc3; 10 Qxa8, cxb2; 11 Bxb2, Qb6 and Black stands rather better (Keres). Better may be **6 e3**.

e2) 5 ..., bxc4; 6 Nc3, d6 (6 ..., e6? Rubinstein-Spielmann, Vienna '22) 7 e4, Nbd7 (Or 7 ..., g6; 8 Bxc4, Bg7; 9 O-O, O-O; 10 Qe2, Nbd7; 11 h3, Nbd7; 12 Bb5, a6; 13 Bd3, e6 Balmazi-Platonov, Ukraine Championship 1965) 8 Bxc4, g6; 9 O-O, Bg7; 10 h3, O-O; 11 a5, Ne8; 12 Qe2, Nc7; 13 Bf4, Rb8; 14 e5 (Zilberstein-K.Grigoryan, 40th USSR Championship 1972).

e3) 5 ..., b4; 6 Nbd2, d6; 7 e4, e5!?; 8 dxe6 (8 g3!?) 8 ..., fxe6; 9 Bd3, e5!; 10 Qe2, Nc6; 11 Nf1, Nd4; 12 Nxd4, cxd4; 13 f4, Be7; 14 Ng3,

O-O with a hard struggle (Balashov
-Platonov, 39th USSR Championship 1971). Korchnoy recommends
15 Nf5 here, but it is not clear who
stands better despite White's two
bishops.

5 ..., g7-g6;

According to Bobotsov, Black
should play **5 ..., e6!**; 6 dxe6 (since
Bg5 is not available) 6 ..., fxe6; 7
cxb5, d5 with a Blumenfeld position that is in Black's favour. Now
some very difficult positions arise.

**6 Nb1-c3, b5-b4; 7 Nc3-e2, Bf8-g7;
8 Ne2-g3, e7-e6; 9 e3-e4, e6xd5; 10
e4xd5, O-O; 11 Bf1-e2, d7-d6;
12 O-O, Nb8-d7;**

115

Bobotsov considers that White
stands slightly better here! Keres is
probably right in thinking that it is
only his next move which spoils
things.

13 Bc1-f4, Nd7-b6?;

Correct is **13 ..., Qb6!** intending ..., Rae8, ..., Bc8, ..., Ne5
(Keres).

**14 Qd1-d2, Rf8-e8;
15 Be2-d3, Bb7-a6;**

According to Keres, **15 ..., a5!**
is best.

**16 Ra1-c1, Ra8-c8; 17 b2-b3,
Rc8-c7; 18 h2-h3, Qd8-e7; 19**

Rf1-e1, Qe7-f8; 20 Re1xe8, Nf6xe8;
21 Ng3-e2, Bb7-c8; 22 Nf3-h2,
Nb6-d7; 23 Bf4-e3, a7-a5;

Here Keres gives **23 ..., f5!**

**24 g2-g4, a5-a4; 25 f2-f4, Rc7-a7;
26 Nh2-f3, Qf8-e7; 27 Kg1-g2,
a4xb3; 28 a2xb3, Ra7-a3; 29
Bd3-c2, Ra3-a2;**

A mistake according to Bobotsov;
but see move 34.

**30 Be3-f2!, Nd7-b6; 31 Rc1-e1,
Qe7-d8; 32 Bf2-h4, Qd8-d7;
33 Qd2-d3, Ne8-f6;**

116

34 Ne2-g3, h7-h5?;

Bobotsov claims a larger White
advantage now, while Keres points
out that **34 ..., Ba6!** (threatening ...,
Nfxd5 and ..., Nbxc4) was very
strong instead.

**35 f4-f5!, h5xg4; 36 h3xg4!,
Nf6xg4?;**

36 ..., Ba6! (Keres) still leaves
the situation unclear.

37 f5xg6, f7-f6;

Forced, since if 37 ..., fxg6?;
38 Re7 and White wins.

**38 Kg2-g1, Ng4-e5;
39 Nf3xe5, d6xe5;**

Not 39 ..., fxe5?; 40 Rf1 and
41 Rf7 etc.

40 Qd3-f5!, Qd7-e8?;

Not 40 ..., Qf5?; 41 Bxf5, Rb2;
42 Re3, Bh6; 43 Rd3 and wins
(Bobotsov), but 40 ..., Rb2! (Keres)
gains an important tempo.

41 Qf5-h5!, Bc8-h3;

There is no denying White's
advantage now. If 41 ..., Rxc2?; 42
Qh7+ (Or 42 Bxf6! Keres) 42 ...,
Kf8; 43 Bxf6!, Bxf6; 44 Rf1
winning (Bobotsov).

42 Bh4xf6!, Bg7xf6; 43 Qh5xh3,

Renewing his main threat.

43 ..., Qe8-e7; 44 Bc2-f5, Kg8-f8;
45 Re1-f1, Kf8-e8; 46 Ng3-e4,
Bf6-g7; 47 Qh3-h7, Bg7-f8; 48
d5-d6, Qe7-g7; 49 d6-d7+!, Ke8-d8

If 49 ..., Nxd7; 50 Bxd7+,
Qxd7; 51 Rxf8+ and wins.

50 Qh7xg7, Bf8xg7; 51 Ne4xc5,

Threatening 52 Nb7+ and 52
Ne6+.

51 ..., Nb6xd7; 52 Rf1-d1, Ra2-a7;
53 Rd1xd7+, Ra7xd7;
54 Nc5xd7, **Black resigns.**

QUASI-VOLGA GAMBITS IN THE
BENONI AND KING'S INDIAN

In this section will be discussed all counter-gambits cognate to the
Volga, i.e. involving the thrust ..., b5 in connection with the typical Benoni
closed centre and Black's king fianchetto. In some cases there are remote
possibilities of transposition to or from the Volga itself.

First there is Lundin's Counter-Gambit, introduced without success
at the 1948 Interzonal Tournament by that Swedish master. Its
distinguishing feature is the omission of ..., a6 by Black, at least until he
has completed his fianchetto.

**Game 57
Stupica - Tringov**
(Lubliana 1969)

**1 d2-d4, Ng8-f6; 2 c2-c4, c7-c5;
3 d4-d5, d7-d6;**

This was the order of moves
adopted by Lundin. However it is
also possible to play 3 ..., b5; 4
cxb5, d6; 5 Nc3, g6; 6 e4 etc.

**4 Nb1-c3, g7-g6; 5 e2-e4,
b7-b5!?; 6 c4xb5, Bf8-g7;**

If Black plays here 6 ..., a6!?
he cannot count on reaching
normal Volga lines, for besides the

possibility 7 bxa6, Bxa6; 8 Be2
White might follow Schiffer-Hug,
Berlin 1971: 7 f4, Bg7; 8 Nf3, O-O;
9 bxa6, Bxa6; 10 Bxa6, Rxa6?
(Better 10 ..., Nxa6) 11 O-O, Qb6;
12 Qe2, Nbd7; 13 e5 with a win in
21 moves.

7 Ng1-f3,

Equally good here is 7 **Be2** e.g:

a) 7 ..., a6; 8 Nf3, O-O see the text
continuation.

b) 7 ..., O-O; 8 h3?! (8 Nf3, a6 see
text, or 8 Bd2!?, a6; 9 a4 with an
unclear position: Lemaire-van

Hoorde, Bruges 1954) 8 ..., a6; 9 bxa6, Nbd7; 10 Be2, Bxa6; 11 O-O, Nb6; 12 Bf4?!, Bxe2; 13 Qxe2, Na4 (Black stands well) 14 Rad1?, Nh5 and wins (Bajec-Forintos, Lubliana 1969).

In the game O'Sullivan-O'Kelly, Dublin 1956, there occurred 7 **Bd3**, O-O; 8 Nge2, a6; 9 O-O, axb5; 10 Bxb5, Ba6; 11 Qd3, Qb6 and if White had now exchanged bishops there would arise one of those typical positions in which Black has pressure, albeit no concrete threats for the time being.

An interesting experiment was 7 **Rb1** in Martens-Gaprindashvili, Gothenburg 1968, continued: 7 ..., O-O; 8 Be2, a6; 9 bxa6, Bxa6; 10 Nf3, Nbd7; 11 O-O, Qc7; 12 h3, Rfb8; 13 Bg5, Rb7; 14 Bxa6, Rxa6; 15 Qe2, Ra8; 16 Rfc1, Qb8; 17 b3, h6; 18 Bf4, Ne8; 19 Rb2, Rb4; 20 Rbc2, Nc7; 21 Na4, Nxd5!; 22 Bd2, Rbxa4; 23 bxa4, Nb4 and Black drew with ease.

7 ..., O-O;

If 7 ..., a6 White can consider 8 **a4!?**, O-O; 9 Bf4, Qa5; 10 Nd2 (Hort-Gaprindashvili, Gothenburg 1972)

8 Bf1-e2,

In a game Pines-Kantorovich, USSR 1959, White tried instead 8 **Nfd2**, Nbd7; 9 Be2, a6; 10 O-O, axb5; 11 Bxb5, Ba6; 12 a4, Qc7 (12 ..., Ne8 was suggested in 'Schach-maty') 13 Qe2!, Qb7; 14 Nc4, Bxb5; 15 Nxb5, Ra6 (Better 15 ..., Ne8; 16 Bd2, Nc7 'Schachmaty') 16 Bg5, Rfa8!; 17 Qc2, Nb6; 18 Nxb6, Rxb6; 19 Bxf6!, Bxf6; 20 Rab1, Rba6; 21 b3, Qb6; 22 Qc4, Qa5; 23 Rbe1 and White stood better.

8 ..., a7-a6;

Move order is very flexible in this gambit; for example Black in the game played 8 ..., **Nbd7**; 9 O-O, **a6** with transposition. It is also to be noted that Black can delay his gambit even beyond move 5, by playing 5 ..., **Bg7**; 6 Nf3 (Or 6 Be2, b5!?; 7 cxb5, O-O; 8 Nf3) 6 ..., O-O; 7 Be2, b5!?; 8 cxb5 etc. as Tringov here did.

117

9 O-O,

The declined form 9 **b6!?** has been seen (Lundin-Akvist, Sweden 1970), but the major alternative is 9 **bxa6, Bxa6** and now:

a) 10 Bxa6, Nxa6 (Also possible is 10 ..., Rxa6 to continue ..., Nbd7, ..., Qa8, ..., Rfb8 although here White can be awkward and play 11 Qe2) 11 O-O, Nd7; 12 Bg5!, Rb8; 13 Qd2, Rb8; 14 Rab1 (Bronstein-Lundin, Saltsjobaden Interzonal 1948) and now Pachman (1962) considers the position to be in White's favour. This may however be a typical case of 'Oldthinkers' unbellyfeel Volga Gambit' as in recent years many such positions have been shown to be satisfactory for Black. The continuation was 14 ..., Qa5; 15 Rfc1, Nc7; 16 Bh6, Bf6; 17 a3, Rb3; 18 Qc2, Reb8; 19 Nd2, R3b7; 20 Nc4, Qa6; 21 Qa4, Qxa4;

22 Nxa4 and now instead of 22 ..., Nb5?; 23 b4! the suggestion of Akvist and Berglund 22 ..., Ra7; 23 Nc4, Ne5 seems quite promising. Anyway, five years later Bronstein himself was playing the gambit in a Candidates Tournament!

b) 10 Rb1, Nbd7 see Martens-Gaprindashvili, above.

c) 10 O-O, Nbd7 (Also playable 11 ..., Qc7 and 11 ..., Qb6) **11 Re1** (White might try 11 Bxa6, 12 Qe2, 13 e5; compared with the text game White is safer with his bishop on c1) 11 ..., Nb6; 12 h3, Bxe2; 13 Qxe2 (Shashin-Berezin, USSR 1958) and now after the correct 13 ..., Nfd7! Black may have some compensation for his pawn.

9 ..., Nb8-d7;

Alternatively Black can try:

a) 9 ..., axb5; 10 Bxb5, Ba6; 11 Nd2 (11 Qe2 of Prokhorovich-Berezin, USSR 1958 should have been met by 11 ..., Qb6! as in the analogous O'Kelly game mentioned above) 11 ..., Qc7 (Or 11 ..., Qb6; 12 a4, Qa6; 13 Ra3) 12 Qe2, Qb7; 13 a4, Nh5; 14 Nc4, Nd7; 15 Qc2, Ne5; 16 Nxe5, Bxe5; 17 Bh6, Rfb8; 18 Rfb1, Qc8 (Laursen-Roos, correspondence 1970) and now 19 h3 (to prevent ..., Qg4) would have left White with a clear advantage.

b) 9 ..., Qa5; 10 Nd2, axb5; 11 Bxb5, Nfd7; 12 Nc4, Qc7; 13 Bf4, Nb6; 14 Ne3, Ba6; 15 Qe2 and White has a slight advantage (Lemon-Foster, Woolacombe 1972)

10 Bc1-g5!?,

The critical continuation is probably still to make the double exchange on a6. A game Eriksson-Akvist, Sweden 1970, went **10 h3** (An useful waiting move) 10 ...,

axb5; 11 Bxb5, Ba6; 12 Bxa6, Rxa6; 13 Qe2, Qa8; 14 Bf4 (14 e5?!) 14 ..., Rb8; 15 e5, Nh5; 16 Bh2, dxe5; 17 Nxe5, Nxe5; 18 Bxe5, Rxb2!? with an unclear position.

10 ..., h7-h6; 11 Bg5-h4, a6xb5; 12 Be2xb5, Bc8-a6; 13 Bb5xa6, Ra8xa6; 14 Qd1-e2, Qd8-a8;

118

15 e4-e5?!,

White has a difficult game anyway, in view of the displacement of his bishop, but the attempt to crack open the centre recoils drastically.

15 ..., d6xe5; 16 Nf3xe5, Nd7xe5; 17 Qe2xe5, Rf8-b8!;

Achieving a high degree of co-ordination in the Black forces.

18 Qe5xe7,

If **18 Rab1** Black might choose 18 ..., Rb4; 19 Bg3, Ne4 (analysis).

18 ..., Nf6xd5;

Not **18 ..., Rxb2?;** 19 d6 and White wins.

19 Qe7xc5?!,

The lesser evil is **19 Nxd5**, Qxd5; 20 Rad1 with drawing chances.

19 ..., Nd5-f4;

White now appears to be totally lost.

20 f2-f3, Rb8xb2; 21 Ra1-d1,

Also on **21 Rf2** Black has 21 ..., Nd3!

21 ..., Bg7xc3!;

In view of the fork on e2.

22 Kg1-h1,

The intended **22 Rd8+** is worthless in view of 22 ..., Qxd8; 23 Bxd8, Bd4!; 24 Qxd4, Ne2+ etc.

22 ..., Ra6-c6; 23 Qc5-e7, Nf4-e6; White resigns.

Quasi-Volga possibilities can also arise from an orthodox King's Indian move-order, or sometimes even from a Pirc. In the notes to the two following games will also be found a few non-Volga gambit ideas for Black in the King's Indian. Firstly we have systems with e4; secondly, the fianchetto variations.

Game 58
Calvo - Benko
(Palma de Mallorca 1968)

1 d2-d4, Ng8-f6; 2 c2-c4, g7-g6; 3 Nb1-c3,

In the game A.Zaitsev-Adorjan, Polanica Zdroj 1971, the continuation was most unusual: **3 f3!?, c5** (Better 3 ..., d5) **4 d5** (According to Pachman 4 dxc5 would give White the advantage) 4 ..., d5; 5 e4, b5!?; 6 cxb5, a6; 7 bxa6, Bg7; 8 Bb5+, Nbd7; 9 Ne2, Qa5+; 10 Nbc3, Bxa6; 11 Bxa6, Qxa6; 12 O-O, O-O; 13 Be3! (Also good is 13 Qc2! intending 14 Bg5! - Zaitsev) and Black was without compensation for his pawn.

3 ..., Bf8-g7; 4 e2-e4, d7-d6; 5 Bf1-e2,

Counter-gambit lines may also occur in other King's Indian lines:

a) 5 f4, O-O; 6 Nf3, c5; 7 d5, e6; 8 Bd3, exd5; 9 cxd5, b5!?; 10 Bxb5, Nxe4; 11 Nxe4, Qa5+!; 12 Kf2, Qxb5; 13 Nxd6, Qb6; 14 Nxc8, Rxc8; 15 Rb1, Nd7 'Black having adequate compensation for the pawn sacrificed' - Pachman.

b) 5 Be3, O-O; 6 h3, c5; 7 d5, b5!?; 8 cxb5, Qa5; 9 Bd3, a6; 10 bxa6, Bxa6; 11 Nge2, Qb4 and Black found some play for his pawn, eventually drawing in Lyavdansky-Vasyukov, USSR Championship 1964.

c) 5 f3, Na6!? (The ensuing sacrifice is also possible but more risky after 5 ..., O-O) 6 Be3, e5; 7 d5, Nh5; 8 Qd2, **Qh4+!?;** 9 g3 (9 Bf2!?) 9 ..., Nxg3!?; 10 Qf2 (Not 10 Bf2 when 10 ..., Nxf1 attacks the White queen) 10 ..., Nxf1; 11 Qxh4, Nxe3. With Black having castled on move 5, a game Kikiani-Goldin (Moscow 1963) continued 12 Ke2 (Or 12 Qf2, Nxc4; 13 Qe2, Nb6; 14 O-O-O, c6 as in a 1956 Gligoric-Bronstein encounter; also possible here is 12 ..., Bh6!?) 12 ..., Nxc4; 13 Nb5, Na6; 14 Rc1 (14 b3!? - Sokolsky; 14 h4!?) 14 ..., Nxb2; 15 Nxc7, Nxc7; 16 Rxc7, b6! Black standing perhaps already better, and winning in 36 moves.

5 ..., O-O; 6 Bc1-g5,

The Averbakh System, designed to prevent **6 ..., e5?** (7 dxe5, dxe5; 8 Qxd8, Rxd8; 9 Nd5) and to lead to either lightning attacks or endgame pressure according to Black's reaction.

6 ..., c7-c5; 7 d4-d5, b7-b5!?;

Black can also consider 7 ..., Qa5, 7 ..., e6 and 7 ..., h6. In the latter case, after **8 Bf4!?** (8 Be3 is more normal) Black tried in the game Uhlmann-Geller, Palma Interzonal 1970, yet another variant on the old theme: 8 ..., a6; 9 Qd2, Kh7; 10 Nf3, b5!?; 11 cxb5, axb5; 12 Bxb5, Qb6!; 13 Be2, Qb4 with a strong initiative (14 e5, Nh5). Geller won in 44 moves.

8 c4xb5, a7-a6;

119

9 b5xa6?!,

According to an article by Boleslavsky in 'Schachmatny Bulletin', September 1972, White should play **9 a4!**, e.g. 9 ..., Qa5; 10 Bd2, axb5; 11 Bxb5, Ba6; 12 Nge2, Nbd7; 13 O-O, Bxb5; 14 Nxb5, Qb6; 15 Qc2, Rfc8; 16 b3! (An improvement upon 16 Bc3, c4 of Uhlmann-Adamski, Polanica Zdroi 1968) 16 ..., c4; 17 bxc4, Ne5; 18 Be3, Qb7; 19 c5!, dxc5; 20 Rfb1, Qa6; 21 h3 and Black does not have compensation for his pawn. It is apparently only very recently that masters have taken the view that the move a4, by maintaining an obstructive outpost at b5, may do more good than harm to White's chances in this and all analogous lines of the Volga Gambit.

9 ..., Bc8xa6;

This was the original idea of Pachman. However Black can also try:

a) **9 ..., Qa5!?** (Geller) 10 Bd2, Bxa6; **11 Qc2**, Nbd7; 12 Nf3!? (12 Bxa6!?) 12 ..., Bxe2; 13 Nxe2, Qa6; 14 Bc3, Nb6; 15 O-O, Na4; 16 Rfc1, Rfb8; 17 b3, Nxc3; 18 Nxc3, c4!; 19 Rab1, cxb3; 20 axb3, Rb4 and White had to fight hard to draw (Harding-Woodcock, Oxford 1967). Here Suetin suggested **11 Nf3** to meet 11 ..., Qb4 by 12 Bxa6 and 13 Qe2; also **10 Qd2!?** may be playable.

b) **9 ..., Nxa6**; 10 Nf3, Qb6; 11 Rb1, h6; 12 Bh4, g5; 13 Bg3, Nh5; 14 O-O, Nxg3; 15 hxg3, Nc7; 16 Bc4, Bg4; 17 Qc2 and White had some advantage (Filip-Calvo, Havana 1966).

10 Ng1-f3,

In Boleslavsky's view, a better plan is probably **10 Bxa6** and 11 Nge2.

10 ..., Qd8-b6; 11 Ra1-b1, Nb8-d7; 12 O-O, Rf8-b8; 13 Qd1-c2, h7-h6; 14 Bg5-f4, g7-g5; 15 Be2xa6,

If **15 Bg3** Benko intended 15 ..., Nh5, while if **15 Bd2?** Black regains his pawn by 15 ..., Bxe2; 16 Nxe2, Rxa2.

15 ..., Qb6xa6; 16 Bf4-e3?,

16 Bd2 was necessary, but Black has strong pressure anyway.

16 ..., Nf6-g4; 17 Be3-d2, Ng4-e5; 18 Nf3xe5, Nd7xe5; 19 f2-f4?,

This makes matters worse, by opening the a7-g1 diagonal.

19 ..., Qa6-d3!;

The position is obscure after **19 ..., Ng4!?** (Or 20 fxg5 (Or 20 e5!?) 20 ..., Bd4+; 21 Kh1, Nf2+; 22 Rxf2, Bxf2 and now either 23 e5 or 23 gxh6 (Benko).

20 Qc2xd3,

He loses after **20 Qc1, Nc4; 21 Rd1, Nxd2!; 22 Rxd2, Qe3+; 23 Kh1, Bxc3** (Benko).

20 ..., Ne5xd3; 21 f4xg5, h6xg5?!;

120

Benko pointed out in 'Chess Life & Review' that **21 ..., Bd4+; 22 Kh1, hxg5** was clearly better for him; but less good would be **22 ..., Nf2+.**

22 Rf1-f3, c5-c4; 23 Rf3-g3, Kg8-f8!; 24 Kg1-f1, Bg7xc3!;

This assures him of some advantage.

25 Bd2xc3, f7-f6; 26 h2-h4,

White cannot maintain his extra pawn (**26 a3?**, Rxa3) and if **26 Re3**, Rxa2; 27 Re2, Rb3 followed by ..., Nc5-a4 (Benko). He prefers activity.

26 ..., g5xh4; 27 Rg3-h3, Ra8xa2; 28 Rh3xh4, Rb8-b3; 29 Rh4-h8+, Kf8-f7; 30 Rh8-c8, Nd3-c5; 31 Rb1-e1,

If **31 Rxc5**, bxc5; 32 e5 White might hold out longer, since the great attenuation of material creates technical difficulties.

31 ..., Nc5-a4; 32 Rc8xc4, Na4xb2; 33 Rc4-c7, Nb2-d3; 34 Re1-d1,

Benko also gives the variation

34 Re3 (Or 34 Ra1, Rxc3!) 34 ..., Rb1+; 35 Be1, Rf2+; 36 Kg1, Rd2!

34 ..., Nd3-c5; 35 Bc3-d4, Nc5xe4; 36 Rd1-e1, Ne4-g3+; 37 Kf1-g1, Nf3-e2+; 38 Kg1-h2, Rb3-b8; 39 Kh2-h3, Ra2-a3+; White resigns.

Either it's mate or the bishop goes with check.

Game 59
Keene - Wade
(Teesside 1972)

1 Ng1-f3, g7-g6; 2 c2-c4, Bf8-g7; 3 d2-d4, Ng8-f6; 4 g2-g3, O-O;

An accelerated form is **4 ..., c5; 5 d5, b5!?;** 6 cxb5, a6; 7 bxa6, Bxa6; 8 Nc3, O-O; 9 Bg2, d6; 10 O-O, Nbd7 transposing into Game 53 of the Volga proper.

5 Bf1-g2, c7-c5; 6 d4-d5, b7-b5!?;

A more normal method of treating this position is **6 ..., d6; 7 Nc3** and now **7 ..., Na6** (Pelikan), **7 ..., a6** or the sacrificial **7 ..., e6!?; 8 dxe6, Bxe6; 9 Ng5, Bxc4!**, first proposed by Stein. After **10 Bxb7, Nbd7:**

a) 11 Bxa8, Qxa8; 12 O-O, d5; 13 Qc2, Re8; 14 Re1, h6; 15 Nf3, Ba6; 16 a4, Qc6 with an obscure position (Donner-Bielicki, Havana 1964). 16 ..., d4!? is also possible, but contemporary analysis suggested it to be inferior.

b) 11 Qxd6, Rb8; 12 Bg2, Re8; 13 Qd1, Ng4; 14 O-O, Bxc3; 15 bxc3, Bxe2; 16 Qd5, Nde5; 17 Re1, Qa5; 18 Bf4, Red8; 19 Rxe2, Rxd5; 20 Bxd5, Qxc3; 21 Rae1 with yet another unclear game (Hollis-Hodos, Students' Olympiad 1963).

If White plays **7 O-O** (Instead

of 7 Nc3) it is not so likely that the sacrifice is playable for Black, since a subsequent Na3 will gain a tempo for White in many variations.

7 c4xb5, d7-d6; 8 O-O, a7-a6; 9 b5xa6, Nb8xa6!?;

Wade's patent. **9 ..., Bxa6; 10 Nc3** gives normal Volga lines. The balanced positions that now arise are almost totally unexplored.

121

10 Nb1-c3, Bc8-b7; 11 e2-e4, Na6-c7; 12 Bc1-f4,

Pressing for the thematic e5 perhaps, but primarily to inhibit ..., e6 which would have left White with a weak centre pawn.

12 ..., Ra8-a5; 13 Rf1-e1, Qd8-a8; 14 a2-a4,

If **14 Qd2**, Rb8 Black has a typical sound position with pressure, while White cannot undertake anything active (15 Bh6, Bh8).

14 ..., Rf8-b8; 15 Nf3-d2, Ra5-a7;

He might lose the initiative to Nc4 otherwise.

16 Nd2-c4, Bb7-a6;

But now he can take immediate counter-action.

17 Nc4-a5,

Other moves lose the pawn at b2.

17 ..., Ba6-e2!; 18 Re1xe2, Ra7xa5; 19 e4-e5, Nf6-e8; 20 Bf4-g5, Bg7-f8

The alternative **20 ..., f6?!** would help White by opening the e-file and 7th rank.

21 Qd1-c2, Nc7-b5!;

This was coming anyway.

22 Nc3xb5, Ra5xb5; 23 Qc2-c1, Rb5-b4; 24 a4-a5, Ne8-c7;

122

Draw agreed.

White has too many weak pawns to worry about, while Black has to be careful that his king does not become too denuded. A fair decision.

6 FROM'S AND BEYOND

So far all the openings we have considered stemmed from 1 e4 or 1 d4. In this chapter the few remaining counter-gambit systems will be discussed, beginning with From's Gambit.

FROM'S GAMBIT (1 f4, e5)

Bird's Opening (1 f4) is comparatively rare, only Larsen among the grandmasters apparently believing it strong. However, if met inappropriately, White's flank attack based on control of e5 by f-pawn, knight and often a fianchettoed queen's bishop can prove very strong. Like some other suspect openings, the Bird has the power to inspire devotion in certain players — the former English international B.H. Wood for example. They are very happy to play White's cumbersome build-up, if only because they know it so well and their opponents in general do not.

Fortunately for Black, he can easily throw White off his programmed strategy by means of From's Gambit, which at the cost of a pawn highlights the weakness created near White's king by the move 1 f4. The theoretical condition of From's Gambit is still unclear, but there is no doubt that Black gets excellent results in over-the-board practice.

In 1961-2 a correspondence tournament was held in Germany, in which the From Gambit was the required opening. The games, together with analysis, have been published in a book; the results can only be described as inconclusive. From's Gambit leads often to wild tactical games, or to lines hard to assess in which Black has steady positional pressure for his pawn. Many From games are marred by blunders and missed opportunities, but I have sought to select the most instructive recent games with the gambit, and to indicate each of the main lines, albeit at the cost of including some bad play at times. The comparatively large amount of space allocated to From's Gambit in this book is justified by its high entertainment value and the need in chess literature for some fairly authoritative treatment of this opening.

1 f2-f4, e7-e5; 2 f4xe5,

If White's temperament is better suited to attacking play than to the defence of material advantage, he would be advised to play 2 e4, with transposition to the King's Gambit. Black might then logically proceed 2 ..., d5, for which see Chapter 2.

2 ..., d7-d6; 3 e5xd6,

White can decline the gambit by 3 Nf3, dxe5; 4 e4 (4 Nxe5, Bd6; 5 Nf3 transposes back to the main line) 4 ..., Bc5 but the resulting King's

Gambit Declined position is not particularly desirable for White in view of the vulnerability of his king. The attempt to establish a classical pawn centre by 5 c3 is best met by 5 ..., Nf6; 6 d4, exd4; 7 cxd4, Bb4+ (Not so clear is 7 ..., Nxe4; 8 dxc5, Qxd1+; 9 Kxd1, Nf2+) 8 Bd2, Bxd2+; 9 Nbxd2, O-O (Better than 9 ..., Nc6; 10 Bb5) and the White centre already seems hollow; e.g. 10 Bc4, Nc6 or 10 e5, Re8; 11 Be2, Ng4!

3 ..., Bf8xd6; 4 Ng1-f3,

123

This is the starting position of all games with From's Gambit. As conceived by the 19th century Danish master Severin From, Black can play 4 ..., g5, threatening to drive away the knight by ..., g4 and then administer checkmate commencing ..., Qh4+. White's attempts to cover this tactical weakness can result in all kinds of wild play, and the first three illustrative games in this chapter will be devoted to the exploration of these possibilities.

However it may be argued that the move 4 ..., g5 weakens Black as much as it threatens White and so the modern positional continuation 4 ..., Nf6 (stemming from Schlechter) is of almost equal popularity; three games will be devoted to this too. At that point also there will be a discussion of Black's rare fourth moves: 4 ..., Nc6, 4 ..., Bg4, etc.

Game 60
Zeh - Rothgen
(Correspondence Tournament
8. DFM/5)

**1 f2-f4, e7-e5; 2 f4xe5, d7-d6;
3 e5xd6, Bf8xd6; 4 Ng1-f3, g7-g5;
5 d2-d4!?,**

The quieter continuation 5 g3, formerly thought too passive, is now generally held to be White's strongest move here. It will be

examined in Game 62.

5 ..., g5-g4; 6 Nf3-g5!?,

Tartakover's suggestion, envisaging a piece sacrifice for an attack reminiscent of the old lines of the King's Gambit. However, this is almost certainly unsound. White should give preference to 6 Ne5: see the next Game.

6 ..., f7-f5!;

Cutting off the knight's retreat

and preparing to win it. Other moves have also been played here, not without success:

6 ..., Be7 was shown up in the game Cording-Lungmuss (thematic tourney) by 7 Qd3, f5; 8 h3 since Black decided he had to play 8 ..., g3? It would have been more interesting to test White's idea by 8 ..., Bxg5 when presumably the intention was 9 Nc3! e.g. 9 ..., Nc6; 10 Bxg5, Qxg5; 11 Nd5!, Qg7; 12 Qe3+ and 13 O-O-O with promising compensation for the piece. None of this, surprisingly, receives any comment in the tournament book.

6 ..., Qe7 is the main alternative. After 7 Qd3, f5 (The English player Mabbs has suggested 7 ..., Nf6) 8 h3 Black has tried:

a) **8 ..., g3?!**; 9 c4, c6; 10 Nc3 should not offer Black adequate compensation for his pawn. After 10 ..., Nf6 White can exchange queens by 11 Qe3, rather than the risky 11 e4?! of Brinckmann-Cording (thematic tourney).

b) **8 ..., Nf6**; 9 Na3!? (9 hxg4, Nc6!; 10 c3, Nxg4 and 9 c3, h6; 10 hxg4, Nxg4; 11 Nh3, Qh4+ both offer Black more chances) 9 ..., Nc6 (Here 9 ..., h6; 10 hxg4, Nxg4; 11 Nh3, Qh4+; 12 Kd1, Nc6; 13 Nc4, Bg3; 14 Bd2, Ne7; 15 Ne3 and Black's attack is broken) 9 ..., Nc6; 10 Nc4, Bd7; 11 Nxd6+, Qxd6; 12 c3, h6; 13 hxg4, Nxg4; 14 Nh3, O-O-O; 15 Bf4, Qd5; 16 e3 turned out well for White in Brinckmann-Gigas (thematic tourney). However one may expect further discoveries to be made in this line.

c) **8 ..., Nc6**; 9 hxg4 (Or first 9 c3) 9 ..., Nf6 (Alekhine analysed 9 ..., Nb4; 10 Qb3, f4; 11 Rxh7!, Rxh7; 12 Qxg8+ and White wins) 10 c3,

Bd7; 11 gxf5, O-O-O; 12 Na3, Nd5; 13 Nc4, Nf4; 14 Qe4, Qg5; 15 Nxd6+ and Black has over-sacrificed (Speer-Kremer, thematic tourney).

7 e2-e4, h7-h6;

Treybal's idea **7 ..., f4?!** is dubious: 8 e5, Bxe5 (Schwarz mentions 8 ..., Bb4+; 9 c3, Qxg5; 10 g3!?) 9 dxe5, Qxg5; 10 Qd4, Qh4+; 11 Qf2, Qxf2+; 12 Kxf2, Ne7 with an endgame that Kremer as Black lost twice in the thematic tourney.

If **7 ..., Be7** immediately then 8 Nh3! etc is stronger than in the game, since the Black king rook is not available for the defence.

8 e4-e5, Bd6-e7;

Rellstab experimented with **8 ..., Bb4+!?**; 9 c3, Ba5 leading to similar play. However one feels that the bishop is worth more on e7.

Popp had some success with the counter-sacrifice **8 ..., Bxe5**; 9 dxe5, Qxd1+; 10 Kxd1, hxg5; 11 Bxg5 and now 11 ..., Be6 should have been met by 12 Nc3, and 11 ..., Rh5 by Lochner's positional continuation 12 h4!, gxh3; 13 Bf4!, hxg2 (13 ..., Be6!) 14 Bxg2, Rxh1; 15 Bxh1 when White has the better endgame.

9 Ng5-h3, g4xh3; 10 Qd1-h5+, Ke8-f8; 11 Bf1-c4,

See Diagram

The starting-point of a controversy in the theory of From's Gambit. Pachman, amongst others, holds the position to be about level. However recent experience suggests that if Black chooses the wrong move here he loses, but if he plays correctly he wins!

124

11 ..., Rh8-h7!;

This is much stronger than the old **11 ..., Qe8?!**; 12 Qxh3 and now:

a) 12 ..., Kg7; 13 O-O, Nc6; 14 c3, Bg5; 15 Nd2, Nge7; 16 Nf3 (Cording-Rellstab) and now if 16 ..., Qg6 (suggested in the tournament book as an improvement upon 16 ..., Bxc1) White is better after 17 Nh4, Qh7; 18 Bd3.

b) 12 ..., Qg6 (Or first 12 ..., Nc6; 13 c3) 13 O-O, Nc6; 14 c3 (Or 14 Be3!?) 14 ..., Kg7 (a slight improvement on 14 ..., h5? which lost four games for Zastrow) 15 Nd2, Bg5; 16 Nf3, f4; 17 e6, Nge7; 18 b4! and White stands to win, e.g. 18 ..., Qf5; 19 Qh5, Bxe6; 20 Bxe6, Qxe6; 21 Nxg5, hxg5; 22 Qxg5+, Ng6; 23 Bxf4 (analysis).

12 Qh5-g6,

How else can White try to justify his piece sacrifice? **12 c3** fails to 12 ..., Bh4+; 13 Ke2, hxg2; 14 Rg1, Rg7; 15 Bxh6, Nxh6; 16 Qxh6, Qg5; 17 Qh8+, Ke7; 18 Qc8, Qg4+; 19 Kd2 (Funck-Halldorsson, Rejkjavik 1971) and now simplest would have been 19 ..., Bf2 as pointed out by Halldorsson in The Chess Player.

His suggested **12 Qxh3?** is quite futile however as Black

replies 12 ..., Qxd4.

12 ..., Be7-b4+!;

White's game is now probably beyond salvation. In the game Hromadka-Gilg, Podebrady 1936, there had occurred instead **12 ..., Rg7**; 13 Bxh6, **Nxh6?** (Better 13 ..., Bb4+ for if 14 c3, Qh4+) 14 Qxh6, Bb4+; 15 c3 with advantage to White since ..., Qh4+ is now ruled out.

13 Ke1-e2,

It would be worse to play **13 c3**, Rg7; **14 Bxh6**, Qh4+; 15 g3, Qxh6 as in Speer-Brinckmann. Or **14 Qh5**, hxg2; 15 Rg1, Qxd4 and Black crashes through.

13 ..., Rh7-g7; 14 Bc1xh6, Ng8xh6; 15 Qg6xh6, Qd8-g5; 16 Qh6xg5;

Conducive to White's ultra-swift demise is **16 Qh8+?** e.g. 16 ..., Ke7; 17 Bd5, Be6; 18 Bxb7, Bc4+; 19 Kd1, hxg2; 20 Rg1, Qg4+; 21 Kc1, Qf4+; 22 Resigns (Zastrow-Heemsoth, thematic tourney).

16 ..., Rg7xg5;

125

17 g2-g3,

Also critical is **17 gxh3?!**, b5!; 18 Bd5 (Not 18 Bxb5?, Bb7 followed by 19 ..., Rg2+) 18 ..., c6; 19 Bf3, Be6; 20 a3, Be7; 21 Nc3, a6; 22 Rag1, Ra7; 23 Rg3, Rd7; 24

Rd1, Rg7; 25 Kf1, Bg5; 26 d5! (Faure-Brinckman). By fine play White held the ending, but one cannot imagine he would choose this line again.

17 ..., Nb8-c6;

Experience in a second From Gambit Tournament suggests that 17 ..., c5 is even stronger here.

18 c2-c3, Bb4-e7!;

But not 18 ..., Ba5? putting the bishop out of play as in Deppe-Paepke, correspondence 1957, won by White.

19 Nb1-d2, Rg5-g4; 20 Rh1-f1, Kf8-g7; 21 Rf1-f4, Bc8-d7;

The final link in Black's plan to exploit his material advantage. The bishop is bound for the king's side.

22 e5-e6, Bd7-e8; 23 Nd2-f3, Rg4xf4; 24 g3xf4, Be8-h5; 25 Ra1-g1+, Kg7-f6; 26 a2-a3?!,

This allows Black to win another pawn - but how in fact is this decisive manoeuvre to be prevented?

26 ..., Be7-d6; 27 Rg1-g5, Bh5xf3+ 28 Ke2xf3, Ra8-h8; 29 Bc4-d3, Nc6-e7;

White resigns, in view of the threatened 30 ..., Bxf4; 31 Kxf4, Rh4+. It is unlikely that the sacrifice 6 ..., Ng5 will be much seen in the future.

Game 61
Bohringer - Eichhorn
(Germany 1961)

1 f2-f4, e7-e5; 2 f4xe5, d7-d6; 3 e5xd6, Bf8xd6; 4 Ng1-f3, g7-g5; 5 d2-d4, g5-g4; 6 Nf3-e5,

This is White's alternative, which is certainly sounder than 6 Ng5. The usual continuation now is **6 ..., Bxe5**; 7 dxe5, Qxd1+; 8 Kxd1, Nc6 with a position generally believed to be even. This should not be taken on trust, though. The critical line appears to be 9 Bf4 (Both 9 Nc3, Be6 and 9 Bg5, Nge7 are easier for Black) 9 ..., Be6; 10 e3, O-O-O+; 11 Nd2, Nge7; 12 Bb5 (This is better than 12 Bd3, Ng6; 13 Bxg6 played in a 1930 Moscow Championship game, Slonim-Zubarev, won by Black) 12 ..., Bd5 (The passive 12 ..., Bd7 lost quickly in Heemsoth-Rellstab, thematic tourney) 13 Ke2 (13 Rhg1 may be worth playing, to preserve the extra pawn) 13 ..., h6; 14 c4, Bxg2; 15 Rhg1, Bh3; 16 Ne4 and White's position may even be superior.

The thematic tourney game Heemsoth-Bohringer, continued 16 ..., Ng6; 17 Bxc6, bxc6; 18 b3, Nh4; 19 Nf6? (A blunder; 19 Nf2 consolidates) 19 ..., h5; 20 Rad1, Nf3; 21 Rxd8+, Rxd8; 22 Rd1, Bf1+! and Black won.

6 ..., Qd8-f6!;

An innovation, allowing Black to create complications after all. A less successful attempt to avoid the line given in the previous note was **6 ..., Nc6?!**. A Tartakover-Spielmann 1913 match game then went 7 Nxc6, bxc6; 8 g3, h5; 9 Bg2, h4; 10 Qd3 and Black has no way of breaking through.

7 Bc1-d2,

Ingeniously guarding his pawn: 7 ..., Bxe5; 8 dxe5, Qxe5?; 9 Bc3 skewers the rook. The alternative **7 Nc4?** (7 Qd3!?) fails to 7 ..., Qh4+; 8 Kd2 (8 g3?, Bxg3+) and now Black can begin to exploit his advantage by 8 ..., g3!? (8 ..., Be7 is also good) 9 Nxd6+, cxd6; 10 e3 (10 c3?, Qxh2!) Nf6 with strong threats

7 ..., Nb8-c6!; 8 Bd2-c3,

8 Nxc6?? allows mate in 3 commencing 8 ..., Qh4+.

8 ..., g4-g3; 9 h2xg3, Qf6-g5; 10 Qd1-d3,

The only way to guard the g-pawn since **10 Kf2?**, besides allowing 10 ..., f6, invites manoeuvres like 10 ..., h5!?, 11 ..., Rh6, 12 ..., Rf6. Events are proceeding by force.

10 ..., Bc8-f5;

Probably the best way to maintain the tempo of the attack. Lots of tactics would follow **10 ..., f6!?** e.g. 11 Nxc6 (11 Rxh7?, Bf5) 11 ..., Bxg3+; 12 Kd1, bxc6; 13 Qe4+!? (13 Nd2 is also crucial) 13 ..., Ne7; 14 Rxh7?! (14 Bb4!) 14 ..., Rxh7; 15 Qxh7, Bf5!?; 16 Qh8+, Kd7; 17 Qxa8, Nd5; 18 Bd2, Ne3+ with a vehement attack (analysis). But it takes a lot of confidence to put one's trust in such wild variations.

11 e2-e4, Bd6xe5; 12 d4xe5,

If 12 e4xf5 then 12 ..., O-O-O! and Black should win.

12 ..., Ra8-d8;

126

13 Bc3-d2!,

White finds a resource. He dare not move his queen to allow 13 ..., Qc1+ or 13 ..., Qxg3+

13 ..., Rd8xd3;

He has no option; there is so much en prise!

14 Bd2xg5, Rd3xg3; 15 Bg5-f4, Rg3-g4; 16 e4xf5, Rg4xf4; 17 Nb1-c3, Rf4xf5; 18 O-O-O, Ng8-e7;

Unfortunately **18 ..., Rxe5** is met by 19 Nd5, Kd7; 20 Nf6+, Kc8; 21 Nxg8 and 22 Rxh7 and White has the better of it.

19 Nc3-b5, Rf5xe5; 20 Nb5xc7+, Ke8-f8; 21 Bf1-d3, Kf8-g7; 22 Rh1-h3, a7-a6; 23 Rh3-g3+, Ne7-g6;

Black is forced to break the ring around the White knight. Probably there was no way for him to win the ending against correct play.

24 c2-c4, Rh8-c8; 25 Nc7-d5, b7-b5; 26 Nd5-b6, Rc8-c7;

Not, of course, **26 ..., Rb8??**; 27 Nd7.

27 c4xb5, a6xb5;

None of the discovered checks win anything.

28 Kc1-b1, Rc7-b7 . Draw agreed as Black cannot win the knight.

An interesting struggle. One may expect to see 6 ..., Qf6 again. However, why should White play 5 d4, since it only creates new chances for his opponent? The next game illustrates a different way to handle the From for White.

Game 62
Larsen - Zuidema
(Beverwijk 1964)

**1 f2-f4, e7-e5; 2 f4xe5, d7-d6;
3 e5xd6, Bf8xd6; 4 Ng1-f3,
g7-g5; 5 g2-g3!?,**

The choice of the grandmaster.
White will make as few concessions
as possible and hope to win on
material.

5 ..., g5-g4;

The normal move, although 5
..., h5 may sometimes be independently significant. A game Gorcha-
kov-Kaiszauri (Niemeyer junior
tournament, Groningen 1972) continued 6 d4, g4; 7 Nh4, Nc6 (for 7 ...,
Be7 see the note to Black's 6th
move, below) 8 c3, Be7; 9 Ng2, h4;
10 Rg1 (if 10 Bf4, Bg5!; 11 Rg1, h3;
12 Bxg5, Qxg5; 13 Nf4, Bf5 with an
unclear position) 10 ..., hxg3 (10 ...,
h3!?) 11 hxg3, Nf6; 12 Bf4, Nd5; 13
e3, Rh2; 14 Nd2, Nxf4; 15 Nxf4,
Bh4!? (presumably not liking 15 ...,
Bg5; 16 Rg2) and now White went
badly wrong by 16 Bd3?, Bg5; 17
Qb3?? allowing 17 ..., Bxf4 and
demolition on the e-file. Critical is
16 Be2!

6 Nf3-h4, Ng8-e7;

Black can try other moves
here, too:

a) 6 ..., Be7!?; 7 Ng2, h5; 8 d4, h4; 9
Bf4 (Hellman-Strautmanis, The
Hague 1928) 9 ..., h3! (suggested by
Schwarz in his book on Bird's
Opening) and after 10 Ne3, Nf6
White's position is so discoordina-
ted that he probably stands worse.
Further investigation of this conti-
nuation would be welcome. White
could play instead 8 d3 (as in a
correspondence game Pulkrabek-
Borowski, 1952); this may be some

improvement.

b) 6 ..., f5!?; 7 e3, Ne7; 8 Bd3, Be6
(Or 8 ..., Nbc6; 9 O-O, Ne5; 10
Nxf5, Nxf5; 11 Bxf5, Nf3+; 12
Rxf3, gxf3; 13 Qxf3, O-O; 14
Qxg4+ and White has three pawns
for the exchange: Chekhover-
Rabinovich, Leningrad Champion-
ship 1934) 9 Nc3, Nbc6; 10 O-O,
Qd7; 11 a3, Ne5; 12 Be2, N5g6; 13
Nxg6, hxg6; 14 Nb5, O-O-O; 15
Nxd6+, Qxd6; 16 c4, Rh3; 17 Rf2,
Rdh8; 18 Bf1? (A blunder, but
against 18 Rg2 Black has the
manoeuvre Be6-d7-c6) 18 ...,
Qxg3+ and Black won (Velibekov-
Halibeili, Azerbaijan Champion-
ship 1964).

c) 6 ..., Nc6; 7 d3, f5; 8 e3, Nge7; 9
Nc3, Ng6; 10 Ng2, h5; 11 Nf4 and
White slowly repulsed the attack in
Loganov-Dus Hotimirski, Russia
1908.

7 d2-d4,

The usual move at this point.
Others:

a) 7 e3, Ng6; 8 Ng2, h5; 9 Nf4, h4;
10 Bg2 is an untried suggestion of
M.Kloss.

b) 7 e4?!, Ng6; 8 Nf5 (8 Ng2!?) 8 ...,
Bxf5; 9 exf5, Qe7+!; 10 Be2 (after
10 Qe2, Ne5; 11 Bg2, Nc6; 12 c3,
O-O-O; 13 O-O chances are
roughly equal) 10 ..., Nc6 (Markland also considered 10 ..., Qe4!?;
11 Rf1, Nh4!?) 11 Nc3 (after 11
fxg6, hxg6; 12 O-O, O-O-O Black
would threaten both ..., Nd4 and ...,
Rxh2) 11 ..., Nf4; 12 Rf1, Nd4; 13
f6, Qxf6; 14 gxf4?! (Black threatened ..., Ng2 mate, but a better
chance was 14 Rxf4 intending 15
Nd5) 14 ..., Qh4+; 15 Rf2, O-O-O;
16 Nd5, Rhe8; 17 Ne3, Bxf4 with a
colossal attack for Black (Frost-
Markland, correspondence 1972-3)

7 ..., Ne7-g6; 8 Nh4-g2,

Apparently Larsen was not impressed by the continuation of the game Heemsoth-Brinckmann in the thematic tourney: **8 Nxg6!?**, hxg6; 9 Qd3! although it is not clear how Black should play now. 9 ..., c5?; 10 dxc5, Bxc5; 11 Qxd8+ favoured White, and Heemsoth's suggestion (in 'Schach-Echo') 9 ..., Nc6; 10 c3, Qe7; 11 Bg2, Bd7; 12 Bf4, O-O-O is also likely to be inadequate. Or if here 11 ..., Bf5; 12 e4, O-O-O; 13 Bf4, but not 13 O-O?, Ne5!; 14 Qe3, Bd7; 15 b4?, Nc4 (Petran-Pancenko, Bratislava 1971)

8 ..., Nb8-c6;

Black threatens a little combination: **9 Nc3?**, Nxd4!; 10 Qxd4??, Bxg3+ etc.

9 c2-c3,

This is Larsen's improvement over the game Schenkein-Spielmann, Vienna 1911: **9 e3?**, h5; 10 Bd3, h4; 11 Bxg6, fxg6; 12 Nxh4, Rxh4; 13 gxh4, Qxh4+; 14 Kd2, Bf5; 15 a3, O-O-O and White's king could not withstand the combined onslaught of the enemy pieces.

127

9 ..., h7-h5;

A quieter plan might have

been possible: **9 ..., Bf5**; 10 Ne3, Be4; 11 Bg2, Qe7; 12 O-O, O-O-O with an unclear position. However, White could then return the pawn by 10 Nd2, Qe7; 11 e4, Bxe4; 12 Nxe4, Qxe4; 13 Qe2 said Larsen, in the Congress bulletins.

10 e2-e4, h5-h4; 11 e4-e5, Bd6-e7;

Larsen must have envisaged the sacrificial attack **11 ..., hxg3!?**; 12 exd6, Rxh2, yet it is not clearly unsound. If 13 Qe2+, Kf8!; 14 Rg1, Qxd6 and White is in trouble (15 Be3, f5). He probably intended 13 Rg1, Qxd6; 14 Bd3 but then 14 ..., Bd7 and if 15 Bg5 (to prevent castling) there comes 15 ..., Qd5; 16 Qe2+, Kf8; 17 Bxg6, Qxg5 and Black still has strong threats.

12 Rh1-g1, h4xg3; 13 h2xg3, Rh8-h2;

Again Zuidema could have offered a piece, this time by 13 ..., **Nh4!?**; 14 gxh4, Bxh4+; 15 Ke2 (Too risky is 15 Nxh4?, Qxh4+; 16 Ke2?, g3 or 16 Kd2, Bf5!; 17 Rg2, O-O-O! while 15 Kd2? allows 15 ..., Bf2 or 15 ..., Nxe5) 15 ..., Bf5! with complications, e.g. 16 Bf4, Qd5; 17 Kd2, Bf2; 18 Be2, Qe4! and not now 19 Na3?? on account of 19 ..., Nxd4! winning for Black.

14 Bc1-e3, Bc8-f5;

The sacrifice was still possible: **14 ..., Nh4?!** with similar play to that in the previous note. Zuidema continues to play simple moves but ends up without compensation for his pawn.

15 Nb1-d2, Be7-g5?;

This move definitely is an error, which has to be retracted with fatal loss of time. 15 ..., Qd7, intending long castling, still offered some chances (Larsen then intending to play 16 Bb5, a6; 17 Qa4), or he could have sought a tactical solution by **15 ..., Nh4**; 16 gxh4 (White now could play 16 Nxh4, Bxh4; 17 Be2) 16 ..., Bxh4+; 17 Ke2, Nxe5!

16 Qd1-e2,

Simple and good. Did Black not foresee it?

16 ..., Bg5-e7;

Sad, but he has to play ..., Qd7 and ..., O-O-O somehow, and exchanging on e3 would be worse.

17 Be3-f2, Qd8-d7; 18 Ng2-e3, O-O-O; 19 Rg1-g2,

If **19 Nxf5**, Qxf5; 20 Nc4 then Black could try **20 ..., Nxd4** - Larsen.

19 ..., Rh2-h1; 20 Ne3xf5, Qd7xf5; 21 Nd2-c4, Be7-g5; 22 Rg2-g1, Rh1-h2; 23 Bf1-g2, Ng6-e7; 24 Bf2-e3,

Now Larsen has accomplished the positional refutation of his opponent's play, and is more or less bound to win another pawn. At last Zuidema goes in for some heavy sacrificing - against a lesser master than Larsen he might yet have had a chance.

128

24 ..., Ne7-d5!;

Hopeless is **24 ..., f6**; 25 Rf1,

Qe6; 26 Bxg5, fxg5; 27 Rf6 with a bind.

25 Rg1-f1, Qf5-g6; 26 Qe2xg4+, Kc8-b8; 27 Bg2xd5, Rd8xd5; 28 Be3xg5!,

Not **28 Qxg5?**, Qd3 threatening mate and the knight on c4.

28 ..., Qg6-d3;

If instead **28 ..., Rxd4**; 29 cxd4, Nb4 Larsen intended 30 Rf5.

29 e5-e6!!,

The killer. Not **29 Nd2?**, Nxe5!; 30 dxe5, Rgxd2! nor **29 Na3?**, Nxe5; 30 dxe5, Rxe5+.

29 ..., Rd5xd4?!;

Nothing is any good now. 29 ..., f5 is met by 30 Qf3! and sacrifices also fail:

a) 29 ..., Rxg5?; 30 exf7

b) 29 ..., Nxd4; 30 cxd4, Rxd4; 31 exf7, Re4+; 32 Qxe4, Qxe4+; 33 Be3!, Re2+; 34 Kxe2, Qc4+; 35 Ke1, Qb4+; 36 Kf2, Qb2+; 37 Kg1 and wins.

c) 29 ..., f6; 30 e7!, Nxe7; 31 Ne5! (analysis).

30 e6xf7, Rd4xg4;

Also **30 ..., Re4+** fails to 31 Qxe4 as in note **c** above.

31 f7-f8 (Q)+, Nc6-d8; 32 Qf8xd8+, Qd3xd8; 33 Bg5xd8, Rg4-e4+; 34 Ke1-d1, Re4xc4; 35 Bd8-g5, b7-b6; 36 Bg5-d2, Black resigns.

An inconclusive game, from the theoretical point of view, but it is indicative of many of the possibilities of both players in this gambit. From what we have seen, 4 ..., g5 is certainly playable for Black, although the focus is now shifting to the more positional lines illustrated by the next three games.

Game 63
Ilgitsky - Vilner
(Odessa Championship 1923)

**1 f2-f4, e7-e5; 2 f4xe5, d7-d6;
3 e5xd6, Bf8xd6; 4 Ng1-f3, Ng8-f6;**

The most usual alternative to 4 ..., g5. Others:

a) 4 ..., Nh6!?; 5 d4, Ng4 transposing back to the text.

b) 4 ..., f5?!; 5 d4?! led to a draw in a game Rothgen-Lochner (thematic tourney).

c) 4 ..., Nc6 (a promising move) 5 e4, Qe7; 6 Qe2, Bg4; 7 c3, Nf6; 8 d3, O-O-O; 9 Bg5, Rhe8; 10 Nbd2, h6; 11 Bh4, Qe6; 12 h3, Bh5; 14 g4, Bg6; 15 Kd1 (So Black has succeeded in his plan of keeping the White king in the centre) 15 ..., Bf4; 16 Kc2, Rxd3!; 17 Qxd3 (If 17 Kxd3, Nxe4 wins easily) 17 ..., Nxe4; 18 Nxe4 (18 Re1 is better but then Black can win either by 18 ..., Nxf2 or by 18 ..., Nb4+; 19 cxb4, Qc6+) 18 ..., Bxe4, 19 Re1, Nb4+!; 20 Resigns (Zastrow-Lochner, thematic tourney) for if 20 cxb4, Qc4+!

d) 4 ..., Bg4 (Or 5 g3, Nf6; 6 Bg2, Nc6 see the next game) 5 ..., f5! (Better than the quiet 5 ..., Nd7; 6 d4, c5; 7 e5, Bc7; 8 c3 of Vasiliev-Timchenko, USSR 1961) 6 Qe2, Bxf3; 7 Qxf3 Nc6!; 8 c3, Qh4+; 9 g3, fxe4 (Lochner-Lungmuss, thematic tourney) and although Black eventually lost, it was not because of the opening.

See Diagram

5 d2-d4,

For White's other moves, see the next two games.

5 ..., Nf6-g4?!;

129

This is still Black's most popular move here, but probably not the best:

a) 5 ..., Ne4?! Here we may quote Larsen, from his book of selected games: 'The books regard this as Black's strongest answer, but I do not like it. Should not the other pieces be developed?'. The games of this variation in the thematic tourney ended 6-1 in White's favour, giving the lie to Pachman's assessment of the position after 6 Nc3 (Also possible 6 Qd3, f5; 7 Nc3, Qe7; 8 Nb5) 6 ..., Bf5; 7 Nxe4, Bxe4; 8 e3, O-O and now 9 Bd3, f5; 10 Qe2, Qe7; 11 Bd2, Nd7; 12 O-O-O was Lochner-Bohringer, White winning in 38 moves.

b) 5 ..., O-O!; 6 Bg5 (6 g3 is recommended by Schwarz and in the tournament book, but it is unlikely to bring White any advantage; also possible is 6 Qd3, Nc6; 7 c3 but this has not been tried) 6 ..., Re8 (Not 6 ..., h6; 7 Bxf6, Qxf6; 8 Nc3! according to Larsen) 7 Qd3 (If 7 Nc3, Bf5) 7 ..., Nc6 (Better than the 7 ..., h6 of Gigas-Heemsoth; Black threatens the d-pawn) 8 a3 (Also after 8 c3, h6; 9 Bxf6, Qxf6; 10 Nbd2, Bf5; 11 e4, Qg6 Black has a good game - Larsen) 8 ..., h6; 9

Bh4? (Correct was 9 Bxf6, Qxf6; 10 e4 and now either the unclear 10 ..., Bg4!?; 11 Nbd2 or 10 ..., Bf5; 11 Nc3 after which Black regains his pawn but has probably no advantage - Larsen) 9 ..., g5; 10 Bf2, Ne4; 11 h3, Bf5; 12 Qd1, Bf4; 13 g4, Nxf2; 14 Kxf2, Be3+; 15 Kg2, Nxd4! and Black wins (Nyman-Larsen, correspondence game in the newspaper 'Dagens Nyheter' 1966)

c) 5 ..., c5?!; 6 Qd3, Ng4; 7 Nc3, Nc6; 8 dxc5, Bxc5; 9 Qxd8+, Kxd8; 10 Ne4, Bb6; 11 c3!, Re8; 12 h3, Ne3! led to a draw in Cording-Faure.

6 Qd1-d3,

White parries the threat of ..., Nxh2 by covering g3 indirectly, and by providing the king with a flight square on d1.

6 ..., 0-0;

This unusual move may merit further examination. Black cannot play 6 ..., Nc6; 7 c3, Nxh2? because of 8 Qe4+, Kf8; 9 Rxh2 (Lipke-Ed, Breslau 1889) but often seen is **6 ..., c5; 7 Qe4+** (7 c3!?; 7 Nc3!?) 7 ..., Be6; 8 Ng5 (8 Bg5!? is a complicated alternative) 8 ..., Bxh2; 9 Nxe6 (9 Rxh2, first, leads to perpetual check) 9 ..., Qh4+; 10 Kd2, fxe6; 11 Rxh2! (Not 11 Qxe6+, Kd8; 12 Kc3, Nf6 which was to Black's advantage in Filip-Fichtl, Czechoslovakia 1958) 11 ..., Qg5+ (Not 11 ..., Qxh2?; 12 Qxe6+, Kd8; 13 Qxg4, Rf8; 14 Qg5+ Gigas-Speer) 12 e3!, Nxh2; 13 Qxe6+, Kd8 (Better than 13 ..., Qe7; 14 Qc8+, Qd8; 15 Bb5+ Ettingen-Sosnik, USA 1967) 14 Qd6+, Nd7; 15 Qxh2, Rf8; 16 Be2, cxd4; 17 Bf3! (Gigas-Faure). Black has some drawing chances but White's two

pieces should prove superior to the rook.

7 Bc1-g5, f7-f6; 8 Bg5-d2, Rf8-e8; 9 Nb1-c3, c7-c6; 10 g2-g3, Qd8-e7;

Inaugurating the theme of the weak e-pawn.

11 Bf1-g2, b7-b5;

Black has some science-fiction ideas in mind for his pawns!

12 a2-a3, a7-a5;

130

13 Nf3-h4, b5-b4!; 14 a3xb4, a5xb4; 15 Ra1xa8, b4xc3; 16 b2xc3, g7-g5;

How much of this would have been possible if White had played **13 0-0** ? Black had anyway good dynamic cohesion in his position.

17 Nh4-f3, Bc8-f5!;

Now the possibility of mate will play a large role.

18 Qd3-c4+, Bf5-e6; 19 Qc4-a4,

More prudent was to play **19 Qd3** and determine whether Black would settle for a draw.

19 ..., Be6-d5; 20 0-0,

Returning a trifle of his great material superiority to induce some simplification. Both players are after the win.

20 ..., Qe7xe2; 21 h2-h3,

So that if the knight retreats, **22 Re1** will win.

21 ..., Ng4-e3; 22 Bd2xe3, Qe2xe3+ 23 Kg1-h2, g5-g4; 24 Rf1-e1,

No choice, for if **24 hxg4, Qh6+; 25 Nh4, Qxh4+ or 25 Bh3, Re2+**

24 ..., g4xf3!;

131

The queen sacrifice, of course. This is a logical game, for all its high fantasy.

25 Re1xe3, Re8xe3; 26 Qa4-a6,

If **26 Bxf3, Rxf3?; 27 Kg1 (27 h4, Rf1!; 28 Kh3, h5)** White might well survive, but **26 ..., Bxf3!; 27 Kg1, Bxg3** closes the net.

26 ..., f3xg2; 27 Qa6-c8+, Kg8-g7; 28 Qc8-g4+, Kg7-h8;

Gaining time on the clock, no doubt.

29 Qg4-c8+, Kh8-g7; 30 Qc8-g4+, Kg7-f8!; 31 Ra8xb8+,

If **31 Qc8+, Kf7!** soon ends the checks.

31 ..., Bd6xb8; 32 Qg4-c8+, Re3-e8; 33 Qc8-g4, h7-h5!;

The last unmoved pawn triumphantly lifts off the back row. White's queen can only remain on the c8-h3 diagonal at the cost of **34 Qd7, h4.**

34 Qg4-g6, Re8-e1; 35 Qg6xf6+, Kf8-e8; White resigns

since he has only a few 'spite checks'.

Instead of **5 d4** White may here also try a plan based on **g3**. There is as yet no good game to exemplify a successful Black plan based upon ..., **O-O-O**, which is what Larsen intended against Nyman. The following game, in which Black castles king's-side is interesting for the way in which White is able by a hairsbreadth to maintain control of the position.

Game 64
Zastrow - Speer
(From Gambit Correspondence
Tournament 1961-2)

1 f2-f4, e7-e5; 2 f4xe5, d7-d6; 3 e5xd6, Bf8xd6; 4 Ng1-f3, Ng8-f6; 5 g2-g3,

The remaining possibilities, **5 e3** and **5 d3**, will be discussed in the next game.

5 ..., Nb8-c6;

Here **5 ..., Bg4** should transpose. Other moves are dubious:

a) 5 ..., h5?; 6 d4, h4; 7 gxh4, Ne4; 8 Qd3, Bf5; 9 Bh3, Bg6; 10 Rg1!, Qe7; 11 Rxg6!, fxg6; 12 Nc3, Nxc3; 13 bxc3, O-O; 14 Qxg6, Re8; 15 Qd3, Nd7; 16 Ng5, Nf6; 17 Be6+, Kh8; 18 Nf7+, Kg8; 19 Bb3, Kf8; 20 Nh8, Resigns (Tartakover-Prins, Zandvoort 1936)

b) 5 ..., Ng4?!; 6 Bg2, h5 (Not 6 ..., Nxh2?; 7 Nxh2, Bxg3+; 8 Kf1, h5; 9 e4 Deppe-Ulfig, 1957) and not now 7 Kf1? allowing 7 ..., Bxg3! (8 hxg3?, Ne3+) as in Zastrow-

Brinckmann.

6 Bf1-g2, Bc8-g4; 7 d2-d3,

132

7 ..., O-O?!;

This seems to be too routine. Other ideas:

a) 7 ..., Bc5!?; 8 Nc3, a6; 9 Bg5, h6; 10 Bxf6, Qxf6; 11 Qd2, O-O-O; 12 Rf1, Rhe8; 13 Qf4, Qe6; 14 e4, Nb4; 15 O-O-O, g5; 16 Qd2, Nxa2+; 17 Kb1, Bb4; 18 h3, Nxc3+; 19 bxc3, Ba3; 20 Ka1, Qb6; 21 Rb1, Qa5; 22 Rb3, Bc1+; 23 Resigns (Kremer-Lungmuss, thematic tourney).

b) 7 ..., Qe7; 8 Bg5, O-O-O; 9 Nbd2, Qe6; 10 e4, h6; 11 Be3, Nd5; 12 Bf2, f5; 13 O-O and White's position is solid (Kremer-Heemsoth, thematic tourney).

c) 7 ..., Qd7!?; 8 Nc3, O-O-O; 9 O-O, h5; 10 Bg5, Bc5+; 11 Kh1, Bh3 is unclear, e.g. 12 Qd2, Rde8; 13 Bxf6, gxf6; 14 Qf4, Bxg2; 15 Kxg2, f5; 16 Rae1, Be3; 17 Qh4, Reg8; 18 Nd1, Rg4; 19 Qf6, Rh6; 20 Qc3, f4; 21 Nxe3, fxe3; 22 Nh4 (Trying to block the advance of the h-pawn.) 22 ..., Qd5+; 23 Kh3! (23 Rf3, Ne5) 23 ..., Qe6! (Not 23 ..., Rxh4+?!; 24 Kxh4! and White still lives.) 24 ..., Rxh4! (This could of course have been played on move 22.) 25 gxh4, Rg6+; 26 Kh1,

Qd5+; 27 Rf3, Ne5; 28 R1f1, Ng4!!; 29 h3 (Or 29 Kg1, Nf2+; 30 Rg3, Qh1 mate) 29 ..., Nf2+; 30 R1xf2 (Or 30 Kh2, Qd6+) 30 ..., exf2; 31 Kh2, Qxf3! and Black wins (analysis).

8 O-O, Nf6-h5; 9 c2-c3,

In order to control d4. In the game Lungmuss-Speer, there occurred instead **9 Nc3,** f5; 10 Nb5, Bc5+; 11 d4, a6; 12 dxc5, axb4; 13 c3, Qxd1; 14 Rxd1, Rfd8 and Black managed to draw the ending.

9 ..., Qd8-d7; 10 Nf3-g5, Ra8-e8; 11 Bg2-f3, Bg4xf3; 12 e2xf3!,

After **12 Nxf3?** Black could build up a formidable attack by 12 ..., Qg4! intending the manoeuvre Re8-e6-h6 in conjunction with a sacrificial break-through on g3.

12 ..., f7-f5;

Piece moves alone could not intensify Black's pressure. Now he has the threat of ..., h6 followed by ..., f4 so White's next is forced.

13 f3-f4, Nh5-f6; 14 d3-d4, Nc6-d8;

While White gains space and completes his development, Black seeks to dislodge the strong Ng5 and so get his own knight to e4.

15 b2-b3, Nd8-f7; 16 Ng5-f3, Nf6-e4; 17 Bc1-b2, h7-h6; 18 Nb1-d2, g7-g5; 19 Nd2xe4, Re8xe4; 20 Nf3-e5, Qd7-e6;

After **20 ..., Nxe5?!;** 21 fxe5 (not 21 dxe5?, Bc5+ and 22 ..., Qc6 with play for Black) 21 ..., Be7; 22 Qh5 and 23 Rad1 Black is extinguished.

21 c3-c4, g5xf4; 22 g3xf4, Kg8-h7; 23 Qd1-h5, Nf7xe5; 24 f4xe5, Bd6-e7; 25 Kg1-h1, Be7-g5;

The alternative plan, of bringing rooks to the g-file, would also be insufficient, so Black avoids exchanges.

26 d4-d5, Qe6-b6; 27 e5-e6, Qb6-d6; 28 Rf1-f2, c7-c6; 29 Ra1-g1, Qd6-e7;

Black's 'threat' of ..., Be3 was of course illusory in view of Qg6+. Now White forces the decision.

133

30 Bb2-a3!,

This deflection is reminiscent of the first move in the famous Botvinnik-Capablanca combination (AVRO, 1938).

30 ..., Qe7xa3; 31 Rg1xg5, Re4-e1+; 32 Kh1-g2, Rf8-f6; 33 Rg5xf5, Rf6-g6+; 34 Kg2-h3, Re1-e3+; 35 Rf2-f3, Qa3-c1; 36 Rf6-f7+, Black resigns.

The final illustrative game for From's Gambit shows White being meted out the usual punishment of the greedy gambit-hog.

**Game 65
Bryntse - Ekstrom
(Correspondence 1971)**
1 f2-f4, e7-e5; 2 f4xe5, d7-d6; 3 e5xd6, Bf8xd6; 4 Ng1-f3, Ng8-f6;

In the actual game, this position was reached with a move lost by each side (3 Nf3, dxe5; 4 Nxe5, Bd6 etc.), but to make comparison with the openings of the other games easier, the usual move numbers are here maintained.

5 e2-e3,

In the thematic tournament, the move 5 d3 was also seen in three games. After **5 ..., Ng4; 6 c3** was played, giving the king a flight square (Not 6 Nc3??, Nxh2!; 7 Nxh2, Qh4+; 8 Kd2 as Black is guaranteed the vital check he needs to unpin). Then there followed:

a) 6 ..., Nc6; 7 Qa4, O-O; 8 Bg5 (As first occurred in a game Wisker-Zukertort, 1872) **8 ..., f6!** (Better than the 8 ..., Qe8 of Faure-Heemsoth) 9 Bd2, Re8; 10 e4, f5; 11 Ng5 (Better than the 11 Bg5 given by Schwarz) 11 ..., Qf6; 12 Be2, Nd4; 13 Qb3+, Kh8; 14 Nf7+, Kh7; 15 Nxd6, cxd6; 16 O-O, Qg6 and the chances are about equal (Faure-Speer).

b) 6 ..., c6; 7 Qa4, O-O; 8 Na3?, Re8; 9 Bf4, b5; 10 Qd4, Bxf4; 11 Qxf4, Qxd3 and Black stands better (Lungmuss-Faure).

5 ..., Nf6-g4;

This was Black's choice four times out of six in the thematic tourney. Other moves were unsuccessful:

a) 5 ..., c5; 6 Bb5+, Nc6; 7 d3, Qc7; 8 Bg4?; 9 Bxc6+, bxc6!? (Speer-Lochner).

b) 5 ..., Nc6; 6 Bb5, Bd7; 7 d3, Qe7; 8 Nc3, O-O-O; 9 Bd2, Ng4; 10 Qe2 (Speer-Heemsoth).

6 Qd1-e2, Nb8-c6;

Again the best move. Others:

a) 6 ..., c5; 7 Nc3, Nc6; 8 d3, O-O; 9 Bd2, a6?; 10 Ne4, Be7; 11 Bc3 (Heemsoth-Lochner).

b) 6 ..., O-O; 7 Nc3, c5; 8 d3, Qc7; 9 Nd5, Qc6; 10 c4, Be6; 11 Ng5 (Speer-Rothgen).

It is rarely good for Black to play ..., c5 in the From. He does better to develop his pieces.

134

7 Nb1-c3,

Two other moves were tried in the thematic tourney:

a) 7 g3, h5; 8 d3, h4; 9 Rg1! (Not 9 Nxh4, Rxh4 with advantage to Black) 9 ..., Nce5; 10 Nbd2, Nxf3+; 11 Nxf3, hxg3; 12 hxg3, Qf6 with adequate compensation for Black in the activity of his pieces (Heemsoth-Cording).

b) 7 d3, O-O; 8 Nbd2, Re8 (8 ..., Nxe3?!) 9 Nc4, b5; 10 Nxd6, Qxd6; 11 g3, Nb4! (threatens 12 ..., Nxe3) 12 Kd1? (Also after 12 e4, f5 White is in difficulties) 12 ..., Nd5 (Speer-Cording). White is lost since 13 e4? is met by 13 ..., Rxe4; 14 dxe4?, Nc3+.

**7 ..., O-O; 8 Nc3-e4, Rf8-e8;
9 Ne4xd6, Qd8xd6; 10 Qe2-d3,**

Ekstrom, in 'The Chess Player' points out that 10 d3, Nb4; 11 a3?

allows 11 ..., Nxe3! (12 Bxe3, Rxe3; 13 Qxe3, Nxc2+ etc.).

10 ..., Qd6-f6!; 11 Qd3-c3,

Here **11 c3** may have been preferable.

**11 ..., Nc6-e5; 12 Bf1-e2, Ne5xf3+;
13 Be2xf3, Qf6-h4+;
14 g2-g3, Qh4-h3!;**

There is a high priority on preventing White's castling.

135

15 Qc3xc7,

White is by now committed to the feckless course of pawn-grabbing.

15 ..., Ng4-e5; 16 Bf3-d5,

In case of **16 Bxb7,** Bxb7; 17 Qxb7, Rac8 Ekstrom gives two lines:

a) 18 Qe4, Rc4!; 19 d4, Rxd4!

b) 18 c3, Nd3+; 19 Ke2, Rcd8; 20 Qf3, Qd7; 21 Rd1, Re6 intending ..., Rf6.

16 ..., Bc8-g4; 17 Qc7xb7, Ra8-b8;

A fourth pawn goes, but the square f3 is conquered.

**18 Qb7xa7, Bg4-f3; 19 Bd5xf3,
Ne5xf3+; 20 Ke1-f2, Nf3-g5;
21 Qa7-a6,**

If **21 Qa5** (to prevent Black's next move) then 21 ..., Re6 will prove potent.

21 ..., Qh3-f5+;

Not now **21 ..., Re6** because of 22 Qe2.

22 Kf2-e1,

22 Ke2 loses a rook to 22 ..., Qf3+ while **22 Kg1** is mated by 22 ..., Qf3+ and 23 ..., Nh3.

22 ..., Ng5-f3+; White resigns.

The two possible continuations given by Ekstrom were:

a) 24 Kd1, Nd4!; 25 Qf1, Qg4+; 26 Ke1, Nxc2+ winning.

b) 24 Kf2, Nd4+; 25 Kg1, Qf3! In all cases, mate can only be staved off at a heavy cost.

In conclusion, it can be seen that the From Gambit is an enterprising way of meeting Bird's Opening. It is not theoretically unsound and gets good results in practice. Anyone proposing to play the gambit, with either colour, is advised to search for original plans, as well as new moves in the more established lines, for there is surely much still to be invented in this exciting counter-gambit.

ENGLISH OPENING (1 c4)

As stated in Chapter 1, the English is one of those modern flank openings in which one will not expect to find many examples of counter-gambits. There is a tendency for the players to develop their games more or less independently, and only come to grips in the middle-game.

Nonetheless occasional examples of early material offers by Black are on record, albeit not in the main theoretical lines.

Game 66
Timman - Browne
(Wijk aan Zee 1972)

1 c2-c4, c7-c5; 2 Nb1-c3, g7-g6; 3 g2-g3, Bf8-g7; 4 Bf1-g2, Nb8-c6; 5 a2-a3,

All this is well-known, although more usual choices for White here are **5 Nf3, 5 e3** and **5 e4.**

5 ..., e7-e6!?;

Formerly this was believed good for White, but according to Taimanov's 'Slawisch bis Reti-Eroffnung' the alternatives are not quite satisfactory:

a) 5 ..., Nf6; 6 Rb1, O-O (6 ..., a5!?) 7 b4, cxb4; 8 axb4, a5; 9 bxa5 (Better than 9 b5, Nb4; 10 Qb3, d5! Hort-Janosevic, Harrachov 1966) 9 ..., Nxa5 (Or 9 ..., Qxa5; 10 Bb2 threatening 11 Ra1) 10 d3, d6; 11 Bd2, Bd7; 12 Nf3, Bc6; 13 O-O (analysis by Taimanov).

b) 5 ..., a6; 6 Rb1, Rb8; 7 b4, cxb4; 8 axb4, b5; |9 cxb5, axb5 and now: **b1) 10 Nh3,** Nh6; 11 O-O, O-O; 12 d4, d5; 13 |Bxh6, Bxh3; 14 Bxg7, Bxg2; 15 Bxf8, Bxf1; 16 Bxe7,

Bxe2; 17 Bxd8, Bxd8; 18 Bc7, Bc2;
19 Rb2, Rb7; 20 Be5, Nxe5 (At
least Black breaks the symmetry)
21 Qxc2, Rxc2; 22 Rxc2, Rxc7; 23
Kf1, g5 (Stolyar-Szukszta, Bulgaria
1969).

b2) 10 Nf3, d5; 11 d4, e6; 12 O-O
(12 Bg5!?, Qb6; 13 e4 Velimirovic)
12 ..., Nge7; 13 Bf4, Rb6; 14 Qd3
(Or 14 Bh3!?, Nf5; 15 Bxf5, exf5;
16 Qd2 Taimanov) 14 ..., O-O; 15
Rfc1, Ba6; 16 Nd1 and White
stands better (D.Byrne-Matulovic,
Lugano 1968).

6 b2-b4, Ng8-e7!;

Browne's improvement upon
the course of the game Garcia-
D.Byrne, Lugano 1968: **6 ..., cxb4?!**
7 axb4, Nge7 (Not 7 ..., Nxb4?; 8
Ba3, Nc6; 9 Nb5) 8 b5, Ne5; 9 c5,
d5; 10 cxd6, Qxd6; 11 Ba3 and
White had the initiative.

7 b4xc5,

The young Dutch master takes
up the gauntlet. In view of the time
he has already expended on queen
side operations, there is hardly any
other consistent continuation (7 b5
perhaps).

7 ..., Qd8-a5; 8 Bc1-b2, O-O;

Of course not **8 ..., Qxc5?**; 9
Ne4.

9 Ra1-c1, b7-b6!;

Since to recapture the pawn
would still allow White the upper
hand.

10 c5xb6, Ra8-b8;
11 Ng1-f3, Rb8xb6;

See Diagram

For his pawn, Browne has a
definite queen side initiative.
Timman fails in the sequel to find
an adequate solution.

12 Bb2-a1, Bc8-a6;

More dynamic than **12 ...,
Qxa3?!**; 13 Nb5 with simpli-
fications.

13 Nc3-a4,

If **13 d3** he could be in trouble
after 13 ..., d5!

13 ..., Bg7xa1;

Of course this is no exchange
sacrifice, since if **14 Nxb6?!** comes
14 ..., Bg7; 15 Nxd7, Rd8 with two
pieces and the initiative for rook
and two weak pawns.

14 Rc1xa1, Rb6-b7; 15 Ra1-c1, Rf8-b8; 16 O-O,

Black threatened to regain the
pawn by 16 ..., Bxc4!; 17 Rxc4,
Rb1; 18 Rc1, Rxc1; 19 Qxc1, Qxa4.

16 ..., Rb7-b3;

This was unstoppable. Black
regains his pawn with clear
advantage.

17 Na4-c3, Ba6xc4; 18 Nc3-e4, d7-d5; 19 Ne4-d6, Bc4-a6;

Forcing White into the following desperation 'attack'.

See Diagram

20 Nf3-g5, Nc6-d4; 21 d2-d3, f7-f6; 22 Ng5-f7, Rb3-b2; 23 e2-e4,

137

Nd4-e2+; 24 Kg1-h1, Rb2-d2; 25 Qd1-e1, Ne2xc1; 26 e4xd5, Nc1-e2; 27 d5xe6, Ba6xd3; 28 Nd6-b7,

On what strange quest are Timman's knights now embarked?

28 ..., Qa5-c3; 29 f2-f4, Rd2-b2; 30 Nf7-d6, Qc3xe1; 31 Rf1xe1, Rb2-b1; 32 Re1xb1, Bd3xb1;

White's position is indeed a wasteland; not even Merlin could save this situation.

33 Nb7-c5, Bb1-a2; 34 Bg2-e4, Rb8-b6; White resigns.

Finally, another original conception for Black in the flank openings. Notes specially contributed by George Botterill.

Game 67
Markland - Botterill
(Robert Silk Fellowship, 1973)

1 c2-c4, g7-g6;

The position that arises after Black's 4th move can also be reached by **1 c4, e5; 2 Nc3, Nc6; 3 g3, g6; 4 Bg2, Bg7.** However White can also play **3 Nf3** and after **3 ..., Nf6; 4 g3** (Or **4 d4**) **4 ..., g6** etc is dubious as White may adopt a line with e4 and d3. An interesting

possibility, though, is **4 ..., Nd4!?** to answer **5 Nxe5** by **5 ..., Qe7; 6 f4** (6 Nd3??, Nf3 mate) and now **6 ..., d6** or **6 ..., Qc5** with some compensation for the pawn in White's vulnerable king and general discoordination (Author's Note).

2 g2-g3, Bf8-g7; 3 Bf1-g2, e7-e5; 4 Nb1-c3, Nb8-c6; 5 Ra1-b1,

Taimanov also considers **5 Nf3, 5 e3** and **5 e4.**

5 ..., Ng8-f6!?;

I think this is rare (Taimanov only analyses **5 ..., a5, 5 ..., d6** and **5 ..., Nh6?!**). The idea is to counter the march White is stealing on the queen side by quick play in the centre.

6 b2-b4, O-O; 7 b4-b5!?,

Two rounds later, Danny Wright improved with **7 e3!** and the game went on **7 ..., d6; 8 b5?!** (This still allows Black to carry out his idea of a quick ..., d5! More testing is **8 Nge2, Be6; 9 Nd5!** and now maybe **9 ..., Ne7!?**) **8 ..., Ne7; 9 Nge2, d5!; 10 cxd5, Nexd5; 11 Nxd5, Nxd5** and the position was already a little better for Black.

7 ..., Nc6-e7; 8 Ng1-f3!?,

Possibly a mistake in view of the reply. Against **8 e4** Black plays **8 ..., c6** and then ploughs ahead with ..., d5!?

8 ..., d7-d5!;

See Diagram

9 Nf3xe5, Bc8-f5; 10 Rb1-b3,

Against **10 d3, ..., Ng4** or **..., Nd7** is unpleasant.

10 ..., Nf6-e4; 11 f2-f4,

After **11 Nxe4?,** dxe4 White cannot cope with the threat of ...,

138

f6, winning the Ne5.

11 ..., d5xc4;

So as to meet **12 Nxc4** with 12 ..., Bxc3; 13 dxc3, Qxd1+; 14 Kxd1 Nf2+ and wins.

12 Nc3xe4!,

A fine exchange sacrifice. On **12 Rb4** I intended 12 ..., Bxe5; 13 fxe5, Qd4; 14 Nxe4, Bxe4; 15 Bxe4 (15 Bb2?, Qc5) 15 ..., Qxe4; 16 O-O, Nd5 without being sure what was going on. But it seems to be good for Black after 17 Ra4, a6!; 18 Bxa6, b5!

12 ..., c4xb3; 13 Qd1xb3, Bf5-e6;

Otherwise White plays 14 Ng5.

**14 Qb3-c2, Be6-d5;
15 O-O, f7-f6;**

Not a pleasant move to opt for, but ..., f5 is very weakening, and on **15 ..., c6** I feared 16 Nc5, e.g. 16 ..., Bxg2; 17 Kxg2, cxb5; 18 Ncd7, Re8; 19 Qb3 and Black is in trouble.

16 Ne5-f3, c7-c6?!;

Still not quite correct. More solid was **16 ..., a6**, as suggested by Danny Wright, also opening a file for the rooks.

**17 Ne4-c3, Bd5-f7;
18 Bc1-a3, Rf8-e8;**

After **18 ..., cxb5**; 19 Nxb5, Qb6+; 20 Nbd4, Black's b-pawn is hard to defend.

**19 Rf1-b1, Qd8-a5; 20 Ba3xe7,
Re8xe7; 21 b5xc6, b7xc6;
22 Nf3-d4, Qa5-c5; 23 e2-e3,
Ra8-c8; 24 Qc2-a4, Re7-c7;
25 f4-f5!,**

If instead **25 Rc1** Black plays 25 ..., Bf8!; 26 Nce2, Qb4!; 27 Qxb4, Bxb4 and should win.

25 ..., Bg7-f8; 26 Bg2-h3,

139

Here White offered a draw - probably too generous of him. However, Black was feeling pigheaded ...

26 ..., g7-g5; 27 Qa4-c2,

27 Rf1!?, intending Ne6 and the occupation of f5, may be stronger. What should Black do then? Maybe 27 ..., Rb7; 28 Ne6, Q somewhere.

27 ..., h7-h5?!;

Mainly bluff!

28 Bh3-g2?,

Too tame. Markland had overlooked that after **28 Ne6**, Bxe6; 29 fxe6 I cannot sort out my pawn-formation by 29 ..., g4; 30 Bg2, f5 because of the simple 31 Rf1. After 28 Ne6! the white-square weaknesses in Black's king side are serious; I haven't found an adequate defence yet!

28 ..., Qc5-e5; 29 Qc2-a4,

To tie Black up again, but he breaks out.

29 ..., c6-c5!;

With the point **30 Ndb5**, Rd7; 31 Nxa7, Rxd2; 32 Nxc8, Qxe3+; 33 Kh1, Qxc3 and White is lost, for Black threatens both ..., Rxg2 and ..., Rxa2.

30 Nd4-e6!,

It appears that this should lead to a draw.

30 ..., Rc7-e7; 31 Rb1-f1,

Forced.

31 ..., Bf7xe6; 32 f5xe6, Rc8-d8; 33 Qa4-c4, Rd8xd2; 34 Nc3-e4,

The alternative was **34 Nd5, Rxe6** and now:

a) 35 Nc7?, Rxg2+; 36 Kxg2, Qe4+ wins.

b) 35 Rxf6?, Rd1+ with a plus for Black.

c) 35 Nxf6+, Kh8?; 36 Ne4!,

Rxg2+ (forced) 37 Kxg2, Qxe4+; 38 Qxe4, Rxe4; 39 Rxf8+, Kg7; 40 Rf5, Kg6; 41 Rxc5, Rxe3

d) 35 Nxf6+, Kg7!; 36 Nxh5+ (Or 36 Ne8+, Kh6!) 36 ..., Kh6; 37 Rxf8, Qxe3+; 38 Kh1, Rd1+ and Black seems to be winning.

Both players were in time trouble now!

34 ..., Rd2-d8; 35 Ne4xf6+, Kg8-h8 36 Nf6-d7, Qe5xe3+; 37 Kg1-h1, Bf8-g7; 38 Qc4xc5??

The blunder that loses. White should play **38 Bd5**. I was then intending **38 ..., Qd4; 39 Qb3, Qc3?** but this looks awful for Black after 40 Qd1! So Black has probably nothing better than **39 ..., c4; 40 Qxc4** (40 Bxc4??, Qe4+ and ..., Bd4+) 40 ..., Qxc4; 41 Bxc4 which looks like a draw.

38 ..., Qe3xe6;

Now the Nd7 must be lost.

39 Qc5xg5, Re7xd7; 40 Qg5xh5+, Qe6-h6; White resigns.

INDEX TO OPENINGS AND VARIATIONS

The numbers denote the page on which the treatment of the line commences. The suffix 'n' indicates that the variation must be sought in a note, whilst 's' refers the reader to additional material in the stop-press supplement below.

STOP-PRESS SUPPLEMENT

Theory is never static, so at proof stage I have added the following notes containing material that has come to my notice since composition.

Falkbeer page 13 (Planinc-Vasyukov) In the tournament book, Rossetto criticised 9 Kd1 and recommended 9 Be2, e.g. 9 ..., Bf5; 10 d3, c6; 11 g4.
Latvian Counter-Gambit A great number of new postal games have appeared in print lately, chiefly in 'Fernschach'. Both the 3 Nxe5 and the 3 Bc4 lines are currently in flux, but 3 exf5 remains reliable.

page 28 (Stockholm-Riga) After **4 Nc4** (instead of 4 d4) Black's best, following the Dane B.Anderssen, is 4 ..., fxe4; 5 Nc3, Qf7!; 6 Ne3, c6; 7 Nxe4, d5; 8 Ng5!, Qf6; 9 Nf3, d4; 10 Nc4, b5 with an unclear position. This supports my preference for 4 d4.

Black's alternative **3 ..., Nc6** was suggested in 1873 by G.B.Fraser and H.Moller, according to Freeborough and Ranken (1910) who give five columns and ten notes of analysis, mostly stemming from Fraser. 6 ..., Rg8 can lead to:

a)- **7 Nxf8**, Rg4; 8 Qh6, Rxe4+; 9 Kd1 (9 Be2, Qe7 draws according to Fraser) 9 ..., Ng4; 10 Qh5+, Kxf8; 11 Qxf5+, Kg7; 12 Qf3, Qh4; 13 g3, Nd4; 14 Qg2, Nxf2+; 15 Qxf2, Qg4+; 16 Be2, Rxe2 'and wins', e.g. 17 h3!, Rxf2+; 18 hxg4, d5!; 19 Ke1, Rg2; 20 Na3, Bxg4 etc.

b)- **7 e5**, Nxe5; 8 Nxe5, Qe7; 9 f4!?, Rg4; 10 Qf2, d6; 11 d4, dxe5; 12 dxe5, Ne4; 13 Qf3, Bd7; 14 Nc3, Bc6; 15 Nxe4, Bxe4; 16 Qf2, Qc5; 17 Be3 with advantage to White.

page 31 (Purins-Englitls) After 3 Bc4 note also:

a)- **3 ..., Nf6!?**; 4 Nxe5, Qe7; 5 d4, Nc6; 6 Nc3!, Nxe5; 7 dxe5, Qxe5; 8 O-O, fxe4; 9 g3? (9 Nd5!) see 'Fernschach' 5/1973, Dravnieks-Morgado.

b)- **3 ..., Nc6!?** (Or 3 ..., f5 to avoid the Giuoco Piano!) 4 d3 (4 d4!), d6; 5 Ng5, Nh6; 6 Nxh7!, Ng4!; 7 Ng5, Nxh2; 8 Bf7+, Ke7; 9 Bh5!, Ng4; 10 Rh3! with White better in the complications, H.Schmid-Boese, 'Fernschach' 10/1964.

c)- **3 ..., b5!?**; 4 Bxg8, Rxg8; **5 d4!**, fxe4; 6 Bg5!, Be7; 7 Nxe5, g6; 8 Bxe7, Qxe7; 9 Qe2, Nc6? but ½-½ in 37, Salnins-Purins; maybe better is 9 ..., c6 and 10 ..., d6, suggested in Milic in 'Informator 15'.

d)- **3 ..., fxe4; 4 Nxe5, d5!** (There are some new ideas after 4 ..., Qg5, but none that affect the assessment of game 9.) 5 Qh5+, g6; 6 Nxg6, **hxg6!?** (The 6 ..., Nf6 main line awaits a real test.) **7 Qxh8**, Kf7!; 8 Qd4 (8 Be2, Bg7; 9 Qh7, Qg5 and 10 ..., Nf6) 8 ..., Be6; 9 Be2 (9 Bb5, a6!) 9 ..., Nc6 occurred in a game Blomberg-Svedenborg, Norway 1972. A 1973 number of the Norwegian 'Skaak' magazine recommended now 10 Qa4 (idea: 11 d3) and if 10 ..., a6 then 11 c3. White's best may be Monck's line, given in Freeborough and Ranken: **7 Qxg6+, Ke7**; 8 d4!, Nf6; 9 Bg5, Qd6; 10 Qxf6+, Qxf6; 11 Bxf6+, Kxf6; 12 Bxd5 with more than enough pawns for the bishop.

Enklaar-B.Anderssen, Clare Benedict 1973, went after 7 Qg6+ instead **7 ..., Kd7**; 8 Bxd5, Nf6; 9 Nc3, Qe7; 10 Bxe4, Kd8; 11 Qg5, Bh6; 12 Qg6,

Bf4?! ('Chess in the U.S.S.R.' suggested 12 ..., Rg8; 13 Qxh6, Nxe4; 14 Qe3, Nxc3.) 13 d3, Rg8? (13 ..., Bxc1 is preferable) 14 Qxg8+, Nxg8; 15 Bxf4 and White eventually won.

Two Knights Defence Estrin's 1973 Bulgarian booklet on the 'Traxler Counter-Attack' (i.e. Wilkes-Barre) includes several additions and corrections to his 1971 Russian work (now available in English). There have also been some new games in 'Fernschach' and 'Informator 15'.

page 37 (Porreca-Ballbe) The main line stands, but also note:

a)- After 5 Nxf7?!, Bxf2+; 6 Kxf2, Nxe4+; 7 Ke3, Estrin now says that 7 ..., Qe7 is met by 8 c3!, Qc5+; 9 d4, exd4; 10 cxd4, Qe7; 11 Kf3 and so recommends 7 ..., Qh4!:

a1)- 8 g3, Nxg3; 9 hxg3, Qd4+; 10 Kf3, d5; 11 Rh4, e4+; 12 Kg2, O-O; 13 Qh5, Be6; 14 c3, Qxc4; 15 b3, Qd3 and Black won, Ostrava-Kutna Gora, Czech clubs' 1959.

a2)- 8 Qf3, Nf6!!; 0-1 Jentzsch-Nosutta, correspondence 1956. If 9 Bb3, Nd4 or 9 d3, d5 or finally 9 Nxh8, Qd4+; 10 Ke2, Qxc4+; 11 Kd1, Nd4. Estrin has apparently overlooked this game, and recommends 8 ..., Ng5 which should also win.

b)- If 5 Nxf7, Bxf2+; 6 Kxf2, Nxe4+; 7 Kg1!, Qh4; 8 g3, Nxg3; 9 Nxh8, d5!? (9 ..., Nxh1; 10 Qf3!   ) 10 Qf3!, Qd4+ (10 ..., Nf5!?) 11 Kg2, Nf5; 12 c3, Qxc4; 13 d3, Qh4 should draw - Estrin.

c)- Or 5 Nxf7, Bxf2+; 6 Kf1!?, Qe7; 7 Nxh8, d5; 8 exd5, Bg4!?; 9 Be2, Bxe2; **10 Qxe2**, Nd4+; 11 Kf2 and now 11 ..., O-O-O! also gives chances to Black. So 10 Kxe2 is best, but after 10 ..., Nd4+; 11 Kf2 Black has 11 ..., Ne4+!; 12 Ke3, Qg5+; 13 Kxe4, Qxg2+ (If 13 ..., Qf5+; 14 Ke3, Nxc2+ Estrin recommends 15 Qxc2, Qxc2; 16 Nc3.) 14 Kd3!, Qh3+; 15 Ke4 (15 Kc4, b5+; 16 Kc5, Qh6!; 17 Kb4, Qd6+) 15 ..., Qg2+ with a draw - Estrin. If White deviates he will lose.

d)- In note b3 to White's 5th, he could try 12 g4!?. Black has 11 ..., Ne4!?.

e)- After 5 Bxf7+!, Ke7 , not 6 b4?, Bxf2+! P.Schmidt-Estrin, Correspondence 1971-72.

f)- After 5 Bxf7+, Ke7; 6 Bb3 Black has tried **6 ..., d6**. White should get back into the main line by 7 Nc3, Rf8; 8 O-O, since Black has done well with 7 Nf7?, Qf8 , 7 O-O, Bg4 and 7 c3, Rf8; 8 O-O, Bg4 whereas after 7 Nc3 the possibility of Nd5+ rules out ..., Bg4.

g)- Note b to Black's 12th (on page 39) After 12 ..., hxg5; 13 gxf6, gxf6 Estrin gives 14 Ba4. Also possible is **12 ..., Bg4** e.g. 13 Nxf6, gxf6; 14 Nf7+, Qxf7; 15 Qxg4, Nxe5; 16 Qe4, Qg7; 17 cxd4, Bxd4; 18 Qxb7, Kd7; 19 Kh1, Bb6; 20 Ba4+ Resigns. Winkelman-Koch, correspondence 1971; after 20 ..., Ke7; 21 f4, White wins a piece.

page 49 (Fishhaimer-Gligoric) In note f to White's 13th, an important possibility is 13 Nd2, O-O; **14 f4!?** 'Fernschach' 1963 gives a game Sundqvist-Kretschmar (not in Estrin!) which went 14 ..., Re8; 15 O-O, Nd5!; 16 Bf3, Ne3; 17 Qe2, Ba6; 18 Re1, Nc2; 19 Qxe8+, Rxe8; 20 Rxe8+, Bf8 (20 ..., Kh7; 21 Be4+, g6; 22 b4! should draw.) 21 Nc5!, Qb6? (21 ..., Nxa1; 22 Nde4, Bc8 was correct.) 22 Ne4!, Na1; 23 Kh1, Qb5; 24

Be3, Qf1+; 25 Bg1, Nb7; 26 Nd7, Bc4; 27 Rxf8+, Kh7; 28 Rb8, Bd5; 29 Nf8+, Kg8; 30 f5!, Resigns.

Rubinstein Four Knights

page 54 (Spielmann-Rubinstein) Dr. W.Alles, in an article published in 'Chess' no.472 (1964), analysed the line 5 Nxd4, exd4; 6 Nd5, considering that after 6 ..., Nxd5 (If 6 ..., c6; 7 Nxf6+ followed by attacking the weak pawn on d4) 7 exd5, Qf6 (Spassky's 7 ..., Qe7+ is dull but level.) 8 O-O, Be7; 9 Re1 (Instead of Wolf's 9 f4?) 9 ..., O-O stand both 10 b3 and 10 Bd3 offer White an excellent game. But in the former case he overlooks after 10 b3, d3; 11 Rb1 the natural riposte 11 ..., Bc5 while after 10 Bd3, not 10 ..., d6 but 10 ..., b6 equalising.

page 57, note to White's 9th: instead of 13 O-O, Henriksen's 13 Ng5! is critical.

page 63: After 6 Be2, d5!? instead of 7 Nd3 White played, in a game Book-Unzicker, Dubrovnik 1950, **7 exd5**. The continuation was 7 ..., O-O; 8 O-O, Re8; 9 Nf3 (9 Nc4, Rxe2!) 9 ..., Nxe2+; 10 Nxe2, Qxd5; 11 Nf4, Qf5; 12 d4, Bd6; 13 Nd3, b6; 14 c4, Bb7; 15 c5 (15 d5, Ba6 regaining the pawn) 15 ..., Bf8!; 16 b4, Ba6; 17 Nfe5, Ng4; 18 Nxg4, Qxd3; 19 Ne3, Qc3; 20 Qb3! with some counterplay for White (0-1, 91).

Philidor Defence

page 79: this gambit was offered in Pollock-Blackburne, Hastings 1895, but White declined it — and lost!

Giuoco Piano

page 80: the line **3 ..., Nd4**; 4 Nxe5, Qg5; 5 Nxf7, Qxg2 is illustrated by the 1929 postal game Kozelek-Holzmann, continued 6 d3, Qxh1+; 7 Kd2, Qg2; 8 Nxh8? (Better 8 Kc3, Qxf2; 9 b4) 8 ..., Qxf2+; 0-1 because of mate in 5 or loss of the queen. My source, Dr. Dyckhoff's 'Correspondence Miniatures', also gave 6 Rf1+, Qxe4+ or 6 Qh5?, Qxh1+ or 6 Nxh8, Qxh1+; 7 Bf1, Qxe4+; 8 Be2, Nxe2+; 9 Kf1, Qh1+.

Ponziani Opening

page 80: The Caro and Leonhardt counter-gambits often succeed in practice. In line a, **8 ..., Qe8** (Novak-Charbakapa, World Individual Blind Championship 1970) proved an interesting alternative 8 ..., Re8; in line b, Black has also tried **8 ..., Bg4!?** A thorough study of Ponziani's Opening is now in preparation, however, in which I attempt to demonstrate that White can weather the storm in all the counter-gambit lines.

Caro-Kann

page 91: right col., note d: After **8 g3** Black may also try Petrosian's 8 ..., Na6; 9 Bg2, Qb6!; see 'Fernschach' 1972, p.80.

Englund Gambit

page 104 (Malich-Muller, note to Black's 1st move) There is an article on this in 'Correspondence Chess' for Spring 1973, by the American player Claude Bloodgood. He considers **2 ..., d6** (Grob's 2 ..., Qe7 should return to Pachman's line after 3 Nf3.) **3 exd6** (3 Nf3, Be6!; or 3 e4, Nc6; 4 Bb5, Be6; 5 Nf3, Qd7; 6 O-O, O-O-O   ) **3 ..., Bxd6; 4 Nf3, Nf6** along the lines of the From.

However White's K-side is not weakened here, so one should expect the pawn to tell. It is not easy to agree with Bloodgood's assessments sometimes, e.g. after 5 Bg5, Nc6; 6 g3, Bf5; 7 Bg2 (How can this be worse than 7 c3, as he claims?) 7 ..., O-O; 8 O-O, Nb4 (8 ..., Re8; 9 Nd4! or 8 ..., h6; 9 Bxf6, Qxf6; 10 Nc3, Nb4; 11 Nd4!, or here even 11 Rc1, Rad8; 12 Nd2!) 9 Nd4! and not 9 Na3 with only slight advantage to White, as in a game Ourednik-Bloodgood, USA 1961.

As a possible improvement for Black, I recommend delaying the development of the KN, viz. **4 ..., Nc6!** and if 5 e4!? then 5 ..., Bg4!

Winawer Counter-Gambit

page 112 (Langeweg-Donner) A probable improvement upon Black's play is **8 ..., Qe7** (Instead of 8 ..., Bxc3) viz:

a)- 9 Qe2, Qa5; 10 Bxd7+, Nxd7; 11 Ne4, Bxd2+; 12 Nxd2, Ngf6; 11 Ngf3, ½-½ was E.Teichmann-Merkel, prelims. 8th German Correspondence Championship 1962-63.

b)- 9 Nd5?, Bxd2+; 10 Qxd2, Qe5; 11 Bxd7+, Nxd7; 12 Rc1, Rd8!; 13 Nc7+, Kf8; 14 Qb4+, Ne7; 15 Qb7, Nc5! threatening ..., Nd3+ and winning - Teichmann in 'Fernschach'.

Teichmann also gives the variation **8 e6** (Instead of 8 Bd2) 8 ..., fxe6; 9 Qh5+, g6; 10 Qe5, Qf6; 11 Bf4, Nc6 favouring Black.

Hennig-Schara Gambit

page 118 (Polugayevsky-Zaitsev) A few more games:

a)- Instead of the usual 11 Be2, White can play **11 Bb5!?** A postal game Clement-Villup ('Fernschach' 1972, page 27) continued 11 ..., O-O-O; (11 ..., O-O!) 12 Qe2, g5; 13 Bd2, g4; 14 Nd4!, Bxd4; 15 exd4, Qd6; 16 O-O-O, Rde8; 17 Be3, Nd5; 18 Nxd5, Qxd5; 19 Qc4, Be6; 20 b3, Rd8; 21 Qxd5, Bxd5 and White won in 50 moves, although the ending is far from easy.

b)- **11 Be2, O-O-O; 12 O-O** 12 Bd2, g5; 13 Na4? favoured Black in a postal game Kornath-Villup. **12 ..., g5** when:

b1)- **13 a3, g4; 14 Nd4, Qe5** and now instead of **15 Ncb5?** (0-1, 24 in Vilela-Rodriguez, Cienfuegos 1972) or 15 b4, Milic in 'Informator 13' suggested the unclear line **15 Bd2!?**, Bd6; 16 g3, h5!

b2)- **13 Bd2** and White won, unconvincingly, in a postal game Nathe-Kornath.

b3)- **13 b4!?, Bxb4; 14 Qb3, Rhg8** (14 ..., g4!? - Jovcic) 15 Rb1, Bf5; 16 Rb2 favoured White (1-0, 30) in another 1972 postal game, Negyesy-Berta.

Budapest Defence

page 122 (Smyslov-Steiner) A good illustration of Black's chances is the game Clarke-Carleton, Birmingham International 1972: 1 d4, Nf6; 2 c4, e5; 3 dxe5, Ne4 (If 3 ..., Ng4; 4 Bf4, g5; 5 Bd2! see 'Fernschach' 1970 pp 208-9.) 4 Nf3 (4 Qc2!) 4 ..., Nc6; 5 a3?, d6; **6 exd6!?**, Bxd6; 7 e3, Bf5; 8 Nbd2, Qe7; 9 Nxe4, Bxe4; 10 Bd2, O-O-O; 11 Be2, g5; 12 h3, h5; 13 Qb3, g4; 14 hxg4, hxg4; 15 Rxh8, Rxh8; 16 Ng1, Rh1; 17 O-O-O, Qh4; 18 g3,

Bxg3; 19 fxg3, Qxg3; 20 Bd3, Bxd3; 21 Qxd3, Rxg1; 22 Qf5+, Kb8; 23 Qxf7, b6; 24 Qd5, Ne7; 25 Qe4, Nc8; 26 c5, Rxd1+; 27 Kxd1, Qg1+; 28 Be1, g3; 29 Qf4, g2; 30 Ke2, Qxe1+; 31 Kxe1, g1(Q)+; 32 Kd2, Qb1; 33 Qe5, bxc5; 34 Qc3, Qf5; 35 Qb3+, Nb6; 36 Qg8+, Kb7 0-1.

Modern Benoni

page 145 (Donner-Planinc) In the tournament book, Rossetto criticises White's 17th and 18th moves. 18 Ne4 would have been better than 18 Qa4? while instead of 17 Bxa8? Donner should have preferred 17 Qd2! e.g. 17 ..., Nc6 (17 ..., Qf6?; 18 Bxa8, Rxb2; 19 Ne4!) 18 dxc6, Qf6 and if 19 O-O-O, Bg7.

Lundin Counter-Gambit

page 171 (Stupica-Tringov) Apparently Lundin was not the pioneer! In note a to Black's 9th move, the game van Scheltinga-Opocensky, Buenos Aires Olympiad 1939, continued **10 ..., Qb6** (Instead of 10 ..., Ba6) 11 Nd2, Ba6; 12 Nc4, Qb7; 13 Bxa6, Qxa6; 14 Qe2?! (14 Ne3!) 14 ..., Nbd7; 15 Be3 (15 Rfe1 intending Ne3) 15 ..., Rfb8 (Intending ..., Nb6; Black stands well now.) 16 Rab1? (16 Rfe1) 16 ..., Ne8!; 17 Rfe1? (17 Bd2) 17 ..., Bxc3!; 18 bxc3, Rxb1 0-1. This game is in Kmoch's 'Pawn Power in Chess' which contains other material, on the Pirc and Giuoco Piano, that theoreticians have ignored.

From Gambit

page 182 (Bohringer-Eichhorn) White might prefer **7 Nc3!?** as a game Dreyer-Pena, Tel Aviv Olympiad 1964, continued 7 ..., Bxe5 (7 ..., Nc6 looks good, meeting 8 Nxc6, b7 , 8 ..., bxc6 or maybe 8 ..., Qh4+?!) 8 dxe5, Qxe5; 9 Qd5, Qe7 (9 ..., Qxd5; 10 Nxd5, Na6; 11 e4, Be6; 12 Bxa6, Bxd5 according to Czerniak) 10 Qd4, f6? (10 ..., Qf6 is quite playable, but again White has the two bishops.) 11 Nd5, Qd8; 12 Bf4, Na6; 13 O-O-O, and White won in 20 moves.

page 187 (Ilgitsky-Vilner) A miniature Fried-Schlechter, New Vienna Chess Club 1894, went 1 f4, e5; 2 fxe5, Nc6; 3 Nf3, d6; 4 exd6, Bxd6; 5 d4 (5 g3 is given by Spielmann in his biography of Schlechter) 5 ..., Nf6; 6 Bg5 (6 g3) 6 ..., h6; 7 Bh4, g5; 8 Bf2, Ne4!; 9 e3, g4; 10 Bh4?, gxf3!; 11 Bxd8, f2+; 12 Ke2, Bg4+; 13 Kd3, Nb4+!; 14 Kxe4, f5 mate.

'BRITISH CHESS MAGAZINE' PUBLICATIONS

(All prices include packing & postage — by surface mail — to any address in the world)

'B.C.M.' Bound Volumes

Complete yearly sets (bound red cloth with gold-blocked spine) are available as follows -
(All previous years are now sold out)

1967	368 pp + 14 p Index **£3.00 US $7.40**	1971	476 pp + 14 p Index **£3.40 US $8.25**
1968	388 pp + 16 p Index **£3.00 US $7.40**	1972	500 pp + 16 p Index **£3.85 US $9.35**
1969	380 pp + 16 p Index **£3.00 US $7.40**	1973	540 p + 16 p index **£4.40 US $10.60**
1970	372 pp + 16 p Index **£3.00 US $7.40**	1974	476 pp + 16 p index **£3.90 US $9.45**

Exceptionally, 1971 is a LIMP cover volume — NOT cloth bound

'B.C.M.' QUARTERLIES SERIES

No.4	**Hastings 1960-61 Tournament**	£0.60 US $1.45
No.5	**Around the Chess World in 80 Years** by Divinsky - Vol.1	£1.73 US $4.25
No.8	**Around the Chess World in 80 Years**, by Divinsky - Vol.2	£1.75 US $4.30
No.6	**Scarborough International Tournament 1930** by H.Golombek	£0.91 US $2.20
No.7	**31st USSR Championship, Leningrad 1963** (algebraic)	£0.93 US $2.25
No.9	**Bognor Regis 1965 International Congress**	£0.81 US $1.95
No.14	**5th Correspondence World Championship**, by Berliner & Messere	£2.07 US $5.00
No.15	**Counter Gambits,**	
No.16	**Tal Since 1960**, by W.H.Cozens. Limp cover; 101 pp.	£1.95 US $5.15
No.17	**Staunton, the English World Champion**	£3.25 US $8.60

The following Quarterlies are now OUT OF PRINT: Budapest 1952, 22nd USSR
Championship, 24th USSR Championship, 1958 Portoroz Interzonal, Spassky's Road to the
Summit, The Ben-Oni Defence, 4th Candidates' Tournament by Golombek, Mir Sultan
Khan (a new edition is in preparation), Flank Openings by Keene .

'BCM' CLASSICS REPRINTS SERIES

No.1	**St.Petersburg 1914** (in English)	**Out of Print**
No.2	**London 1899 International Tournament** (in English)	£2.46 US $6.00
No.3	**Der Internationale Kongress Paris 1878** (in German)	£1.27 US $3.10
No.4	**London 1862** (in German)	**Out of Print**
No.5	**Leipzig 1877 Schachkongress**, by E.Schallopp (in German)	£1.45 US $3.50
No.6	**Caxton's Game and Playe of the Chesse** (1474)	£2.46 US $6.00
No.7	**Der erste Wiener Schachkongress 1873** (in German)	£1.77 US $4.35
No.8	**Rice Memorial Tournament 1916** by P.W.Sergeant	£1.13 US $2.70
No.9	**Das zweite internationale Schachturnier in Karlsbad**	
	1911, by Dr.M.Vidmar (in German) — Volume 1	£2.05 US $4.95
	Volume 2	£2.05 US $4.95
No.10	**Coburg 1904** (the 14th Congress of the German C.F.)	£1.85 US $4.50
No.11	**London International Tournament 1883** (in English)	£3.16 US $7.70
No.12	**AVRO Tournament 1938** (in algebraic with figurines)	£0.70 US $1.70
No.13	**Alekhine: '200 parties d'echecs'** — Tome 1 (in French)	£2.75 US $6.60
No.14	**Die Schacholympiade von Hamburg 1930** (in German)	
	(See Review on page 104 of March 1975 BCM)	£1.50 US $3.75
No.15	**Das internationale Turnier Nurnberg 1896** by Dr.Tarrasch	
	and C.Schroder (See Review on page 55, Feb 1975 BCM)	£3.26 US $8.70
No.16	**Baden Baden 1925** (See page 200, May 1975 BCM	£2.84 US $7.50

All orders should be sent direct to
British Chess Magazine Ltd., 9 Market Street, St.Leonards on Sea, Sussex TN38 0DQ
Great Britain

THE BRITISH CHESS MAGAZINE LTD.
9 MARKET STREET, ST. LEONARDS-ON-SEA
SUSSEX

BRITISH CHESS MAGAZINE

Monthly